Codeword
BARBAROSSA

אבי רבנו

מזל טוב 7026 ₪3, ₪

כסי ד ש' 1

03 268426

בבה אני

The MIT Press
Cambridge, Massachusetts, and
London, England

Codeword
BARBAROSSA

Barton Whaley

This book was set in Linotype Baskerville,
printed on Mohawk Neotext Offset
and bound in GSB Book Cloth S/535/96
by The Colonial Press Inc.
in the United States of America.

First MIT Press paperback edition, August 1974

Library of Congress Cataloging in Publication Data
Whaley, Barton.
  Codeword BARBAROSSA.
  Bibliography: p.
  1. World War, 1939–1945—Secret service.
2. World War, 1939–1945—Germany. 3. World War,
1939–1945—Russia. I. Title.
D810.S7W447   940.54′13′43   72–10882
ISBN 0–262–23062–3 (hardcover)
ISBN 0–262–73038–3 (paperback)

Contents

In order to pluck . . . victory on the front, several spies somewhere on the enemy's army staff . . . capable of stealing the operational plans and giving it to the opponent, is all that is necessary.

—Stalin, unpublished speech
to the Central Committee
of the CPSU, March 1937

Preface

Many books have been written about the origins and course of the Russo-German war of 1941–1945. But none have looked only at the element of initial surprise. Yet Hitler's achievement of total strategic surprise over Stalin remains a major unsolved problem for historians, political scientists, and intelligence specialists.

This book is an intensive study of the eleven-month period preceding the German attack of 22 June 1941. The standard sources were culled, the intelligence warnings were collated, the networks of information flow were reconstructed, and the interpretations were analyzed.

What emerged was not only an account of the intricacies of intelligence networks and communications systems in this critical period, and of the world leaders and intelligence experts who both ran these systems and were misled by them. What also emerged were the refutation of the generally accepted Wohlstetter communications model, and the development of a new theory of strategic surprise.*

How to Read the Book
This book is designed to be read straight through by the general reader. Intelligence analysts and the consumers of strategic information will probably prefer to skim or even omit the specific intelligence warnings in Chapters 3, 4, and 5. Social scientists and historians will probably find their professional curiosity best served by reading Chapters 1 and 9 and then browsing at leisure. And those mystery story fans who cheat will, naturally, want to read the ending first.

Acknowledgments
I acknowledge my very special indebtedness to Dr. William R. Harris of Harvard University for his several helpful theoretical discussions and many bibliographic references. For their critical readings of the final draft, I warmly thank Dr. Joan Rothschild of

---

* The generality of this theory for other cases was subsequently validated in over 100 instances of strategic and tactical surprise from 1914 to 1972.

the Center for the Study of Public Policy and Mrs. Jean Clark of Weston, my editor. The encouragement of Professors Lucian Pye, Donald L. M. Blackmer, and, particularly, Ithiel de Sola Pool made possible the initial transmutation of this work from a thin draft chapter in a monograph on Soviet intelligence sponsored by the Advanced Projects Agency of the U.S. Department of Defense to my doctoral dissertation at M.I.T. I also thank Professor H. Roberts Coward of the Case Institute of Technology for reminding me of an apt quotation from Ustinov and Dr. Harold C. Deutsch of the University of Minnesota for some stop-press additions and a correction.

Barton Whaley

Cambridge, Massachusetts
October 1972

PLAN BARBAROSSA

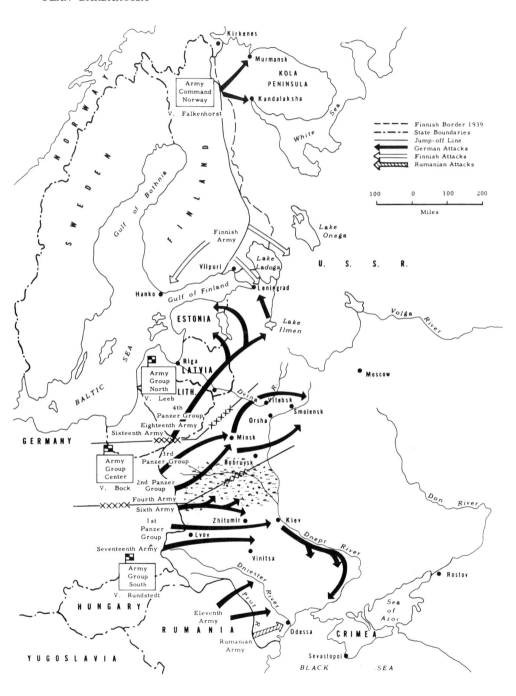

In the Kremlin on 23 August 1939 Germany and Russia astonish the world by signing a nonaggression pact. *Left to right:* Ribbentrop, Stalin, Gauss, Hilger, Molotov, and Schulenburg. Nine days later, assured of Russian neutrality, Hitler invades Poland; Britain and France declare war.

The frontiers of the Nazi and Soviet empires now meet in occupied Poland, but mutual hatred and suspicion continue. During 1940 Hitler grows increasingly annoyed by Stalin's land-grabs in Finland, the Baltic states, and the Balkans.

Nazi Foreign Minister Ribbentrop gives a warm smile to Ambassador and Mme. Dekanozov on his visit to the Russian embassy in Berlin on 29 January 1941. But Hitler has already decided that Russia will be crushed in May.

Hitler's chief war planners were Field-Marshal Keitel and Lt.-Gen. Jodl, shown here at the "Wolfsschanze" headquarters on the Eastern Front, 9 July 1941. *Left to right:* Christians, Göring, Hitler, Keitel, Jodl, Jeschonnek.

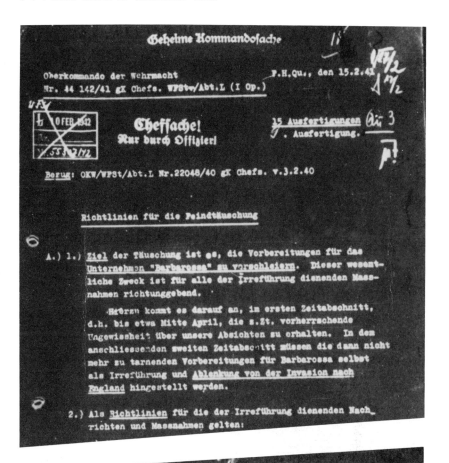

This previously unpublished photograph of the key document issued on 15 February 1941 by Hitler's personal staff (OKW) gives the first detailed "Guidelines for the Deception of the Enemy"—Russia. (Complete translation on pp. 246–251.)

The specially designed photoreconnaissance planes of the Luftwaffe begin in March 1941 to map the Russian defenses. The Russians detect over 300 of these ominous border violations.

(*Top*) Junkers Ju-88D1 overflying Russia on preinvasion photo mission. (*Bottom*) The high-flying Junkers Ju-86P2 (ceiling 39,000 feet).

(*Left*) "The Director": Lt.-Gen. Filipp Golikov, head of GRU, Soviet military intelligence.
(*Right*) "Le Grand Chef": Leopold Trepper, head of GRU in Western Europe.

East Germany issued a posthumous set of postage stamps in 1963 honoring the Berlin "Red Orchestra." Arvid Harnack and his American wife, Mildred, were tortured and hanged by the Gestapo in 1942.

The USSR followed in 1965 with this belated epitaph for their master spy inside the German embassy in Tokyo. Caught in late 1941, Dr. Sorge was executed by the Japanese in 1944.

General Ōshima, Japan's master spy in Germany, presents his ambassadorial credentials to Hitler and Ribbentrop in the Berghof, Hitler's retreat in the Austrian Alps above Berchtesgaden, 27 February 1941. Ōshima predicts Hitler's attack on Russia but is not believed in Tokyo.

The British warn the Russians but are suspected of being mere provocateurs. (*Left to right:* Mrs. Eden, British Foreign Secretary Eden, and Soviet Ambassador Maisky on the day of the invasion.)

The Americans also warn Soviet Ambassador Umansky (shown with Gen. Golikov at the White House on 31 July 1941).

GERMAN PARATROOPS IN CRETE

Hitler, enraged by the Yugoslav anti-Nazi coup in March, crushes Yugoslavia and Greece during May. But this diversion forces a month's delay of the Russian campaign. BARBAROSSA is put off to 22 June. The rumor mills depicted the eleven-day airborne and amphibious assault on the Greek island bastion of Crete as a rehearsal for the imminent invasion of Britain.

"Hi, Joe! I Wonder If You'd Do Me a Favor . . ."
In the weeks before BARBAROSSA it was obvious to all that Russo-German relations had reached a crisis. But most journalists, statesmen, and intelligence
chiefs expected Hitler to deliver an ultimatum—not a surprise attack.

(*Left*) Among the many visible indications that Hitler's attention had turned eastward was the sudden demand in Berlin bookstores for Russian maps and guidebooks, German-Russian phrase books, and copies of de Caulaincourt's famous memoir of Napoleon's campaign in Russia.

(*Right*) *Aleksandr Nevsky*, Eisenstein's anti-Nazi cinema masterpiece, was suppressed when the Nazi-Soviet Pact was signed. In May 1941, *Nevsky* was suddenly readied for rerelease—one of the few actions showing Stalin's growing apprehension over Hitler's intentions.

Although *Time* had sold its readers the "ultimatum" theory, the editors did have famous illustrator Boris Artzybasheff prepare a cover of Stalin and Red Army chief Marshal Timoshenko just in case.

The Russians also conclude that Hitler will deliver an ultimatum rather than a surprise attack. (Photo taken of Soviet mission leaving the War Office in London on 9 July 1941. *Left to right:* Ambassador Maisky, Lt.-Gen. Golikov, Rear-Adm. Kharlamov.)

German Stuka dive-bombers rise to the attack at dawn on 22 June 1941.

"WE HARDLY BELIEVED OUR EYES. ROW AFTER ROW OF . . . PLANES . . . STOOD LINED UP AS IF ON PARADE."—*Luftwaffe Captain Hans von Hahn*

On the first day alone, over 1,811 Russian aircraft were destroyed—at least 1,489 on the ground. Only 35 German aircraft were lost. This triumph of surprise was the greatest single day's victory in the history of military aviation.

Red bombers destroyed on 22 June.

Remains of Soviet aircraft at Kaunas.

"This miserable ape of Napoleon."—Radio Moscow
Punch, *24 Sept. 1941*

Codeword
BARBAROSSA

1 Introduction:
The BARBAROSSA Puzzle

Modern historiography has tended to overlook the role of police and intelligence services in the great social movements of history. Yet, since the days of Fouché, this has been a factor that historians ignore at the peril of gross error.

–R. G. Colodny, The Struggle for Madrid *(1958)*

The researcher is a detective, and his research task is to unravel a mystery; but he must first find and recognize that mystery—his "research problem." [1]

The research problem grew out of my wrong solution to quite another problem. In December 1966 I had completed a draft history of Soviet intelligence networks.[2] It was a structural analysis, limited to the channels through which foreign information flowed into and within the Soviet intelligence and decision-making system. I then realized the need for a short section on function as a caveat to any unwary reader not to assume that the vast size and far-flung operations of the Soviet strategic information system necessarily indicated that it was either efficient or effective. Once stated, the point may seem obvious, but mistaking omnipresence for omnipotence did fairly represent the logical pitfall of nearly all recent writings on Soviet intelligence and espionage. The apocalyptic cold war visions of *The Net That Covers the World, The Great Spy Ring,* and *Pattern for World Revolution*—to cite some typical titles of the period—seem almost hysterical compared with the bumbling reality.

Faced with a pressing deadline, I had the happy thought of demonstrating my point about the shoddy reality of Soviet intelligence with a short chapter limited to a single case study, one I could quickly write up. The best example to crib from the literature was obvious: Operation BARBAROSSA, that monumental instance of strategic surprise inflicted by Hitler on Stalin when at first light on Sunday, 22 June 1941, the Wehrmacht struck across the Russian frontier. Strategic surprise was complete and, except for the Soviet Navy and some scattered Red Army units, tactical surprise as well. The *Feldgrau* horde slashed its way forward through unprepared and disintegrating resistance, sweeping up 400 miles along the entire front in only four weeks. More than 1400 Russian aircraft were caught on the ground and destroyed in the first day alone. The Red

Army barely survived this initial stunning blow. Yet Stalin had received repeated warnings: from Churchill, from the U.S. State Department, from his own agents. Seemingly, only the monstrous fatuity of a Byzantine dictator and his authoritarian system could explain such blindness.

Moreover, *all* the authorities were agreed that this explanation— Stalin's unwillingness to face simple facts—did full justice to the scenario. Senior participants like Winston Churchill, Anthony Eden, Eduard Beneš, Cordell Hull, and Sumner Welles publicly complained after the war that their warnings had gone unheeded. The postwar revelations of documents and defectors had added that similar warnings had come through such top Soviet agents as Richard Sorge in Tokyo and Alexander Rado in Switzerland. The same version was accepted in their postwar studies by professional intelligence officials such as William Langer (OSS), Lyman Kirkpatrick (CIA), F. W. Deakin (S.O.E.), J. R. M. Butler (M.I.), Kenneth Strong (M.I.), L. A. Nicholson (M.I.6), and Peter Fleming (London Controlling Section).* Even Khrushchev added his concurrence in his "secret" denunciation of Stalin in 1956. Soviet historians (such as M. A. Nekrich), memoirists (I. M. Maisky, Valentin Berezhkov, Admiral N. G. Kuznetsov, and Marshal N. N. Voronov), and even the KGB itself quickly agreed and eagerly supplied new supporting evidence. (At least that was the Russian trend until 1967, when Stalin ceased to be fair game for either self-serving calumny or cautious scholarship.) All Western Sovietologists— Max Beloff, John Erickson, Raymond L. Garthoff, David Dallin, Bertram D. Wolfe, Colonel Albert Seaton—agreed, as did such sober scholars as Arnold Toynbee, Trumbull Higgins, Chalmers Johnson, and Gerhard L. Weinberg and such popular journalistic historians and memoirists as Paul Carell, Alan Clark, Ernest K. Lindley, Sefton Delmer, Ladislas Farago, Ronald Seth, William L. Shirer, Alexander Werth, Harrison Salisbury, and Louis Fischer, to name only the better known. Even Stalin admitted his surprise, after recovering from the nervous breakdown brought on by the

---

* Abbreviations are explained in the "Glossary of Abbreviations, Acronyms, Codewords, and Definitions," which precedes the Index.

unexpected invasion. Only the ever-foolish Anna Louise Strong had the nerve to rush into print in 1941 with a book titled *The Soviets Expected It.*

I could think of no historical event of comparable magnitude that had found such overwhelming consensus of informed authority. Overconfident, I winked away Shaw's admonition that "forty million Frenchmen *must* be wrong," and set about summarizing BARBAROSSA. Knowing from earlier readings that this consensus existed, I decided to limit my research to surveying the dozen or so standard accounts most readily at hand.[3] That task was allotted a mere fortnight.

I then made a fortunate blunder in "methodology." I should have adopted that hoary method appropriate to such secondary analysis as précis of a textbook or comparative case study in which the writer does not impeach his selected authorities. However, in my haste, I unthinkingly employed my usual research method, namely, an inductive one that treats all empirical generalizations as tentative hypotheses to be tested against all available instances. This method is of course both pointless and wasteful when faced with proven conclusions of the type BARBAROSSA seemingly fitted. However, it is a most efficiently productive method for tackling doubtful or controversial questions.

Accordingly, I began systematically collating the intelligence warnings contained in the sources. After about a week a curious point emerged: although all authorities presented the same conclusion, they varied rather wildly in the evidence presented. That is, while most authorities tended to merely repeat the same narrow set of four specific warnings, a few included one or two others that had turned up in their research. Taken together, these sources supplied twelve separate warnings. Moreover, by arraying the contributions of each authority in chronological order of publication, it became obvious that most later writers had failed to make full use of even the more readily available published sources. With few exceptions,[4] these authorities had impeached one another. Such contempt for evidence is a red flag for any bullheaded empiricist. In stubborn annoyance, I abandoned my arbitrary schedule and chose a more open-ended one. But my intention was still to do only enough research to provide the first comprehensive and critical survey of *all* known warnings of BARBAROSSA. It had not yet occurred to me that my authorities' *conclusions* could also be fundamentally wrong.

By late January 1967 I had spent about three weeks rummaging my original sources, discovering some of the main memoirs, and beginning to browse in such basic published documentary collections as the transcripts of the Nürnberg war crimes trials, *The Foreign Relations of the United States,* and *Documents on German Foreign Policy.* A startling fact had emerged: the standard authorities had all misrepresented their data. Two widely cited warnings had never been uttered (warnings 27 and 56);* another was a simple forgery.[5] But far more serious than occasional scholarly lapses was that *all* the warnings had been universally assigned an unwarranted degree of specificity and credibility. That is, even the authentic warnings were mutually inconsistent, individually ambiguous, and often transmitted by less than credible sources. With unexpected insight, I suddenly recognized that the data fitted the Wohlstetter model of the role of intelligence in surprise attack.[6]

During the 1950s Roberta Wohlstetter wrote her brilliant analysis of the antecedents of the surprise attack on Pearl Harbor. She did this at the RAND Corporation. When her study finally emerged in 1962 from "the clutches of an interminable, capricious clearance process," [7] it made a deserved stir among historians, political scientists, and intelligencers. It was the first explicit statement of a systematic hypothesis about the nature and cause of strategic surprise. She showed quite conclusively how strategic surprise *could* result from ambiguous information, information that only the wisdom of hindsight makes seem explicit. Moreover, her theory of surprise also requires a specific research method, which she has summarized as follows: "To understand the fact of surprise it is necessary to examine the characteristics of the noise as well as the signals that after the event are clearly seen to herald the attack." [8]

Wohlstetter also entered a tentative claim that her Pearl Harbor

* Eighty-four warnings are given in Chapters 3, 4, and 5.

analysis explained "many [other] examples of effective surprise attack," including specifically BARBAROSSA.[9] (Unfortunately, her own tentative and unsubstantiated generalization was uncritically accepted by most of us as a model for *all* cases of strategic surprise.)

Having long urged colleagues and students of the need and ease of replicating Wohlstetter's study,[10] I realized I now had a superb opportunity to do so myself. I immediately increased the fineness of my net to catch the BARBAROSSA "noise" as well as the "signals" to which I and all previous investigators had hitherto limited ourselves. The next two months were occupied with a more careful and critical screening of the literature to establish the magnitude, quality, and relative balance of both the signals and the noise.

In late March the second plateau in the research was reached. I had completed first rough drafts of the following basic chapters:

1. An outline of the German development of the BARBAROSSA plan (the present Chapter 2), which was intended only as a chronological summary of the actual decisions and actions taken by the Germans vis-à-vis Russia.

2. A chronologically organized description of the BARBAROSSA security leaks known to have reached foreign ears (Chapters 3 to 5). (Nearly half the final eighty-four instances and types of warnings had by then been identified.)

3. An account of the channels, both national and international, through which intelligence was diffused in the first half of 1941 (Chapter 6). The research covered the strategic information and intelligence systems of fourteen countries. This study yielded the unexpected finding that, perhaps uniquely in history, nearly every first- and second-class power was intercepting and reading most of the secret communications of nearly identical information about German actions.

4. A compilation of the rumors, inconsistencies, and ambiguities comprising the noise that confused the various non-German intelligence services (Chapter 7), which showed for the first time that, as with Pearl Harbor, much noise was associated with BARBAROSSA.

5. A discussion of Soviet perceptions, expectations, and decisions regarding the various indications of German intentions (Chapter

8). The main findings here were that while (1) the Soviet leadership did indeed generally fail to sense the imminence of war, individual perceptions and responses varied somewhat, and (2) Stalin did finally come to believe on D-minus-1 that attack was imminent, the abysmal lack of contingent preparations and the cumbrous inefficiency of his bureaucracy meant that even with a few hours' advance warning at the top, the system as a whole remained unwarned.

6. I also compared (in Chapter 9) the estimates of all other major national intelligence services and foreign-policy makers with those of Stalin. An important, original, and quite unexpected finding emerged. Previously, all commentators had ascribed Stalin's blind disregard of the warnings either to his authoritarian rule in general or to his personal paranoid tendencies. That is, they had presumed that Stalin stood alone in stubborn ignorance while the rest of the world's informed leaders clearly perceived the shape of the coming invasion. My research showed that, in fact, the great majority of world leaders and intelligence services had miscalculated Hitler's intention quite as badly as Stalin. Nor could their failure be written off any more than Stalin's on the grounds of insufficient information: as Chapters 3 to 5 and, particularly, 6 prove, their conclusions were all based on virtually the same data. Consequently, we have in BARBAROSSA a general and not an idiosyncratic case of failure in intelligence estimating. Authoritarianism or paranoia were not necessary conditions for this particular surprise attack.[11]

Proportionately few individuals and intelligence organizations had early and consistently read Hitler's intention to attack Russia: British Prime Minister Churchill, U.S. President Roosevelt, U.S. Secretary of State Hull, and Undersecretary Welles. These four were the only examples known to the standard authorities and were the sole basis, other than hindsight, for the hard historical judgment against Stalin. In addition, my own research was able to extend this list of more or less prescient leaders to include Czechoslovak President-in-exile Beneš, Pope Pius XII, and the following disbelieved persons: Japanese Ambassador to Berlin Ōshima; Italian chief of military intelligence (SIM), Cesare Amè; chairman of the British Joint Intelligence Committee (J.I.C.), Victor Cavendish-Bentinck; and members of the Advanced Planning Enemy Section of the J.I.C. But those were about all, and they represent a very small proportion of the foreign policy leaders and intelligence experts in 1941. And, as the test of fact neared, some such as Hull grew *less* certain, and others such as Cripps wavered.

The research had succeeded only in disclosing a mystery. The warnings were available in profusion, yet nearly everyone had failed to understand them. Almost no one realized that Hitler had decided to smash Russia, no matter what. And the few such as Churchill and Beneš who had correctly fathomed Hitler's intent did not know why they had guessed right. Consequently, they could not present their warnings to Stalin in a convincing way. Why? I was now, for the first time, able to pose a key research question: *How* was Stalin surprised? As the reader will discover in following through the story, this initial question proved just off the mark—but close enough to lead easily to the right one. The question that ultimately gave the solution to the puzzle is: How did *Hitler* inflict surprise—on Stalin as well as on almost all the world's national leaders and intelligence analysts?

Up through Chapter 6 all the clues and all the "red herrings" available to world leaders and intelligencers on the eve of the invasion are presented. Thus at this point it should be *possible* for the reader to guess the solution, or at least to identify a set of alternative solutions, including the correct one. The person who succeeds will have done better than anyone did at the time. Chapters 7 and 8 give the additional evidence needed to *choose* the correct solution. Anyone who succeeds in doing this will also have outguessed all the military historians.

The reader can approach this book as, what Graham Greene would call, "an entertainment." It is, after all, a tale of strategic intelligence and, particularly, of counterespionage. But BARBAROSSA was not fiction. It was the most important international mystery of 1940/41. Its human costs and political consequences literally changed the world. Moreover, an understanding of *how* Hitler surprised Stalin in 1941 gives us a far deeper understanding of how most of the puzzling cases of strategic surprise have been brought about—from Pearl Harbor six months after BARBAROSSA to the Arab-Israeli Six Day War in 1967. It may even help us understand and perhaps avoid future strategic surprises.

2 Hitler's Intentions and German Secret Planning

We terminate the endless German drive to the south and west of Europe, and direct our gaze towards the lands in the east. . . . If we talk about new soil and territory in Europe today, we can think primarily only of Russia and its vassal border states.

—Hitler, Mein Kampf (*1924*)

Russia had been on Hitler's agenda of conquest since he wrote *Mein Kampf* in 1924.[1] The vast lands and grains and natural resources of Russia formed the coveted heart of the territorial *Lebensraum* that Hitler dreamed would someday be the empire of the Thousand Year Reich.

Before 1940: Hitler and Stalin—Cautious Enemies, Uneasy Allies

Russia was coveted, but a Bolshevik Russia was anathema to Hitler. His road to power in Germany was red-carpeted with Communist blood. One of his first acts as chancellor in 1933 had been to break the long-standing, mutually useful covert rearmament cooperation between the German and Soviet armies. And three years later, in 1936, Germany and Japan signed the Anti-Comintern Pact whose ostensibly secret military provisions directed against Russia were known to Soviet intelligence. Finally, late that year, Hitler came into direct military confrontation with Stalin in the Spanish Civil War, albeit both men thinly disguised as "volunteers" their thousands of regulars—airmen, tank crews, artillerymen, and naval officers. Stalin desperately reached out for allies against the rising threat of Hitler. He sought mutual security pacts and promoted Popular Front alliances between Communist and other anti-Fascist political parties within other nations. In May 1938 Stalin stiffened the resistance of Czechoslovakia and briefly helped thwart Hitler's intent to invade that country. But mutual security crumbled four months later at Munich when France and Britain, trusting Hitler's promises of peace, "appeased" the Führer with the Czech Sudetenland. Just six months later Hitler's lies were exposed and the trust lost when, in March 1939, the Wehrmacht seized the rest of Czechoslovakia.

Hitler's next target was Poland, but that take-over required Stalin's acquiescence. Stalin's international position was weak. While the Wehrmacht's strength was waxing, the Red Army's had waned —a crippled victim of Stalin's grisly consolidation of absolute power in the Great Purge of 1937/38. Britain and France, having belatedly learned the lesson of Munich, now resolved to defend Poland, by war if necessary. Stalin had earlier courted Britain and France as allies for the most practical reasons of self-defense, even though many powerful voices in the West talked hopefully of a full-scale, mutually destructive Russo-German war. But now that Britain and France had committed themselves to defend Poland against further German aggression, Stalin saw his opportunity to make an about-face in foreign policy. He could simply sit by and watch three of his main enemies exhaust each other in battle.

Thus on 23 August 1939, at Stalin's initiative and with eager response from Hitler, the Nazi-Soviet Pact was signed in Moscow. The pact, scheduled to run for five years, guaranteed mutual non-aggression. The attached "Secret Additional Protocol" assigned to the Russian sphere of influence Finland, Estonia, Latvia, the Bessarabian section of eastern Rumania, and, most important, eastern Poland. Nine days later Hitler invaded Poland, and Britain and France declared war. When Warsaw fell the next week, Stalin telephoned his congratulations to the German ambassador in Moscow. Nine days later the Red Army moved in to occupy its share of Poland.

Stalin's sense of security was to prove false and short-lived. On 23 November 1939, three months to the day after the signing of the nonaggression pact with Russia, Hitler revitalized his fifteen-year-old dream of conquering Russia. He informed a select group of his senior officers that he would move against the Soviet Union at the first opportunity after his conquest of Western Europe.[2]

The German Führer and the Russian Vozhd continued to divide the spoils. But their overweening greed led each to grow increasingly nervous about the stability their pact had been intended to ensure. Thus the very speed with which Hitler's Wehrmacht had conquered Poland was an unwelcome surprise to Stalin. Similarly, Russia's brutal attack on Finland in the winter of 1939/40 caused concern in Berlin. Then, in April 1940, while Hitler was busy in the West conquering Denmark and Norway, Stalin imposed Red Army bases on the three Baltic states of Estonia, Latvia, and Lithuania. Stalin was made truly uneasy by the Nazi blitzkrieg across Holland, Belgium, and France during May and June. In only six weeks and at negligible cost to the Wehrmacht, the West European armies that Stalin had counted on to preoccupy and wear down Hitler had been driven from the continent. So, while the Wehrmacht was still deployed in the West, Stalin in late June took not only Bessarabia from Rumania but, to the annoyance of Berlin, northern Bukovina as well. Moreover, these moves were accompanied by strong reinforcement of Russia's western frontier zone. Ribbentrop later recalled that some time around the beginning of July—after the French campaign—Hitler expressed vague unease at these acts.[3] Next, on 2 July 1940, the commander in chief of the German Army High Command (OKH), General Walther von Brauchitsch, directed the chief of the Army General Staff, Lieutenant-General Franz Halder, to introduce planning— alongside but second to Britain—on "how a military blow against Russia is to be executed to induce her to recognize the dominant rôle of Germany in Europe." It is thought that Brauchitsch did this in response to Hitler's private instructions.

But Stalin went further yet. On 21 July he simply annexed Estonia, Latvia, and even Lithuania, part of which Hitler thought to be in his preserve. That same day Hitler ordered new feasibility studies of the conquest of Russia.

Still, as the summer of 1940 waned, the international balance did not look too unfavorable to Stalin. True, Germany was strengthened rather than exhausted as Stalin had intended. But Hitler was preoccupied with beating Britain. Thus Stalin's main concern was that Britain might negotiate peace with Germany. At that time neither Stalin nor anyone else believed Hitler would fight a two-front war. As long as Britain fought, surely Germany would not attack Russia. But Stalin was wrong. Hitler had now reached the complicated conclusion that what was keeping Prime Minister Churchill in the fight was the hope that, by holding out long enough, Russia would eventually be drawn into the war against

Germany. Therefore, to Hitler, the road to London passed through Moscow. Operation SEA LION, the planned invasion of Britain, was postponed indefinitely.

Attack Contingencies: AUFBAU OST and OTTO

Preliminary planning by the OKW (Hitler's personal military high command) and the OKH culminated in November–December in an OKH wargame directed by then Lieutenant-General Friedrich Paulus.[4] Some time during this period Hitler told his OKW chief, General Wilhelm Keitel, that he intended the invasion of Russia to occur in the "fall of 1940," but even the servile Keitel summoned enough courage to point out the complete logistic and climatic impossibility of such a forced schedule. Consequently, on 29 and 31 July, the OKW staff planners, General Alfred Jodl and Colonel Walter Warlimont, were told by Hitler that the attack was to be made ready for "the spring of 1941," specifically, May. Accordingly, on 9 August, the OKW issued the preliminary detailed order, AUFBAU OST, that began the Wehrmacht's shift toward Russia. As Warlimont later recalled, AUFBAU OST was "entirely camouflaged, not mentioning the U.S.S.R. nor the eventual attack." [5]

The code designation itself, AUFBAU OST,[6] is a revealing indicator of Hitler's intention. Its manifest or public meaning is rather neutral: "Reconstruction (or Development) East" or, better, "Buildup East." Taken in this literal dictionary sense only, it is merely descriptive of the overt activity of the Wehrmacht—its eastward deployment—and tells nothing of its purpose. However, the term carries an esoteric connotation that virtually reveals Hitler's purpose, although I have not found any intelligence experts or scholarly writers or Germans who have noted it. The word *Aufbau* held a very special and highly specific meaning for Hitler and some of his earliest cronies in forming the Nazi program. In its sense of "reconstruction," Aufbau was the name of an eccentric, fanatical Russo-German political-economic association. The Aufbau group was the creation of Max Erwin von Scheubner-Richter, a Baltic German who was one of Hitler's closest confidants until killed, literally at Hitler's side, in the 1923 putsch. Scheubner-Richter and his fellow Russian monarchist émigrés provided the initial source of Hitler's violent anti-Bolshevism and his plans for the conquest ("reconstruction") of Russia.[7] Because none of this original group were in the OKW—by 1940 most were in Alfred Rosenberg's circle of anti-Russian, anti-Semitic fanatics —the codeword AUFBAU OST was surely Hitler's own invention. Hitler was unable to resist a codeword that proclaimed his overweening ambition; luck still lingered with him. Its ominous hidden meaning was missed by all.*

In October 1940 the Wehrmacht launched its major program for the development of rail and road facilities throughout Central and Eastern Europe in anticipation of the heavy military traffic for the planned invasion of Russia. That was the so-called OTTO-PROGRAMME, "Otto" for *Ost* ("east").[8]

The Decision: Plan BARBAROSSA

Hitler's determination to eliminate Russia was virtually set during the fall of 1940, if not already in July.[9] His last serious effort to achieve some modus vivendi occurred during Soviet Foreign Commissar Vyacheslav Molotov's negotiations in Berlin on 12 and 13 November 1940. These meetings between Molotov (with Ambassador Dekanozov) and Hitler (with Foreign Minister Joachim von Ribbentrop) were intended by Hitler to reach preliminary agreement on nothing less than the division of the world among Germany, Russia, Japan, and Italy. The Russians were interested but, not sensing the finality of the offer, resisted Hitler's efforts to redirect their interests southward to the Middle East and India and stubbornly pressed their claims in Europe, particularly the Baltic. The discussion between Hitler and Molotov grew quite ill-tem-

---

* In naming their more routine military operations the Germans, like the British and Americans, chose codewords randomly from predetermined lists. But few war leaders could refrain from christening the major acts. As we have just seen, Hitler seemed to have picked his for their talismanic aura. Churchill also flaunted security by such giveaway coinage as TORCH, OVERLORD, and DRAGOON, but he implied that his were picked with an eye to future historians. On World War II codewords for military operations, see Kahn (1967), 501–503.

pered and apparently ended with Hitler concluding that it would be impossible to reach any viable accommodation with the Russians. This was the eyewitness impression of Dr. Paul Otto Schmidt, Ribbentrop's aide and personal translator, and—in part—of Ribbentrop himself, Ernst von Weizsäcker, and Gustav Hilger. At this juncture diplomacy ceased in all but its outward forms. Henceforward, Hitler's concern was only in pressing BARBAROSSA, and diplomacy was subordinated to it as one of many deception operations to lull Stalin.[10] Accordingly, he allowed the Foreign Ministry to bumble along with Ribbentrop's deluded efforts to maintain Russo-German friendship. Only on (or about) 20 April 1941 did Hitler summon Ribbentrop to Vienna to inform his foreign minister of his firm decision to attack Russia. Hitler cautioned that no démarche was to be sought by the Wilhelmstrasse: "no diplomacy, he said, would make him change his mind about Russia's attitude, which was quite clear to him, and it might well deprive him of the weapon of tactical surprise for an attack." [11]

This initial, yet entirely firm, all-the-way type of decision was very much part of Hitler's decision-making style. Thus on 27 March 1941 when he again found himself frustrated and infuriated— this time by a Yugoslav coup the previous day—he bluntly told his assembled senior High Command officers that he was "determined, without waiting for possible loyalty declarations of the new Government, to make all preparations to smash Yugoslavia militarily and as a state. No inquiries regarding foreign policy will be made or ultimatums presented." [12] *

Meanwhile, military planning had continued. On 6 December 1940 Jodl instructed Warlimont to prepare a general plan for the operations against Russia.[13] On the twelfth this draft was desig-

* Hitler exhibited a similar single-minded purpose earlier, in May 1938, when momentarily frustrated in his aggressive schemes by Czechoslovak general mobilization. On that occasion he wrote: "It is my unalterable decision to smash Czechoslovakia by military action in the near future," awaiting only "a convenient apparent excuse." As Louis Fischer remarks, "In the face of [such] documentation a shopful of A. J. P. Taylors will find it difficult to mend Hitler's reputation as a warlover." For Hitler's Czechoslovak directive of 30 May 1938, see *DGFP*, 2 (1949), 357–362; also Fischer (1969), 311.

nated "Directive No. 21" and was initially given the undistin-
guished cover name of FRITZ.[14] Five days later, Hitler redesignated
FRITZ by the term by which it would henceforward be known: *Fall*
(that is, "Case" or, loosely, "Operation") BARBAROSSA.[15] Again we
see Hitler's personal intervention with his humdrum OKW
flunkies. He chose as his paragon the Germanic hero and twelfth-
century Holy Roman Emperor Frederick I, known as "Barbarossa," from the Italian for "redbeard." On 10 June 1190, while
leading the Third Crusade through Asia Minor, Barbarossa was
drowned and his corpse—or at least the site of burial—lost. A late
legend had it that Barbarossa lived on, awaiting the summons of
his country, in a cave in Kyffhäuser Mountain at the traditional
geographic center of Germania. Ironic of Hitler to choose such a
murky symbol: a Crusader who failed in his holy mission to the
East and whose very legend as the sleeping hero is ersatz, a folk
transferral from that of his truly remarkable grandson, Frederick
II.[16] And the final irony: Hitler's disastrous emulation of Barbarossa led not only to his own death but to a similar legend of mysterious survival (a legend now happily exploded by the long-suppressed evidence of the Soviet intelligence team assigned to capture
Hitler in his bunker).[17]

Finally, on 18 December Hitler ordered his reluctant but compliant General Staff to implement the detailed and explicit "Directive No. 21." That set the attack—or, rather, the completion of all
preparations—for 15 May 1941. This D-day was unofficially designated B-*Tag*, B for BARBAROSSA.[18] However, the unanticipated
Yugoslav campaign during April forced delays in the BARBAROSSA
schedule, first (on 27 March) postponing B-day "up to four weeks,"
and finally (on 30 April) to 22 June.[19]

Although proof is lacking that the last date was picked for other
than logistic reasons, it is curious that 22 June was the day Napoleon's Grand Army began its three-day crossing of the Niemen
River into Russia in 1812. However, this coincidence—if that is
what it was—did figure in some of the rumors and leaks that circulated about BARBAROSSA in diplomatic circles. (During this period
Hitler had become quite disillusioned with the court astrologers

who were mainly associated with the coterie of Deputy Führer
Rudolf Hess and was no longer particularly attentive to their
prognostications and omens.) It is tempting to suppose that Hitler,
or someone in his circle, chose the 22 June B-day for its symbolic
value. It was not only the date of Napoleon's invasion—a poor
omen, I would have thought; it was also the first anniversary of
Hitler's greatest triumph, the defeat of France, marked by the
signing of the armistice at Compiègne. There, the day before the
signing, as the defeated French generals arrived, Hitler had made
his famous, odd jump for joy beside the historic railway carriage.
Somehow, none of the contemporary rumors or subsequent writers
have noted this last coincidence, although the date 21 June appears as BARBAROSSA-*Tag* in some of the contemporary rumors and
later memoirs.*

The revised redeployment schedule started the German troops
moving eastward toward their assembly areas on 22 May. On 6
June the OKW issued its final "Timetable BARBAROSSA." This remarkable document noted among its many details the following
points. It stated that the need to camouflage the attack applied
only until 18 June, after which the OKW assumed that the Russians would unequivocally perceive the shape of the operation. It
noted that 1300 hours on the twenty-first was the latest time at
which the operation could be canceled. The cancellation codeword was designated ALTONA; the go-ahead, DORTMUND.† Finally,
it specified "H-hour for the start of the invasion by the Army and
crossing of the frontier by the Air Force. 0330 hours." [20] On 14
June, H-hour was advanced to 0300.[21]

Hitler gave final all-day briefings to his forty-five most senior
military commanders on 14 June at the Reich Chancellery,[22] and
on the seventeenth the timetable was reconfirmed by the OKW.[23]

Lest there be any persisting doubt of the unyielding firmness of

---

* In 1941 the twenty-first of June was also the first day of summer.

† These two codenames have no esoteric meaning. They are merely the names
of northwestern German towns. Indeed, since Dortmund lies a bit west of
Altona, they do not even hint at the direction of attack. However, ALTONA did
not go to waste. The SS used it in 1943 to designate the roundup and execution of 786 Russian Partisan suspects and 126 Jews.

Hitler's resolution to attack Russia *regardless of any concessions* by Stalin, consider the following: in the final week before the invasion, Hitler (and Ribbentrop) simply severed all possibility of a last-minute Soviet approach through diplomatic channels. This was achieved by the simple, secret device of instructing their staffs to inform any approaching Russian officials that they were out of town and hence unavailable. They even had their private railroad cars alerted for immediate evasion in such an eventuality. However, on his two final approaches—on 18 and 21 June—Ambassador Dekanozov was quite satisfied to speak with State Secretary Weizsäcker and then only on pathetically inconsequential matters.[24]

The point of no return was reached sometime during the evening of the twentieth, when OKW flashed the final, fateful go-ahead parole, DORTMUND.[25] Mechanically, according to the final plan, the Army crossed the Russian frontier on 22 June at 0300 hours, the Luftwaffe following at first light at 0315. However, some twenty to thirty of the most experienced blind-flying bomber crews had been sent across the frontier at maximum altitude at 0300 so that they could hit the main Soviet aerodomes, causing enough confusion to delay aircraft dispersal before the main German air strike fifteen minutes later.[26] *

Although closely matched in the zone of battle in troops (3 million Russians to 3 million Germans) and divisions (139 to 123),† and heavily outnumbered in aircraft (6,000 to 1,800) and tanks

---

* Hours throughout are given according to local times. Thus 0300 German summer time equaled 0400 in Moscow. The chaotic presentation of time in the histories of BARBAROSSA results from both their authors' unawareness of the revised German timetable and their inattention to such simple matters as time-zone differences.

† That is, according to the more critical Western historians who give careful accounting of the Russian versus *German* deployments. However, by some odd arithmetic these same writers usually omit supplementing the German figures with those of her allies who were also available at the front on B-day: the Finns (17 division equivalents and 600 aircraft) and the Rumanians (10 divisions and 1,000 aircraft). To these were soon added the Italians (3 divisions), the Hungarians (1.5 division equivalents), the Spanish (1 division), the Slovaks (1 brigade), and the Croats (1 regiment). See Anders (1953), 7, 18, 32–35.

(10,000 to 3,350), the blitzkrieg—prepared, coordinated, and purposeful—smashed the frontier defenses, destroyed 800 planes on the ground by noon, and swept forward 400 miles in only four weeks.

Soviet intelligence had known the German plan for some time. Yet total tactical and almost complete strategic surprise had been achieved.[27] Why? The answer, as we shall see, exposes the complex reality of intelligence.

3 Warnings:
Early Indications

One of the first rules of war is: don't march on Moscow.

—Field-Marshal Montgomery

This and the next two chapters seek to list all the warnings of BARBAROSSA reported to have circulated before the invasion itself. Although the inventory is long and detailed, such close examination is needed for two purposes. First, its sheer volume dispels the widely held myth that there was any dearth of relevant information, thus sharpening the real question, namely, how decision makers can make faulty interpretations of even ample intelligence. Second, by their rich detail the warnings supply an all too rare example of the varied and complex ways by which even the most secret operations may be disclosed. Furthermore, the presentation enables the reader to derive inductively his own insights about some of the realities of the functioning of intelligence collection and its relationship to evaluation. The subsequent chapters make explicit the manner in which this information was interpreted and acted on.

The numerous warnings are presented in chronological order except where it has proved convenient to combine some because they represent a series: one emanating from a single source, or being transmitted through a single intermediary, or constituting a single type of special information. Counting such series as a single warning, eighty-four "warnings" are identified and separately described.

1. "Perfidious Albion"

The British Government was the first to begin a series of warnings to Russia about the German threat. They were initiated with a personal letter dated 25 June 1940 from Churchill to Stalin, merely pointing out that Hitler's insatiable drive posed a common problem. When Stalin received the newly arrived British ambassador on 1 July, Stafford Cripps delivered Churchill's note and added his concurring remarks. Stalin was "formal and frigid" toward Cripps, and he never replied to the note.[1]

Churchill's warning was not based on intelligence reports, nor did it pretend to be. Like President Roosevelt's similar warning to the Russians preceding the Hitler-Stalin nonaggression pact, it was based only on an accurate appraisal of Hitler's thinking and a prescient reading of the developing events. Furthermore, on 13 July Foreign Commissar Molotov, on explicit instructions from Stalin, saw German Ambassador Friedrich von der Schulenburg in order to give the Germans a written memorandum of this private conversation—for which indiscretion Ribbentrop soon replied that he "greatly appreciated this information." [2] Stalin had thereby assured the Germans that he "was not of the opinion that German military successes menaced the Soviet Union and her friendly relations with Germany. . . ." [3]

This was only the first of several such British (and American) warnings that Stalin disclosed to the Germans. He evidently feared that such warnings concealed a provocation, regardless of their accuracy, and sought to forestall any German suspicions of secret connivance by his prompt admission of such approaches. He probably reasoned that, even if German intelligence did not ferret out these contacts, the British might well see to it that the Germans were told. In early 1941, Britain desperately needed to divert Hitler.

2. Order of Battle

The large and rapid physical redeployment eastward of virtually the entire Wehrmacht[4] was one early and continuing indication of some sort of change in German intentions that could not be concealed from any functioning intelligence service.* (Tables 3.1 and 3.2 compare the German and Russian troop strength in the period preceding BARBAROSSA.) This highly visible movement was

* A simple mathematical model of train-watching demonstrates that a quite small number of observers can, by infrequent and random monitoring of key rail junctions, effectively monitor virtually all traffic, even in a large and complex network such as led eastward to the Russian border. (See Richard E. Barringer, "Industrial Simulation Model of the Soviet Economy" [Waltham, Mass.: Raytheon Corporation, Strategic Studies Department, 1963].) A detailed account of the train-watching techniques developed by British Military Intelligence in World War I is given by a former practitioner, Ivone Kirkpatrick (1959), 15–17.

Table 3.1 Deployment of German Forces

Date	No. of Divisions Facing Russia	Total Divisions	Percentage Facing Russia
25 May 1939	—	51	—
1 Sept.	58	—	—
18 Sept.	65	117	56
c. Feb. 1940	7	—	—
10 May	4	156	3
14 June	negligible	c. 150	(c. 3)
31 July	negligible	130	(c. 3)
26 Aug.	5	—	(c. 3)
Oct.	17	—	—
18 Dec.	34	146	23
Jan.–Feb. 1941	c. 70	—	—
Mar.	c. 65	—	—
May	87	—	—
1 June	80	—	—
21 June	123	c. 180	68

Sources: Mainly Erickson, Churchill, and the published German records and memoirs. There is surprisingly poor agreements among these sources on specific numbers. This seems mainly due to the elementary failure of the German (and British) military and intelligence experts to define the readiness or mission of units and the boundaries of the front. The most detailed published statistics of the Wehrmacht order of battle are in Burkhart Mueller-Hillebrand, *Das Heer, 1933–1945*, 2 vols. (Frankfurt: Mittler, 1954, 1956), and in Jacobsen, 1 (1965), 97E.

directly observed and reported by Russian, British, Polish underground, and even Japanese intelligence. In its later stages it was evident even to the more perceptive foreign correspondents.[5]

The only difficult problem with this form of direct surveillance, aside from the high attrition rate among inspectors,[6] is how to evaluate the purpose of such movements. The sheer signals are indeterminate. They may signify an attack. But equally they may signal a demonstration of force to extort some condition in lieu of attack, a demonstration used only as a bluff, a staging for subsequent movement against some other target, or even a mere training maneuver. Collateral evidence is needed to determine the

Table 3.2   Deployment of Russian Forces

Date	No. of Divisions Facing Germany	Total Divisions	Percentage Facing Germany
Sept. 1939	65	138 (+30) = 148	44%
Dec.	106	—	—
Aug. 1940	64 (+10) = 69	183 (+38) = 196	35%
Apr. 1941	—	210 (+40) = 223	—
22 June	139 (+37) = 151	—	—
1 Dec.	235 (+40) = 248	303 (+50) = 320	78%

Note: Parentheses give number of armored (or mechanized) brigades. Totals count three Russian armored brigades as one division.
Sources: Erickson (1962a), 767–768. See also Blau (1955), 7, and Kesselring (1954), 93. These are, at best, rough figures. There are wide discrepancies among the sources. The contemporary German estimates were based on weak intelligence, and comprehensive Soviet figures are still awaited.

significance or intention of force deployments. Nevertheless, military deployments do affect military capabilities; and major changes in such deployments normally reflect *some* change in broad political or military policy.

By late November 1940 the Wehrmacht's eastward deployment had already become widely known and was a subject of nervous speculation on the diplomatic circuit in Moscow.[7]

A special part of the Wehrmacht's—and later BARBAROSSA's— lines of communication crossed neutral Sweden. In July 1940 Germany demanded and received transit rights on the Swedish railways for troops moving between Germany, Norway, and Finland. Almost 300,000 German troops had been shuttled back and forth across Sweden by 22 June 1941. To monitor the German deployment, Soviet intelligence recruited Swedish railwaymen, presumably even before the German attack on Russia. In any case, immediately after that event it became convenient to use the Swedish Communist party with its new-found anti-German policy. NKVD collaborators in the party, particularly peripatetic journalists, traveled about recruiting Communist railwaymen as train-watchers. It was in this manner that the subsequently famous spy Fritiof

Enbom was recruited in the fall of 1941. Enbom, then a railway lineman, continued to serve as a train-watcher until August 1943, when Sweden could safely defy the flagging Germans by withdrawing the transit privilege. Originally reporting directly to the party "cutouts," in February 1943 Enbom was finally taken under the direct control of his real masters, the NKVD office in the Soviet embassy in Stockholm.[8]

Presumably, Russian agents in Finland were maintaining a similar watch on the German deployments there and of Finnish mobilization itself. At least, the number of Soviet agents there greatly increased during late 1940 and early 1941.[9] This German deployment was obvious to the foreign press corps in Berlin by May 1941.[10]

The agreement among Red Army documents captured by the Wehrmacht, Soviet defectors, and recent official Soviet histories leaves no doubt that the Red Army had adequately detailed tactical intelligence on German troop movements and deployments along and behind the frontier.[11] For example, the Germans recovered a complete, up-to-date copy of their own entire order of battle on the first day of the war from the abandoned safe of the commander in chief of the First Cossack Army at Lomza.[12] It is quite possible this last material was one of the fruits of Rudolf Rössler's magnificent GRU intelligence line from Berlin to London (?) to Switzerland to Moscow.

3. Mobilization

As indicated in Table 3.1, the German buildup for BARBAROSSA required not only the vast redeployment already described but also a substantial mobilization. Undermanned divisions were brought up to strength; semiactive units were returned to active duty; and the conscription of new recruits was pressed more intensively than ever.[13]

German peasants were alerted from late December 1940 on by the suddenly increased requisitioning of horses upon which the blitzkrieg depended for its supply train. All this increased activity was quite apparent to Germans and to the foreign press and diplomatic corps in Germany. For example, the foreign wire service bureaus in Berlin were alerted in early January 1941, when their formerly easily deferred German office staffs lost their exemptions and were drafted.[14]

Mobilization on this scale clearly indicated that Hitler intended some new use for the Wehrmacht. But the signal, once again, was ambiguous. It did not tell *how* Hitler intended to use this force: as a threat or for attack. Nor did it tell *where* it was to be used: Russia, Britain, the Mediterranean, or several places at once.

4. Frontier Fortification

Early and visible indication of a less friendly German attitude toward Russia came in the form of extensive preparations for war on the eastern frontier zone. In late December 1940 the peasants of that portion of East Prussia immediately adjoining the Russian frontier were ordered to evacuate farther inland, and those farther back were told not to prepare for spring planting. Property and draft animals were confiscated (with compensation). The same procedure was undertaken in eastern Poland (but without compensation for these "inferior" souls).[15]

Although false rumors circulated in Berlin that "Organization Todt"—the Nazi's efficient corps of engineers under Major-General Dr. Fritz Todt—was erecting an eastern Siegfried Line, heavy construction was indeed required: airfields, depots, road improvements, and some fortified posts.[16] Actually, we now know that the Germans intended Soviet intelligence to learn of the few static defenses, hoping thereby to deceive them that the deployments indicated a purely defensive policy.[17] And the Soviet NKGB was indeed observing and reporting these activities, if we can believe the often wildly mendacious memoirs of Konon Molody, the notorious Soviet agent. Molody, who claims he was in the Communist underground in German-occupied Poland in 1940–1941, states he had penetrated Organization Todt in Warsaw as a messenger boy with false papers as a *Volksdeutscher*. Molody alleges that, beginning in April 1941, all the messages he carried to the German Army and Gestapo headquarters were photographed en route by fellow Communist agents.[18]

East Prussia and Poland were the main centers for Hitler's POW camps. Rumors reached Berlin in early 1941 that nearly a million prisoners of war were being transported to new camps farther west and that the old camps were being enlarged to twice their original capacity. By early May they were said to be standing ready to receive 3,000,000 new inmates.[19] These rumors were an ominous warning. Moreover, they were substantially true.[20] Some time late in February 1941 Lieutenant-General Hermann "Little Keitel" Reinecke, the infamous chief of the OKW's General Armed Forces Department, including its POW section, summoned over twenty chiefs of district POW sections to OKW headquarters in Berlin and notified them in strictest secrecy "that a tentative invasion of the Soviet territory had been planned for the beginning of summer 1941 and that in this connection OKW had elaborated essential measures, including the preparation of camps for Russian prisoners of war. . . ." [21]

One odd clue pointing to Russia as the target of this intense military activity was the sudden demand for all maps of Russia that emptied the German bookshops in spring 1941. Books on Russia also disappeared from circulation, General de Caulaincourt's memoirs of the Napoleonic campaign and books on the Russo-Polish war of 1920 becoming very popular at German army headquarters in the east.[22] Moreover, books of German-Russian phrases were printed in large numbers for the Wehrmacht. It is most unlikely that the Soviet diplomatic and press corps in Berlin missed such pointed evidence.

5. Border Violations

Another early indicator of Hitler's aggressive design was the Luftwaffe's reconnaissance flights over the Russian defense zone. These flagrantly provocative intelligence operations were necessary to BARBAROSSA planning because the German intelligence services had woefully neglected the development of conventional agent networks in Russia and could not improvise them effectively on the short notice given by the BARBAROSSA timetable. It is quite clear from the captured German archives that the Nazis had no effective intelligence nets or fifth column in Russia, much less the vast conspiratorial networks of Quislings in the Kremlin depicted by Stalin's then widely credited purge propaganda.[23]

The effort to supplement inadequate agent networks in Russia with aerial surveillance was a similar problem and a similar solution that fifteen years later faced the American CIA in mounting its U-2 program. The OKH, in the persons of von Brauchitsch and Halder, had recommended aerial photoreconnaissance of Russia in September 1940, but Hitler refused to authorize flights so early on the grounds that they would prematurely disclose his intentions.[24] Germany's aerial espionage program was launched by a personal and secret order of October 1940 from Hitler to Luftwaffe Lieutenant-Colonel Theodor Rowehl.* This order, according to a popular and possibly inaccurate account, specified: "You will organize long-range reconnaissance formations, capable of photographic reconnaissance of Western Russian territory from a great height. This height must be so exceptional that the Soviets will not notice anything. You must be ready by 15th June 1941." [25]

This top secret "Rowehl Squadron" or, to use its official cover name, the Reconnaissance Group under the Commander in Chief Luftwaffe, became operational about February 1941 but was limited to short-range penetrations. By early March, the OKH was receiving Rowehl's valuable reports.[26] This program used specially adapted reconnaissance bombers: the Heinkel He-111 with a 28,000-foot ceiling, the Dornier Do-215-B2 with a 30,000-foot ceil-

---

* Actually, in 1939, before the war, the then Captain Rowehl commanded a special unit, the so-called Bildstaffel Rowehl based secretly in Hungary, that flew secret high-altitude photoreconnaissance missions over Britain. See Generalleutnant H. J. Rieckhoff, *Trumpf oder Bluff? 12 Jahr deutsche Luftwaffe* (Geneva: Verlag Interavia, 1945), p. 149. See also testimony of General Lahousen in *TMWC* (1947), 2:467–468, and 3:26–27, and Eyermann, 2 (1963), 35–44, 131–140, 264–269.

ing, the Junkers Ju-88B with a 33,000-foot ceiling, and the Ju-86P with the then sensational ceiling of 39,000 feet.* These planes, organized in four squadrons, flew numerous successful missions across the entire frontier zone as far as Lake Ilmen, Minsk, Kiev, and the north coast of the Black Sea. A fortnight before B-*Tag*, their missions were extended to deep penetration flights.[27] Only one of these planes was lost over Russia—a forced landing near Minsk just two days before the invasion—but the crew destroyed the plane with its incriminating photographic evidence before their capture.[28] It is evident from the location of some of the targets and the short range of the particular aircraft that most of the flights were made from German or German-occupied territory, contrary to the assumption of most writers that they were all still based in Hungary.[29]

The Soviet frontier defenses first detected the German reconnaissance flights on 27 March 1941. An informal protest was made the next day to Reichsmarschall Hermann Göring by the Soviet deputy military attaché in Berlin. By 18 April, 80 such violations had been observed, one involving the emergency landing on 15 April of a German airplane complete with camera, exposed film, and a topographical map of the Russian frontier zone. The Soviet government cited these cases in a formal protest to the German government on 21 April. However, this "protest" was in fact virtually an acquiescence, because the Russian note reminded the Germans of the standing order to Soviet forces "not to fire on German planes flying over Soviet territory so long as such flights do not occur frequently." [30] The third and final and useless Soviet protest was delivered in Berlin on 21 June by Ambassador Dekanozov and simultaneously repeated by Molotov to the embarrassed German ambassador in Moscow. This pathetic *note verbale* cited 180 additional violations since 19 April and concluded from their systematic nature and depth of penetration—sometimes 100 to 150 kilometers—that they were not "accidental." [31] After the invasion the Russian Informburo alleged that a total of 324 such overflights

---

* By comparison, the Lockheed U-2, operational since 1956, cruises at 70,000–90,000 feet, and later models can reach 100,000 feet. See John M. Carroll, *Secrets of Electronic Espionage* (New York: E. P. Dutton, 1966), pp. 167–187.

had occurred in 1941, asserting that they "cannot be explained otherwise than as a desire to make reconnaissance." [32]

Incidentally, the occasionally overzealous efforts to prove Nazi war guilt have almost universally overlooked the fact that the Red Air Force itself was responsible for a substantial number of border violations against her Western neighbors. However, these reconnaissance sorties do seem to have followed, not preceded, the comparable Luftwaffe efforts. In either case, the Russians were reportedly offering such provocation at least as early as 1 March 1941.[33] Molotov, in his historic broadcast of 22 June announcing the invasion, probably lied in categorically denying that any Russian aircraft sorties had been previously authorized beyond the border.[34]

Although British R.A.F. intelligence had been flying photoreconnaissance aircraft over Germany since the beginning of 1939, this endeavor made only a peripheral contribution to their knowledge of the redeployment of the Wehrmacht. Thus the superb strippeddown Spitfire's often undetected photo missions at 33,000 feet partially verified the Germans' cancellation of SEA LION, the vaguely planned invasion of Britain. However, Air Vice-Marshal Medhurst, the director of Air Intelligence, was not able to get his short-range Spitfires and medium range Blenheims over Poland or Rumania where they would undoubtedly have contributed to the overall redeployment picture that was emerging from train-watching and other reports.[35]

6. Increased German Espionage and Patrolling

As part of their effort to obtain better tactical (and strategic) intelligence on the assigned target, the German army and intelligence services gradually stepped up two activities that were highly visible to their Soviet counterparts: espionage inside Russia and military probings of her border defenses.

German intelligence on the Soviet military system was rather weak and too out of date for purposes of BARBAROSSA operational planning. Accordingly, in September 1940, the OKW directed Admiral Wilhelm Canaris to expand his Abwehr's coverage. By early

1941, Reinhard Heydrich's SD was doing the same. Since it is not feasible to create secure espionage nets on a crash basis, the more or less effective Soviet counterespionage service (KRU) of the NKGB was soon enjoying great success in seizing the majority of the several hundred German agents being smuggled into the country.[36] The number of German agents apprehended increased steadily between January 1940 and June 1941, the rate in the last three months being some twenty-five to thirty times that of the same period in the previous year.[37]

Border patrolling, particularly by Abwehr-recruited anti-Communist Ukrainian nationalist guerrilla groups, increased as well; and some 1,300 of these border violators were killed or wounded while crossing.[38]

7. A Christmas Present

On 18 December 1940 Hitler issued the initial detailed order for the invasion of Russia. This was his "Directive No. 21: Operation BARBAROSSA." It was TOP SECRET, prepared in just nine copies, and issued to only five offices: two to the OKW and one to each of the operations staffs of the three services.[39]

Seven days later, on 25 December, an accurate summary of (what I presume to be) that specific document reached the Soviet military attaché in Berlin. The summary was in the form of a letter that reported Hitler's decision to prepare for the war, gave a detailed and (as subsequently appreciated) generally accurate outline of the plan of operations, and indicated that the invasion was scheduled to begin in the spring of 1941. The letter was anonymous and the Russians evidently had no clue to the identity of the generous donor of this most remarkable Christmas present.[40] While this event borders on the fantastic, it is almost certainly true because it reflects no credit on the alertness or industry of the Soviet intelligence services, which was the main purpose of the Russian article in which the incident was first disclosed in 1965.

8. To Russia with Love

The Soviet embassy in Berlin was again the recipient of a free gift of intelligence about six weeks later, some time in mid-February.

This time the gift was brought in person by the donor, a German printer. It was a copy of a conversation manual, or phrase book, that he said was just then rolling off the presses in large numbers. It consisted of sentences in German with their Russian equivalents given in Latin letters. The sentences, however, indicated the very special purpose of the phrase book: "Where is the kolkhoz Chairman?" "Are you a Communist?" "What is the name of the secretary of the Party district committee?" "Hands up! I'll shoot." "Surrender!" And so forth. The phrase book was promptly forwarded to Moscow in the embassy pouch.[41]

9. Admiral Canaris

Several unauthorized disclosures of BARBAROSSA originated with Admiral Wilhelm Canaris, the chief of the Abwehr, the OKW's military intelligence department. This strange anti-Nazi allegedly disclosed some warnings in Berne in casual conversation in the home of a Polish gentlewoman whom he had rescued and settled in Switzerland. In the winter of 1941 he informed her that Hitler would certainly attack Russia sooner or later. The following spring he told her that the German military deployments in the Balkans were not directed against Turkey but "perhaps" Russia. Whether Canaris made these disclosures by indiscretion or design is now unknowable, but probably the latter because he surely knew that Madame J—— had registered with the Free Polish movement and was in close contact with the Polish legation in Berne and, through them, the British to whom she recounted his statements. Indeed, in October 1940 Canaris had specifically instructed her to repeat their conversations to no one, *except the British*.[42]

10. Another Warning from Cripps

Alexander Werth alleges that in "February, after his visit to Ankara," British Ambassador Cripps warned the Soviet Foreign Commissariat that Germany was preparing invasions both of the Balkans now and of Russia "in the near future."[43] While there is no direct confirmation for Werth's assertion, there is strong circumstantial evidence supporting it. First, Cripps did hold this view at the time. (He acquired it during his consultations on 27 February

1941 in Ankara with Foreign Minister Eden and C.I.G.S. General
Sir John Dill.)[44]

Second, and more important, Cripps did make this point to the
British and American press on the day of his return from Ankara,
the last day of February—hence the very day he would have notified the Russian Foreign Commissariat, if Werth is correct in his
facts. In any case, Cripps extemporaneously tacked the following
astounding coda to his off-the-record press conference:

Wait a minute, there is something else I'd like to tell you. I am
convinced that Hitler will attack this country before the end of
June. Hitler will not dare to wait, because he knows that the Soviet
industrial progress and defense preparations are advancing too
rapidly. You think he will strike at England first, and as I told you
confidentially, General Dill appears to agree with you. But I say
that Hitler must deal with this country first, and that he will
launch an attack not later than the end of June.[45]

A remarkable piece of guesswork. Or was it mere guess? Cripps got
the month (June) right only by accident. Hitler's timetable for
BARBAROSSA was then still set for 15 May. As we shall see later,
Cripps may have known much more of Hitler's moves than he revealed to the journalists.

Regardless of how well-founded Cripps's prognostication may have
been, it was not credited by the Anglo-American press corps in
Moscow. Nor, seemingly, by the Russians. Indeed, for them it
became only one of a series of marks against him as a provocateur,
a charge that they were to make both publicly in a TASS release
on 13 June and privately to the Germans.

The KGB now admits that, "In February of 1941 information was
obtained that the invasion of the British Isles was being postponed
until the end of the war against the USSR." [46] While the KGB
does not identify the source, it could well have been Cripps. Even
more interesting is that the KGB implies that this warning had
been recognized by Soviet intelligence as authentic at the time.

11. At GRU Headquarters in Moscow
Soviet military intelligence, the GRU, had been receiving several
warnings at its Moscow headquarters on the square at Kropotkin

Gate. Some time in February the following important and partly accurate message arrived:

> For the attack on the USSR, three army groups are being set up: the 1st group under the command of General Field Marshal von Bock will strike in the direction of Petrograd; the 2nd group under the command of General Field Marshal von Rundstedt, in the direction of Moscow; and the 3rd group under the command of General Field Marshal von Leeb, in the direction of Kiev. The tentative date for beginning the attack on the USSR is May 20.[47]

Although otherwise generally accurate, this message transposed the commands of the three field-marshals. The actual plan—in effect since December 1940—had Wilhelm von Leeb commanding Army Group C in the north, Fedor von Bock commanding Army Group B in the center, and Gerd von Rundstedt commanding Army Group A in the south.*

12. The Amateur from Texas

While the Soviet intelligence services were desperately rebuilding their shattered espionage networks in Germany, some of the earliest concrete warnings of the impending German attack were those passed to Stalin from American intelligence. The American contribution is particularly remarkable because unexpected and improbable, given the fact that U.S. foreign intelligence itself was almost nonexistent at the time, having only begun to reconstitute itself in 1939. Indeed, the earliest American intelligence coups vis-à-vis BARBAROSSA were entirely the effort of a remarkable amateur, Mr. Sam E. Woods.† He had been in Berlin since 1937 as the U.S.

---

* On 1 April 1941, these three formations were retitled Army Groups North, Center, and South, respectively.

† Sam E[dison] Woods (Texas, 1892–1953). By turns a college teacher, engineer, businessman, and, since 1928, diplomat; assistant trade commissioner, Prague, 1928–1934; commercial attaché, Prague, 1934–1937; in Berlin as commercial attaché-at-large, 1937–1939; commercial attaché, Berlin, 1939–1941, when interned for five months; and consul-general, Zürich, 1942–1945. During this tour in Zürich, Woods reestablished contact with his superb sources in Berlin. Through them he obtained some of the earliest and more important intelligence on the new German magnetic mine and on their atomic research on heavy water. He also personally arranged the escape of nearly 1,700 Allied

commercial attaché, a post not then in use as an espionage cover. However, this forty-eight-year-old, unassuming, cosmopolitan Texan had a talent for making well-placed friends in key offices of the Nazi regime. One of these friends was Erwin Respondik.[48] Another even more important informant was the career diplomat Hans Heinrich Herwarth von Bittenfeld. The latter was, as "Johnny Herwarth," well known to the Americans. Since 1936, while serving in Moscow as Schullenburg's second secretary, he was the most valued informant of his American counterparts, "Charlie" Thayer and "Chip" Bohlen. Called to active military service in 1939, he then acted as Woods's main informant.* Both men were anti-Nazis with close connections to several ministries, the Reichsbank, and senior Nazi party members.

In August 1940, only one month after the critical, initial planning meetings for war against Russia, Herwarth von Bittenfeld informed Woods in general terms of these conferences at Hitler's headquarters. Over the next four weeks his information, which he passed to Woods in a darkened cinema, became increasingly specific. He even correctly assured Woods that the continuing prep-

---

aviators interned in Switzerland. I presume Woods was by then a "professional" with the OSS, although this has never been officially acknowledged. In 1945 he went briefly to Istanbul as consul-general; was again in Zürich, 1945–1946, with that title; and was consul-general with rank of minister, Munich, 1947–1952, when retired. Woods should not be mistaken for the pseudonymous "Stallforth" with whom von Hassel had covert dealings in 1941. Judging from Sherwood (1948), Stallforth must have been James D. Mooney, president of the General Motors Overseas Corporation. See Hull, 2 (1948), 967–968; Shirer (1960), 842–843; Long (1966), 182–184, 312–313, 326, 335; and *The National Cyclopaedia of American Biography*, vol. 45 (New York: White, 1962), pp. 55–56, with photograph. Unfortunately, his lengthy Associated Press obituary notice filed from Munich cast no new light on the problem. For a contemporary reminiscence see Russell (1941), 71–72. For his exfiltration operations see Graham H. Stuart, *American Diplomatic and Consular Practice* (New York, 1952), p. 329. Obviously, Woods deserves a biographer.

* Although Herwarth von Bittenfeld (b. 1904) was involved in the 1944 plot to blow up Hitler, he survived the Gestapo's manhunt to become the West German ambassador to London and Rome. He now lives in retirement in Munich. I am indebted to Dr. Harold C. Deutsch for this previously unpublished information about Herwarth von Bittenfeld, whom Deutsch has recently interviewed.

arations for SEA LION (the invasion of Britain) was only a deliberate blind. Further details also pointed eastward; they concerned the Wehrmacht's formation of shadow regional occupation governments, including the earmarking of personnel to act as economic staffs and the actual printing of bales of ruble bank notes. Finally, some time between early January and mid-February, Herwarth von Bittenfeld was able—through a friend in the OKW—to supply the details of what must have been the recent "Directive No. 21" itself or, possibly, minutes of Hitler's meeting on 9 January with his top military chiefs, including its strategic operations plan and the fact that all planning was to be "completed in the spring of 1941." By 21 February when Woods's impressive packet of reports finally reached the secretary of state, Cordell Hull immediately understood its sensational nature but—suspecting it to be a German "plant"—passed it to FBI Director Hoover for comment. Hoover thought it seemed authentic. Then, in late February, Hull had Assistant Secretary of State Breckinridge Long verify the reputation and connection of Woods's contact with a "prominent German exile" in the United States whose name had been given as a reference.[49] This person was no less than Heinrich Brüning,* the former Catholic Center party chancellor, who owed his loss of office in 1932 to the intrigues of General Kurt von Schleicher and Hitler.[50] Brüning, then a professor of public administration at the Harvard Business School, was invited by Long to Washington to view and discuss this information. Satisfied with the verification of Woods's document by Hoover and Brüning, Hull and Welles took the matter to Roosevelt.[51] They agreed this definitive intelligence

---

* Brüning (1885–1970), in exile in the United States since 1933, was often used as the liaison man in foreign contacts by members of the German Catholic opposition and even some disgruntled Foreign Office officials. The Catholic Centerists also maintained liaison with General Beck and Admiral Canaris. Active Catholic Centerist conspirators included such people as Dr. Josef Wirmer, who were also collaborating with Carl Goerdeler's circle. For Brüning's connections with the German underground, see the books by Schlabrendorff (1947, 1965); Hans Rothfels, *The German Opposition to Hitler: An Appraisal*, new rev. ed. (Chicago: Henry Regnery, 1962); Terence Prittie, *Germans against Hitler* (Boston: Little, Brown); Dulles (1947, 1963); Ritter (1954); and Boveri (1963).

be communicated to the Russians.[52] Accordingly, on the morning of 1 March, Hull telegraphed a summary to U.S. Ambassador Laurence Steinhardt, urgently recommending that he convey its substance to Molotov or, failing him, to Deputy Foreign Commissar Andrei Vyshinsky. However, Steinhardt—like Cripps later—was reluctant, and on the third he advised Hull that this not be done, on the perceptive grounds that the Russians would only interpret it as a British provocation. The next day Hull replied that he fully accepted the reservations of this man on the spot, canceled the offending message, but with charming frankness informed Steinhardt that, anyway, the home office had already given the message to the Soviet ambassador in Washington.[53]

Welles's opportunity had arisen because he was then engaged with Soviet Ambassador Konstantin Umansky in a series of bitter conversations on several outstanding U.S.-Soviet differences. When at their next meeting, on 1 March, Umansky was—on Hull's instructions—told this warning by Welles, he visibly blanched, thanked Welles for this confidence, averred that "I fully realize the gravity of the message," and promised to forward it to Moscow immediately.[54] At the end of their next conversation, on 20 March, Umansky asked Welles if he had any further confirmation. Welles assured him of this but seemingly did not volunteer details.[55] If true, this is unfortunate because the new intelligence was most illuminating. The previous day, the Greek minister in Washington, Cimon Diamantopoulos, had given Welles a memorandum asserting that the Greek government had learned that the Swedish government had been informed by its diplomatic missions in Berlin, Bucharest, and Helsinki that certain German sources said serious discussions were under way indicating that "Germany could attack Russia." [56]

Although the Russians made no further response, Hull believed their sudden signing of a nonaggression treaty with Japan three weeks later reflected Stalin's effort "to protect himself in the Far East in his new-found belief that Hitler intended attacking him in Europe." [57]

13. A Misperceived Clue from Vienna

On 5 March, Reichsmarschall Hermann Göring and General Ion Antonescu, each accompanied by some officials, met in the Belvedere Palace in Vienna to discuss the question of Germany's oil needs from Rumania and Russia. Although Antonescu expressed his usual fears of Russia, Göring went out of his way to stress that the only conceivable difficulty that might arise in Russo-German relations was specifically over the delivery of oil and not at all their general relationship.[58] All in all, a rather pacific meeting. Yet, at least in 1965, the Soviet KGB implied that it constituted a warning, saying, "In March the meeting of Antonescu with one of the German officials, Bering [Göring!], became known [to Soviet intelligence] during which the question of war against the Soviet Union was discussed." [59] Unless Russian intelligence received a different transcript of the meeting than that recorded for posterity by the near-perfect 300-words-per-minute German rapporteur, Dr. Paul Otto Schmidt, it is difficult to understand how they could have seen any relevance to BARBAROSSA, even afterward. In fact, Antonescu did not become witting until June; and, although Göring was more or less witting, he leaned over backward to avoid catering to Antonescu's desire for just such a German move.

14. Activities of the Soviet Military Attaché in Berlin

The Soviet military attaché in Berlin throughout this crucial period was Major-General V. I. Tupikov. Like all military attachés he was a "legal" spy: his espionage was sanctioned by tacit international convention, his freedom from arrest was guaranteed by diplomatic immunity, and his communications to his government were assured of prompt and secret handling by the local embassy's code clerks and radio transmitter.[60] And, like all Soviet military attachés, Tupikov reported directly to the GRU—military intelligence—whose director was Lieutenant-General Filipp Ivanovich Golikov.

General Tupikov had already received, and faithfully passed on, his first warning of BARBAROSSA the previous December.[61] Now, on

14 March, Tupikov transmitted the statement of a German major: "We are changing our plan completely. We are going east, against the USSR. We will seize the USSR's grain, coal and oil. Then we will be invincible and can go on with the war against England and America." [62] Less than six days later, Tupikov also reported that the invasion was to be expected between 15 May and 15 June 1941.[63]

15. Washington "Magic"

The memoirs of the senior U.S. State Department officials who sought to alert the Russians to the German threat—Hull, Welles, and Long—do not describe the nature or identify the sources of the confirmation of Sam E. Woods's original warning or warnings. All commentators have assumed that these also originated with the same source, Woods. This is not the case. Or at least the followup messages of Woods were no longer the only, much less the best, source. Quite spectacular verification was now reaching Washington through an entirely new channel.

The story remained hidden for so long because it fell within one of the innermost rings of state security, involving the electronic interception and cryptanalysis of secret communications. While the story has been in great part publicly revealed with regard to "Magic," to the Americans' magnificent breaking of the Japanese diplomatic ciphers in 1940–1943, its full extent and implication, particularly that part concerning BARBAROSSA, have only recently been disclosed.[64]

The general problem of unauthorized interception and reading of others' secret communications is so necessary to understanding the international intelligence picture in 1941 that it is treated as a separate section in Chapter 6. However, it is useful to single out one particular aspect for discussion at this point, because it involves a major disclosure of BARBAROSSA to the Russians.

Since 1940 the U.S. government had become quite dependent on the broken Japanese ciphers for its intelligence on Japanese foreign and military policy. William F. Friedman and his fellow "magicians" of Section B (Code and Cipher Solutions) of the

Army's Signal Intelligence Service (SIS) had succeeded in doing something their Japanese counterparts believed impossible: they had reconstructed the Japanese ciphering machines. Moreover, the American-built models were so superior that U.S. intelligence was henceforward able to decipher the Japanese messages faster than the Japanese code centers themselves. Consequently, it caused a great flap among the security-minded American cryptologists when on 28 April 1941 they intercepted the following top secret ciphered telegram from the German chargé d'affaires in Washington to his Foreign Ministry:

AS COMMUNICATED TO ME BY AN ABSOLUTELY RELIABLE SOURCE, THE STATE DEPARTMENT IS IN POSSESSION OF THE KEY TO THE JAPANESE CODING SYSTEM AND IS THEREFORE ABLE ALSO TO DECIPHER INFORMATION TELEGRAMS FROM TOKYO TO AMBASSADOR NOMURA HERE REGARDING AMBASSADOR OSHIMA'S REPORTS FROM BERLIN.

THOMSEN [65]

This message was intercepted and read that same day by the U.S. SIS with some apprehension, because they feared that a change in the Japanese codes would surely follow the warning, if the Germans chose to pass on this information.[66]

Prompted by Dr. Hans Thomsen's warning, the Wilhelmstrasse's official in charge of German-Japanese relations, Dr. Heinrich Stahmer, did indeed speak on this matter to Ambassador Hiroshi Ōshima five days later. As we shall see, the German decision to warn the Japanese was taken not for any altruistic reasons but only to seal off the leakage of BARBAROSSA information through them. That same day, 3 May, Ōshima sent Foreign Minister Yōsuke Matsuoka an eyes-only wire in his most sophisticated cipher, PURPLE-CA, stating:

STAHMER . . . SAID THAT GERMANY MAINTAINS A FAIRLY RELIABLE INTELLIGENCE ORGANIZATION [IN THE U.S.] AND, ACCORDING TO INFORMATION OBTAINED FROM THE ABOVE MENTIONED ORGANIZATION, IT IS QUITE RELIABLY ESTABLISHED THAT THE U.S. GOVERNMENT IS READING AMBASSADOR NOMURA'S CODE MESSAGES. . . .[67]

This key transmission was monitored by the U.S. Navy. The U.S. monitors and cryptanalysts were now urgently following this security crisis through to its curious ending. Two days later Japanese Foreign Minister Matsuoka passed the warning to Nomura, his ambassador in Washington. Matsuoka also ordered Ōshima in Berlin to ask Stahmer for the source of his information, but Ōshima replied that the German Foreign Ministry had refused to disclose it. The upshot was that the Japanese decided that their prized diplomatic machine cipher was unbreakable. Therefore, they did not change ciphers but merely tightened internal embassy security, on the false assumption that the messages were, at worst, being pilfered.[68]

Although this denouement astonished and delighted its secret American audience, the Americans feverishly sought to discover their own very real initial security leak that had reached Thomsen on 28 April. An urgent but detailed investigation revealed many gaps in security. For example, Roosevelt's military aide had lost two monitoring summaries, one of which was recovered from his unclassified wastebasket. But the crucial breach was discovered in the State Department. Hull had virtually ignored his part of the solemn interagency agreement of January that had been designed to ensure the most limited and carefully guarded distribution of both the original intercepts and the summaries and evaluations explicitly based on them.[69] Hull had not only extended access to at least ten of his staff but, to facilitate access, had permitted the reproduction and circulation of additional mimeographed copies.* One of these pirated copies was traced to the files of Undersecretary Welles. He was the leak.

Sumner Welles (as described in warning 12) had been assigned by Hull and Roosevelt to warn the Russians of BARBAROSSA. Welles on 1 March had passed Woods's information to Ambassador Umansky. However, he withheld the name and nature of the source, and

---

* Distribution among the senior officials was to Hull, Welles, Stanley Hornbeck, Hamilton, Ballentine, Adolph Berle, and Dunn. Junior officers with access included W. R. Langdon, M. W. Schmidt, J. M. Jones, and John P. Davies, Jr.

he and Hull were disappointed that Umansky did not rise to their delicious bait. At first, Welles observed similar routine precaution in passing Umansky the new intelligence that had begun to come in. This material was the intercepts of telegraphic traffic from the Japanese embassies in Berlin, Rome, and Moscow. The first was a telegram on 19 March from Moscow in which Ambassador Yoshitsugu Tatekawa reported a radical change in Russo-German relations. Similar material accumulated to the point that SIS on 22 March issued a memorandum (I.B. 1–155) that, after summarizing all the relevant "Magic" intercepts, flatly predicted "a German attack on the U.S.S.R. within two months." Next, on 3 and 4 April two telegrams were intercepted from Ambassador Ōshima in Berlin. They outlined Germany's "preparations for war with Russia." [70]

Welles presumably decided that this was the sort of more or less hard intelligence that was required to convince the skeptical Russians. Accordingly, he took the potentially disastrous risk, seemingly entirely on his own, of showing Umansky his unauthorized copies of the original decrypted translations and the SIS memorandum of 22 March.[71]

Unknown to Welles, the Russians were intensely fearful of Anglo-American provocations directed toward what the Russians falsely believed to be a precariously balanced Russo-German relationship, not knowing that Hitler had already decided to end the whole balancing act. Moscow's fear was so great that Molotov had immediately notified the Germans of Churchill's initial vague warning in July 1940. Ambassador Umansky, undoubtedly on instructions from Moscow, now emulated his foreign commissar. Accordingly, he soon informed Dr. Thomsen, his German counterpart in Washington, that the Americans had evidence of a German plan to attack Russia that they had culled from Ambassador Ōshima's wires to Tokyo.[72] This was the factual basis of Thomsen's wire to Berlin on 29 April as well as the guarded warning to Ōshima embodied in Stahmer's 3 May wire to Tokyo. Thus Welles's supreme indiscretion had triggered both the Japanese and the American security investigations.

There is some curious, partial verification of this tale in an early leak to the U.S. press and its official Soviet denial.[73] The July 1942 issue of the *Ladies' Home Journal* carried the first of a two-part article coauthored by Forrest Davis and Ernest K. Lindley, on America's road to Pearl Harbor. Both were prominent Washington journalists; indeed, Lindley was then the Washington bureau chief for *Newsweek*. This remarkable piece, a sort of unofficial White Paper, clearly was written with rather full access to U.S. officials—White House, State Department, and even OSS sources being most evident. As mentioned earlier, Davis and Lindley had made the first public reference to the fact that Welles had given Ambassador Umansky intelligence warning of BARBAROSSA. Although their reference was a somewhat garbled "leak," it appears to refer to the intelligence from Woods rather than that from reading Ōshima's telegrams. However, they added the explicit remark that Ambassador Umansky had passed Welles's warning to the German chargé d'affaires (Thomsen) in Washington.[74] Umansky, then back in Moscow, promptly issued a formal public denial of the charge, counterattacking it as a provocation designed to split the wartime allies. (Incidentally, after denying the charge he admitted that he had forwarded Welles's warning to his home government.)[75] The charge about Umansky's trafficking with the German embassy was dropped from the subsequently published book version of the Davis-Lindley article.[76] I do not know whether this was done because Umansky's official denial was believed or because the authors or their publisher bowed to his countercharge.*

16. The *Chicago Daily News* Skips a Beat

There is a curious footnote to the U.S. State Department's information and disclosures on BARBAROSSA. While Hull and Welles with President Roosevelt's approval were trying to warn Ambassador Umansky, another senior State Department official tried un-

---

* At that time the deliberate suppression of anti-Soviet material was very common among American publishers, who confused the U.S.-Soviet wartime *alliance* with *friendship*. Thus *Harper's* did not hesitate to suppress the publication of Trotsky's biography of Stalin until after the war. See the publisher's note in Leon Trotsky, *Stalin* (New York: Harper & Brothers, 1946).

successfully to alert the American press. This official was Adolf A. Berle, Jr., the assistant secretary of state handling intelligence affairs. In that capacity he was officially charged with liaison among the president, the State Department's own communications, intelligence, and security divisions, the Office of Naval Intelligence, the Military Intelligence Division, and the FBI. Berle was certainly receiving all or most of the BARBAROSSA intelligence. For example, we have seen that he was one of the seven men in the State Department who was on the formally authorized distribution list for the Army-Navy "Magic" intercepts. Moreover, I presume he was familiar with the Woods material and with the disclosures to Umansky.

In any case, some time in late March, Berle told Edgar Ansel Mowrer, the famous foreign correspondent of the *Chicago Daily News,* that Hitler would soon attack Russia. However, to protect his real and highly credible sources, Berle foolishly lied that this information had been given the State Department by T. V. Soong, the official Chinese purchasing agent in the United States. Mowrer was not impressed, only astonished that Berle would have credited such an unlikely source. Consequently, the intended leak aborted and Mowrer threw away a newsbeat of a lifetime.[77]

17. Polish Underground Intelligence

Although their army was swiftly crushed in 1939 by the Wehrmacht and the Red Army, the Poles were soon able to build a clandestine resistance movement loyal to their government-in-exile in London. From the beginning, its intelligence service was most sensitive to any indications of a Russo-German break because the Poles realized that this was their best hope of victory over their joint conquerors. As with the other intelligence services, their earliest indicators came from observing the Wehrmacht's buildup.

During this period the underground formed its army, the ZWZ (Union of Armed Warfare, renamed the Armja Krajowa or "Home Army" in 1942). This force, commanded by professional Polish officers then under General Rowecki (alias "Grot"), maintained its own large intelligence corps to provide the information essential for the day-to-day survival of the fiercely hunted underground.

The Warsaw underground headquarters had established effective communications with the London government-in-exile and its head of military intelligence, Colonel Mitkiewicz. Several clandestine radio transceivers were available for forwarding urgent, brief messages, and a variety of courier routes (to Portugal, Sweden, and Turkey) channeled bulky dispatches between Warsaw and London in a fortnight.[78]

The Polish underground intelligence was getting many of the BARBAROSSA clues. It detected the visible, preliminary movements of AUFBAU OST in the summer of 1940. Late that fall it noted but could not ferret out the content of a major interservice conference held at Spała between Field-Marshals von Brauchitsch and Walther von Reichenau and General Albert Kesselring. However, it recognized that the conference signaled a renewed German military interest in Eastern Europe. These early warnings were promptly radioed to London.[79]

Ordered by London to increase surveillance of all such indicators, the Polish intelligence corps had established by the winter of 1940 a systematic network of agents to monitor the entire Polish transportation, depot, and warehouse complex. These agents were recruited particularly among the Polish railway workers themselves. Consequently, accurately detailed reports of nearly all German troop deployments were inundating the Warsaw headquarters and being promptly forwarded to London.[80]

From about March 1941, all of this material bearing on BARBAROSSA was given by the Poles to their British hosts;[81] and they, in turn, passed it on to the Russians with the knowledge of the Poles.[82] Polish Prime Minister Władisław Sikorski was as anxious as Churchill that the Russians, if they were drawn into the war, would not be easily or quickly defeated.

Beginning in February, Poland was rapidly filling with German troops, and Polish intelligence was quickly discovering their unit designations, numbers, and locations.[83] Finally, toward the end of March the Polish intelligence in Warsaw concluded that 15 April was the probable date for the German attack on Russia. All German troop leave had been canceled from that date; transport and

other construction activities were ordered to fulfill current orders
by mid-April, and a hectic pace of conferences was reaching a peak
among the local German staffs. Consequently, London was informed by Warsaw of its conviction that B-day would be 15 April.[84]
A wrong date, but one upset like the then actual one—15 May—
by Hitler's spastic decision to interject Yugoslavia into his agenda
of conquest.

18. A Leak to British Intelligence
Some time in March, a senior British S.I.S. (M.I.6) officer, Captain
Leslie Arthur Nicholson, was flown to Barcelona to meet an anti-
Nazi (German?) diplomat who, having received proper permission
to retire and emigrate, was on his way to Argentina. During several
days of conversation the diplomat spoke freely of Hitler's plans
and actions. The most stunning information was a detailed and accurate account of BARBAROSSA. Although S.I.S. requested and received full details, they were quite skeptical. And so was the staff of
the Directorate of Military Intelligence (M.I.) when Nicholson
discussed the report with them. Their attitude was: "Why should
Hitler answer our prayers?" Nicholson's claim that this was the
first indication of BARBAROSSA received by British intelligence is
not wholly correct.[85]

19. The Red Air Attaché Seeks Proof
On 21 March, the Soviet air attaché in Berlin, Colonel Skorniakov,
engaged in conversation one of the German officials dealing with
Russo-German economic relations.* Skorniakov tried to pump
him about a German attack on Russia. He repeated this performance on 9 April, apparently without results.[86]

20. An Economic Clue
The Russians disclosed in the mid-1960s that their intelligence
service had received reliable information on 22 March stating that
"Hitler has issued a secret order to cease filling orders for the

---

* The German official, a Herr Immisch, was evidently with Alfred Rosenberg's
office.

USSR." [87] Although no other details are revealed, it would appear from the particular archive cited (the Defense Ministry) that the recipient was the GRU. Moreover, it may well be that the Soviet agent involved was the vice-president of the Škoda Works, Škvor, who was reporting similar information to the GRU office in Berlin around that same time. (See warning 32 for the ostensibly later but possibly misdated and hence identical warning from Mr. Škvor.)

21. Swedish Intelligence in Berlin

By 24 March, the Swedish ambassador in Berlin, Arvid Richert, had accumulated an impressive collection of intelligence on German intentions and plans. He summarized this information in the following rather accurate estimate.[88] Hitler had virtually abandoned his plan to invade England, preferring to take control of the main productive areas of Russia, probably in May. [All quite true.] Hitler was motivated to this decision by a conviction that the inevitable entrance of the United States into the war would be intolerable as long as Russia remained free to cut off her flow of essential supplies to Germany. Moreover, growing Soviet strength would soon enable her to reject German demands. [True.] Consequently, the Wehrmacht would, while maintaining aerial and submarine warfare against England, conduct a blitzkrieg against Russia. [True.] The detailed operational planning has been completed and the Wehrmacht has already been deploying by night in strength toward the Soviet border, a fact confirmed during the past ten days by Swedish engineers working in Warsaw. [True.] The invasion would be conducted by three groups: von Rundstedt's pushing off from Königsberg in the north, von Bock's driving from Warsaw in the center, and Wilhelm List's thrusting from Krakow in the south. [Some garbling here.] * However, the Rus-

* The actual plan called for von Leeb (Army Group C) in the north, von Bock (Army Group B) in the center, and von Rundstedt (Army Group A) in the south. However, List was correctly identified as being assigned to the south, but only in his subordinate position (under Army Group A) as commanding general of the Twelfth Army. Richert's information on order of battle seems to resemble the earlier Marcks's Plan more than the final BARBAROSSA "Directive No. 21."

sians would be offered a chance to avoid invasion by accepting a German ultimatum that would be presented, "probably in May," before the final attack order. The ultimatum would give Russia the following alternative to war: enter into a full alliance with the Axis (including joining the Tripartite Pact with Germany, Italy, and Japan) and receive a free hand in Finland and Iran. [This "ultimatum" notion was sheer fiction.]

The Swedish ambassador transmitted his report to his counterpart in Moscow, Minister Vilhelm Assarsson, and, I presume, to Swedish Foreign Minister Christian Günther. Then, on 24 March, Assarsson passed on this information to his American colleague, Ambassador Laurence Steinhardt, who promptly forwarded the intelligence to U.S. Secretary of State Hull.[89]

I do not know if this much traveled report also reached the Russians. Although the Swedish assistant air attaché in Moscow at that time was Captain Stig Wennerström, it was another eight years before he was recruited by Soviet military intelligence. In 1941, his private liaison was mainly with Wehrmacht attachés.[90]

22. The Commissar Order

On (or about) 30 March, Hitler verbally directed his 200 or so assembled BARBAROSSA military chiefs to conduct the forthcoming Russian campaign with "unprecedented, unmerciful and unrelenting harshness" and to execute out of hand all political commissars, in flagrant breach of international law.[91] When the dismayed Prussian gentlemen conveyed the gist of this infamous so-called Commissar Order (*Kommissarbefehl*) to Admiral Canaris and Colonel Hans Oster, these two Abwehr chiefs promptly made it known among their fellow anti-Nazi conspirators.[92] Although I have found no specific evidence, it is possible that this information was then passed on by one of the latter to their British contacts. It is known that the conspiracy's principal civilian leader, Carl Goerdeler, did not transmit it abroad but used it only to goad his German collaborators again to seek peace terms from Britain through his Swiss intermediaries.[93] In any event, this secret *Kommissarbefehl* was initially leaked only at high level, as even corps commanders such as Infantry-General Erich von Manstein did not receive the order until the week of the invasion.[94]

23. A Glimpse of Stalin

On 6 April, the Yugoslav minister in Moscow, Dr. Milan Gavrilović, concluded a six-and-a-half-hour discussion with Stalin immediately following the signing of the provocatively anti-German Soviet-Yugoslav Treaty of Friendship and Nonaggression by asking if he had heard the "rumors" that Germany intended to attack Russia "in May." Stalin merely replied, "Let them try it." [95] Incidentally, German intelligence in Budapest was intercepting—and soon selectively published—Gavrilović's running telephone conversations with Belgrade during the final negotiating sessions that night.[96]

4 Warnings:
A New Timetable

Wars and rumours of war.

–Matthew 24:6

Hitler's sudden decision on 27 March to invade Yugoslavia inevitably disrupted the hitherto smooth timetable for BARBAROSSA. Until then, B-day had been set for 15 May. Now, Hitler declared, it was "postponed up to 4 weeks." Then, on 30 April, B-day was finally set for 22 June. This change—not of plans but only of timing—would now prove particularly confusing to the world's intelligence services in their efforts to fathom Hitler's intentions.

24. Warnings from the Czechs

When the Czechoslovak government went into exile—first in France, then in London—its excellent military intelligence service accompanied it virtually en masse. Furthermore, the director of military intelligence, Colonel František Moravec, maintained uninterrupted contact with his well-organized espionage networks in the underground resistance movement in occupied Czechoslovakia and among anti-Nazi circles in Berlin, including direct access to the German Abwehr itself. The information from Germany was brought to Czechoslovakia where UVOD (Center of Military Resistance) radioed it to the Czechoslovak General Staff in London.[1] Czechoslovak President Eduard Beneš freely shared this material with the British who, he avers, were greatly astonished by its quantity and quality.[2]

It was through these channels that Colonel Moravec's service learned of BARBAROSSA, enabling President Beneš to warn the British and the Russians.

In early February 1941 Beneš had acquired definite indications that Germany intended to make war on Russia, and he reported his early estimate to both the British and the Russian governments about that time.[3]

Beginning in early March (or, perhaps, early February), there was an uninterrupted flow of information to Moravec regarding German preparations against Russia. Most of these reports came from Prague: from underground workers, civilians, and members of the Czech military intelligence organization there, which even included some German officials among its many informants. Those who particularly distinguished themselves in this connection were Ministerial Councillor Dr. Jaroslav Papoušek, Colonel Josef Balabán, and Zdeněk Bórek-Dohalský. In addition, Ukrainian emigrants in Czechoslovakia provided much relevant information, although it often was of a rather fantastic nature. Even the Czechoslovak Communists in Prague sometimes gave information.[4]

Finally, at the beginning of April, Colonel Moravec received the following precise report from Prague:

> The campaign against the Soviet Union is said to have been definitely decided upon; as soon as Germany has finished the Yugoslav campaign, i.e. in the first half of May at the latest, the German attack on the Soviet Union will begin; it is reported in Berlin that all the necessary military arrangements have been made and there has already been a conference of all the higher commanders of the German Eastern front at which the opening moves of the campaign were precisely determined and explained; the date of the "Kriegsbereitschaft" (alert) for the whole Eastern front is said to have been fixed for May 15th; some technical details of the military plan of the whole Eastern campaign were appended to this report.[5]

President Beneš immediately recognized the value and significance of this report but deemed it "so fateful" that he "did not even dare to pass the news on immediately in *all* details to the Allies." Fortunately, this odd failure of nerve passed; and "in due course" he disclosed the "essence" to all—to the British, the Americans, and the Russians.[6]

President Beneš dramatically presented this intelligence report to Churchill on 9 April at a postlunch discussion at Ditchley. Those present included Mrs. Churchill; Roosevelt's special envoy, Averell Harriman; Churchill's parliamentary private secretary, Brendan Bracken; Czech Prime Minister Monseigneur Jan Šrámek; the Czech chief of staff; U.S. Army Air Corps commander Major General H. H. Arnold; and several other Britons and some Czechoslovak military officers. Beneš concluded that Russia would be drawn into the war by Hitler. Churchill was most excited because, as he subsequently told Beneš, he had just received similar reports— presumably Woods's material and the Japanese radio intercepts— from the United States.[7]

Unfortunately, Beneš does not specify when he notified the Russians, but presumably it was at about this time. In any case, he had ample opportunity and several channels to the Russians. First, and most likely because it was a direct and secure channel, he could (as he occasionally did on routine matters at this time) just informally advise the Soviet embassy in London.[8] A second point of contact was in Istanbul. There Colonel Heliodor Pika of the Czechoslovak General Staff and Lev Klučka maintained permanent contact with Soviet intelligence from October 1940, when they arrived from Rumania, until late April 1941, when they went to Moscow to establish an informal diplomatic mission.[9] A third channel is implied by the assertion that the émigré government was heavily infiltrated by Communists and that Moravec's intelligence service sometimes collaborated with the NKVD.[10]

Subsequently, Czechoslovak intelligence learned that the German General Staff had grossly underestimated the strength of the Red Army and was counting on a quick campaign of about sixty days. They also learned of the intention to establish administrative centers in the Soviet Union.[11]

Although Czechoslovak intelligence had several excellent informants, Agent A–54 (alias "Frantas") was outstanding because he gave direct and regular access to the middle level of the German OKW. A–54 was the main and best source of the Czechoslovaks' warnings on BARBAROSSA. He was a German, a native of Saxony, and a baker's son. He had lived in Prague since 1939, where he was well known as a playboy lawyer whose social climbing had netted him many contacts in artistic, diplomatic, and government circles. He called himself "Dr. Steinberg." In fact, his real name was Paul Thummel, and his real job was no less than that of Abwehr chief for Southeast Europe. He was an early Nazi party member (card no. 61,574) who had been coopted by the Abwehr, first as a minor agent (a so-called honorable agent) in 1928 and later, in 1933, as a regular officer. Then, in 1936, while serving as chief of the Abwehr's Dresden office, he became a double agent for Czechoslovak military intelligence. Following the flight of the Czechoslovak government into exile, Thummel worked through the left-behind remnant of Czechoslovak military intelligence, headed by Lieutenant Colonel Josef Masin, although his true name and identity were known only to his contact, Masin's deputy, Major Vaclav Moravek.* [12]

25. Leaks to Russian and Ukrainian Émigrés

Hitler's Europe was filled with hundreds of thousands of political émigrés from Bolshevik Russia. One was the chief Russian cryptanalyst in Ribbentrop's Foreign Ministry. Others formed the core of Soviet experts gathered around Joseph Goebbels in his Propaganda Ministry and around Alfred Rosenberg in his Eastern Office of the Nazi party's Foreign Policy Office (APA). Some circulated socially in German elite circles such as that of General Friedrich Paulus. Many were organized into political-social organizations aspiring—quite ineffectually—to replace the Bolshevik government or, in the case of the Ukrainians, to obtain national independence. All these groups were prime targets for penetration by the NKVD; and some members, including senior leaders, were Soviet agents.[13] Although I have been unable to identify specific émigré infiltrators in the BARBAROSSA information channels, we should assume that any information on BARBAROSSA that reached such émigré groups had a high probability of soon being passed on to Soviet intelligence. For example, the socially prominent Anna and Vassili Maximovich, sibling children of a tsarist general, were active agents of the Soviet Trepper-Gilbert GRU espionage network in Paris.[14] (See warning 31.)

A circumstantial case can be built that does link the diffusion of information on BARBAROSSA with Ukrainian émigrés and rumors of Soviet espionage. The head of Rosenberg's APA Political Department was his fellow *Volksdeutscher*, the Odessa-born Dr. Georg Leibbrandt. While Leibbrandt's Nazi loyalty is unchallenged, that of his two principal Ukrainian émigré confidants and advisers is suspect. These men were Alexander Sevriuk and Peter Kozhevnikov. Sevriuk died in December 1941 in a railway crash,

* Thummel was finally captured by the Gestapo in 1942 and executed on 20 April 1945, only nineteen days before the liberation of Prague by the Red Army.

amidst rumors that he had been liquidated by the SS as a Soviet agent; and Kozhevnikov was placed in a concentration camp by the SS in late 1942, allegedly on the suspicion that he was also a Soviet agent.[15] The APA and particularly its coterie of Eastern experts was drawn into the BARBAROSSA planning on 31 March 1941. The militant nationalist faction, led by Stephen Bandera, was alerted in the spring by the Abwehr in return for its military and clandestine collaboration. A Ukrainian legion was secretly formed under the Abwehr's Brandenburg Regiment, its military character camouflaged under the sign "Reichsarbeitsdienst" (German Work Section) at their training camps in the Carpathians.[16] On 9 April Sevriuk notified the "pro-Polish" UNR and "Prometheus" nationalists in their Warsaw headquarters. And on 11 June the OUN-M faction, led by Andrew Mel'nyk, was presenting its liberation program to Hitler.[17]

26. An OKW Leak

On (or about) 13 April Harry W. Flannery, William Shirer's successor as CBS's correspondent in Berlin, received a tip from within the OKW itself that the German attack "had been planned to begin within the month, but that the Yugoslav trouble had interfered with the time schedule." Recognizing the authenticity of this information, Flannery hinted at it in his broadcasts to America but could not speak openly because of the German censorship.[18]

27. A Leak from Berchtesgaden?

On 16 April 1941 British Foreign Minister Eden disclosed to Soviet Ambassador Maisky the alleged substance of the top secret discussions between Hitler and Ribbentrop and the yielding Yugoslav Prince Regent at the Berghof on 4 March.[19] Hitler, Eden reported, had told Prince Paul he planned to attack Russia in June or July. This report had reached the British Foreign Office from three seemingly independent sources: from Belgrade on 31 March, from Sumner Welles on 2 April, and from the king of Greece on 6 April.[20] Hull had been informed of these bare details by the U.S. ambassador in Belgrade, Arthur Bliss Lane, in a telegram sent and received on 30 March, which credited only the usual "reliable source." [21] What could this source have been? One possible source was Yugoslav Air Force Commander General Dušan Simović, who, as leader of the anti-German conspirators, later overthrew the Prince Regent. During his visit to Yugoslavia in late January, President Roosevelt's personal agent, Colonel "Wild Bill" Donovan, had established close relations with Simović that encouraged his coup on 27 March.[22] It is likely that Simović maintained the contact.[23]

In any case, we do know that one series of diplomatic "leaks" was from Dr. Milan Gavrilović, the Yugoslav minister to Moscow. Gavrilović's story was that Hitler had won over the violently anti-Bolshevik Prince Regent Paul by assuring him that German action in the Balkans was intended only to secure the German flank for the imminent attack on Russia. Gavrilović retold this story at least once more, following his expulsion from the USSR. The occasion was an afterdinner conversation in Ankara on 16 June with a gathering of the Yugoslav, Polish, and American ambassadors in Turkey. However, American Ambassador John van A. MacMurray did not think to pass on this altogether intriguing news to Washington until driven by hindsight a half day *after* the German invasion of Russia.[24] Even then MacMurray sent it by sea mail. It reached Washington on 10 July. President Roosevelt did, however, appreciate the new Turkish stamps his ambassador was sending.

Whatever the source, the Americans and British were deceived. Quite aside from the inherent unlikelihood of Hitler making such an early disclosure of BARBAROSSA to Prince Paul, no record of it has been found in any German files,[25] and the many German and Yugoslav records and memoirs make it quite clear that the agenda was limited to the negotiation of a German-Yugoslav agreement. Hitler's alleged revelation of BARBAROSSA was only a rumor, one that probably originated in the Simović-Gavrilović circle.

Since Eden and the official Foreign Office historian *still* believe this tale,[26] we may assume that it was not a British effort to dupe the Russians.

Happily for the credibility of British intelligence, the Russian

NKGB had already independently acquired their own false report of the meeting. Although we do not really know how either the NKGB or Stalin perceived this report in 1941, it is significant that it was accepted as authentic in 1965 and 1967 by the successor organization, the KGB. In 1965 an anonymous KGB historian revealed: "On 10 April the organs of state security [NKGB] sent intelligence information to J. V. Stalin and V. M. Molotov about the content of Hitler's talks [sic] with Prince Paul of Yugoslavia, from which it appeared that Hitler had decided to open military operations against the USSR at the end of June." [27] Much the same point was made two years later by KGB Deputy Director Pankratov in an interview in which he said: "in April 1941, we [Chekists] learned of a conversation between Hitler and the Yugoslav Prince Paul, in which the Fuehrer disclosed his intention to begin military operations against the USSR in late June." [28] There is no acknowledgment that this report had also come from Eden by way of Maisky, but Pankratov's motive for his revelation was to document the industry and alertness of his organization even "in the environment of the personality cult." [29]

In fact, Soviet writers have much trouble with this whole incident. Thus one Russian historian, Nekrich, writing in 1965 asserts that Hitler had told Prince Paul specifically "that the attack on the Soviet Union was scheduled for June 30" and that this information not only was known to Churchill but was one of the bases for Churchill's warning to Stalin sent on 3 April (see warning 28).[30] Nevertheless, in 1967 a Soviet critique of Nekrich's book raised the question whether Churchill even had this information to pass on.[31]

28. Churchill: All His Own Work

On or just before 30 March 1941 Churchill, who wisely insisted on reading occasional raw intelligence reports "in their original form," was stunned by a single "Intelligence report from one of our most trusted sources." This report presumably was based either on British agent train-watchers in Rumania and Poland or, more likely, on the deciphered intercept of a German military order.* It described the redeployment of three Panzer divisions. The details and timing and circumstances were interpreted by Churchill as meaning that it had been "Hitler's intention to invade Russia in May" but that he would now have to delay until June. To his unrepressed delight, events proved Churchill right and his professional intelligence chiefs wrong in the interpretation of their own data. The Joint Intelligence Committee (J.I.C.) and the Chiefs of the Imperial General Staff (I.G.S.) had long remained firmly committed to the notion that Hitler would not so irrationally overreach himself as to attack Russia at any time in the near future. However, the rapid amassing of verification eventually began to force even the professionals to modify their judgment. On 31 May the Chiefs of Staff concluded that the eastward deployment of German forces foreshadowed an imminent Nazi ultimatum, further major Russian concessions, or war. Only on 5 June did the Joint Intelligence Committee begin to shift its position, concurring with the Chiefs of Staff on 10 June,[32] and on the twelfth concluded that:

Fresh evidence is now to hand that Hitler has made up his mind to have done with Soviet obstruction and intends to attack her. Hostilities, therefore, appear highly probable, though it is premature to fix a date for their outbreak. It remains our opinion that matters are likely to come to a head during the second half of June.[33]

The "fresh evidence," which arrived at the end of the first week in June, consisted of detailed information on the relocation of

---

* British intelligence, as noted, was receiving train-watching reports from the Polish underground intelligence. However, this particular report seemingly came from a British network in Rumania, although Churchill is a bit veiled in his disclosure. However, Churchill later explicitly confirms that there were British "agents" in Rumania during the war. See Churchill, 6 (1953), 227. The agent in question is, I presume, the same quiet "illegal" who was David Walker's S.I.S. boss there during 1939–1941. See Walker (1957), 62–64.

For the British reading of these messages see chap. 6. It is now known that Churchill identified the several references in his memoirs to these intercepts by just such oblique phrases as this one used on Stalin.

various higher Wehrmacht headquarters: Field-Marshal List's Twelfth Army's move from Athens to the Lublin area in Poland, the identification of the Eleventh Army headquarters in Bucharest, and reliable evidence of the creation of an Army Group head-quarters in Rumania. This evidence, particularly the arrival of List, was deemed decisive by the J.I.C., whose initial shift of view on 5 June had been predicated on intelligence in the last week of May that the Luftwaffe was redeploying units, depots, and com-munications networks eastward.[34] In all fairness to his intelligence chiefs, who unlike himself were forever silenced by the Official Secrets Acts, Churchill conceded that the total intelligence picture did not suggest BARBAROSSA. Thus Churchill was right, but per-haps for the wrong reasons.

Upon recognizing Hitler's intentions, Churchill "cast about for some means of warning Stalin" and thought to "arrest his atten-tion and make him ponder" with the following "short and cryptic" but truthful message:

I have sure information from a trusted agent that when the Ger-mans thought they had got Yugoslavia in the net—that is to say, after March 20—they began to move three out of the five Panzer divisions from Rumania to Southern Poland. The moment they heard of the Serbian revolution this movement was counter-manded. Your Excellency will readily appreciate the significance of these facts.[35]

This message was telegraphed on 3 April to Sir Stafford Cripps in Moscow with explicit instructions to deliver it in person. Through a notable series of blunders by Ambassador Cripps, Foreign Secre-tary Eden, and the permanent staff of the Foreign Office, this urgent personal message sat on Cripps's desk until 19 April, when he de-livered it to Deputy Foreign Commissar Vyshinsky (*sic*), who on the twenty-second informed Cripps by note only that he had passed Churchill's message to Stalin.[36] (The comedy of errors was ad-vanced by the further bumbling of the Foreign Office permanent staff in London: they neglected to forward the Cripps-Vyshinsky return receipts. The sorely tried prime minister had to jog his care-less foreign secretary three times to even get the clerical paperwork on his note processed.)[37] There was no reply from Stalin, for what in Whitehall was farce was tragedy in the Kremlin.

Denied its contrivedly dramatic presentation to assure salience, Churchill's brief message did indeed prove "cryptic." When only six months later Lord Beaverbrook, then of the War Cabinet, was in Moscow, Stalin asked him: "What did Churchill mean by saying in Parliament that he had given me warnings of the impending German attack?" [38] On 15 August 1942, during Churchill's first wartime trip to Russia, Churchill reminded Stalin of this query and passed him a copy of the original telegram of 3 April 1941. Stalin shrugged and said, "I remember it. I did not need any warnings. I knew war would come, but I thought I might gain another six months or so." [39] Moreover, we now know from Zhukov that Stalin had received Churchill's warning "skeptically." Zhukov, who was working closely with Stalin during this period, speculates that Stalin was strongly prejudiced against any such "information coming from imperialist circles," particularly from Churchill, whose open anti-Communist views were known and whose then secret contingency plans to invade the North Caucasus and bomb the Baku oil fields were also known.[40]

Incidentally, the Germans were quite aware of Cripps's warnings to the Russians.* On 24 April the unwitting German naval attaché in Moscow, Captain Norbert von Baumbach, notified the Navy High Command in Berlin that the counselor of the Italian embassy, Luciano Mascia, reported that "the Ambassador [Cripps] predicts June 22 as the day of the outbreak of the war." [41] There is a small mystery here, since Hitler himself did not set the 22 June date until six days *after* the naval attaché's signal, the existing original text of which was both sent and logged in on 24 April. Seemingly, Cripps merely made a lucky guess, probably based on the current rumor that Hitler would attack on the anniversary of Napoleon's invasion in 1812.

---

* For example, Cripps's communications to Vyshinsky in March 1941 were disclosed to the German Foreign Ministry by "a reliable, strictly secret source" by 7 April. And again, Cripps's note of 11 April was similarly disclosed within eleven days. See *DGFP*, 12 (1962), 604–605.

On 17 April, while Churchill's note was still lingering on
Cripps's desk, the third secretary of the American embassy, Charles
W. Thayer, wrote a private letter to "Chip" Bohlen, then second
secretary in Tokyo. Thayer mentioned that an English source had
asserted that Germany would attack the USSR on 20 May.* By 3
May the German ambassador in Tokyo, Major-General Eugen Ott,
"had the opportunity through [a] confidential source" to read
Thayer's letter. Ott immediately telegraphed its substance to the
Foreign Ministry in Berlin, which sent an information copy to its
Moscow embassy two days later.[42] Ott's source was surely either
Japanese intelligence itself, which was intercepting just such mail
at the Post Office (see Chapter 6), or, conceivably, a German agent
infiltrated into the Japanese system. Since Richard Sorge was also
a confidant of Ambassador Ott, it is quite possible that Thayer's
information became further grist for Sorge's expanding file of
invasion warnings to Moscow (warning 37).

Eden had five personal talks on international problems with
Ambassador Maisky between mid-April and mid-June. At each
of these private meetings, the foreign secretary included warnings
of the German buildup, stressing the rapid accumulation of
confirmatory reports.[43] Maisky subsequently assured Alexander
Werth that he had passed Eden's warnings to Moscow.[44]

29. The Rumanian Underground Warns Baker Street

Some time in April, London received a wireless signal from Rumania that the German attack on Russia was scheduled for 15
June.[45] This significant piece of intelligence was received not by
the regular Secret Intelligence Service (S.I.S.) but by the new
Special Operations Executive (S.O.E.), specifically its S.O.2 division, whose mission was limited to sabotage and guerrilla operations. Operationally separated from S.I.S. and having negligible li-

---

* Just as Baumbach in his report of 24 April noted that "others" (that is, foreigners in Moscow other than Cripps) were rumoring that B-day would be
20 May.

aison with it, S.O.E. had by the spring of 1941 failed to develop its clandestine nets outside Britain, except in the Balkans. Even there they had only one radio transceiver in operation. When the British embassy left Rumania that February, the S.O.E. representative had supplied a transceiver to their local collaborator. This man was no less than Iuliu Maniu, the leader of the National Peasant party and former premier, who had been recruited the previous year. Although Maniu proved reluctant to organize the type of active subversion that London had intended, he did supply a steady flow of intelligence over his radio.* He transmitted to the S.O.E. field office in Istanbul, which relayed his messages to its Middle East and Balkans headquarters in Cairo and thence to the head office on London's Baker Street—this entire radio network being in the hands of S.I.S., which still monopolized all British secret radio communications.

30. Verification of Woods?

On 22 April a U.S. consular report from Vienna summarized the rumors of a Russo-German conflict that were current there. The American consul, Harry E. Carlson, concluded that the only elements that "can probably be accepted as actual facts" were that (1) the Germans had begun a limited evacuation of some civilians and administrative offices near the Soviet-Polish border, (2) some 60 to 80 German divisions had been moved into that area, and (3) "all Russian deliveries to Germany have apparently ceased." [46] State Department officials noted a close similarity between this report and Woods's earlier document but expressed their faulty judgment that the rumors might be a German plant.[47] Indeed, they may have been—but by German traitors, not obedient Nazis —since this report coincided in time and place with a Ribben-

---

* In 1947 Maniu was arrested, tried, convicted of treason, and sentenced to life imprisonment as part of the Communists' successful postwar effort to break his National Peasant party. He died in prison in 1952. Maniu had also been in touch with the British through Colonel Jan Kowalewski's Polish underground liaison office in Lisbon. See Listowel (1952), 141–143, 151.

trop-Ciano conference where the topic was a lively one within the German staff if not between the two Axis foreign ministers.[48]

31. Soviet Espionage Reestablished in Western Europe

The Soviet foreign espionage system was devastated by Stalin's Great Purge in 1937–1938. It suffered not only a complete change of experienced top intelligence personnel in the various Moscow headquarters of the NKVD, GRU, Foreign Ministry, and Comintern but also the systematic destruction of most of its overseas espionage networks. In all but a few, key personnel of the foreign networks were recalled to Moscow and executed or—for a few lucky ones—imprisoned. Stalin did not trust these persons with their long years of experience (read "contamination") in the outside world.[49]

This state of affairs was particularly evident in Western Europe. There, little remained of the large espionage network. However, if Stalin had nothing to fear from his espionage services except a rather low level of efficiency for all their effort, he feared, and quite legitimately so, the political maneuverings of the British and French. He needed up-to-the-minute intelligence on their political position vis-à-vis Germany and Russia. Consequently, the newly appointed chiefs of the NKVD (Lavrenti Beriya) and the GRU (Lieutenant-General Filipp Ivanovich Golikov) pushed for the reestablishment of intelligence networks in Western Europe.

In March 1939, Leopold Trepper arrived in Western Europe to rebuild the GRU's covert network in France, Belgium, and Holland.[50] Trepper was "le Grand Chef" of the network, and the Big Chief's network soon became known in the Abwehr as the Rote Kapelle—the "Red Orchestra." Operating out of Brussels and Paris in the guise of two international import-export firms, Trepper (now known as Monsieur Jean Gilbert) quickly developed his contacts and sources. Although the Red Orchestra was originally targeted only against France and the Low Countries, Hitler's blitzkrieg of May–June 1940 immediately put Trepper's network up against the Germans.

One of Trepper's minor agents was Ludwig Kainz, a German

junior engineer working in Organization Todt, the Nazi government's vast military construction enterprise. Herr Kainz had
previously worked on the German fortifications along the Bug
River frontier with Russia after the Polish campaign. Then, in
April 1941, he was sent again to the Bug for a quick inspection
trip. On his return to France later that month he told Trepper of
the intense warlike preparations under way there, and he bet "le
Grand Chef" a case of champagne that a Russo-German war would
begin before the end of May.

Another of Trepper's informants was an Austrian colonel in the
Wehrmacht's supply service in France. In the spring he told
Trepper the curious news that his job was getting easier—because
so many German occupation troops were leaving. A quick check
with other informants (French railway employees) confirmed this
movement and added the information that they were all shipping
east, to Poland.[51] Due to bureaucratic inefficiency, Trepper's network in Paris did not yet have its own radio. So Trepper was
forced to transmit this intelligence through Major-General I. A.
Susloparov, the military attaché in the Soviet embassy in Vichy.

32. Soviet Intelligence in Berlin

The Soviet espionage nets in Germany were virtually emasculated
during the three years before BARBAROSSA partly to avoid provocation of Hitler, partly because Stalin underestimated the need, and
partly as an inadvertent consequence of the purge that struck so
deep into the experienced ranks of the security services themselves.[52] Despite its weakened condition Soviet intelligence continued to count some notable coups in penetrating BARBAROSSA.

Mr. Škvor, the patriotic vice-president of the Škoda Works in
Czechoslovakia, voluntarily contacted the GRU (apparently in
Berlin) and became a GRU agent. In April 1941, Škvor reported
the Wehrmacht's massive eastward redeployment and the fact that
the huge Škoda munitions factory had been ordered by Berlin to
stop its deliveries of arms to Russia because war had been scheduled for the second half of June. When this report was passed to
the Politburo on 17 April, Stalin affixed in red ink his assessment:

"This information is [an] English provocation, find out who is making this provocation and punish him." The task was assigned to GRU Major Ismail Akhmedov, who promptly set off to Berlin with cover as TASS correspondent "Georgi Nikolayev." [53]

33. An American Diplomatic Cocktail Party

Mr. Jefferson Patterson (later U.S. ambassador to Uruguay) had been the first secretary of the U.S. embassy in Berlin since 1939. His personal wealth afforded him a luxurious three-story house in the Charlottenburg section of Berlin. His taste ran to large dinner groups and even larger cocktail parties. It was now the end of April 1941 and Patterson was due to leave this post before the month's end. So another one of his famous 300-person cocktail parties was in order.

Valentin Berezhkov, the first secretary of the Soviet embassy, arrived. Patterson greeted him and said, "There's a man here I'd like you to meet." Taking the Russian by the arm he led him to the fireplace where a tall, lean man was standing, whiskey glass in hand, chatting with a cluster of American diplomats. The man was in the uniform of a Luftwaffe major. Patterson introduced them. The major was an old friend; they had met in the States before the war. The loquacious German major was saying that he was a veteran combat pilot just arrived on leave from North Africa. He spoke pessimistically of Rommel's success there.

As the party was ending, the German major was finally alone with Berezhkov. The major now revealed:

There's something Patterson wants me to tell you. The fact is I'm not here on leave. My squadron was recalled from North Africa and yesterday we got orders to transfer to the east, to the region of Lodz. There may be nothing special in that, but I know many other units have also been transferred to your frontiers recently. I don't know what it might mean, but I personally would not like to have something happen between my country and yours. Naturally I am telling you this completely confidentially.

Berezhkov was startled. Here was a German officer giving top secret information to a Russian diplomat. "However," as Berezhkov recalls, "at that time we feared provocation above all [so] I decided to make a discreet, stock answer: Thank you, Major, for this information. It is extremely interesting. But I assume Germany will observe the nonaggression pact. My country is also interested in preserving the peace between us. Let us hope for the best." The German major merely replied: "You know best." Berezhkov was nonplused by this odd conversation. But he included it in the regular embassy report to Moscow.[54]

34. Soviet Naval Attaché in Berlin

According to Khrushchev's "secret" speech, the Soviet naval attaché in Berlin, Rear-Admiral M. A. Vorontsov, signaled Moscow on 6 May that:

Soviet citizen . . . Bozer communicated to the deputy naval attaché that according to a statement of a certain German officer from Hitler's headquarters, Germany is preparing to invade the U.S.S.R. on 14 May through Finland, the Baltic countries and Latvia [Rumania]. At the same time Moscow and Leningrad will be heavily raided and paratroopers landed in border cities. . . .[55]

As noted earlier, the original mid-May attack, actually scheduled for the fifteenth, had in fact already—on 27 March and 30 April—been deferred to mid-June. Thus this particular intelligence report was at least six weeks old; and, unless it told more than Khrushchev chose to reveal, would have been only a source of confusion. About a month later, another report from Vorontsov supplied a less anachronistic date (warning 54).

Incidentally, the naval attaché system seemingly reported directly to Soviet naval intelligence, which was then an independent service, directly subordinate to People's Commissar for the Navy Admiral Nikolai Kuznetsov.

35. Soviet Intelligence in Warsaw

Soviet agent Konon Molody (alias Lonsdale), according to his far from trustworthy memoirs, was a member of a Polish Communist underground network in German-occupied Poland. This group, led by one "Pyotr" (Peter) and headquartered in Warsaw, was evidently an NKGB apparatus. In any case, it ran a number of agents throughout Poland, who were connected with the Warsaw headquarters by an effective courier system. In turn, the headquarters were linked to Moscow by clandestine radio. This network had been closely monitoring the Wehrmacht's eastern deployment since some time in early 1941. At the beginning of June, Pyotr had recognized that the German preparations were nearing completion and concluded that an attack was imminent. They also "learned the actual date of the attack and had passed it on" to Moscow.[56]

36. A Befuddled Diplomat

Lord Casey was appointed Australia's first diplomatic representative in Washington in early 1940. Being quite out of his depth in intelligence, the minister hardly helped matters by his peculiar approach to Soviet Ambassador Umansky. In his own words:

From mid-April to June 1941, one heard progressively more in informed quarters about German demands on Russia. Late in April, I heard a number of estimates of the date on which the attack would take place. I averaged the dates that I heard from responsible people and told Oumanski, the Russian Ambassador, in early May that it would happen on June 30th, which he airily dismissed as nonsense.[57]

Quite so. Such amateurish degradation of hard, reliable intelligence into vague, discreditable rumor or speculation plagues the entire intelligence process. Lord Casey's contribution was not the first such instance presented in this volume, nor will it be the last. It is just the most self-evidently foolish. Not only does this incident illustrate how a new and false rumor can originate—in this case the meaningless yet specific date of 30 June—but, far more seriously, how the credibility of a genuine source can be undermined. Soviet intelligence services do treat the diplomatic cocktail circuit as a major source of authentic leaks; and Umansky would very probably have assumed that such a remark, coming as it did from so senior a person as the Australian minister, was an official leak from British intelligence. Consequently, the perpetration of such unverifiable "noise" could only serve to further discredit in Russian eyes the already highly suspect motives and credibility of the intense Anglo-American effort to warn them.

37. Stalin's Man in Tokyo

Soviet military intelligence had been receiving indications of BARBAROSSA since late April 1941 from its superb "illegal" espionage network in Japan. This group was created and led by Dr. Richard Sorge, the brilliant grandson of Friedrich Sorge, a nineteenth-century secretary-general of Karl Marx's First International. Richard Sorge had joined the German Communist party in 1920, been recruited into the Comintern's clandestine intelligence service (OMS) in 1924, and been transferred to military intelligence in 1929. He had directed a major GRU network in China from 1930 to 1932. His final assignment was Japan, where he operated from 1933 until his arrest in October 1941. Despite his lineage and long-standing Communist activities, Sorge spent these eight years in Japan effectively protected by his deep cover as a brilliant Ph.D. in political science (Berlin, 1920), as a prestigious contributor to Professor Karl Haushofer's *Zeitschrift für Politik,* a loyal member of the Nazi party (since 1934), ace correspondent for the *Frankfurter Zeitung,* a bon vivant, and a trusted friend and close adviser of German Ambassador Ott himself.[58]

Situated at the heart of the German embassy in Tokyo, Sorge was quickly and systematically privy to the incoming evidence on BARBAROSSA. He was at least as well informed as anyone on the embassy staff. According to the unsupported assertion of *Pravda,* his first indications were summarized in microfilm strips that he sent off on 5 March 1941 to Moscow—presumably by means of his Soviet embassy contact, Viktor Zaitsev, the second secretary and GRU *Rezident.* This filmstrip contained photographs of telegrams from Foreign Minister Ribbentrop to Ambassador Ott, allegedly alerting General Ott that Hitler was planning an attack on the Soviet Union in May.[59]

Sorge's first confirmation came in late April from his conversa-

tion with the German senior military attaché, Colonel Max Kretschmer, who disclosed that:

although it was uncertain whether or not the situation would
lead to actual hostilities, Germany had completed her preparations on a very large scale; and I understand (from Kretschmer)
that, with her concentrations of military forces, Germany would
be able to induce the Soviet Union to acquiesce in her hitherto
unspecified demands. I also learnt that the decision on peace or
war depended solely on Hitler's will, and was quite irrespective of
the Russian attitude.[60]

Further confirmation arrived the next month, borne by a special
envoy of the German War Ministry, Colonel Oskar Ritter von
Niedermayer, a leading Soviet expert. Disarmed by a personal
letter of introduction to Sorge from their mutual friend and
former ambassador to Japan, Dr. Herbert von Dirksen, Niedermayer sought out Sorge and revealed that war had been decided
on.[61] Incidentally, Niedermayer was even then outspoken against
his Nazi bosses. Indeed, he was denounced and sentenced to death
in 1944, but freed by the Americans and imprisoned by the Russians.[62]

Later, on 20 May, the third loose-lipped German officer brought
further confirmation directly to Sorge's open ears. Lieutenant-
Colonel Scholl was passing through from Berlin via the Trans-
Siberian Railway to take up his new post as military attaché in
Bangkok. Sorge later recalled that this close friend—from his
earlier posting in Tokyo as assistant military attaché—required
only a drink to disclose the confidential and substantially accurate
information he had just brought Ambassador Ott:

Scholl gave me a detailed account. The attack would begin on
June 20; there might be a two or three days' delay, but preparations were complete. 170–190 German divisions were massed on
the Eastern frontier. There would be no ultimatum or declaration of war. The Red Army would collapse, and the Soviet régime
would fall within two months.[63]

Finally, on 15 June, Sorge, presumably in receipt of additional
information, radioed the correct B-day: 22 June.[64]

After his arrest, Sorge pridefully told his Japanese secret police
interrogators that he had received a special commendation by

radio from the GRU director for his warnings about BARBA-ROSSA.[65] While this may well be true, it must be remarked that (never known to Sorge) his radio operator, Max Klausen, had begun to permit his increasingly remunerative cover as a capitalist businessman to take precedence over his Marxian duty. Throughout 1941, Klausen had often failed to forward messages from Sorge, and by way of example to his interrogators he cited one of those concerning BARBAROSSA. Since the GRU had neglected to incorporate any systematic receipt- or acknowledgment-of-message procedure, Sorge and the GRU remained unaware of Klausen's failing. However, as Sorge personally radioed many of the more important messages, we should presume that most of the BARBAROSSA ones did get sent. Nevertheless, we do not know which specific messages were lost.[66]

38. The *Herald Tribune*'s Scoop

During May, an astonishing disclosure of BARBAROSSA occurred in Tokyo.[67] It was authentic and freely offered information ferreted from innermost sources by a reliable Soviet GRU agent. Yet it went begging until the end of the month and when finally published was buried in obscurity. It is an instructive case of the degradation of hard intelligence to discredited rumor.

Branko de Voukelitch was a correspondent of the leading French press agency, Havas. Stationed in the Tokyo bureau headed by Robert Guillain, the popular and intelligent "Vukie" had close official contact with the Japanese news bureaus and good personal relations with the foreign correspondents, particularly the Americans. Indeed, he was Richard Sorge's personal liaison with these two secondary but important sources for Sorge's GRU intelligence network.

Voukelitch was probably privy to at least some of the intelligence on BARBAROSSA that Sorge was getting at the German embassy. While it is not known just which—if indeed any—specific bits of this information the often close-mouthed Sorge was revealing to Voukelitch, we know that Sorge was briefing his two other key agents, Ozaki and Klausen, on BARBAROSSA so that they could be alert for any confirmation.[68] It is particularly reasonable that Sorge would have similarly alerted Voukelitch. On the other hand, because Voukelitch was not enjoying the best relations with or closest confidence of Sorge during this period, it is just possible that some of his information may—as he claimed—have been from his own sources.[69]

In either case, in the first week in May, Voukelitch began guardedly leaking incoming material to his acquaintances among the American contingent of the foreign press corps. That this was at most a fortnight after Sorge had begun to receive similar material suggests that Sorge was probably Voukelitch's original source. Why was Voukelitch making these wider disclosures, urgently encouraging foreign publication? His actions could easily have been noted by the watchful Japanese "Thought Police" and could have soon led to "blowing" the entire Sorge ring. Since Sorge would not deliberately have taken such a risk,[70] it must be that Voukelitch was acting on his own initiative; and it may be a measure of the degree to which he had begun to disassociate from his GRU loyalties.

Voukelitch had settled on the Americans as his confidants because, as he himself plausibly argued, his other press outlets (including the Vichy French Havas) would only suppress the story. He urged the Americans to warn the world so it could be prepared to counter the Nazi move. In all, he passed his story to the Tokyo correspondents of the Associated Press, United Press, the *New York Times* (Otto Tolischus), and the *New York Herald Tribune* (Joseph Newman). He initially disclosed that Hitler was prepared to attack some time before the end of June, before the Russian harvest.

However, the Americans would not touch this story. Rendered overcautious by the then rising flood of such rumors, they dismissed it as at best a British provocation. The only journalist to treat it seriously was the most junior one, Joseph Newman of the "Trib." But he decided to try out the story that first week in May over lunch at the American Club with the three locally available Russo-German experts: Otto Tolischus of the *New York*

Times (recently transferred from Berlin), Walter Duranty of the *Times* (London) and the *New York Times* (newly arrived from his Moscow assignment), and Charles "Chip" Bohlen of the U.S. embassy (also recently posted from Moscow). Bohlen led off by arguing that the story must be untrue. Hitler could gain all his demands from Stalin by mere blackmail, because Stalin knew a German invasion would topple his regime. Duranty pontificated that "The chance of war between Germany and Russia is about as good as frying snowballs in the summertime." [71] Overwhelmed by these voices of authority, Newman sat on the story for weeks.

Then, in late May, he received some independent confirmation while interviewing a Norwegian who, having recently escaped the Nazi occupation via Finland, described the intensive road construction and other German activities indicating invasion preparations directed against Russia. Checking with a Japanese informant who had close connections in the government, Newman learned that Japanese officials had themselves grown increasingly apprehensive about an attack on Russia.

Voukelitch now pressed Newman. He warned that delay could cost the scoop of a lifetime and stressed that his sources were deliberate leaks from anti-German Japanese in the Foreign Office and armed services. Newman was impressed by these arguments, particularly since Voukelitch with these same sources had proved accurate and detailed a month before in his leaks to Newman about Foreign Minister Matsuoka's negotiations in Berlin and Moscow in March. Thereupon, on 31 May 1941, Newman finally telephoned his story to New York, but well-watered by his lingering skepticism. Due to the Tokyo–New York time difference it appeared in that morning's edition of the *Herald Tribune* headlined:

TOKYO EXPECTS HITLER
TO MOVE AGAINST RUSSIA

but lost among business items on page 21. [72] Newman is still proud of his scoop and fails to realize that it was spoiled not by an editor's faulty sense of news value but by the degrading of the credibility of the story by the self-defeating efforts of both Vou-kelitch and Newman to protect their sources and themselves.

39. Treason by the German Ambassador

In early May,* an unauthorized warning, emanating directly from the German ambassador in Moscow, was issued to the Russians. Although Ambassador Count Friedrich von der Schulenburg and his equally anti-Nazi counselor, Gustav Hilger, did not yet have any concrete confirmation of BARBAROSSA, they were already convinced that Hitler was determined to wage war on any military pretext. They agreed that peace could perhaps be saved if the Soviet government would take the diplomatic initiative by involving Hitler in extended negotiations of an appeasing nature. At the moment Soviet Ambassador Dekanozov was in Moscow for briefings, and Hilger decided he must be warned. Hilger convinced Schulenburg that the risk of execution for treason was a worthwhile gamble. Accordingly, Dekanozov was invited to a confidential luncheon at Schulenburg's residence. Besides Schulenburg, Hilger, and Dekanozov, only V. N. Pavlov, the then chief of the German section of the Soviet Foreign Commissariat and Molotov's permanent interpreter, was present. Since Pavlov was widely—but falsely—rumored in German circles to be Stalin's illegitimate son,[73] his presence may have been welcomed by the two Germans as perhaps giving direct access to the Soviet dictator. Despite their assurances of their own unilateral initiative and of the urgent necessity for the Russians to open conciliatory negotiations, they were seemingly not believed. Their desperate gesture was apparently taken as a provocation to induce the Russians into a position of negotiating from weakness, damaging both Soviet prestige and its bargaining position. In retrospect, Hilger concedes that this brave, foolhardy performance must only have confirmed the Russian belief that Hitler was bluffing, hoping to draw further concessions.†

* Specifically, some time between 30 April when both Schulenburg and Dekanozov arrived in Moscow and 13 or 14 May when Dekanozov returned to Berlin. Other evidence implies the meeting was after 5 June.

† Hilger states that Dekanozov insisted he could not communicate the

Hilger was right. They were not believed. Pavlov himself stated privately in 1967 that he still believed the warning was a "blackmail" attempt.[74] Moreover, Soviet historians have recently denounced it as "fantastic."[75]

40. Abwehr Leaks in the Vatican

In the fall of 1939 the Abwehr deputy chief, Colonel Hans Oster, succeeded in opening a liaison channel to the pope. Although it was initially created only to preserve a last, indirect link between the Anglo-French governments and the anti-Nazi German opposition in the latter's continuing efforts to bring about a peaceful end to the war, it soon became a major channel for leaking Hitler's aggressive intentions and operational plans. These leaks included detailed warnings of the invasions of Scandinavia, the Low Countries, and Russia.

The link between Colonel Oster and Pope Pius XII was effected through two principal intermediaries. Oster's man was the official Abwehr representative in the Vatican, the courageous Dr. Josef Müller. He was a Munich lawyer, prominent Roman Catholic, former leader of the Bavarian People's party, and one of the main conspirators against Hitler. The agent of the Sovereign Pontiff was his principal personal aide, the very discreet Jesuit priest Father Robert Leiber. The pope's willingness to enter into this astonishing collaboration had been substantially facilitated by the happy circumstance that Cardinal Pacelli, while serving in Germany before he became pope, had been a riding companion of Admiral Canaris and General Beck and an acquaintance of Müller.[76]

This remarkable Abwehr-papal intelligence liaison lasted from the fall of 1939 until Müller's arrest by the Gestapo in April 1943.

Schulenburg-Hilger statements to his superiors unless they admitted they were speaking at the behest of the German government. However, we must assume that Dekanozov and Pavlov both informed their respective bosses, Beriya and Molotov, and eventually Stalin. Incidentally, the treason of the two Germans was not disclosed by the Russians, since Schulenburg was not arrested and executed until after his implication in the 1944 bomb plot against Hitler. See Hilger and Meyer (1953), 331–332.

It had endured that long only through the protective cloak thrown over the enterprise by Canaris. Since 1936 the SS, in the person of the SD chief, Reinhard Heydrich, had held Müller in grave suspicion for his clandestine Roman Catholic lay activities. Indeed, Heydrich (wrongly) suspected Müller of being a disguised Jesuit priest. Müller's link to the pope had first been imperiled in early 1940 by the investigative efforts of the venal SD agent, the pro-Nazi Reverend Hermann Keller, the former prior of the great Benedictine Abbey of Beuron. On that occasion Canaris managed to throw glittering dust into the eyes of Hitler by submitting a counterfeit report that effectively discredited Reverend Keller. The second threat to Müller materialized in June 1940, when Heydrich learned from decrypted intercepts of Belgian diplomatic communications from the Vatican that there had been OKW leaks of critical strategic political-military intelligence through the German mission in Rome. Canaris audaciously misdirected the ensuing investigation by appointing Müller himself to head it.

During the three and a half years of his wartime activity, Müller was not only the sole conduit for the warnings from Oster but also the Vatican's main courier for the secret intelligence reports from the Roman Catholic hierarchy in Germany and Poland.

During early 1941 Müller was passing to Father Leiber the increasingly specific warnings from Oster of Hitler's plans to invade Russia.[77] These BARBAROSSA warnings were passed to the pope, who —misinformed by Leiber—mistakenly thought they originated with Canaris rather than Oster.[78] (Oster was the source of the warnings, Canaris only the willing protector of the covert channel.) Some time around early June, the pope told Mr. Harold H. Tittmann, Jr., the assistant to Special Representative Myron C. Taylor, that war between Germany and Russia was imminent,[79] at least according to an Abwehr agent in the Vatican (Müller himself?).[80] Thus fully crediting his Abwehr intelligence source, the pope at least was not surprised by BARBAROSSA.

Müller himself has asserted that some time in the same period he had notified British authorities in Vatican City of the BARBAROSSA B-day date.[81]

41. Another Abwehr Leak to the British

Some time in the spring or summer of 1941, the Abwehr opposi-
tionists sought again to warn the British of BARBAROSSA. For this
purpose Nikolaus von Halem of Canaris's personal staff was selected.* He traveled in his professional guise as a wholesale merchant to Moscow, where he succeeded in contacting an English
resident, an old acquaintance.[82]

42. The "Motorized Parsifal" in Scotland

One potentially superb but unexploited source for British intelligence parachuted into Scotland on 10 May 1941: Rudolf
Hess, the Deputy Führer and Hitler's intimate friend. His bizarre
purpose, possibly with Hitler's approval, was simply to open peace
negotiations with Britain.† Mr. Ivone Kirkpatrick was hastily
brevited from his recent appointment as B.B.C.'s controller of
European services to function as an ad hoc case officer for the
Foreign Office. At his first rambling interrogation (13 May) Hess
volunteered that Germany had demands of various kinds on Russia that must be met, "either by negotiation or as the result of a
war," but he specifically denied the truth of the rumors that an
early attack on Russia was planned. At the third interrogation
(15 May) Kirkpatrick explicitly raised this point:

> Hess replied that it was out of the question. I pressed him again
> and again, but he assured me that Hitler was a man who stuck
> scrupulously to his engagements. I got the impression that Hess
> was so much out of things that he really did not know.[83]

Kirkpatrick's judgment that Hess either knew nothing of BARBA-
ROSSA or, at least, did not know of its imminence was uncritically
accepted by Churchill and Eden, and this official Anglo-German
version has been almost universally accepted by the American
president (to whom Churchill communicated it on 17 May) and

---

* Von Halem had been one of the most active conspirators from 1934 until
his execution for high treason in 1944.
† This widely discounted point—Hitler's prior knowledge—now seems plausibly established. See Leasor (1962), 74–81, 122–127, 132, and J. Bernard Hut-
ton, *Hess* (New York: Macmillan Co., 1971).

by subsequent historians.[84] Only one knowledgeable insider has pointed out that nothing of intelligence value was gotten from Hess simply because of the unprecedentedly incompetent interrogations.[85]

Nor did the British make effective propaganda from the Hess episode. Even the editor of *The Times* noted in his diary for 14 May: "The Ministry of Information [are] more incompetent and variable than ever."[86] But this was unfair comment; Duff Cooper's hands were quite tied by the prime minister. Churchill, surprised and fearful of the inflammatory potential of the whole affair, directly imposed many political constraints. They certainly thwarted any major propaganda campaign and added to the general mystification. And they may well have inhibited any effective interrogation of Hess.

In fact, Hess did know something of BARBAROSSA. We have the recent categorical disclosure to this effect by his personal adjutant, Captain Karlheinz Pintsch.[87] True, Hess was somewhat displaced from power by the growing number of parvenus around Hitler, but Hess was still Deputy Führer, leader of the Nazi party, Reichminister without portfolio, a member of the Secret Cabinet Council, and a member of the Ministerial Council for the Defense of the Reich and still enjoyed Hitler's table and confidence.[88] Moreover, the senior Nazi party officials under Hess were already deeply involved in BARBAROSSA, dividing up their eagerly expected spoils. For example, Alfred Rosenberg and Martin Bormann had both become witting in April.[89] However, this last point is inconclusive because, given the intensely competitive decentralization of the Nazi party, it should not be assumed that either Rosenberg or Bormann would have automatically shared such information with their nominal chief, Hess. In addition to the credible testimony of Pintsch, others of varying degrees of authority knew of or presumed Hess's witting participation in BARBAROSSA. Thus SD chief Schellenberg presumed Hess knew the details, possibly including the recently set final B-day of 22 June.[90] Franz von Papen even asserts that Hess promptly disclosed BARBAROSSA to his British captors; however, the then ambassador to Ankara was not privy to these secrets, and his account should thus probably be discounted as rumor.[91] British historian Alan Clark compounds error with anachronism in asserting that "Stafford Cripps [sic] presented to Stalin comprehensive evidence of the German plan (supplied by Hess). . . ."[92] Clark cites no source, for of course there is none. Hjalmar Horace Greeley Schacht also thought Hess knew of the attack plan, but Schacht was no longer in the Nazi inner circle.[93] Even the Italian ambassador in Berlin, Alfieri, believed in Hess's prior knowledge.[94] And the perennially credulous American journalist Waverly Root also believed that the Hess flight somehow proved to the British that the invasion of Russia was certain.[95]

In any case, Schellenberg and others assumed that the Russians would interpret the whole Hess affair as a warning. Indeed, the Russians well may have, as suggested by the fact that Stalin throughout the war queried qualified British visitors (Beaverbrook and Churchill himself) about what Hess had "really" revealed.[96] Stalin's suspicions were presumably fed by his own intelligence services, which must have been aware that this rumor was being credited in the highest diplomatic circles abroad. Indeed, we know of one such report filed by the GRU's best agent in Japan, Richard Sorge. At that time, Sorge's contacts in the German embassy alleged that Hitler had sent Hess as a final effort to negotiate peace with Britain before attacking Russia. Sorge concluded from this allegation that war was inevitable.[97]

The coincidence that Hess dropped in on the British Government just a month before BARBAROSSA was widely interpreted as having a particularly sinister connotation.[98] The Nürnberg Tribunal thought that it was "significant to note that this flight took place only 10 days after the date on which Hitler fixed June 22, 1941, as the time for attacking the Soviet Union."[99] Yet, as his defense counsel unsuccessfully tried to point out, coincidence it was. Hess had been planning his flight since the previous June and had even made two or three full-scale tries that aborted, one in January 1941 and one or two others soon afterward.[100]

The NKVD eventually had the full truth—from Hess's disgraced adjutant Pintsch, when they captured him on the Eastern Front a few weeks after he was sent there, presumably on a suicide assignment. Captain Pintsch readily confessed, and the NKVD was seemingly satisfied that they had extracted all he knew because after ten days of unrestrained torture and eleven years of imprisonment he was finally repatriated in 1955.[101] Nevertheless, Stalin sought full vengeance: he had his judge at Nürnberg issue a vociferous dissenting opinion in which he unsuccessfully demanded the death penalty for Hess.[102]

43. Chinese Intelligence

Even the Chinese Nationalist intelligence service had picked up a possibly authentic warning. At a dinner in Chungking on 10 May (while Hess was piloting his Me-110 to Scotland) Generalissimo Chiang Kai-shek took U.S. Ambassador Nelson Johnson aside and asked him to inform Hull that the Chinese had "good information" that Germany planned to attack Russia some time between the end of May and the middle of June. The delighted Generalissimo enlarged on this news three days later. The two messages were sent to Hull by Johnson on the eleventh and fourteenth, respectively.[103]

I have been unable to trace Chiang's source. However, the Chinese Nationalist secret service operated centers at their diplomatic missions in Berne, Vichy, London, Stockholm, and Moscow; and, given the amount of authentic information readily available by May in the diplomatic and intelligence circles in those cities, it would be remarkable only if the Chinese had failed to acquire some of it. Moreover, they had some excellent lines flowing from the British Cabinet (at least in 1940), War Office, and London diplomatic circles, as well as some liaison with the German SD both in Vichy and in Berne (at least in 1942) and with one or more of the Russian services in Moscow.[104] Chiang's informant may very well have been Quo Tai-chi, his ambassador to London who had just returned to Chungking. Quo held that some 200 German divisions would invade Russia in late June.

He had acquired this information in London some time before his departure on 2 April.[105]

It is interesting that later, on 23 May, the remarkable German minister without portfolio, Hjalmar Horace Greeley Schacht, informed the Chinese in Berlin that it was his personal belief that Germany would attack Russia some time during the course of the summer.[106]

44. The Drunken Propagandist

Despite German security precautions, many inadvertent leaks occurred simply through loose talk. One spectacular case is authenticated. It occurred during a well-attended reception on 15 May at the Bulgarian legation in Berlin. There Dr. Goebbels's confidant, Professor Dr. Karl Bömer,* the able, kindly, alcoholic head of the Propaganda Ministry's Foreign Press Section, got drunk and prattled on about the German plans for invading Russia, announcing that he was scheduled to be appointed Gauleiter of the Crimea.[107] Moreover, he specifically mentioned, according to one secondhand source, the 22 June jump-off date. Later that evening the Bulgarian ambassador sent an open telegram to Sofia stating that a senior official of the Nazi party had disclosed to him that war with Russia was imminent.[108]

Incidentally, this particular leak was an inadvertent result of a plot by Bömer's enemies in the rival News Service and Press Department of the Foreign Ministry. These men, seeking to entrap Bömer into expressing his frank views against such top Nazi leaders as Ribbentrop, took calculated advantage of these liquid social occasions. They succeeded at the Bulgarian legation affair, but at the risk of a potentially disastrous security leak. Bömer's befuddled betrayal of BARBAROSSA brought his downfall. His indiscreet remarks were immediately reported by Dr. Emil Rasche to his boss, Dr. Paul Karl Schmidt, the Foreign Ministry's News Service and Foreign Press chief, who gleefully denounced Bömer to the Gestapo. Dr. Bömer was summarily dismissed in

* Commonly misspelled Boehmer and Böhme.

May, arrested for treason in July, and on 17 October given a two years' concentration camp sentence. (It would have been death but for Goebbels's intercession.) He was released in 1942 at the age of forty-two on the condition that he serve as a private in his old regiment on the Russian front. Bömer was soon fatally wounded.[109]

The essential details of this indiscretion, presumably as well as others in diplomatic and other international and elite social circles, quickly reached Soviet intelligence nets. In this particular case, the news had immediately reached Ivan Filippov, the chief of the TASS Berlin bureau and a senior NKGB intelligence officer.[110]

45. A Forgery

A potential new source of warning to the Russians developed during the last two months before the attack, when the OKW widened its planning to include the exploitation of the captured Russian economy. This program was launched on 29 April by General Georg Thomas, the chief of the OKW War Economy and Armaments Office. Thomas's Oldenburg Plan specified in great detail the seizure of Soviet agricultural and industrial produce.[111] Then, on 22 May, the so-called Four-Year-Plan Office, the military-industrial complex directed by Reichsmarschall Hermann Göring, issued the first of a series of secret instructions on the actual utilization of captured crops, oil, and factories. Göring's planning culminated on 1 June with the detailed "Green File" program.[112]

This enlargement of planning beyond the OKW necessarily increased the number of persons aware of BARBAROSSA and thereby enhanced the chances that leaks to Soviet intelligence would occur. Although no authentic leaks are known, one flagrant forgery alleging leaks from Göring and the Oldenburg Plan does exist. Moreover, this specific allegation has been repeated by one of the several credulous scholars deceived by the forgery.[113]

This forgery is the spurious memoir of the nonexistent "Cyrille D. Kalinov," who purports to have been a colonel on the Soviet

General Staff who escaped to the West in 1949. "Colonel Kalinov" claims there were two leaks to Soviet intelligence some time before June 1941. Both were allegedly received by the NKGB office in Berlin, in the person of Soviet Ambassador Dekanozov. The first leak was supposedly from Göring himself, who told one of Dekanozov's agents—Max Bauer, a former friend of the recently purged Karl Radek—that while Germany would soon have 150 divisions at the Russian frontier they would be there only to render credible the "greatest blackmail undertaking in history," namely, a "colossal hoax" of an ultimatum demanding more petrol, manganese, rare metals, and raw materials. The second alleged leak was a copy of a document acquired through Alexander Rado's network in Switzerland. This was purportedly the OKW's Oldenburg Plan of 29 April. Kalinov states that Dekanozov discounted this document as a deception because he had already accepted the blackmail ultimatum view.[114]

46. A Mercenary Press Attaché

Neutral Portugal sheltered a main field office of the Polish military intelligence service. Its Lisbon bureau not only was one of the more effective liaison offices between the Polish government-in-exile in London and the underground in Poland but also provided neutral ground for unofficial contacts with Axis officials. This office was founded and directed from June 1940 until April 1944 by Colonel Jan Kowalewski, an experienced Polish General Staff intelligence officer.[115]

Colonel Kowalewski had noted the current Lisbon rumors of Russo-German trouble. As early as 22 April 1941 he had reported to London: "The Russo-German idyll is at an end." [116] Then, on 15 May 1941, his principal collaborator, the secretly anti-Nazi Rumanian minister in Lisbon, Jean Pangal, arranged a meeting with Hans Lazar, the press attaché of the German embassy in Madrid. Lazar was an Austrian journalist who had joined the Nazi Foreign Ministry following the *Anschluss*. For entirely personal motives— quite unconnected with the anti-Nazi resistance—Lazar now sought to protect himself by forestalling what he believed would prove to be a disaster for his country. Accordingly, he approached his acquaintances from the mid-1930s in Bucharest, Pangal and Kowalewski, the latter having served there as Polish military attaché.[117] Left alone with Kowalewski, Lazar excitedly but hesitantly disclosed that he had just returned (by 12 May) from meetings in Berlin with Ribbentrop, Goebbels, and their aides and OKW officers from whom he had learned that it had been decided to invade Russia and that the invasion was set for some time between 20 and 25 June. Kowalewski immediately dispatched a preliminary coded telegram to London through the Polish legation in Lisbon and on the seventeenth sent by the diplomatic bag a detailed report and analysis supporting the 20–25 June B-day.[118]

Kowalewski now began sounding out his various Hungarian, Rumanian, and Italian diplomatic contacts for confirmation of Lazar's news.[119] The Hungarian minister, Andre de Vodianer, confirmed on 20 May that Russo-German relations were tense and that a major Wehrmacht movement to the Soviet frontier was under way. That day or the next, Italian Minister Renato Bova-Scoppa also indicated that a crisis was near but that its peaceful resolution depended on whether Russia could agree to economic collaboration with Germany in the Ukraine. On 12 June Vodianer told Kowalewski he had just been alerted by Budapest to expect a German surprise that would "explode on the world" in ten days, on 22 or 23 June. Vodianer reported: "My people have the impression that the Germans are getting ready for a sensational enterprise of the vastest dimensions, a super *Blitzkrieg*. There is tremendous agitation in Germany and fantastic preparations are being made." [120]

Fortified by such confirmation, Kowalewski sent his final appreciation to his government in London:

Massive German troop movements began on June 7th. The Germans are concentrating troops on their eastern border. These concentrations will be completed about June 20th. Between June 20th and June 25th operations against Russia will begin. The Germans have chosen this date because they want to occupy the Ukraine before the harvest has been cut, so as to prevent the Russians from destroying it. The Germans say that their war against Russia will be of short duration.[121]

Dispatched by the Polish diplomatic bag on 13 June, Kowalewski's report reached London on the fifteenth.

47. AP and TASS

Fifty-four-year-old Louis P. Lochner had worked in Germany for twenty years and since 1928 had been chief of the Associated Press Berlin bureau. Doyen of the foreign press corps, he was rated by most of his colleagues as the best in Germany, a judgment authenticated by the Pulitzer Prize Committee in 1939. In addition to his superb contacts in press, diplomatic, social, and business circles, he was more closely connected with and trusted by German resistance groups than any other foreigner. Lochner was a veritable one-man intelligence service. Thus it is appropriate that he was the only journalist in Berlin both to have received *B-Tag* from an informant and to have passed it on to his Russian colleagues in TASS.

During the first week of his repatriation to America in mid-1942, following his release from German internment, Lochner disclosed that, "Late in May [1941] one of my informants whose information had always proved true came to tell me that at 3 a.m. on the fourth Sunday in June [i.e., 22 June] the Germans would march into Russia." [122] In his book, written two months later, Lochner specified that he had received this intelligence "thirty days" before the event, that is, on 23 May.*

Who was Lochner's remarkable informant? Lochner implies he was a German and a member of the anti-Nazi resistance.[123] Having a healthy fear of the Gestapo's thoroughness and vengefulness, Lochner was careful to camouflage the identities of his many anti-Nazi informants in all his wartime writings. Despite this caution, Lochner let slip one clue that simultaneously establishes both the informant's identity and his credentials as a highly credible source. In his 1942 book Lochner stated, "My informant seldom visited

---

* This seemingly precise date is not necessarily exact, as Lochner routinely disguised such circumstantial details that might assist the Gestapo to identify his informants. In any event, while 0300 was the correct time, H-hour had tentatively been set at 0330 during the period before 14 June. See Lochner (1942*b*), 1.

me, but when he came it was always on legitimate business which he was careful to announce in advance over our tapped telephone. Even today nobody in Germany suspects him." [124] Lochner also disclosed that before this man had given the warning on BARBAROSSA he was the man "who not only gave me the zero hour for the outbreak of World War II, but who later informed me of the exact day and minute for the attack on Crete." [125] Moreover, it was the same man who, a week before Hitler's invasion of Poland, passed Lochner a three-page typescript version of Hitler's sensational speech to his senior military commanders at Obersalzberg on 22 August 1939.

Lochner's BARBAROSSA warning has been entirely missed by historians, but the typescript of the 1939 speech enjoyed a growing fame. The American embassy refused to receive such "dynamite," [126] but the British were decidedly interested. Lochner gave a copy to Sir George Ogilvie-Forbes, the counselor of the British embassy, and identified his informant (by name) as "a Staff Officer who received it from one of the Generals present at the meeting who is alleged to have been horrified at what he heard and to have hoped for the curbing of a maniac." [127] While Ogilvie-Forbes was also careful to conceal the name of this "Staff Officer" he later specified that he was an "Army" officer, thereby pinpointing him in the OKH.[128]

In December 1945 Lochner drove Major Wilfred Byford-Jones, the British information officer in Occupied Berlin, down to observe the Nürnberg trials. Major Byford-Jones recalled in his memoirs, published the next year, that Lochner told him then that the L–3 document had been passed by "a confidant" of retired Colonel-General Ludwig Beck, former chief of the OKH.[129]

The key identification finally came from Lochner in an affidavit submitted on 25 July 1949 at the trial of Field-Marshal Erich von Manstein, who had been one of those present at Hitler's 1939 speech. Lochner affirmed that the controversial L–3 document had been given him by Hermann Maass, at the instigation of Colonel-General Beck.[130] Later, by 1954, Lochner replied to Professor Gerhard Ritter's query that he had received the L–3 transcript from Maass, who had it from Beck, who in turn had obtained it from an officer (presumably) known to Beck but unnamed to Lochner.[131]

Thus Hermann Maass was Lochner's immediate source for the L–3 document and, inferentially, his informant on the Polish, Crete, and Russian D-day warnings. Maass was deeply involved in the anti-Nazi resistance. Born in 1897, he had been a life-long Social Democrat (SPD), prominent in its trade union and youth work. From 1924 until succeeded by the Nazi's Martin Bormann in 1936, he had been the secretary of the Association of German Youth Movements. Denied direct access to political life, Maass eventually went to work, some time around the late 1930s, in an aluminum factory in Berlin. This new job was also his entrée into conspiracy since the factory was simply a cover for an underground network run by its manager, Wilhelm Leuschner, the former SPD trade union leader. Leuschner recruited his staff from among political friends such as Maass and used the factory as a cover, source of funds, and base of operations. It was through Leuschner that Maass had contact with Colonel-General Beck. Maass continued to operate until arrested by the Gestapo on 8 August 1944; his execution followed on 20 October.[132]

Perhaps it is not important that the trail of the L–3 document ends with an unnamed staff officer, for he may not be the same man who passed the MERKUR (Crete) and BARBAROSSA warnings to Beck for Maass and Lochner. General Beck was an old conspirator with many contacts in the OKH. Nor is it certain that Beck was Maass's channel for these last two warnings to Lochner. Professor Ritter speculates that the L–3 bearer may have been either Captain Fritz Wiedemann or a representative of Admiral Canaris.[133] However, while a Canaris Abwehr man is a plausible guess, Captain Wiedemann must be absolved of even unwitting participation in this near treason because he had recently been transferred from his position as Hitler's adjutant to that of consul-general in San Francisco.[134]

At the time Maass gave his sensational warning of BARBAROSSA,

Lochner was already aware of vague rumors of possible war. But now he was more than half-convinced due to the credibility of his source and the categorical precision of the information. He immediately sought verification from the U.S. military attachés (presumably including Colonel Truman Smith, who was then the senior military attaché). They confirmed that all the reports available to them concurred that virtually the entire Wehrmacht was deploying along the Russian frontier, and concluded that this evidence indicated a "blowup" soon.[135]

Lochner's office was also now receiving other evidence that tended to support this intelligence and assessment, but "nothing else so precise on timing."

At this point, Lochner disclosed the L–3 information to his "Russian colleagues," by whom I presume he means the TASS correspondents Filippov, "Nikolayev," "Tarasov," and Kudryavtsev. Lochner repeatedly pressed this information upon them and asserts that he knew "they inquired of their own embassy about it." However, they insisted to the very end that Russo-German relations were "quite normal and that Soviet Russia was supplying all the raw material that Germany had asked for."[136]

By warning TASS, Lochner was—unwittingly it seems—directly reaching the NKGB, since virtually all TASS correspondents were then state security officers, TASS being merely a cover because *all* Soviet professional foreign correspondents had "crashed" in the Great Purge three to four years earlier.[137] And the only two non-NKGB men with the TASS Berlin bureau, Deputy Bureau Chief "Georgi Nikolayev" and Sergei Kudryavtsev, were GRU officers.

48. A GRU Coup in Berlin

Khrushchev has also revealed that on 22 May Deputy Military Attaché Khlopov signaled from Berlin that "the attack of the German Army is reportedly scheduled for 15 June, but it is possible that it may begin in the first days of June. . . ."[138]

While this report seemingly represented recent intelligence, it was evidently partly garbled, as a B-day of 15 June was never contemplated.

49. A Warning from Tito

In mid-May, while the German divisions in conquered Greece and Yugoslavia were hurriedly being routed through Belgrade toward Rumania, another opportunity for a credible disclosure existed. Vladimir Dedijer reveals in his official biography of Tito: "A senior German officer told a Russian refugee that Hitler was preparing to attack Russia. This information reached Tito, who sent a radiogram to Dimitrov toward the end of May bringing it to his notice." [139] Dimitrov, in Moscow in his 'capacity as secretary-general of the Comintern, would have immediately informed the NKVD, if not other Soviet authorities, of such intelligence.*

50. Ribbentrop Squeals

An unexpected warning allegedly emanated from no less a person than Ribbentrop himself. This apparently happened sometime after March or April 1941. Anxious to preserve his dream of enduring Russo-German friendship, Ribbentrop asserted from his Spandau cellroom:

I let the Kremlin know through an intermediary in Stockholm that in view of the evidence of Soviet aggressive intentions the Führer was very skeptical concerning further agreements with Moscow. The Russian reply was that the question of where the blame was to be sought was really immaterial; disquisitions on "which came first, the chicken or the egg" were "typically German." [140]

Although Ribbentrop's claim has never been verified, it is just possibly true. In the last week of April he was agonized over whether to oppose Hitler in this venture.[141] Moreover, there is little doubt that by 1943 he had gone against Hitler's explicit wishes by making just such contacts with the Russians in Sweden.[142]

---

* Tito's transmitter, by the way, was the clandestine one set up by Vladimir Velebit in Zagreb before the war. Tito, then in Belgrade, had to use the Zagreb set because the only other one, in Belgrade, had been destroyed— together with its operator—during the Luftwaffe's terror raid of 6 April. Another rumor of BARBAROSSA had also reached Dedijer on 11 June. See Vladimir Dedijer, *With Tito through the War: Partisan Diary, 1941–1944* (London: Hamilton, 1951), p. 23.

51. Evidence in Camera

A curious, informal omen of BARBAROSSA appeared at the end of May in the window of the Berlin studio of Hitler's "court" photographer, Heinrich Hoffmann, directly under the official portrait of the Führer. It was a large map of Eastern Europe. The studio was on Unter den Linden, near the Soviet embassy. Its sudden appearance was taken as a warning by Valentin Berezhkov of the embassy staff because it had been Herr Hoffmann's custom since 1940 to display the map of that part of Europe in which military operations were current or contemplated.[143]

52. Counterfeit Rubles and the British Listening Post
in Berne

In anticipation of their occupation of western Russia, the Ukraine, and the Caucasus the Nazis began counterfeiting Soviet ruble bank notes some time after 28 May 1941.[144] Incidentally, this effort seems to have been unconnected with that of the well-known, superbly imitated £10,000,000 in British bank notes that were flooded into international markets by the Sicherheitsdienst from 1943 on;[145] although its Technical Department (SS Amt VI–F) did also issue at least some rubles, according to Schellenberg.[146]

Taken by itself, such counterfeiting is a good example of an ambiguous signal, that is, the sheer fact does not point to a single motive. It may be intended as occupation currency (as in this case), a means of economic warfare (the SD's pounds), as a source of precious foreign exchange (Stalin's faked U.S. dollars in the 1930s), or to supplement the counterfeiter's own income (the SD's British pounds and U.S. dollars). Direct evidence or additional circumstantial evidence is required to draw a conclusion.

This German fabrication of ruble bank notes was soon made known to the British listening post in neutral Switzerland. H.M. Minister David Kelly and his effective staff at the legation in Berne correctly interpreted a report that "the Germans were printing rouble notes . . . for future use" as one of "nine or ten pointers" that Germany was busily planning an invasion of Russia.[147] This particular report about the rubles almost certainly came directly to British intelligence in Berne through one of their several contacts reaching into German officialdom. Moreover, it is quite probable that this indicator (and the other unspecified ones) was shared with Soviet and U.S. intelligence networks in Switzerland with which the British there had liaison at that time.

It was noted earlier, in passing, that Sam E. Woods's German informant, Respondik, had included news of the printing of Russian rubles, but we do not know the time of that information.

5 Warnings:
The Last Month

You can't believe everything in intelligence reports.

—Stalin, 14 June 1941

It was now June, the last month. B-day-minus-22. The foreshadowings of the German invasion were becoming ever more frequent.

53. The Napoleonic Clue

On 1 June 1941, a leak occurred of a type I presume was common. Dr. Hasso von Etzdorf, Ribbentrop's disgruntled anti-Nazi liaison officer between the Foreign Office and the OKW, had long informally known of BARBAROSSA. When queried about the rumors of a war on Russia by Michele Lanza, the first secretary of the Italian embassy in Berlin, Etzdorf replied with the pseudocryptic remark that to know the date of the invasion one need know only the date Caulaincourt's famous diary states that Napoleon crossed the Niemen into Russia: 23 June.[1] *

54. More from the Naval Attaché, Berlin

The Soviet naval attaché in Berlin, Rear-Admiral M. A. Vorontsov, had forwarded an earlier and somewhat misleading warning (34). Now, about June first, he telegraphed more exact information to Admiral Kuznetsov, the commissar of the Navy. Vorontsov cited the latest German preparations and asserted that they would attack about 20–22 June, that is, as Kuznetsov observes, "almost the exact date of the start of the war." Kuznetsov forwarded this report to Stalin and checked to verify that it had, in fact, been received by him.[2]

Commissar Admiral Kuznetsov, as throughout his voluminous memoirs, shows himself as ever alert and Stalin as rather dense in not accepting this warning at face value. However, an equally anti-Stalinist officer on the Soviet army staff, V. A. Anfilov, has revealingly commented: "True enough, but in what light did he [Kuz-

---

* Etzdorf was involved in the 1939 bomb plot against Hitler and in 1962 became Bonn's ambassador in London. Napoleon, with an advance patrol of his Grand Armée, had reached the Niemen on 22 June; and the three-day unopposed crossing began at 10 P.M. on the 23rd, the emperor himself crossing on the morning of the 24th. All these optional dates were covered by the various rumors that linked Napoleon with Hitler in predicting a date for BARBAROSSA.

netsov] present it [his report]? If you could read it, you would see that he claims Vorontsov's communication to be a trick of German counter-espionage." [3]

55. In Vichy Backwaters

By early June, intelligence that Hitler would invade Russia on the twentieth reached even the Vichy regime.[4] Admiral François Darlan —deputy premier and minister of foreign affairs—assured the American ambassador, Admiral William Leahy, on 4 June that a Russian campaign would be as swift as that against Yugoslavia and Greece.[5] Leahy apparently took this remark to be one merely dropped into a general conversation as a hypothetical case, owing its origin to the flood of vague rumors he knew to be current in Vichy. He casually reported it without comment in his telegram to Hull on the conversation, and he omits it entirely from his post-war memoirs.[6] However, Darlan was evidently better informed than Leahy realized, for on 14 June General Weygand, the delegate-general of the French government in North Africa, first learned "authoritative news of the approaching execution of the German plan against Russia" from Darlan's own liaison officer, a Captain Gandin.[7] Admiral Darlan, having recently added minister of interior to his other excellent conspiratorial qualifications, was well placed to learn such matters, even though the Germans had not officially told him. For example, there was no hint of this from Hitler and Ribbentrop in their conversations with Darlan on 11 and 12 May. Gandin's intelligence was defective only in that it presumed the attack was the alternative to Stalin's refusal of an ultimatum.

What was the source of Darlan's conviction about BARBAROSSA? That is not disclosed. It is quite possible it did not come through any specific source but merely arose from a growing perception of the generally available clues. This is suggested by the fact that ever since March 1941 the racist-imperialist Vichy ambassador in Moscow, Erik Labonne, was hinting broadly to acquaintances about a coming German attack.[8] His successor, Gaston Bergery, arrived in May with similar views obtained from talks en route in Berlin with

German officials, but he implied that war could be forestalled if Stalin met certain political demands.[9]

56. The Berlin Orchestra Is Silent

It has been asserted that on 4 June 1941 the fact and date of BARBAROSSA were transmitted to Moscow by the 100-man Berlin branch of the Soviet Rote Kapelle ("Red Orchestra") espionage network headed by Arvid Harnack and Harro Schulze-Boysen.[10] However, this statement is surely false. This particular group of patriotic leftist and Communist conspirators had received their espionage assignment, radio equipment, codes, and crude training only a month or so before and were still fumbling their way by trial and error toward the professionalism that they would achieve by the time of their arrest in August–September 1942. Schulze-Boysen and his fellow radio operator, Hans Coppi, had been able to make merely intermittent radio contact with the GRU center in Moscow prior to the German invasion. During that period Harnack had managed to get off just a few messages—all important, but dealing only with deployments, not attack per se.[11] Thus the Berlin Rote Kapelle's "warnings" were just more instances of many such tactically useful but strategically ambiguous clues.

57. The NKGB Does Its Bit

The Soviet Russian authorities continue to disclose bits and scraps of data about the intelligence picture that was emerging in Moscow before the German invasion. One such tidbit emerged in 1965 in a belabored defense of the role of the state security (NKGB, later KGB) before and during World War II. The anonymous KGB author reveals that, "On 6 June the NKGB presented to J. V. Stalin intelligence information on the concentration of an army of four-million men on the Soviet-German border." [12]

58. The Most Mysterious Source

The most effective single Soviet espionage network during World War II was centered in Switzerland. Like all the better Russian intelligence nets at the time, it was a military intelligence (GRU) rather than a state security (NKVD-NKGB) apparatus.[13] The Swiss network was the superb GRU ring directed by Alexander Rado. Throughout the war it was acknowledged by Stalin and the GRU to be the main source of crucial intelligence, supplying a steady large volume of accurate, up-to-date details of virtually every secret of the OKW. It also provided some of the most detailed and accurate forewarnings of BARBAROSSA. On this last point, however, the story is particularly complicated.[14] I shall recount this part of the tale by moving from the more clearly established facts, through some dubious evidence, to an exposé, and I end on a note of speculation.

Otto Pünter was a Swiss Social Democratic journalist who had worked actively in anti-Fascist conspiracies since 1930. By 1940 he was working both with French resistance members and with John Salter of British intelligence in Switzerland. Pünter recalls: "In January or February 1941 I learned from the de Gaullist 'Neger' (a French resistance group) that German army divisions situated in Bordeaux were being shipped to the East. This was obviously a step toward an attack on Russia." [15] Pünter promptly informed "Carlo," a Soviet GRU agent in Grenoble, France. He also agreed at that time to work for Soviet intelligence while continuing his collaboration with the French and British. Under these conditions and with the approval of the GRU director in Moscow, he was introduced by "Carlo" into Rado's network, in which he was henceforward known as "Pakbo."

The altogether remarkable Rudolf Rössler was a Bavarian leftist journalist who in 1934 immigrated to Switzerland where, in Lucerne, he managed the anti-Fascist but non-Communist publishing house of Vita Nova. In 1939 Rössler was recruited by Dr. Xaver Schnieper into the intelligence service of the Swiss General Staff. Schnieper was working as a journalist in Rössler's firm and had himself been recently recruited into Major Hans Hausamann's so-called Bureau Ha that reported directly to Brigadier Roger Masson, the efficient chief of Swiss military intelligence, the Nachrichtendienst. Through Bureau Ha, Rössler was also linked to both French and British intelligence as a willing, witting, and active collaborator. He had access to superb intelligence on the operational plans and order of battle of the Wehrmacht, although the exact nature of his sources has never been disclosed, least of all to the Russians.

As intelligence began to accumulate that indicated an impending German attack on Russia, the Swiss intelligence decided—probably with the knowledge and approval and possible connivance of the British—to let Rössler act as a conduit of such warnings to the Russians. The initial contact is described by Otto Pünter:

About a month before the German attack on Russia a de Gaullist connected with the Swiss ND came to tell me that, according to reliable information obtained by the ND, the German attack on Soviet Russia would be launched on June 15. The ND looked for a way to inform Moscow of this. I went to see Alexander Rado and repeated to him what I had been told about the German schedule. Rado was somewhat skeptical, however, and asked me, in turn, to chcck the source of the news. I did so and was told that a serious and well-informed man was the source of the information.[16]

This anonymous informant was, of course, Rössler, who thus became recruited into the Rado network under his famous *nom de guerre* of "Lucy" (L for Lucerne).[17]

During early June, Foote recalls transmitting to Moscow a flurry of radio messages that struck him as "ominous" signs of an early German war against Russia. Most of this information was from Rössler and specifically from his anonymous source with access to the OKW, "Werther." Rössler-"Werther" were reporting wholesale Wehrmacht troop movements to the east as well as what the Germans believed were some of the Russians' countermoves.[18]

Then, as recalled by Foote, the key message came "toward the middle of June," possibly on the tenth (as Flicke asserts). That morning Rachel Dubendorfer ("Sisi") had brought Rado the message from Schneider ("Taylor"). It was, in turn, from Rössler and was explicitly based on Rössler's key secret source of OKW intelligence, the still-mysterious "Werther." The message categorically "stated that a general German attack on Russia would take place at dawn on June 22 and it gave details of the army groupings and the primary objectives." Rado immediately summoned Foote to a rendezvous to discuss it. Rado was skeptical—of Rössler as a source and of the possibility that Hitler could seriously intend war with Russia—and was cautiously inclined to not send it. Fortunately, Foote convinced him otherwise, after much discussion, and that night Foote radioed the message to GRU headquarters.[19]

Up to that time, Rössler-Lucy had been treated as highly suspect by Moscow. His insistence on the ambiguity of his own position and his consistent refusal to name his sources assured this suspicion. The GRU suspected he was an Abwehr agent planted in Switzerland to lure the Russians on by the old trick of supplying much correct but relatively minor information while awaiting a decisive moment to suddenly feed crucially damaging misinformation.[20] As Foote learned later in Moscow, Rössler's message naming the 22 June B-day was the first piece of his that the GRU took "seriously," because it "fitted in with information that the Russians had got from other sources and they took it into account in making their troop dispositions." [21] By July or August the Soviet Supreme Staff (Stavka) and Stalin personally had come to have full confidence in all Rössler messages, and the GRU gave them top priority handling and gave Rössler the then magnificent monthly salary equivalent to U.S. $1,700.

These radioed cryptograms from Rado, as all GRU radio and telegraphic communications, were received by the GRU Information Branch located in the NKVD intelligence headquarters in Moscow during that period of partial NKVD control of the GRU.[22] From there, they went to the "Director," the chief of the GRU, who (from mid-July 1940 until sometime after the German invasion) was Lieutenant-General Filipp Ivanovich Golikov.[23] From him, as we shall see in Chapter 8, they went directly to Stalin.

I shall now look at one sensational message that may be a postwar fiction. In his account of the Rado ring, ex-Abwehr Major Wilhelm Flicke alleges that the following message was sent on 10 June:

DORA TO DIRECTOR, THROUGH TAYLOR [i.e., Rado to GRU Chief, from Schneider, Rössler's courier]. HITLER DEFINITELY FIXED D-DAY OF ATTACK ON THE SOVIET UNION AS JUNE 22. HITLER REACHED DE-

CISION TWO DAYS AGO. REPORT ARRIVED HERE VIA DIPLOMATIC COURIER
OF SWISS GENERAL STAFF TODAY. WILL CONTINUE 0130. DORA [Rado].[24]

There are two problems with the text of this message of 10 June
from Rado. First, the 22 June D-day had in fact already been set
by Hitler on 30 April 1941.[25] Hence the implication that that decision had not been made until 8 June is wrong. Second, the specific text quoted may be an outright fiction. Major Flicke was the
Abwehr radio security officer in charge of investigating the Rado-
Rössler case at the time, and his book uniquely supplies much
highly original but factual material, including the authentic "plaintexts" of many intercepted radio messages. However, Flicke's account is written quite openly as a seminovel, the author freely in-
serting imagined conversations *and* texts of those key messages of
which he did not have transcripts.[26]

Next, we must dispense with a fictitious account invented in the
mid-1960s by two French journalists. This occurs in their fantasy-
biography of Rudolf Rössler, Rado's main source.[27] Although this
book has been generally exposed by the European press and its
more pretentious absurdities confessed by the authors, it has gained
a small foothold in American scholarly circles.[28] Consequently,
readers must be cautioned about its serious errors regarding BAR-
BAROSSA warnings.

Accoce and Quet allege that Rössler received by radio a "complete copy" of Hitler's key "Directive No. 21: Operation BARBA-
ROSSA" within a week after it was issued on 18 December 1940.
Moreover, so they assert, it was with this message that Rössler
opened his service with the "MGB . . . the Ministry of State Security in Moscow" by passing it to Rado "in the spring of 1941." [29]
In addition to the gross illiteracy of confusing the MGB (actually
an anachronism—they mean the NKGB) with the GRU and the
unlikely chronology, the direct and reliable testimony of both
Pünter and Foote suggest that whatever the content of Rössler's
first BARBAROSSA warning, it was *not* a full text of "Directive No.
21."

Although perhaps as much detail is publicly available on Rado's
GRU network as on any other single espionage group, the central

mystery remains, namely, who or what were Rössler's remarkable sources? Rössler evidently did not disclose any of them before his death in 1958. The greatest mystery and speculation have centered on the identity of "Werther," his source of intelligence from the OKW. Until 1967 all public speculation comprised, at best, educated guesses about the person or persons *in the OKW* who could have had the opportunity and motive. All efforts have failed to convincingly pinpoint such people, except for the tentative and highly controversial identification of Lieutenant Dr. Wilhelm Scheidt, the War Diarist of the Operations Section (WFSt) at OKW. (The categorical if veiled naming of ten senior officers by Accoce and Quet in 1966 is now admitted by the authors to have been sheer invention.) Despite the previous failures, one more effort should be made—a *systematic* analysis along conventional "damage assessment" lines.[30]

Then in 1967 an entirely new possibility was suggested by ex-S.I.S. counterespionage officer Malcolm Muggeridge.[31] He disclosed that the S.I.S.'s Government Communications Headquarters had been systematically intercepting and reading the German military cryptograms, and suggested that Rössler's key source was not some agent in place in Berlin but the S.I.S. in London! There is much to commend this hypothesis. The British had the capability. They also had the motive. After all, as we have seen, Churchill, Cripps, and the Foreign Office had been passing similar intelligence to their hypersuspicious Soviet opposite numbers. What then could be more credible than to simulate a situation in which Stalin would believe his own espionage service was rummaging the OKW? Muggeridge's hypothesis drew immediate favorable attention in Germany, where any allegation of treason in the OKW is still excitedly rationalized away in many circles.[32] More recently, Muggeridge has raised his original tentative speculation to outright assertion, although he gives no evidence for this change in status.[33]

59. Two Colonels in Vichy

Deputy Premier Darlan and his clique in the Vichy regime had their own sources of foreign and military intelligence (as seen in warning 55). However, they did not include the best intelligence services, those responsible directly to the Army of the Armistice. Darlan was not Germanophile but he was Anglophobe, while the army and particularly their intelligence services were both intensely Germanophobic and somewhat Anglophilic. These nuances of political and ideological bias were the bases of the several factions that constituted the Vichy regime, and they were sufficient to impair the free flow of strategic intelligence among factions.

The two main French military intelligence services were the Second and Fifth Bureaus of the staff of the miniscule Army of the Armistice. The Second Bureau—the renowned Deuxième Bureau—was the conventional army intelligence organization, comparable to U.S. Army G-2. Its chief was then Lieutenant-Colonel Louis Baril. The Fifth Bureau, on the other hand, was the mobilization designation of the two very secret so-called Special Services, the "S.R." (Service de Renseignements) and the "C.E." (Contre-Espionnage). Despite German displeasure, the Fifth Bureau continued its virtually autonomous existence in Vichy France and North Africa under its brilliant chief, Colonel Louis Rivet.[34]

As early as 14 January 1941, Baril had informed his superiors that the Russians were uneasy in their pact with Germany.[35] He had been led to this conclusion by highly questionable reports from Colonel Rivet's "S.R." espionage service that the collaboration between British and Russian intelligence had now become complete since their early establishment of contact in August 1940.* Then, on 28 April, after reviewing the accumulated evidence, Colonel Baril reported that the Germans would soon attack Russia.[36]

Colonels Baril and Rivet, sharing a deep hatred of Germany, were close collaborators who freely pooled their intelligence. Moreover, both had established liaison with British intelligence in Marseilles

---

* This charge of Anglo-Russian intelligence liaison in 1940–1941 is quite unsubtantiated. Indeed, we now know that Stalin and his GRU and NKVD chiefs in Moscow would not have knowingly permitted it. However, this story may be a distant echo of the tangled web of international intelligence liaisons in Switzerland that vaguely linked Swiss, British, Gaullist, German Abwehr, and Russian GRU nets.

and Lisbon. Their own sources reported on German troops in France, Germany itself, and even in eastern Poland. From studying the information from their sources, both concluded that Hitler intended an early invasion of Russia. On their own responsibility, Baril and Rivet twice approached the Soviet military attaché in Vichy, Major-General I. A. Susloparov, to warn him. The Russian complacently replied: "We are too strong: Germany will not dare attack us." [37]

Although his manner struck the French intelligence chiefs as decidedly offhand, that was only because Major-General Susloparov was receiving similar warnings throughout April and May from a wide variety of sources, including "the Yugoslav, Chinese, American, Turkish, and Bulgarian military attachés." From these sources he reported to Moscow in April that the German attack on Russia was planned for some time between 20 and 31 May. He learned subsequently that "in connection with the late spring" the offensive had been postponed a month, that is, until June. Accordingly, in mid-May, Susloparov sent a followup report to Moscow summarizing his most recent indicators of the German design and preparations.[38]

I presume the warnings passed to the Russian military attaché in Vichy by Baril and Rivet incorporated the intelligence added to the pool by Lieutenant-Colonel Ronin, the chief of the Second (that is, intelligence) Bureau of the Air Ministry.* If so, one specific item comprising the estimates made by Baril and Rivet is now known: On 9 June 1941 the Vichy French air attaché in Bucharest, X. de Sevin, sent the following telegram to the Deuxième Bureau of the Vichy Air Ministry:

WAR IS CERTAIN BETWEEN GERMANY AND RUSSIA VERY SOON: PRESUMABLY 17 JUNE. PLEASE DISREGARD THE CONTRARY INTELLIGENCE FURNISHED BY THE FOREIGN AFFAIRS AND WAR MINISTRIES.[39]

---

* This presumption is founded on the fact that Vichy Air Intelligence under Lieutenant-Colonel Ronin was an ally of the army's Second and Fifth Bureaus, and that Ronin shared his intelligence with them as well as with the British. See Stead (1959), 41, 56, 73, 76–77.

60. A Swedish Message

The Swedes were easily the most successful cryptanalysts among the World War II nonbelligerents. Their Defense Ministry's magicians were systematically intercepting and reading the Red Army's ground and air tactical communications, the German Foreign Office and military ciphers, the American and British U-boat warning code, the French diplomatic codes, and the Italian military attaché code.[40]

In the spring (late May?) the Swedish cryptanalysts had pieced together enough German military messages to conclude that an invasion of Russia was scheduled for some time between 20 and 25 June. This intelligence was passed to the Swedish Foreign Ministry, as an admirable matter of routine interministerial liaison. In turn, on 7 June the secretary-general of the Foreign Office, Erik Boheman, informed his distinguished dinner guest, Sir Stafford Cripps, who was passing through Stockholm on his way to London for consultations, that he had concluded Germany would force a "showdown" about 15 June, with an even chance of war.[41]

Boheman's information apparently reached Cripps at a timely moment, for the British ambassador to Moscow seems inexplicably to have been in a brief but ill-timed period of doubt about the likelihood of a German attack on Russia.* Boheman had heard from the Swedish minister in Moscow, Vilhelm Assarsson, that Cripps had recently expressed such doubts to him.[42] Accordingly, Boheman took the occasion of his own meeting with Cripps to verify the Briton's opinion[43] and, as seen earlier, attempt to reverse it. Cripps's aberrant view at the time was also known to the Germans. The German minister in Stockholm, Wipert von Blücher, learned that Cripps had told the British minister to Helsinki (who was then also visiting in Stockholm) "that it will not come to a conflict between Germany and Russia."[44]

61. Some Undelivered American Warnings

During the weekend of 7–8 June, U.S. Secretary of State Hull received cables from the American legations in both Bucharest and

* For Cripps's earlier and later views see warnings 1, 10, 28, 42, 60, 75, 80.

Stockholm asserting that Germany would invade Russia within the fortnight. The skeptical Hull had these reports sent that Monday (the ninth) to Ambassador Steinhardt in Moscow for his information and comment. They were not submitted to the Russians, contrary to William Shirer's assertion.[45]

62. B-day through Königsberg

Two or three weeks before the German invasion (George Kennan recalls) the U.S. consul in Königsberg, Kuykendall, relayed a report specifically naming 22 June as B-day.[46] * This is probably the report that was received in Washington on 10 June, having been flown there from Berlin by one of the American military attachés.†

63. London Tries Again

By 10 June it had become as clear to British intelligence as it had been for some time to Churchill that Hitler was about to attack Russia. A more explicit warning to Stalin was deemed in order. Accordingly, on that day Permanent Under-Secretary Sir Alexander Cadogan asked Ambassador Maisky to see him at the Foreign Office.

Cadogan announced: "On the instructions of His Majesty's Government, I have to make an important communication to you. Please take a sheet of paper and put down what I tell you." He then proceeded to dictate from documents a detailed inventory of the recent German eastward deployment, giving the specific dates and places of movement of division after division. At the end of

* This report is possibly the material telegraphed to State on 8 June by the U.S. chargé d'affaires in Germany, Leland B. Morris. If so, it is not surprising that Morris's impressive start—"I have received rather impressive testimony that within a fortnight Germany will invade Russia"—attracted little attention, given his concluding reservations, caveats, and citing of a contradictory report, albeit from "less impressive sources." *FRUS: 1941,* 1 (1958), 148.
† Suggested by Whitaker (1943), 306. Whitaker, then a *Chicago Daily News* correspondent in Lisbon, asserts that the report was considered too sensitive to confide to a coded cable. Whitaker also asserts that this message specified the correct hour as well as day of the invasion. Whitaker's H-hour and military attaché details suggest that this warning may have been the one given by Hermann Maass to Louis Lochner on 23 May. See warning 47.

this long monologue, Cadogan rose and added: "The Prime Minister asks you urgently to communicate all these data to the Soviet Government." [47]

The astonished Russian hastened to his embassy and dispatched an urgent cipher telegram to Moscow, giving the "precise and concrete" details of the British intelligence. Maisky was impressed. Although he made some discount for British error and motive, Maisky believed the report "should give Stalin serious food for thought, and lead him urgently to check them and, in any case, give strict instructions to our Western frontier to be on guard!" Therefore, Maisky recalls, he felt "extreme amazement" when the only apparent response was the TASS communiqué of the fourteenth publicly denouncing "the British and foreign press . . . rumours" about "the imminence of war between the USSR and Germany." [48]

64. A Leak from the German Embassy in Rumania

Shortly before 11 June, the Italian embassy in Bucharest learned from the German naval attaché that the operation against Russia would be ready to launch on 15 June.[49] This confirmed the date already settled on about 14 May by the chief of the Italian military intelligence (SIM), General Cesare Amè, based on information acquired in Budapest.[50] Since Amè enjoyed close personal relations with Admiral Canaris, it is possible that the earlier information represented a leak from the Abwehr.[51]

65. A Nazi Indiscretion in Sweden

Dr. Hans Draeger was an indiscreet Nazi official. He was originally with Goebbels's Propaganda Ministry as chief of the Foreign Affairs Department but had switched to a high post in Frick's Interior Ministry. He was also president of both the German-Swedish Society in Berlin and the Scandinavian Association. In these last positions he was a frequent visitor to Sweden, where he had a knack for blurting out his nation's innermost secrets before rather large audiences. As early as 2 October 1940 he spoke of the probability of a war between Germany and Russia.[52] Finally, on 11 June

1941, Dr. Draeger arrived in Stockholm and "announced straight out, without beating about the bush, that war with Russia was imminent." [53]

66. Tips from Danzig

A small Soviet intelligence net operating out of the Soviet consulate in Danzig had been transmitting by radio to Moscow right up to the invasion. The bulk of their reports had been concerned with troop deployments; and, in the weeks immediately preceding the invasion, their transmissions included—in the SD's judgment —"vital information about troop concentrations in East Prussia, and also about the movements of our Baltic Fleet." The ring's leaders, two senior members of the consulate's staff, had recruited nearly fifty Germans and Poles and had extended their *apparat* as far as a Wehrmacht supply office in Berlin. The two Russian leaders and some twenty-five of their agents were arrested by the Gestapo and Abwehr during the week or so following 22 June, but the German investigators were unable either to decipher the code used or to locate the transmitter, which was apparently being personally operated by the two Russians from somewhere in the Danzig area.[54] The two intelligence officers were repatriated through Turkey with the rest of the Soviet diplomatic corps on 13 July.[55]

67. The German Embassy Burns Its Bridges

From twelve days to a week before the invasion, the Russians received a tacit, conventional clue of impending war from the German Moscow embassy itself. The wives, children, and pets had begun a hurried return home. This was the result of instructions received on 9 June[56] from the Reich Foreign Ministry ordering the embassy to secure its secret archives and authorizing the "inconspicuous departure of women and children." [57]

This evacuation order was somehow picked up by the Soviet NKGB within two days. In any case, on 11 June the NKGB reported directly to Stalin that this order from Berlin was received on the ninth and directed the German embassy to prepare itself for evacuation to begin in seven days, that is, the sixteenth. The NKGB report to Stalin also verified that the embassy had already begun burning its records.[58] Further confirmation came quickly when the Germans did, in fact, begin evacuation.

All German dependents were evacuated by 22 June except Frau Hilger, the wife of the counselor of embassy.* The rush was of course most conspicuous: the Soviet officials giving full cooperation on the exit formalities, and the frontier officials showing exceptional politeness. On 21 June Molotov summoned Schulenburg to the Kremlin at 9:30 P.M. to complain of German overflights and to pry into German intentions, specifically asking why all German businessmen and embassy dependents had left. The embarrassed ambassador lamely replied that they had all gone on vacation because of the rigors of the Moscow climate and, besides, "not *all* women," had gone, citing Frau Hilger. Molotov shrugged and abandoned his fruitless quest for enlightenment.[59] However, the absurd cover story fooled no one. U.S. Ambassador Steinhardt recognized its significance as did the State Department.[60] † Even the usually uninformed Italian embassy in Moscow panicked and began its evacuation during that last week,[61] Ambassador Rosso having belatedly concluded that war was imminent.[62]

68. Ghost Ships

On 5 June Field-Marshal Keitel issued the BARBAROSSA timetable. This *Zeitplan* BARBAROSSA specified all the carefully coordinated final German deployments and related activities. Section 19 di-

---

* During the opening fortnight in May, directly following Ambassador Schulenburg's return from Berlin on 30 April, tension in Moscow was such that premature rumors were persistent in Moscow's foreign circles that the Germany embassy was packing and leaving. See Scott (1942), 240.

† Steinhardt even read special significance into the fact that a secretary of the German embassy, Gebhart von Walther, had evacuated his otherwise inseparable pet boxer. This prompted Steinhardt to evacuate all eight American embassy wives on the twenty-first. See Cassidy (1943), 57–58. See also *FRUS: 1941*, 1 (1958), 405–406, and Winter (1963), 261. Scott (1942), 266, apparently was misinformed in his assertion that the evacuation of the U.S. embassy was prompted by a warning on 20 June from "one of the secretaries of the German Embassy" who told Steinhardt that "war was imminent."

rected that the Navy from 17 June on would arrange the "inconspicuous withdrawal of German merchant shipping from Soviet Russian ports." [63] The German Naval War Staff promptly conformed and on 12 June issued its own directive canceling—on fictitious grounds—the sailing for Russian ports of any more German merchant vessels.[64]

In a then rare example of the use of statistical operational research, the Soviet Central Naval Staff was graphing this shift of German shipping away from Russian ports. The naval staff correctly read this graph as an ominous sign that "suggested a plan drawn up and implemented with characteristic German precision." [65] On 21 June the last German ship had sailed for home. But the Russians did nothing, and B-day found more than forty Soviet ships totaling 123,000 gross tons in German ports. All were promptly confiscated.[66]

69. Japanese Net Some Clues

Although the Japanese government was not formally notified by Germany of BARBAROSSA until B-day itself, it was getting nearly all the correct signals. Furthermore, while their intelligence services were generally overrated, they were performing magnificently in Central Europe. Consequently, the leaks to the Japanese are important to examine, particularly because some evaluations made in the Berlin embassy were being intercepted by British and American intelligence (see warning 15), and those made by the highest echelons in Tokyo were being passed to Moscow by Sorge.

Rather surprisingly, Japanese intelligence was directly acquiring its own detailed and completely accurate reports on the early German deployments eastward, on the Wehrmacht's order of battle in occupied Poland, and on the political situation in the Russian as well as the German zone of Poland. This was the work of a highly effective Japanese network operating briefly in Poland itself from some time shortly after the defeat of Poland until at least as late as the summer of 1940 when broken by the German SD. This group was headquartered in Warsaw and controlled from the Manchukuoan embassy in Berlin. It consisted of a small number

of Poles with Manchukuoan diplomatic passports. They had excellent connections—obtained in return for financial, technical,
and courier support—with both the political and military secret
services of the General Staff of the Polish resistance movement and
with the pro-German Mel'nyk faction of the Ukrainian nationalist
OUN underground organization in the Soviet zone of Poland.
However, they did not collaborate with German intelligence.[67]

These superb reports from Poland were collected in the Manchukuoan embassy in Berlin and transmitted to the very effective
Japanese European intelligence center in Stockholm operated by
the Japanese military attaché, Major-General Makoto Onodera.
These materials were of course forwarded to Tokyo. However, it
was Onodera's standard practice to barter his highest quality information with other intelligence services, including the British,
Italian, Jesuit, and—most significantly—one of the Russian services. His Soviet client was in the Russian embassy in Stockholm,
and his liaison man was a former Polish officer named Piotr who,
while employed by the Japanese legation was suspected by the
German SD of also being an NKVD agent. The SD later discovered
that Onodera's material traded with the Soviet embassy in Stockholm included intelligence on the German buildup in Poland.
The SD was then able to infiltrate Onodera's network with an
agent who fed in disinformation that Onodera unwittingly passed
to the Russians and other clients.[68] Undoubtedly, some of Onodera's mixed bag of information also eventually reached the GRU
through Sorge's key agent, Ozaki, with his contacts in the Japanese
War Cabinet.

There was also a close and continuing liaison between Admiral
Canaris and Japanese intelligence in Berlin. It had developed
while Colonel Ōshima Hiroshi was military attaché there and continued after his appointment as ambassador (and promotion to
general officer rank). However, whether Canaris ever used this
channel to warn the Japanese of BARBAROSSA is not recorded. Furthermore, the Japanese were quite parsimonious in giving the
Abwehr intelligence on Russia.[69]

Japan received its first veiled official warnings back on 27 March

1941, during the initial private meeting between Ribbentrop and Japanese Foreign Minister Matsuoka Yosuke. Ribbentrop intended only to notify the Japanese that Russo-German relations had cooled and thereby discourage Matsuoka from his planned further improvement in Russo-Japanese affairs. However, the ever-indiscreet Ribbentrop seemingly overplayed his hand by his constant repetition that Russo-German relations had become "correct, but not exactly very friendly," and he visibly alarmed Matsuoka by stating too frankly: "If the Soviet Union should one day adopt an attitude which Germany regards as a threat, the Führer will destroy Russia." [70] And Hitler's own parting words to Matsuoka on 4 April were ominous: "When you get back to Japan, you cannot report to your Emperor that a conflict between Germany and the Soviet Union is out of the question." [71]

Even if Matsuoka found the Hitler-Ribbentrop warnings ambiguous, he was simultaneously getting much clearer messages from the anti-Nazi German opposition. Some approaches were made directly to Matsuoka. In addition, Ernst von Weizsäcker and Erich Kordt managed to reach one of Matsuoka's entourage,[72] Sakamoto Ryuki, the director of the European Department of the Japanese Foreign Ministry. A few days later in Moscow, Mr. Sakamoto talked openly of that conversation with the Slovak minister there. Steinhardt's "confidential source" reported Sakamoto as having said:

Germany wished and was capable of destroying the Soviet Empire, would attack as soon as the Balkan campaign was over, or as soon thereafter as German armies were in shape; further that he was under the impression that the Russians were well informed about the Germans' designs.[73]

However, Matsuoka did not permit these flagrant clues to impinge on his confident dreams that all was going well.[74]

Throughout early May, Ambassador Ōshima in Berlin was tapping all his many resources seeking confirmation of his deep suspicions that Hitler was planning to attack Russia.[75] Finally, on 18 May, he telegraphed Tokyo, warning categorically that a Russo-German war was to be expected momentarily.[76] Ōshima was subsequently told by the German High Command that the war would be a quick affair—concluded within four weeks.[77]

On both 3 and 4 June Ambassador Ōshima was invited to Berchtesgaden, where he learned directly from Hitler of his intention to attack Russia, "to eliminate Communism . . . for the sake of humanity." Ribbentrop was present and gave similar information. Although neither of the Nazi leaders specified the date of the war,[78] both were quite explicit that it was imminent and virtually decided.[79] Ōshima telegraphed the substance of these startling revelations on 5 June, and the Japanese Liaison Conference considered them at its meeting on the seventh. Astoundingly, Foreign Minister Matsuoka almost entirely discounted the report. He preferred to believe that the matter was not imminent.[80]

The fact, rough date, and substance of the Ōshima-Hitler-Ribbentrop conference was soon learned by British intelligence, either in Tokyo or, more likely, from its radio intercepts of Ōshima's telegrams. We know this from a still unpublished letter dated 20 June 1941 to U.S. Secretary of State Hull from Anthony J. Drexel Biddle, Jr., the American ambassador to the governments-in-exile in London. Biddle reported that the British had intelligence from Tokyo that Ribbentrop had disclosed BARBAROSSA to Ōshima some ten days earlier.[81] Because Ōshima's reports were forwarded in three Foreign Office telegrams[82] and because Biddle's letter mentions only a Ribbentrop-Ōshima conference, it seems that British intelligence had not intercepted the entire series.

Finally, on Saturday, 16 June, Ambassador Ōshima cabled home categorically and accurately that a Russo-German war would occur during the coming week.[83] In the discussion by the Liaison Conference that day, Matsuoka at long last seemed to have accepted Ōshima's judgment.[84]

70. London Tries Yet Again

On 10 June British Foreign Secretary Eden met for the fourth time since April to apprise Soviet Ambassador Maisky of the accumulating signs of impending German aggression.* At that meeting,

* 16 April and 2, 5, and 10 June. See warning 28.

Eden's warning had been reinforced by a detailed briefing on Wehrmacht deployments from Sir Alexander Cadogan, who, as the Foreign Office's permanent under-secretary, was Eden's expert on intelligence matters.*

Over the next two days "the information reaching [Eden] had become more significant," so on 13 June Eden again summoned Maisky to his office at the Foreign Office for his last effort to warn the Russians. This step was taken in agreement with Churchill and Cripps with whom Eden had discussed this matter the previous evening. On this occasion Eden backed himself with the expertise of Mr. Victor Cavendish-Bentinck, the prescient Foreign Office's chairman of the Joint Intelligence Committee.

Eden told Maisky that:

> in the past forty-eight hours the information reaching us had become more significant. The troop concentrations might be for the purpose of a war of nerves, or they might be for the purpose of an attack on Russia. I did not know, but we were bound to consider, in the light of this very formidable build-up, that conflict between Germany and Russia was possible.[85]

Eden also reassured Maisky of Britain's intentions to assist Russia should invasion materialize. Cavendish-Bentinck added: "I spent half-an-hour with Anthony Eden . . . trying to convince Maisky that the Germans were going to attack and that this attack would take place on either 21/22 June or 28/29 June. I added that I would put my money on 22 June."[86]

Maisky formally said he would communicate this information to his government. But Eden records that Maisky "betrayed no personal reaction to the message and still professed not to believe in the possibility of a German attack"; and Cavendish-Bentinck recalls more tersely that "Maisky refused to believe this." Although Maisky chooses to completely overlook this extraordinary warning

* See warning 63. There is an old myth that the permanent under-secretary (Lord Vansittart in the 1930s and Cadogan in World War II) was ex officio chief of the British Secret Intelligence Service. This story arose from the fact that all intelligence did pass across that official's desk. In other words, the permanent under-secretary was the Foreign Office's most senior "intelligence watch officer."

—as well as the other four from Eden—in his otherwise detailed memoirs, the Soviet historian Nekrich freely summarizes and cites the published record.[87]

Eden, however, blunders in suggesting that Maisky's chilly attitude was in any way determined by the publication of the sensational TASS communiqué that rather blatantly dismissed reports of Russo-German conflict as a British provocation. Maisky was a far more deceitful man than his ostensibly frank memoirs are designed to imply, but he was not apprised of the TASS communiqué until its public release, *after* his meeting with Eden. (See Chapter 9.)

71. "The Shadow" Knows

Ambassador Ōshima's futile telegrams to alert Tokyo of BARBAROSSA were intercepted not only by Russian and British intelligence but by American intelligence as well. The American intercepts of the Japanese messages on BARBAROSSA from their embassies in Berlin and Rome had continued after Welles's disclosure of these to Soviet Ambassador Umansky in April, as described in warning 12. While the Americans were sharing at least the substance of this material with the British, they had abandoned their efforts to pass it to the seemingly disinterested Soviet ambassador. Nevertheless, as this traffic may well have reached Russian ears by some indirect route, it is at least worth summarizing here.

On 30 April a new summary of intercepts had been prepared by Lieutenant Commander Alwin "The Shadow" Kramer, the head of Op-20-GZ, the translation unit of the Office of Naval Communications. Kramer's "Memo No. GZ-32" apparently concurred with the Army SIS reports in outlining, as specified by its title, "Early Indications of Germany to Attack Russia." [88]

Next, on 3 June, came a telegram from Ambassador Horikiri in Rome informing Tokyo that "Germany had completed all preparations for attacking Russia." Then, as German deployments became more evident to the Japanese or, at least presumably, to Ōshima in Berlin, Kramer issued three new memorandums based on the Japanese intercepts:

1. Memo No. GZ-1, of 14 June, titled "German Plans to Attack Russia."
2. Memo No. GZ-9, of 16 June, titled "Crisis in German Soviet Relations."
3. Memo No. GZ-15, of 17 June, titled "German-Soviet Crisis" with a subtitle or annotation indicating the possibility of "German surprise attacks." [89]

72. The NKGB Gets a Wehrmacht Operational Order

On 16 June the NKGB learned that the concentration of German troops in East Prussia had received an operational order to take up by 13 June initial deployments for attack. Subsequently, this ready date was reset to the eighteenth.[90]

The reference here is to German Army Group North commanded by Field-Marshal von Leeb.

73. Reichsmarschall Göring and the Interloping Swede

Birger Dahlerus was a Swedish manufacturer who delighted in dabbling in diplomacy. Since 1939 he had several times served as an intermediary between the Germans—specifically, his "peacemaker" friend Hermann Göring—and the British. But given the delicacy of his assignments he was notoriously indiscreet, a quality that annoyed the British but delighted Göring, who fully exploited that flaw. Indeed, since 1939, Göring's superb interception service, the Forschungsamt, had been tapping Herr Dahlerus's phone.[91]

In mid-June 1941, after a five-hour conversation in Berlin with Göring, Herr Dahlerus returned to Stockholm. He rushed off on 18 June to the British minister, Mr. Victor Mallet, to spread the word. Dahlerus told Mallet that the Reichsmarschall had stressed Germany's absolute need for steady food and oil supplies from Russia and that, to ensure this before Russia became strong enough to resist, Germany was now prepared to move. Göring then described the German demands—drafted, he said, by himself: Russian demobilization, establishment of a separate government in the Ukraine, control of the Baku oil fields, and perhaps an outlet to the Pacific. Dahlerus concluded that these demands would be presented to Russia as an ultimatum in the very near future, possibly within the week, since Göring was scheduled to meet with Hitler.[92]

Dahlerus's information was repeated to the U.S. embassy in Stockholm and through them to the State Department in Washington. There, Sumner Welles concluded—as he told British Ambassador Halifax—that this formed part of Germany's "pressure tactics" and that Russia would agree to almost anything except the demand for demobilization.[93]

As usual, Göring had simply used Dahlerus to leak a calculated lie. There were no German demands, drafted by Göring or anyone else.

74. A Deserter at the Front

By 18 June many of the German officers and men at the frontier had received their operational orders. These soldiers would have been worthwhile targets for Soviet interrogation. But none were kidnapped, since Beriya's NKVD frontier troops were under strictest restraining orders to avoid provocations.[94] Nevertheless, one German sergeant deserted early that evening, surrendering to the Red Army 15th Rifle Corps deployed at the frontier before Kiev. Under interrogation at corps headquarters in Kovel, this soldier said he had deserted because he expected to be shot for striking an officer while drunk. He added that his father was a Communist. He also stated that the Wehrmacht would invade at 4 A.M. on 22 June. The local corps commander, Major-General Ivan Fedyuninsky, promptly telephoned this last item to his superior, Major-General M. I. Potapov, commanding the Fifth Army, who labeled it a nonsensical "provocation." [95] It does not appear that Potapov forwarded this intelligence through other than routine channels.*

---

* There is much confusion in both Soviet and Western literature about this deserter. Bialer, Salisbury, and Kladt are wrong in supposing there was only one deserter. In fact there were three: this one on 18 June, one in the afternoon of the twenty-first, and one later that night. See warnings 83 and 84.

75. A Late Warning from the Soviet Embassy in London

On 18 June 1941, according to Khrushchev, the Soviet embassy in London cabled Moscow that:

As of now Cripps is deeply convinced of the inevitability of armed conflict between Germany and the U.S.S.R. which will begin not later than the middle of June. According to Cripps, the Germans have presently concentrated 147 divisions (including air force and service units) along the Soviet borders. . . .[96]

This cable does indeed fairly represent Ambassador Cripps's view at that juncture, while back in London (11–28 June) for urgent consultations,[97] and probably in part the fresh cryptanalytic readings given him by the Swedish Foreign Ministry a fortnight earlier (see warning 60). This message about Cripps's view would seem a local Soviet espionage coup rather than a British unofficial leak or official disclosure because Cripps did not raise the question explicitly with Ambassador Maisky until 21 June, although he had already seen Maisky twice since returning from Moscow on the eleventh.[98]

76. Polish Intelligence Gets B-day

By 20 June, even the Polish prime minister-in-exile, General Sikorski, had acquired an intelligence report that the attack would come on 22 June. Sikorski—or his staff—informed the U.S. ambassador to the governments-in-exile, Mr. Anthony J. Drexel Biddle, Jr., who on the twentieth sent this news to Secretary of State Hull.[99]

77. Finland and Rumania Notified

Although conclusive evidence is unavailable, we may assume that Soviet intelligence picked up additional authentic warnings from Hitler's initial allies in BARBAROSSA: Rumania and Finland. The Germans were, as discussed in Chapter 6, careful to conceal BARBAROSSA from the Italians, Slovaks, and Hungarians on the wise presumption that such information would soon pass to the Russians by some more or less devious path. However, because the Rumanian and Finnish armies were an integral part of BARBAROSSA planning, a gradual disclosure to those two governments was necessary.

In the case of Finland, the first veiled notification took the form of a guarded conversation on 20 May 1941 between the German ambassador and Finnish President Ryti. The partial mobilization begun on 10 June was coordinated with Germany, and on the fourteenth the Finns were told war was certain. B-day—22 June—was finally disclosed to the Finnish command on 17 June.

It is quite likely that Soviet intelligence got no more out of the Finns than their visible military preparations, since the Finns managed to limit the circle of witting planners to a mere handful of key individuals—all loyal, all enthusiastically anti-Soviet, all taciturn, and all quite aware of the high political and military risks involved in any premature disclosure to the Russians of any Finnish plotting against them. However, the Finnish preparations for war were highly visible. Everyone was aware of the increasingly frequent German-Finnish military contacts from January on. By the end of May, the improvement of strategic roads and bridges and the stockpiling of munitions and supply dumps were widely known. Then, from June 8 on, large numbers of German troops began conspicuously arriving at Finnish ports and deploying to northern Finland. Two days later the Finns began partial mobilization, and general mobilization began on the seventeenth.[100]

The Russians were quite aware of all this activity. For example, on 19 June the Soviet minister in Helsinki, P. G. Orlov, concluded that a Nazi attack was imminent. Accordingly, he warned General S. I. Kabanov, the commanding officer of the Soviet base on the Hangö peninsula on Finnish-leased territory. At the same time the Soviet military attaché and Minister Orlov evacuated their families who were then sharing a villa near the targeted Hangö base.[101]

The case of Rumania is even more noteworthy. On 27 May 1941 Colonel-General Ritter von Schobert had arrived in Rumania, fully briefed on BARBAROSSA, to coordinate military planning with the Rumanian General Staff without explicitly disclosing the operation to them. General Ion Antonescu, the chief of state, was overjoyed to learn from Hitler in Munich on 11 June that Hitler had decided to attack and, from a subsequent courier message of 18 June, that it would occur "in the near future." [102] (Indeed, Antonescu was so impatient to attack Russia that he later incorrectly recalled that Hitler had already communicated his intent at their two earlier fall and winter meetings.)[103]

On 19 June American Ambassador Franklin Mott Gunther wired Hull from Bucharest that the French air attaché, X. de Sevin, had disclosed that Rumanian officers were openly saying they expected the German attack against Russia to be launched on the morning of the twenty-first.[104] * Thus the Rumanian General Staff was a veritable sieve for secret information and, given the loose-mouthed diplomatic corps in Bucharest, we should assume Russian intelligence immediately knew, particularly as their Balkan service was of the best.[105]

78. A Fumbled Scoop by the *New York Times*

Ray Brock of the *New York Times* was something of a one-man intelligence service. A young but veteran correspondent, he had covered the European war since its first act in Spain during the later stages of the civil war and foreign intervention there in 1938. But such was the foreign correspondence system that his remarkable series of scoops on BARBAROSSA were overlooked, discounted, diluted, or buried by his editors. No effort was made by these men to follow up or double-check Brock's spectacular information. It was a quite typical case of a major news-gathering agency failing to use its superb capabilities for the collection, collation, analysis, and verification of information.

Brock had received his first intimations of BARBAROSSA in December 1940 while stationed in Bucharest. His ever-reliable tipster then was "G——" from the staff of Gafencu's pro-British daily, *Timpul*.† Next year, about 17 or 18 May, he alerted Brock to its certainty and imminence:

* For de Sevin's earlier estimate submitted to the Vichy Deuxième Bureau (when on 9 June he gave B-day as "presumably 17 June"), see warning 59.
† On "G——" see Brock (1942), 89 and 90. Circumstantial evidence makes Alex Coler (described in the Balkan memoirs of Parker and St. John) a very

The Yugoslavs fought and postponed it—maybe for as long as six weeks—but from the information I have been receiving here from Moravia and from reports trickling in from all along the Russo-German frontiers, I would bet the Germans attack not later than July.[106]

"G——'s" file was so extensive that Brock spent two hours in his apartment merely copying partial notes on concentrations of German troops and matériel.[107]

Brock then joined Cyrus Sulzberger as his number two man in Ankara. Sulzberger was skeptical but sufficiently impressed by Brock's evidence to approve a series of articles for the *New York Times* that appeared in late May. Brock's articles summarized his material and gave a carefully hedged prediction of a German attack on Russia that summer.[108]

In the second week of June a new source became available to Brock when his old informant of Spanish Civil War days, Geoffrey "Tommy" Thompson, arrived as the new counselor of the British embassy. Thompson carefully and deliberately disclosed to Brock on an "exclusive" basis news of German Ambassador von Papen's current peace feelers toward Britain. Brock discussed this information with his fellow foreign correspondents; but, excepting the astute Winston Burdett of CBS and Mr. Wallis of Reuters, this story was rejected by Brock's colleagues as ridiculous propaganda. Burdett shared Brock's belief that this German démarche represented an effort to close down military activities in the West and the Mediterranean before striking at Russia. (In fact, these "peace feelers" were quite unconnected with BARBAROSSA, being entirely made at the initiative of von Papen and Turkish President Ismet Inönü.) Burdett also told Brock that Thompson's disclosures verified his own sources, including the correspondent of *Signal* (the German pictorial weekly for occupied Europe), Herr Weber, who had been publicly suggesting an imminent German attack on Russia.[109]

---

likely candidate for Brock's "G——." See Robert Parker, *Headquarters Budapest* (New York: Farrar & Rinehart, 1944), and Robert St. John, *From the Land of Silent People* (Garden City, N.Y.: Doubleday, Doran, 1942).

During this period Sulzberger had managed to organize a news pool with some of the other foreign correspondents in Ankara. It consisted of Sulzberger and Brock of the *New York Times,* Wallis of Reuters, Walter Bossard of the *Neue Zürcher Zeitung,* and, from CBS, Farnsworth Fowle and Winston Burdett. Around 18 June, Burdett contributed the startling news that his Finnish sources were predicting imminent war between Germany and Russia. Brock went scurrying for verification. He took the night train to Istanbul to get the latest information about the German military concentrations from his reliable Yugoslav émigré sources. Brock returned to Ankara on Friday afternoon, 20 June, and immediately telephoned for an interview with the Finnish military attaché, Major Arvo Wiitanen,[110] who agreed to see Brock at 7 P.M. With his aristocratic Polish wife interpreting, Wiitanen incautiously admitted that a German attack was certain along the entire front, including Finland (after a suitable wait), "within forty-eight hours." At this point the German military attaché, General Hans Rohde, was announced. Brock slipped out the back.[111]

Brock's Ankara chief, Sulzberger, radioed Brock's new information, omitting the source, to their New York office that night. He "slugged" Brock's story as item A: ". . . and a German attack upon the entire Russian front, from Finland to the Ukraine, will begin within forty-eight hours, according to a well-informed foreign military source tonight in Ankara. . . ."[112] The following day, Saturday, they received no confirmation other than the observation that the local German embassy staff was in an unusually conspiratorial and self-congratulatory mood. Therefore, for his Sunday "situationer," Sulzberger nervously "toned down the forecast a trifle, but [still] underscored the imminence of Russo-German hostilities."[113] Brock is too gentle on Sulzberger. In fact, Sulzberger's editorial efforts went beyond a merely more skeptical reassessment of the likelihood of war to stress an overriding precondition. Thus the dispatch stressed what I have called the "ultimatum" hypothesis (see Chapter 9), namely, that war was contingent on Soviet rejection of an alleged recently presented German ultimatum. Three hours later, the unfortunately watered-down forecast was fulfilled.[114]

However, Soviet intelligence in Turkey apparently did not have to depend on reading the *New York Times* to get Brock's excellent information. Sulzberger later discovered that one of the American broadcasters in his Ankara circle was a "minor spy" who "regularly informed the Soviet embassy." [115]

79. Accelerating Rumors from Slovakia

Two or three days before the attack, the puppet minister of interior of Slovakia, Sano Mach, publicly announced at Nitra (or perhaps in Bratislava) that a "German liberation" of the Ukraine was "imminent." At least, so the young *New York Times* man, C. L. Sulzberger, reported from Ankara on 20 June.[116] Unfortunately, there is too little published information on Mach's specific relations with his Nazi masters even to speculate, much less reconstruct, the basis of his curious leak. (Sulzberger's information probably came from his number two man, Ray Brock, who had sources reaching into Czechoslovakia; see warning 78.)

80. The Final Warning from London

At 1 P.M. on Saturday, 21 June, Ivan Maisky, the Bolshevik Russian ambassador to the Court of St. James left his embassy for a quiet weekend in the suburbs. He arrived in Bovington, where he was a regular houseguest of Juan Negrin, the prime minister of the Spanish Republican government-in-exile. Maisky was quietly reflecting on the accumulating signals of a German invasion when an embassy secretary rang through to say that Sir Stafford Cripps, the ambassador to Moscow who had returned for consultations eleven days earlier and had twice visited Maisky, was urgently trying to reach Maisky. An hour later Maisky was back at his office and Cripps excitedly announced:

You remember that I have already warned the Soviet Government more than once that a German attack was imminent. . . . Well, we have reliable information that this attack will take place tomorrow 22 June, or at the very latest 29 June. . . . You know that Hitler always attacks on Sundays. . . . I wanted to inform you of this.[117]

Maisky immediately sent an enciphered telegram to the People's Commissariat of Foreign Affairs reporting Cripps's warning. He then returned to Negrin's home to uneasily await the outcome.

81. A Final Warning from "Le Grand Chef" in Vichy

Leopold Trepper, the indefatigable chief of the GRU's espionage network in France and the Low Countries, had been busily collecting further information on the German threat to Russia since his first warning late in April (warning 31). The German engineer informant, Ludwig Kainz, had lost to Trepper his wager of a case of champagne that a Russo-German war would break out by the end of May. But now in early June Kainz insisted that the German attack had merely been postponed a month because of Hitler's Balkan campaign. Kainz now bet Trepper double or nothing that Hitler would strike in June. Trepper soon got confirmation in a series of drinking bouts with some senior SS officers who on the eve of their departure for Poland toasted the imminent defeat of Russia.[118]

In Paris early on Saturday, 21 June, Trepper learned that the Wehrmacht would attack that very night. He still did not have access to a radio transmitter, so for the second and last time Trepper was forced to the dangerous expedient of communicating his most urgent message through the Soviet embassy in Vichy, specifically, through the military attaché, Major-General Susloparov (see warnings 31 and 59). Arriving in Vichy that evening, Trepper told Susloparov: "Here is a message of vital importance, for immediate transmission!" The complacent general burst out laughing and replied: "Why, you must be out of your mind. It's unthinkable, altogether impossible. I refuse to transmit such a telegram. You would simply be making a fool of yourself!" But, at Trepper's insistence, Susloparov did send the message. Three days later the assistant military attaché arrived from Moscow and told Trepper:

I saw the Director [of the GRU] the evening your telegram arrived. He assured me that it had immediately been shown to the Boss [Stalin]. The Boss was very much surprised. "As a rule," he said, "Otto [Trepper's code name] sends us worthwhile material that does credit to his political judgment. How could he fail to detect at once that this was merely a piece of British provocation?" [119]

82. The Picnic Is Off

Finally, as GRU Major Akhmedov later testified, the Soviet embassy in Berlin received a last-minute warning:

Saturday, June 21, 1941 we got another information that the Germans were going to declare war on Soviet Russia the next day, that is Sunday, June 22. That was sent immediately to Moscow headquarters and reported to [Ambassador] Dekanozov . . . who . . . still did not believe in that information and we were ordered to forget it and go to a picnic party the next day. . . .[120]

The following morning, at 3 A.M., Dekanozov was summoned before Ribbentrop, who formally notified him of Germany's declaration of war. The picnic did not take place.*

83. A Warning Heeded

Early on the evening of the twenty-first, a second German army deserter—a sergeant-major—crossed the frontier and surrendered to Soviet Border Guards. He disclosed that the German troops had begun moving up to their final departure areas for the attack, which had been ordered for the coming morning. This report soon reached the chief of staff of the Kiev Military District, Lieutenant-General M. A. Purkayev, who immediately telephoned it to Army Chief of Staff Zhukov in Moscow. Zhukov at once telephoned both Defense Commissar S. K. Timoshenko and Stalin. Stalin summoned them to the Kremlin. On the short drive over, Timoshenko, Zhukov, and Zhukov's deputy, Lieutenant-General N. F. Vatutin, agreed on the need to get Stalin's permission to alert the troops.

* Similarly, Ambassador Nikolai Gorelkin and the entire senior staff of the Soviet embassy in Rome was away that day—bathing at Fregene. See Ciano (1946), 369.

When they arrived, Stalin was alone, looking worried. He asked: "But perhaps the German generals sent this deserter to provoke a conflict?" His senior officers stated their belief in the deserter's report. Just then several Politburo members arrived, and Stalin asked, "What are we to do?" No one spoke until Timoshenko said, "A directive must immediately be given to alert all the troops of border Districts." At Stalin's request, Zhukov read the draft of the alert directive that he had brought along. Stalin revealingly rejected it, saying:

It's too soon to give such a directive—perhaps the question can still be settled peacefully. We must give a short directive stating that an attack may begin with provocative actions by the German forces. The troops of the border Districts must not be incited by any provocation, in order to avoid complications.

Zhukov and Vatutin hurriedly drafted a directive along these lines, announcing that "a sudden German attack is possible" along the frontier on the 22nd–23rd, ordering all border Military Districts to be in "combat readiness," but specifying that "the task of our troops is not to be incited by any provocative action which may cause serious complications." This rather ambiguous directive was approved by Stalin. At thirty minutes past midnight, the General Staff had sent the directive off to all the Military District headquarters.[121]

84. Last Warning

Meanwhile, as Khrushchev later revealed, "on the eve of the invasion" (the night of 21 June), "a certain German citizen" crossed the border to warn that the German attack was due the next morning at 3 A.M.[122]

It is appropriate that this last of all the many warnings was also the first one published, for it was far from a new revelation that Khrushchev had made, although none of the commentators on his "secret" speech have mentioned this. A few days after the German attack, Comrade Walter Ulbricht addressed the German Comintern students in Moscow. Wolfgang Leonhard recalls that Ulbricht said:

We are living through the early days of war, but already I have an encouraging announcement to make to you. As early as 22nd June, the first German soldier deserted to the Soviet side! This soldier was stationed in Rumania on the River Pruth. On the night of 21st–22nd June, he heard the order issued to his unit to attack the Soviet Union. He left his unit at once and swam by night across the Pruth, to join the Red Army and to tell us that a few hours later the Nazi attack on the Soviet Union was about to begin.[123]

Within days this information became public knowledge. It was printed in one of the early Soviet war communiqués, and *Pravda* published the defector's photograph and statement. The soldier, Alfred Liskov, was quoted as declaring:

I have long been against the Hitlerite system. As soon as I learned that the attack was imminent, I took my decision to go over to the Red Army. Even on the very day before the attack on the Soviet Union, no one really believed that such treachery was possible. . . .[124]

Additional details of Liskov's defection have more recently been published by the Soviet historian Nekrich and by Marshal Zhukov. Liskov was with the 222nd Infantry Regiment of the 74th Infantry Division when, at 9 P.M. on the twenty-first, he was picked up at Vladimir-Volynsky on the frontier by troops of the 90th Border Guard Detachment. He was interrogated at 11 P.M. that night. His warning of the final German preparations and their order to attack at 4 A.M. (all these times being local Russian time) was immediately reported by NKVD Major Bychevsky to the chief of the Border Guards of the NKVD of the Ukrainian Military District at Kiev and relayed to the headquarters of the Fifth Army at Lutsk.[125]

This information was then transmitted to Zhukov over his high-frequency telephone by Colonel-General M. P. Kirponos, the commander of the Kiev Military District. Kirponos was ordered to hurry along the earlier alert directive to his subordinate headquarters. At the General Staff headquarters, it now did seem that the Germans were indeed moving to the frontier. Stalin was notified by Zhukov at thirty minutes past midnight. Stalin merely asked if the alert directive had been received by all military districts.[126]

It was 0030 hours. But the German attack would begin in 150 minutes. The alert reached few operational echelons. Soviet military communications, with less than half the needed radio facilities, were not up to the task.[127] Moreover, the cable communication lines from all frontier Military District headquarters to their subordinate units were cut just before daybreak by special German sabotage teams.[128]

Summary of Warnings

These many reports, and undoubtedly others that reached Stalin, constitute an impressive mass of largely independent and firm verification of both Hitler's decision to attack and the nearly exact timetable of that attack. On the evidence it seems incredible that Stalin neither understood this nor set in motion an appropriate alert. He apparently did not appreciate that attack was imminent, and he certainly took no decisive action. We could—like Khrushchev, Churchill, William Shirer, and Drew Middleton—explain these facts by attributing "monumental complacency" or downright irrationality to Stalin, brought on by his stubborn unwillingness to concede that he had lost his ability to manipulate Hitler. Witness Stalin's remark to Churchill the next year, Dekanozov's behavior in Berlin on 21 June, and Molotov's gratuitous reply ("Surely we have not deserved that.") to the German ambassador when told by him at 4:00 A.M. on the fateful twenty-second of Hitler's declaration of war.[129] * All these facts suggest an ostrich syndrome at the peak of the Soviet system. Yet quite another interpretation can emerge if some other, more subtle facts are admitted in evidence.

---

* Eyewitness Hilger says the German telegram reached the embassy at 3 A.M. and was delivered to Molotov "shortly after four in the morning." Molotov replied that an attack had already been under way for one and a half hours.

I am full of leaks, and I let secrets out hither and yon
                    —Terrence, Eunuchus, *act 1, sc. 2*

The previous three chapters have arrayed the known warnings of BARBAROSSA circulating in international intelligence circles before the invasion. Although only a minority of these warnings were conclusively linked by direct evidence to the Kremlin, I asserted that virtually all must have reached Soviet intelligence channels. The present chapter presents the evidence supporting this assertion.

German Security and Internal Diffusion

You will never learn what I am thinking. And those who boast most loudly that they know my thought, to such people I lie even more.
                        —Hitler, to Halder, August 1938 [1]

Paralleling their planning and deployments, the Germans took special steps both to conceal BARBAROSSA from foreign intelligence services and to mislead them about it. These two efforts represent "negative" and "positive" security. The first, the German security efforts to assure the diffusion of the secrets of BARBAROSSA within proper "need to know" channels, is the subject of this section. The second, their deception operations, is deferred to the following chapter.

The German counterintelligence services of the SD and Abwehr took unusual precautions to prevent unauthorized disclosure of BARBAROSSA. The circle of knowers was to be kept as small as possible for as long as possible. For example, only nine closely guarded copies of the original operations order (Führer "Directive No. 21") existed: one to each supreme command of the three service arms (OKH, OKL, OKM), the rest remaining at OKW headquarters. Senior field commanders were to be told only that the plan was a contingency "in case Russia should change her previous attitude toward us." Actually, the bureaucratic channeling of BARBAROSSA messages was quite effectively restrained. Even the final major coordinating memorandum, "Timetable BARBA-

ROSSA" (issued twelve days before B-day) existed in only twenty-one copies, limited to the OKW, OKH, OKL, and OKM.[2]

The then chief of Abwehr III (security), Colonel Franz von Bentivegni, summarized his role in BARBAROSSA to his Soviet interrogators after the war. He mentioned the following directives from Admiral Canaris received in March 1941:

a) Preparation of all links of Abwehr III for carrying out active counterintelligence work against the Soviet Union, as for instance the creation of the necessary counterintelligence groups, their distribution among various fighting units intended for taking part in the operations on the Eastern front, and paralyzing the activity of the Soviet intelligence and counterintelligence organs.

b) Spreading false information via their foreign intelligence agencies, partly by creating the semblance of an improvement in relations with the Soviet Union and of preparations for a blow against Great Britain.

c) Counterintelligence measures to keep secret the preparations being made for war with the Soviet Union and to ensure that the transfer of troops to the East be kept secret.[3]

Usually, only persons privy to a secret can disclose it. Consequently, one effective starting point for an investigation of the channels through which Soviet intelligence learned of BARBAROSSA would be to reconstruct the expanding organizational chart of German officials who were formally briefed on this operation. The ideal procedure is to note the dates, addressors, and addressees listed on (1) all surviving BARBAROSSA formal written directives,* (2) persons involved in oral briefings mentioned in memoranda, diaries, testimonies, and memoirs, and (3), as spot checks, the fragmentary data showing those who were unwitting at particular periods. For BARBAROSSA the documentation is adequate to achieve a nearly complete record. Appendix B illustrates one way by which the data can be displayed. Another would be

---

* Caveat: It was not revealed until 1962 that some OKW and German Foreign Ministry documents have falsified dates and addressors. Thus it was Jodl's practice to issue many OKW papers over the signature of subordinates, sometimes without even the courtesy of informing the nominal "sender." See Warlimont (1964), 592n5.

an information flow chart, although such a chart could show only *some* of the knowers and trace only *some* of the links with Soviet intelligence. More thorough descriptions and analyses of this type would yield clearer clues to the identities of the specific individual officials responsible for the numerous premature disclosures to foreign intelligence. As will be apparent in the next section, most of the leaks occurred at early stages while the total number of knowers was still quite small.*

As noted earlier, it was during the spring of 1940 that Hitler first redirected his private planning to an invasion of Russia. It is likely that his preliminary thoughts were communicated at that time to such intimate members of his immediate entourage as Colonel Rudolf Schmundt, his chief adjutant. It is known that on 2 June 1940—two days before the fall of Dunkirk—he informally discussed this question with Generals Rundstedt and Sodenstern, respectively the commander and the chief of staff of Army Group A, who later commanded the southern front in the initial attack. However, as with so many of Hitler's generals during this period, Rundstedt either conveniently "forgot" or never understood the significance of Hitler's maunderings.[4]

The High Command of the Army (OKH) was the first group drawn into BARBAROSSA, although it was only in the second echelon of the military system. The OKH commander in chief, General von Brauchitsch, was inducted into its mysteries, seemingly sometime toward the first of July 1940, and presumably by Hitler himself. In any event, at Fontainebleau on 2 July von Brauchitsch directed his chief of staff, Halder, to begin prelimi-

---

* That is, knowing roughly which secrets were betrayed, our problem is to identify their betrayers. This method is the reverse of the standard procedure in the "damage assessment" committees used by intelligence services for tracing back which secret documents may have been compromised by a subsequently exposed agent in place. In the case of BARBAROSSA we do not yet know any of the specific infiltrated Soviet agents, except Lieutenant Schultz-Boysen in the Air Force Ministry and Oberreigierungsrat Harnack in the Ministry of Economics. Consequently, it is premature to apply this particular "damage assessment" procedure. For a description of this intelligence procedure see Thomas Whiteside, *An Agent in Place: The Wennerström Affair* (New York: Viking, 1966), pp. 141–147.

nary plans for an invasion of Russia, as described in Chapter 2.[5] From this point forward, the OKH was the focus for all detailed planning of BARBAROSSA.

The second group drawn, belatedly, into the BARBAROSSA planning was Hitler's personal military staff, the High Command of the Armed Forces (OKW). At least, the OKW heads, Keitel and Jodl, are not known to have been aware of Hitler's intentions toward Russia until late July 1940, although the OKW was the apex of the military chain of command. From then on, however, these two toadies so faithfully assured Hitler's continual interference in the planning at lower echelons that they were awarded rapid promotion from an appreciative Führer and the hangman's noose from a vengeful International Military Tribunal.

The ill-fated Colonel-General Friedrich Paulus was immediately made witting upon his appointment to the long-vacant post of deputy chief of the OKH on 3 September 1940. Paulus soon revealed BARBAROSSA to his immediate family—his daughter Olga, his twin sons Captains Friedrich and Ernst Alexander, and his wife Elena Constance, an independently minded Rumanian noblewoman who had opposed the invasion of Poland and now objected to BARBAROSSA. There is no suggestion here that Paulus's immediate family included traitors. However, there is no reason to assume that they were any less indiscreet than the father and husband. Furthermore, the intimate friends of the family included many aristocratic White Russian émigrés such as Prince and Princess Vassilchikov, Prince Gagarin, Count Zubov, and Baroness Hoyningen-Huene.[6] Although such circles might have seemed above suspicion, they were prime targets for infiltration by NKVD provocateurs and, at least among the White Russian groups in Paris, were so infiltrated at their highest levels.[7]

The most senior Luftwaffe officers and planning staffs were early on made privy to BARBAROSSA. The Luftwaffe commander in chief, Reichsmarschall Göring, was apparently witting at least as early as the AUFBAU OST order of 9 August 1940 and certainly knew of the 18 December "Directive No. 21." [8] Field-Marshal Kesselring, then commanding the cross-Channel air operations against

Britain, was earmarked as commander of the Luftwaffe for the Russian front (that is, Air Fleet 2) and accordingly was made witting by the beginning of the new year, although he delayed informing his own staff a month or two.[9]

Jodl notified the Abwehr by 6 September that the OKW was "preparing an Eastern offensive." [10] Although this notice was to initiate appropriate counterespionage and counterintelligence, Jodl also was unwittingly alerting two of the most active sources of security leaks to the anti-Nazi underground and foreign intelligence: Abwehr chief, Admiral Canaris, and his deputy, Colonel Oster. Canaris promptly notified his more trusted section chiefs that the invasion was being planned and, in January 1941, he told them that it had been scheduled for 15 May.[11]

The OKH passed the first general alert to Army Group level and Army level staffs at a day-long briefing at its headquarters at Zossen on 13 December 1940. The assembly comprised the chiefs of staff of three Army Groups and ten of the Armies, the others being OKH staff or liaison officers. Of the 37 officers present, my accounting indicates that 26 were then receiving their first official notification of BARBAROSSA.[12] I presume that these officers promptly reported the news to their various commanders.*

The Navy High Command (OKM) was among the last to know Hitler's intentions toward Russia. Hitler kept his naval commander in chief, Grand-Admiral Erich Raeder, long in the dark. Surprised in August 1940 to learn of the major transfer of army and navy units to the eastern frontier, Raeder had asked Hitler their purpose; but Hitler lied that they were mere feints to camouflage SEA LION. Raeder first learned of BARBAROSSA at Hitler's briefing for the commanders in chief of the three service arms on 18 December, although he admits to receiving earlier intimations.[13] †

In this case, Hitler was probably additionally motivated to de-

---

* For example, the chief of staff of the First Army, Colonel Röhricht, reported this news to his commanding general, Colonel-General Blaskowitz. See Edgar Röhricht, *Pflicht und Gewissen* (Stuttgart: Kohlhammer, 1965), p. 172.
† Admiral Dönitz writes his memoirs as if he had never even heard of BARBAROSSA. He may even be truthful.

ceive Raeder by the negligible role assigned the Navy in BARBA-
ROSSA as well as by his annoyance with the Grand-Admiral's outspoken resistance to such taut extensions of German armed
strength.

Reichsführer-SS Himmler was, to his great delight, informed of
BARBAROSSA at least as early as 1 January 1941.[14] However, the
chief of the SD's Counterintelligence Department, Walter Schellenberg, was brought into the full picture—through a verbal
briefing by SD chief Heydrich—only toward the end of January
1941, although he had received an intimation of it (also from
Heydrich) in early December.[15]

Joseph Goebbels and his Ministry of Propaganda were drawn
into the planning by early April 1941, possibly because of the
valuable contributions his machine could make toward "filling
the empty Soviet space with propaganda." (As we shall see in
Chapter 7, Goebbels even contributed his personal part to the
deliberate German deception campaign.) From early April on,
Eberhard Taubert, head of the Eastern Section of the ministry and
secret director of the Anti-Komintern, expanded his personal staff
and created a new office under the codename VINETA to prepare
and stockpile broadcasts, posters, leaflets, moving pictures, and
phonograph records to flood Russia. To ensure security, the staff
of VINETA was under virtual arrest during their feverish work in
the preinvasion weeks.[16] It was characteristic of Goebbels's administrative style that he not only hid this information from the
other, regular senior members of his staff but actually lied to them
to conceal the fact of the impending invasion of Russia.[17]

Conquest implied occupation, but the military was unwilling
to undertake the odious tasks of civil administration of captured
Russian lands. On 31 March, with Hitler's concurrence, the OKH
defined its role virtually to exclude this task.[18] Accordingly, on
2 April Alfred Rosenberg, the Nazi party's racist ideologist, was
called in by Hitler. On that occasion Hitler explained his intention to attack but did not indicate the schedule, although Rosenberg gathered that it would be soon. As chief of the party's Foreign Policy Office, this Baltic German grasped at the chance to

apply his hitherto dormant theories regarding Russia and to revive his waning bureaucratic powers. He hastily formed and briefed his "Political Office for the East," a team composed largely of Soviet "experts." On 20 April it was renamed the Central Department for the Treatment of Eastern Questions. This was the cover for the huge Ostministerium (with Rosenberg as shadow minister) that was formally promulgated as the civil administration of Russia a month after the invasion.[19]

The number of Wehrmacht officers fully apprised of BARBAROSSA suddenly jumped to about 250 by the Sunday morning of 30 March. The occasion was a two-and-a-half-hour harangue by Hitler to indoctrinate the Wehrmacht with his political and military views on the forthcoming campaign. The assembled officers packing the Great Hall of the New Reich Chancellery consisted of the commanders in chief of the three services, the senior Army, Navy, and Air Force commanders selected for BARBAROSSA, and their senior staff officers—200 to 250 being present.[20] * On returning to their units, at least some of these senior officers alerted key members of their staffs.[21]

Martin Bormann, who controlled the Nazi party machine even before he replaced Hess as Deputy Führer, was witting by April 1941 (and probably earlier), when he began to scheme with Rosenberg and Himmler over their eagerly awaited Russian perquisites.[22]

The Foreign Ministry was one of the last German bureaucracies initiated into the mysteries of BARBAROSSA because the superficial continuance of normal diplomatic relations with Russia was deemed integral to concealment of Hitler's real intentions. The internal aspect of this deception was facilitated by the enthusiasm with which the Wilhelmstrasse—from Ribbentrop down—had protected the Russo-German démarche since August 1939. By merely keeping his plans secret from his Foreign Ministry, Hitler avoided their objections while using their wholehearted desire for

---

* At that time the Wehrmacht had 320,000 officers, including 3,000 generals. In 1940 the OKW alone numbered 4,000 officers and over 7,000 civilians.

rapprochement. As noted earlier, Hitler did not bring Ribbentrop into the cluster of knowers until late April 1941.[23] *

The independent-minded anti-Nazi state secretary in the Foreign Ministry, Ernst von Weizsäcker, was not officially informed of the new policy until he forced the truth from Ribbentrop in Vienna on 21 April, although about the beginning of the year his private sources had alerted him to its likelihood.[24]

However, once the official news began to spread within the Foreign Ministry, security apparently was quite forgotten. Thus the day before the invasion, while the Russians were desperately seeking clues to Hitler's intentions, Ribbentrop's Soviet expert, Dr. Peter Kleist, was discussing this question in the Central Office for Eastern Europe (Zentralstelle Osteurope) as if it were an open matter.[25]

With a single exception, no one in the German embassy in Moscow officially knew anything of BARBAROSSA until 3 A.M. on 22 June when Ambassador Schulenburg received the announcement of war for transmission to Molotov.[26] The exception was the military attaché, Lieutenant-General Ernst Köstring, who had been fully briefed on BARBAROSSA by Halder at Fontainebleau on 3 September 1940 but severely cautioned to disclose nothing of it to his embassy colleagues on his return to Moscow. There is no hint that he did not strictly obey this order.[27] Nor did the wily ambassador to Turkey, Franz von Papen, know until awakened that same fateful morning by Ribbentrop's telegram.[28] The one great exception to delayed knowledge in the German legations

---

* Ribbentrop was also rather close-mouthed with his own staff. This fact may account for the impression of State Secretary Weizsäcker that his chief already knew of BARBAROSSA at least as early as the visit in March of Japanese Foreign Minister Matsuoka. See Weizsäcker (1951), 249–250, 253. Note, however, that it seems unlikely that Ribbentrop and the head of his personal staff, Walter Hewel, did not get at least a fairly clear indication of Hitler's intentions when on 27 March they were brought in at the end of Hitler's announcement to his staff that he had decided to attack Yugoslavia, explaining that this new action would mean that "the beginning of Operation BARBAROSSA will have to be postponed up to 4 weeks." See *DGFP,* 12 (1962), 372–373.

\

abroad was, as seen earlier, the embassy in Tokyo. The personnel there were receiving official word of BARBAROSSA from April 1941 on. Ironically, this was the one German embassy deeply infiltrated by Soviet intelligence.

Colonel-General Heinz Guderian first learned of BARBAROSSA "shortly after" Molotov's visit to Berlin (12–13 November 1940). Guderian, then commander of Panzer Group 2, was brought into the planning through a briefing by his own chief of staff and his first general staff officer, who had themselves been instructed personally by the enthusiastic OKH chief, General Halder. When Guderian was informed that day, he considered the whole scheme so militarily inappropriate that he had a lingering belief that it must be part of some "bluff." [29]

At corps level, information was even slower coming. The first hints of BARBAROSSA did not reach General Erich von Manstein until February 1941, when he was transferred from command of Corps 38 on the Channel coast to Panzer Corps 56 in Germany. Even then, von Manstein received just the specific orders of Panzer Group 4 to which his corps belonged. It was only at 1300 hours on 21 June that Manstein's headquarters was notified that the offensive was scheduled for the next morning.[30]

About 2 June, in Paris, Göring briefed a meeting of all Luftwaffe unit commanders in France. Following this "pep talk" on the imminent invasion of *Britain,* he called two wing commanders aside and admitted jovially that it was all a lie. Under seal of the greatest secrecy he disclosed the truth to these two fighter aces: General Adolf Galland and General Werner Mölders. Göring revealed that SEA LION had become a mere deception to conceal the real goal: the imminent invasion of Russia.[31]

Despite the closest security precautions over BARBAROSSA planning, the ever-widening network of participating military and civil officials inevitably included proportions of paid informers, secret Communists, anti-Hitler conspirators, and some such as Lieutenant-General Paulus of the OKH and Dr. Bömer of the Propaganda Ministry who were merely loose tongued. For example, Schacht, the disgruntled minister without portfolio, learned of it in mid-April through his "indirect connections" with high political and military circles.[32]

Furthermore, the secrets of BARBAROSSA were well known to the members of the anti-Hitler clandestine opposition even if sometimes delayed and somewhat distorted by the nature of their conspiratorial word-of-mouth diffusion.[33] This information reached them through their several members and sympathizers located within the higher commands and ministries (as identified by asterisk in Appendix B).

German counterintelligence increased its surveillance of all known and suspected Soviet and other foreign agents, and wholesale arrests were made of those along transportation routes who might be counting military traffic. Finally, the OKW ordered a "general clampdown on foreign intelligence" for 21 June.[34]

German security on BARBAROSSA was rather dysfunctional, as it was in most of their strategic operations. Although this is likely true of most operations of parts of most governments, the Nazi system's failings in this regard permeated the bureaucracy from the top to the bottom. In any case, it is an instructive cautionary tale. Hitler, ever secretive about his strategic plans, long concealed his early intentions about Russia from such top leaders as Ribbentrop and Raeder and even from many of his most intimate associates. This was in part a consequence of the mystical *Führer-Prinzip*; in part, of the calculated technique of divide and rule that suffused the compartmentalized, conspiracy-ridden Nazi regime. Thus the Wehrmacht was cut off from high politics,[35] the professional diplomats from foreign policy,[36] and so forth throughout the government. For example, Field-Marshal Kesselring evaluated the Wehrmacht's security on BARBAROSSA with unintended irony as "strictly top secret. Nothing leaked out. Staffs were as much in ignorance of what was in the wind as the troops." [37] True, the German security system effectively concealed its military secrets from the whole middle ranks of officers and senior allies. However, their knowing participation might well have led to more effective planning and would probably have elicited more accurate and appropriate intelligence. For example, the newly appointed commander of the Afrika Korps, Lieutenant-General Erwin Rommel, being ignorant of the overall strategic plan and having been given tenuous orders, unilaterally launched his first desert offensive on 31 March 1941. Although achieving a brilliant success locally, Rommel thereby unwittingly disrupted the higher strategy to draw the British into the Greek trap (Operation MARITA) and drained precious resources from BARBAROSSA.[38] *

Informing the Axis Partners

If you would keep your secret from an enemy, tell it not to a friend.
    –Benjamin Franklin, Poor Richard's Almanac (1741)

Great caution was observed in informing Germany's allies of BARBAROSSA. Hitler realized that any disclosures to his foreign allies would immediately pass outside German security control. He further believed—and, as seen, quite rightly—that such disclosures would quickly spread and reach Russian, British, or American intelligence. Consequently, on Hitler's explicit orders, the Finns, Japanese, Rumanians, Hungarians, Croats, and Italians were told guardedly, selectively, and belatedly.

Finland

Although Finland was the first foreign state drafted to join Hitler in his *Drang nach Osten,* the Finnish leaders were unwilling to commit themselves formally. They realized they were playing a most dangerous game. They reasoned that, if Hitler forced enough concessions from Stalin so that BARBAROSSA would be canceled, then Finland would be left alone facing a thoroughly provoked Russia. Indeed, to this day the Finns still publicly pretend they did not conspire with Germany on BARBAROSSA. Reasons of state continue to suppress this controversial truth.[39]

However, the point at issue here is not whether the Finns were

---

* In fact, the British evacuation of Greece had been determined entirely by local circumstances. This, however, was not known to Paulus and the others who were annoyed by Rommel's independent action. See Whaley (1969b), case A26.

committed to aggression but only whether they were witting. On this question there can be no reasonable doubt, despite the general patriotic dissimulation by Finnish politicians, generals, and historians.*

The Germans began laying the groundwork for Finland's military cooperation in BARBAROSSA in January 1941 but camouflaged it from the Finns as mere insurance against the contingency of a *Russian* attack.† [40] Only from 20 May on did the German diplomatic and military negotiators explicitly raise the possibility of their attacking Russia, and then only if their diplomacy failed to gain Russian concessions. By the end of May, all the top Finnish political and military leaders were quite aware of BARBAROSSA but had residual doubts whether it would materialize. To allay these fears and doubts, Hitler authorized his negotiators on 14 June to disclose that war was quite certain.

Throughout this period the closest liaison on BARBAROSSA was maintained between the OKW and a very small but growing group of senior Finnish military and political leaders. Even such key officials as the Finnish ministers in London[41] and Stockholm were kept completely in the dark.

Although the German troops stationed in northern Finland moved across the Soviet frontier and took the port of Petsamo on 22 June, the Finns delayed their own aggression until the twenty-fifth, when the Russians, provoked in a suitable *casus belli,* launched major bombing raids on cities in southern Finland.[42]

Hungary

The Hungarians were not fully informed until quite late because Hitler believed they could not be trusted to keep silence, in view

---

* See, for example, Mannerheim's memoirs (1954). In this claim of innocence the Finns are quite flatly contradicted by both contemporary German documents and postwar German memoirs.

† Postwar allegations by Paulus and Buschenhagen that Halder (with Paulus) had disclosed BARBAROSSA in mid-December 1940 to the Finnish chief of staff, Lieutenant-General Heinrichs, are now known to be false on two counts. First, the meeting actually took place on 30 January 1941. Second, the Germans were only pumping Heinrichs for information about the condition of the Finnish armed forces.

of their close contacts with Britain and other hostile powers.[43] On 15 June, Ribbentrop sent the Hungarians a slightly veiled warning of an ultimatum to be presented "by the beginning of July at the latest." Full notification came only at 10:30 A.M. on the twenty-second with the delivery of a letter from Hitler to Hungarian Regent Admiral Nicholas von Horthy.[44] However, the Hungarians had their own sources. Thus by early May the chief of staff of the Hungarian Army, General Henrik Werth, minuted to Prime Minister László de Bárdossy that Germany would soon attack Russia.[45] And at the end of May General Werth announced to a secret meeting of his eight corps commanders that Germany would attack Russia. He reportedly added that the invasion was due in a few weeks and stated that the Hungarian Army must join promptly to benefit from the spoils.[46] While I do not know what specific information led General Werth to this categorical certainty, it seems to have come through official if, perhaps, unauthorized German OKW and OKH channels.[47] Werth had been alerted in November 1940 by his German counterpart, General Halder, to the likelihood of a "preventive war, possibly against Yugoslavia and definitely against Soviet Russia," sometime in the spring of 1941.[48] From that point on, the closest liaison existed between the German and Hungarian general staffs. In March 1941 Halder notified Werth that the time was imminent for Hungary to begin partial mobilization for war with Yugoslavia and Russia.[49] On 9 June the Hungarian defense minister, General Karl Bartha, told Italian Foreign Minister Ciano that the attack was imminent.[50]

However, the Germans were quite selective about which Hungarians they informed. They had proceeded quite openly with the army leaders and more guardedly with Prime Minister Bárdossy; but they managed to keep Admiral Horthy quite in the dark. In fact, Hungary was brought into the war behind Horthy's back on 27 June through the collusion of Bárdossy, Werth, and the Luftwaffe: Premier Bárdossy suppressed word of a major Russian effort to buy Hungarian neutrality, and General Werth conspired with the Germans to present the *casus belli*—an attack by three bombing planes on the Hungarian city of Kassa—as having been carried out by the Red Air Force and not the Luftwaffe. Horthy did not learn the truth of these two successful deceptions until 1944.[51]

Slovakia

Hitler's Slovakian satellite was only belatedly and seemingly inadvertently made witting. On 19 June OKH chief General Halder arrived in Bratislava, where he paid an incognito visit to General Paul Otto, chief of the German Army Mission to Slovakia. Halder informed Otto of the Führer's wish that the Slovak Army contribute to "an operation [against Russia] that might take place." Two days later, when General Otto mentioned this to the German minister to Slovakia, Hans Ludin, the latter viewed it as a political as well as a military question. Consequently, without seeking instructions, he immediately called on Slovak Minister President Tuka and State President Tiso to explain the situation and obtain their agreement in principle. Thus did the subservient Slovak figureheads learn of BARBAROSSA only on the eve of its execution.[52] Formal notification of hostilities was by the circular telegram that Ribbentrop sent at 4 A.M. on the twenty-second, one hour after the invasion.

Japan

On 5 March Hitler had Keitel issue explicit instructions that while Japan was to be induced to attack Singapore and other British (and, if need be, U.S.) bases in the Far East in conjunction with BARBAROSSA, "no hint of the *Barbarossa Operation* must be given to the Japanese." This prohibition was observed despite Grand-Admiral Raeder's objection; Hitler considered the Japanese too unreliable to have such information.[53]

Rumania

The Rumanians were not informed of BARBAROSSA until 11 June, when Hitler personally spoke to Premier Antonescu. Thenceforward Rumanian and German officials were talking openly of the details and date of attack to the Italians, French, and probably anyone else who would listen (see warning 77). However, the Rumanian government did manage to keep one key official in the dark: wise, pro-peace minister in Moscow (and former foreign minister), Grigore Gafencu.[54]

Italy

The Italians were simply never told until literally the last minute. Hitler believed the Italian royal family was actively collaborating with British royalty,[55] and the trumpeted Rome-Berlin Axis did not include the joint planning of any grand strategy. Mussolini's first official word arrived in a letter sent by Hitler on the afternoon of 21 June that reached Foreign Minister Ciano at 3 A.M.—just when the invasion was beginning—and was immediately telephoned by him to Il Duce.[56] However, Mussolini and Ciano had been quite aware of the generally deteriorating relationship between Germany and Russia since Molotov's visit the previous November.[57] Then, on 15 June 1941, Ribbentrop met Ciano in Venice and told him, in effect, that:

The Fuehrer will shortly be forced, and that presumably toward the end of the month, to make certain requests to Russia having the character of an ultimatum. If they are refused, Germany will find means of receiving justice herself.[58]

Reflecting on these deceitful words, Count Ciano correctly concluded: "The tone and the words used by Ribbentrop are such as to leave very little doubt as to the decision which the Fuehrer has now taken to attack Russia." [59] Thus Ciano implies some measure of independent knowledge, for which Ribbentrop's words formed only a final, authoritative confirmation.[60] Indeed, as early as 30 May, Mussolini had ordered some minor Italian redeployments in Yugoslavia in anticipation of the "possibility of a conflict between Germany and Russia," and there is unverified evidence of planning for an Italian expeditionary corps in Russia.[61] And, as noted in warning 53, on 1 June Ribbentrop's anti-Nazi aide, Etzdorf, privately told the first secretary of the Italian embassy in Berlin that the German attack was set for 23 June.

Ironically, it was precisely in this one example of more or less successful German security that Hitler's goals might have been better served by early disclosure. For Mussolini in equal secrecy had also prepared an attack on Greece. Hitler—warned only at the last moment—went to dissuade the Duce, possibly by disclosing

BARBAROSSA.* However, Hitler alighted from his train in Florence on 28 October 1940 to be met by an elated Mussolini who immediately announced that the Italian Army had crossed the Greek-Albanian frontier.[62] Hitler's deepening involvement in the Balkans, which was partly caused by his partner's adventures, cost valuable, possibly decisive, time for BARBAROSSA.

Treason

We have not talked treason—only discussed the safety of the Reich.
—Admiral Canaris to von Schlabrendorff

German security procedures were, if anything, too effective in limiting the official disclosure of plans and directives about BARBAROSSA. As shown in Appendix B, the number of German soldiers and officials who were made officially witting grew only very slowly over the many months of planning. This is a rare example of a gigantic military operation being effectively concealed from the very civil-military bureaucracy conducting it. Yet these elaborate security measures were quite unable to conceal the plans from foreign intelligence and some unauthorized domestic citizens. Nearly every key BARBAROSSA decision was soon disclosed to hostile eyes. Earlier chapters have described the widening diffusion abroad of the secrets of BARBAROSSA through intercepting and decrypting messages, directly observing and interpreting the visible effects of secret orders, and sharing intelligence among professional intelligence services. Here, however, is an appropriate place to discuss the leakage of these secrets from the narrow circles of the BARBAROSSA planners themselves, for they represented the starting points of most known disclosures. The topic is treason.

Even a third of a century after the event, the question of treason in Hitler's Thousand Year Reich is a mantrap for the historian. Students of the German resistance have yet to give systematic atten-

---

* Weizsäcker asserts that Hitler had foreknowledge from his intelligence and had simply decided to avoid openly thwarting Mussolini. Weizsäcker says Hitler merely feigned surprise. See Weizsäcker (1951), 244; also see Wiskemann (1966), 276.

tion to the many publicly known details, much less to examine the captured Gestapo and Abwehr files and the archives of the U.S. and other diplomatic services that were in contact with members of the resistance. Aside from the books by Harold Deutsch, Allen Dulles, John Wheeler-Bennett, Gerald Reitlinger, and Terence Prittie, the subject has received little notice from non-German writers. And it is instructive that while German writers proliferate the literature on their small but (in part) heroic resistance movements, they are still almost completely unwilling to admit that treasonable disclosures to foreign intelligence were often involved.

Many German writers make a convenient ethical distinction between two types of treason: *Hochverrat,* mere treason against the state—in this case a tyrant, Hitler—from *Landesverrat,* treason against the country, particularly by warning or otherwise aiding and abetting a foreign enemy. The writers who make this distinction, and they include most except the unreconstructed Nazis and a handful of amoral former generals, judge the former to have been ethically acceptable and the latter to be deplored.[63] Even the magnificent von Schlabrendorff demeans himself and his cause by attacking the Communist Rote Kapelle for their espionage while conveniently overlooking evidence of similar activities by his own group.[64]

For their part, the Communists—particularly the East Germans—take great and understandably justifiable pride in their Rote Kapelle, but even they tend to hide the espionage aspect of that group, choosing to stress its patriotic resistance aspect. The proven accusation of espionage, that the Rote Kapelle was a virtual *apparat* of the GRU, comes from the West. However, for the purposes of this study of BARBAROSSA, the case of the Communist resistance may be overlooked for two reasons: the Communists did not begin their resistance until after the invasion of Russia; and, although some had already been recruited into espionage, seemingly none then occupied any key positions in the German bureaucracy that would have given them access to the major secret decisions or directives.

For our purposes, the important instances of treasonable dis-

closure to foreign intelligence all came from the non-Communist
resistance groups loosely termed the July 20th Movement, in honor
of the last and most disastrous of several bumbled attempts to as-
sassinate Hitler. The partisans of July 20th admit to a creditable
high treason against the tyrant but still conceal or are unwilling to
face up to the numerous clear cases of international trafficking in
military and political secrets conducted by members of their movement. Only the numerous, flagrant, and incontrovertibly documented cases of Colonel Oster's *Landesverrat* are acknowledged.
Otherwise, these writers would have us believe that the contacts
with foreigners were limited to prewar plotting (in 1938–1939)
and, during the war, to mere negotiations for honorable conditions
of surrender.

The protestations of innocence by the honorable men of July
20th are contradicted by the evidence.* Considering only the evidence of the disclosure of BARBAROSSA, we have seen that a civilian
in Heinrich Brüning's circle had been freely passing highly secret
documents to U.S. Commercial Attaché Woods from mid–1940
until early 1941. Furthermore, this agent's contacts within the
German military and civil bureaucracies should be presumed to
have known what they were doing. Moreover, because no money
changed hands, their motives were clearly those of patriotic treason. Similarly, Czech military intelligence was receiving almost
identical reports from Paul Thummel, a willing agent within the
German General Staff's Abwehr in early 1941. Again, it is clear
that the Rössler-Rado GRU ring in Switzerland had several sources
in German government staffs. And most conclusive is Gustav
Hilger's open confession in his otherwise widely quoted memoirs
published in 1953 that he and Ambassador Schulenburg in Moscow conspired to warn the Russians directly in early May. Yet,
remarkably, their comrades of July 20th somehow ignore this evidence.

---

* It is, for example, clear from the autobiography of Sefton Delmer that Otto
John was talking quite freely to British intelligence following his escape to
Britain in 1944, after having played his small part in the 20 July bomb plot
against Hitler. See Delmer (1962), 180.

Although few of the specific persons within the Nazi regime who disclosed military intelligence to foreigners are known by name, except Herwarth von Bittenfeld, Respondik, Oster, Thummel, Müller, Hilger, and Schulenburg, it is clear that a number of likely candidates are available. Of the thirty-nine German officials who were witting before December 1940, seven are known to have been already active in the July 20th Movement: Admiral Canaris himself, Colonel Franz von Bentivegni, Colonel Hans Piekenbrock, Infantry General Georg Thomas, Colonel Hans Oster, Major-General Eduard Wagner, and General Erich Fellgiebel.[65] Of course, it may have been the personal aides or private secretaries of some of these men who actually conducted the espionage.

Remarkably, information on BARBAROSSA evidently diffused to foreign ears more easily and more frequently than it did by friendly gossip among different sections of the Nazi bureaucracy. I have found few cases in which this information spread among Nazi officials other than through authorized channels. Ironic that the self-serving competition within the Nazi machine was so bitter that it instilled greater hostility and discretion toward colleagues in other German bureaucratic units than it did toward complete outsiders.

On Reading Other Gentlemen's Mail

General: . . . Incidentally, they know your code.
American Ambassador (Beaming): We know they know our code.
. . . We only give them things we want them to know.

General: . . . Incidentally, they know you know their code.
Soviet Ambassador (Smiling): . . . We have known for some time that they knew we knew their code. We have acted accordingly— by pretending to be duped.

General: . . . Incidentally, you know—they know you know they know you know. . . .
American Ambassador (Genuinely alarmed): What? Are you sure?
                    –Peter Ustinov, Romanoff and Juliet, *act 2*

It would be instructive for historians to compile tables, such as Table 6.1, showing who could and who did read whose secret communications at what times. Such background studies would be useful—sometimes essential—for understanding the international diffusion of such strategic "secrets" as negotiating positions and surprise attack plans.

Almost nothing has been written on this topic outside of books specifically devoted to espionage or cryptology, and they seldom comprehend the political or diplomatic side of the problem.[66] Those few books and articles that do touch on the role of intercepted communications in the conduct of foreign relations were until recently confined to the use that Mussolini and Ciano made of the foreign intercepts supplied *before* World War II by their military intelligence, the SIM.[67] This section will demonstrate not only that the Italian operations extended into the war but that *all* countries were involved.

Intercepts

For the purposes of this case study we need review the state of the art of interception of secret communications only in early 1941, that is, in the half year preceding BARBAROSSA. Let us begin with radio and telegraphic intercepts:

1. In general, the Germans could decrypt all enemy and neutral *diplomatic* messages (except some Russian, British, and American ones) plus those of their Italian allies.[68]

2. Specifically, the Germans (and the British) had easily solved the ciphers of the French Maquis.[69]

3. On 13 August 1941, Vichy Premier Darlan told American Ambassador Leahy that the Germans could read the U.S. diplomatic codes, including the very messages Darlan wished to conceal from his German masters, so Leahy judiciously switched to his still secure naval codes.[70] But the Germans continued to read the communications between the State Department and the American embassies in Moscow, Ankara, Algiers, and Budapest as well as occasional ones from Leahy in Vichy.[71]

4. By March 1941, the Turks realized the Germans were reading their diplomatic codes, a fact also learned by the American am-

Table 6.1 Reading of Opponents' Cryptographic Communications, January–June 1941

	Readers						
Read	Russia	Germany	Italy	Britain	U.S.A.	Japan	Sweden
Russian		d					A
German	a		d	ANi	d		DA
Italian	d	D		dN			D
British		Dni	Dn			da	n
American		Dn	n	D		D	n
Japanese	d	d	d	Dn	Dn		
Swedish		d					
Yugoslav	d	DA	A				
Turkish		d	d				
Vichy French		d		d			
Rumanian			d				
Bulgarian		d					
Portuguese		d					
Swiss		d					
Irish		d					
Free Polish		d					
Egyptian		d					
Iranian		d					

Key:
capitals = intensively read
lowercase = occasionally read

Type of code
D or d = diplomatic
A or a = army
N or n = naval
I or i = intelligence

Note: Too little information is available about solved air force ciphers to warrant inclusion in the table. However, they were notoriously simple in 1941. For example, the Italian SIM could read both the Luftwaffe and British naval air arm messages, and the British were reading those of the Luftwaffe and the Italian Air Force. See Bragadin (1957), 101. The Swedish cryptanalysts were regularly reading the Red Air Force codes. See Kahn (1967), 644–645.

bassador in Ankara and duly communicated by him to Washington.[72] It is not recorded whether the Americans warned the Turks.

5. The Italian naval ciphers were purchased by the British S.I.S. in late 1940. This was accomplished by William Stephenson, the chief of the British Security Co-ordination (B.S.C.) office in New York City, in fact the S.I.S. Western Hemisphere branch and liaison office with U.S. intelligence. To achieve this valued coup, Stephenson reverted to the famous but in fact rare device of insinuating a female agent into the enemy camp. She was Amy Thorpe, the spectacular American wife of British Commercial Attaché Arthur Pack. The happily willing victim was no less than the sexagenarian Admiral Alberto Lais, the Italian naval attaché in Washington and former chief of Italian naval intelligence. S.I.S. retained the full cooperation of Admiral Lais until 2 April 1941, when the State Department declared him *persona non grata* after receiving information through the FBI from Stephenson regarding the admiral's efforts to sabotage merchant ships lying in U.S. ports.[73] However the British did it, their victory over the Italian fleet at Cape Matapan on 27–29 March 1941 was not due to B.S.C.'s efforts, as Hyde asserts, for Lais had not received the codes used at Matapan.[74] But after Matapan the Italians realized that the frequency of British anticipations meant that Italian naval secrets were somehow being disclosed.[75] However, their naval intelligence chiefs remained quite unconvinced that the British had their codes, because they knew a British intelligence agent in Switzerland maintained an open offer of £40,000 sterling for these same codes.[76]

6. The Germans did not warn their Italian allies that their diplomatic code was easily broken. Foreign Minister Ribbentrop reasoned that if the Italians were warned they would change their codes; he could then no longer read his Axis partner's mail either. Only around 25 May 1941 did the counselor of embassy in Rome, Prince Otto von Bismarck, privately tell Ciano's chef de cabinet, Filippo Anfuso, that their codes were being read by the German Foreign Office. Ciano remarked: "This is good to know; in the future, they will also read what I *want* them to read." The game was given a farcical ending by the ever-foolish Ribbentrop him-

self. On 3 October 1941 the Italian ambassador in Berlin sent a long telegram to Rome in what he assumed to be his most secret code, the IMPERO. The telegram unfavorably judged Hitler's latest speech, a lame apologia for the failure to reach a quick victory in Russia. Ribbentrop, piqued on reading this on 14 October, took the first occasion (17 October) to begin berating Ambassador Alfieri, reading to him the full, authentic text of his own secret message. The indignant Alfieri abruptly terminated Ribbentrop's absurd conversation and immediately provoked an official investigation of cryptographic security that led to the quick substitution of a new code.[77] Fact proved more absurd than Ustinov's satire.

7. The Germans, specifically Göring's Air Ministry "Research Office," were also reading all the Japanese embassy's enciphered communications. The decrypted and translated messages were circulated in typescript to selected government and military officials.[78] One of the Foreign Ministry officials on this *Braun* distribution (so-called from the light-brown typing paper used) was State Secretary Baron Ernst von Weizsäcker. This old-fashioned, aristocratic, non-Nazi diplomat was so outraged to learn that German intelligence had stooped to reading the mail of a friendly power that he promptly warned the Japanese ambassador. Somewhat disguising his warning, he told Ambassador Ōshima only that he had reason to believe that Japanese ciphers in their diplomatic mission in Egypt were being read by a "foreign power." Ōshima notified his ministry of this on 14 April 1941, but the Japanese—who had an overweening pride in the excellence of their ciphers—did nothing beyond tightening the *internal* security procedures of their Near Eastern missions. Incidentally, the U.S. Signal Intelligence Service was simultaneously reading this flurry of triple-priority telegrams between Ambassador Ōshima and the chief of the Cable Section of the Japanese Foreign Ministry.[79]

8. In general, the Japanese diplomatic codes and ciphers were a sieve of information for anyone who could intercept the messages. Unknown to them, much of their diplomatic traffic was being regularly read by every major power: Germany, the United States, Britain, Italy, and Russia.[80]

9. Italian naval intelligence (SIS) was able to intercept and de-
code the British fleet signals, at least during the Battle of Cape
Matapan on 27–29 March 1941.* That did not save them from
defeat because the British had radar and, as we have seen, the
Italian fleet codes.

10. In May 1941, Mrs. Pack, William Stephenson's extraspecial
S.I.S. agent, turned her attentions to the Vichy French embassy in
Washington. Posing as an American journalist, she quickly won
the confidence of the anti-Laval press attaché, Captain Charles
Brousse. The much-decorated attaché was soon on the S.I.S. roster,
although he was told it was *American*; and after July 1941 he was
supplying a daily report on embassy affairs plus already deciphered
copies of all current and selected past telegraphic traffic.†

11. The U.S. G-2, ONI, and State Department could read all
Japanese diplomatic codes.[81] ‡ Furthermore, the German Foreign
Ministry was tipped off to this by "an absolutely reliable source"
in (or with access to) Washington. As with the Italians, the Germans did not notify the Japanese of this critical leak in their communications.[82]

12. The Germans also evidently intercepted and decoded at least
some of the lower-grade Russian diplomatic telegraphic traffic between the Foreign Commissariat in Moscow and its overseas legations. The interception and decoding apparently occurred in—of
all unlikely places—Harbin. In any case the already decoded and

---

* This feat was the accomplishment of Section B (radio interception and
cryptology) of the Italian SIS. See Maugeri (1948), 27, 31, 32.

† Subsequently, in June 1942, Mrs. Pack and Captain Brousse even managed
to purloin the French naval code from the embassy coderoom safe. Romantics
may wish to know that Captain Brousse was followed by his mistress to Paris,
where they were married in 1946 after his divorce and her husband's suicide.
See Hyde (1962), 108–110, 115–120, and Hyde (1965), 159–210.

‡ The U.S. Army Signal Corps "magicians" broke PURPLE, the top priority
Japanese diplomatic code, in August 1940 although some partial readings had
been available earlier. However, the U.S. had not broken any of the Japanese
Army or Navy codes prior to Pearl Harbor, breaking the naval codes only in
1942 and after. Moreover, it was only after Pearl Harbor that the FBI and
Federal Communications Commission received authorization to intercept foreign radio and telegraphic communications.

translated messages were being forwarded to State Secretary Weizsäcker in Berlin by August Ponschab, the German consul in Harbin. The time from interception through decoding to forwarding varied between one and four days.[83] (Incidentally, no one could break the NKVD and GRU codes or the higher-grade diplomatic ones, as they were of the unbreakable "one-time pad" type. Undecipherable radio intercepts continued to accumulate until 1942, when the captured Rote Kapelle network in Holland, France, and Germany yielded cooperative GRU radio operators and their cipher keys.)[84]

13. The German Abwehr and SD were regularly intercepting the Yugoslav military traffic, including the superb reports of the Yugoslav military attaché in Berlin, Colonel Vladimir Vauhnik. They had read these codes since at least January 1940.[85] They were also reading some of the Yugoslav diplomatic traffic, for example, that between Washington and Belgrade and between Berlin and Belgrade.[86]

14. The Germans were at that time also reading the diplomatic codes of Vichy France, Bulgaria, Ireland, Egypt, Iran, Sweden, Switzerland, Portugal, and the Free Polish regime in London.[87]

15. Italian army intelligence (the SIM) had, independent of the Germans, solved the Yugoslav military ciphers. This was the achievement of General Vittorio Gamba, the distinguished cryptanalyst who headed SIM's Section 5, its cryptological section. It kept the radio intercept monitors of Section 6 busy collecting the Yugoslav traffic. The SIM deliberately compromised their secret, but only after launching the Italo-German invasion of Yugoslavia in April 1941, by counterfeiting retreat orders to the routed Royal Army.[88]

16. The British Foreign Office's Secret Intelligence Service managed to obtain and break the code used by the German Abwehr undercover agents in the Baltic states. This information was available to the S.I.S. from the winter of 1939/40 until July 1940 or, possibly, through to the German invasion. The coup was the result of a tip an Abwehr agent supplied to a Latvian agent of the S.I.S.'s man in Riga.[89]

17. Finally, the most important and least known of the radio intercepts was a British coup. A large team of British cryptographers had succeeded in breaking the German military ciphers by at least late in 1940.[90] They were thus able to read the voluminous German OKW, OKH, OKL, and OKM movement and operations orders and reports—everything but the most secret messages sent "by officer only."

This cryptanalytic achievement was that of the Government Communications Headquarters (GCHQ, now called the Government Communications Centre), then directed by Royal Navy Captain Edward Hastings jointly for the Foreign Office and the Admiralty. It was located at Bletchley Park near London.[91] These British cryptanalytic efforts were greatly aided by obtaining in 1940/41 three German Enigma cipher machines: one captured in North Africa, another salvaged from a surrendered U-boat, and the third seized in a Commando raid on the German-held Lofoten islands.[92]

This magnificent coup in codebreaking was one of the few perfect secrets of the war. Indeed, the British have only recently disclosed some of the bare facts. It raises serious questions about some of the sources that they had previously alleged to have used on BARBAROSSA. For example, Churchill's "one of our most trusted sources" may not, as implied, have been a British agent running train-watchers in the Balkans but the unwitting OKH itself. Moreover, it has revolutionized the recent speculation on "Lucy"-Rössler's mysterious source, since Malcolm Muggeridge suggested early in 1967 that it may have been the GCHQ and not a traitor in the OKW or OKH. (See warning 58.)

Penetration

Radio and telegraphic interception was the main source of secret messages, but other means were used as well. Thus since 1935 Francesco Costantini, the omnipresent Italian majordomo of the British embassy in Rome had exploited an enterprising sideline: selling the contents of the embassy wastebaskets and safe. He systematically acquired copies of all the diplomatic correspondence, both cabled and carried by the King's Messengers. These he gave to his Italian masters and also to the NKVD in the person of the counselor of the Soviet embassy, Leon Helfand.* Furthermore, the Italian government passed much of this booty to the Germans. This profitable operation was ended only by Italy's entry into the war on 10 June 1940, for a warning to the British from the prominent Italian journalist Luigi Barzini, Jr., that their embassy was penetrated had been filed and forgotten. But it led to Barzini's quiet arrest on 26 April 1940. Italian intelligence had of course also gotten the British memorandum of Barzini's warning.[93]

The British had received an earlier and credited warning that the Germans had "broken" their diplomatic ciphers. Presumably, they then changed them, but the Italian source would have immediately disclosed the new ones. This warning had been told to Mr. Ivone Kirkpatrick, the head of chancery at the British embassy in Berlin, on 11 December 1938. His informant was an anti-Nazi retired state secretary, then a member of the anti-Nazi salon, the *Solf Kreis* maintained by Frau Hanna Solf, the widow of the former ambassador to Japan.[94] †

Like the British, the Italians had an SIS, but theirs was the intelligence branch of the Navy.[95] The resourceful Italian Commander Max Ponzo, head of SIS Section D (espionage), managed thoroughly to infiltrate the office of the U.S. naval attaché in Rome. With the appointment of Captain Thomas C. Kinkaid as attaché in November 1938, Ponzo found a gallant line officer but one unprepared to cope with security. Kinkaid made the gross mistake of giving occasional access to his safe to an Italian on his staff, who took the opportunity to make a duplicate key. Not surprisingly, this senior clerk was also an employee of Commander Ponzo, who from then until Italy declared war on the United States on 11 December 1941, knew all that the safe contained.[96] Indeed, the situation only deteriorated further when Captain Kinkaid left in March 1941 for a glorious and well-rewarded combat career in World War II. His

---

* Although Costantini wisely retired into the lumber trade in 1937, he obviously passed on his expertise to some successor in the embassy.

† The informant was probably either Artur Zarden (1888–1944), former state secretary in the Finance Ministry, or Dr. Franz Kempner (died 1945), former state secretary in the Ministry of Reconstruction. Frau Solf survived the war despite a death sentence, and her papers may disclose this informant.

successor, Captain Laurance N. McNair, set out to recruit a network of local agents. By the time of his retirement in July of that same year McNair had succeeded in acquiring three: one courtesan who immediately "doubled" to Ponzo's Section D, and two men planted by Major Carlo Pontani, the chief of Section E (counterintelligence).[97]

Thus Italian naval intelligence (SIS) had effectively penetrated U.S. naval intelligence (ONI). However, the American secrets were not forwarded to the German Nazi or the Italian Fascist governments, for the Italian SIS was a more or less willing collaborator of British intelligence. The Italian Navy had a strong pro-British tradition among its officers, a tradition that was little affected by the coming either of fascism or the war. Furthermore, the SIS was a focus of this attitude. In particular, its durable Section D chief, Commander Ponzo, was in friendly liaison with British intelligence, especially through his admired father-in-law, Giovanni Sèrrao, who in 1930 had been knighted (as Sir John Serrao) by the British monarch, the only Italian so honored. Liaison became even more intimate with the appointment on 24 May 1941 of the pro-British and subsequent resistance leader, Admiral Franco Maugeri, as director of the SIS.[98]

The similar rummaging in the safe of his master by the famed "Cicero," valet to the gentle, doddering British ambassador in Turkey, occurred much later—throughout the period from October 1943 to February 1944.[99] The Russians were also adept at this technique. Sometime *after* Russia's entry into World War II, the GRU "legal" *Rezident* in Chungking managed to suborn a secretary of one of the Allied embassies, who supplied similar materials from his unsuspecting ambassador's safe until 1942 or 1943.[100]

In some unspecified clandestine manner, the German ambassador in Turkey, von Papen, was receiving at least occasional copies of reports of Turkish Ambassador Ali Haydar Aktay in Moscow to Aktay's home government.[101]

Throughout the BARBAROSSA planning period, German intelligence had managed a partial penetration of the NKGB office in the Soviet embassy in Berlin. This infiltration had been arranged by Rudolf Likus, Foreign Minister Ribbentrop's old crony and his intelligence liaison officer with the SS. By late 1940 Senior Counselor Likus had somehow managed to "double" a young junior NKGB agent operating out of the embassy and reporting directly to Counselor of Embassy (and NKGB chief *Rezident*) Bogdan Kobulov and later to Ivan Filippov, ostensibly the TASS bureau chief in Berlin. This double agent, a former Latvian journalist named Orests Berlings, regularly reported to Likus his orders from Kobulov and Filippov. Berlings was specifically required to obtain confidential documents and other indications of German intentions toward the USSR. Likus's reports were carefully read by Ribbentrop and Hitler, but the Germans got as little information from their man as did the Russians. Berlings was either quite incompetent or, as Hitler eventually came to suspect, a *triple* agent feeding back trifling disinformation. In either case, Hitler ordered the "swindler" placed under close surveillance and, immediately after the invasion of Russia, arrested.[102]

Other Means
Outright raids to obtain secret communications were also undertaken. Such an effort by Stephenson (abetted by Ian Fleming of the N.I.D.) at 3 A.M. sometime in June 1941 netted the British S.I.S. the diplomatic codebooks from a safe of the Japanese consul-general in Rockefeller Center.[103] In May the Abwehr had first tried out its intelligence commandos (a unit of the Brandenburg Regiment) in Crete, a special paratroop unit whose sole mission was to capture British intelligence codes, maps, and other materials.[104]

Even the telephone was fair game for most in 1941. For example, the land line between the Yugoslav embassy in Moscow and Belgrade was regularly the subject of unauthorized "conference calls." It not only was tapped by the NKVD in Moscow[105] but was simultaneously listened in on in Budapest by the Germans.[106] The German SD was also regularly tapping the lines of such interesting personalities in Berlin as Yugoslav Military Attaché Vauhnik[107] and the Abwehr chief Canaris himself.[108] Göring's "Research Office" was also wiretapping the Italian, French, and Balkan diplomats with great success, but it found the Americans to be rather discreet, while the Russians and Japanese were totally secure in their use of the telephone.[109] And the Italian secret police (OVRA) had all Vatican telephone and mail communications under close surveillance in its imperfect efforts to isolate that center of papal intelligence and international intelligence liaison.[110] Italian intelligence, at least in 1939–1940, was also tapping the German diplomatic line between Rome and Berlin.[111] However, contrary to widespread belief, the Germans did not begin to unscramble the Churchill-Roosevelt transatlantic radio-telephone calls until March 1942.[112] In general, ciphony ("scrambling") simply does not provide secure communications.[113]

The mails were also frequently intercepted in this period. The Japanese post office was systematically opening and reading the official and private overseas mail of the American embassy in Tokyo. Nor were they deterred from this practice by Ambassador Grew's repeated protests. Indeed, they were passing some of these mail intercepts to the Germans.[114] And in 1940–1941 the British S.I.S. in Bermuda was systematically intercepting German SD and Japanese naval intelligence mail from the United States to Berlin, Madrid, Lisbon, and Buenos Aires.[115]

Even that most conventionally inviolable means of communications, the diplomatic pouch, was seemingly being tampered with by the Russians. There is some circumstantial evidence that the NKVD had managed to steal one set of American pouches (from a Finnish aircraft they shot down in the Baltic on 14 June 1940).[116] They also bungled an effort to acquire the text of the 1941 Tripartite Pact by stealing it from the Japanese courier on the Berlin-Moscow Nord Express.[117]

In fact, the Germans applied to the wartime interception of secret communications the full range of their skills in industrial espionage (the term was coined in the Weimar Republic).[118] For example, the Gestapo had "bugged" the walls of the Adlon Hotel adjoining the British embassy.[119]

A pet social espionage project of SD Chief Reinhard Heydrich from late 1940 on was his fashionable, discreet, superbly appointed "Salon Kitty" or "House of Gallantry" on Giesebrechtstrasse, personally managed by SS-Brigadeführer Walter Schellenberg. The hostesses—recruited by Arthur Nebe, appropriately the chief of the Criminal Police and former vice squad detective—comprised elite European prostitutes and patriotic German society matrons. The unsuspecting clientele comprised a significant proportion of the diplomatic corps (including Japanese Ambassador Ōshima), visiting VIPs (including Count Ciano), and prominent Germans (including Ribbentrop). The battery of microphones and recorders was shut down only during SS-Obergruppenführer Heydrich's frequent personal inspections. Surprisingly, this institution did collect some valuable diplomatic indiscretions, but its main use was for the type of political blackmail against colleagues by which Heydrich flourished.[120] Unknown to his colleagues in this enterprise, SS-Gruppenführer Nebe had been a determined and active anti-Nazi since 1938, the one exception in the senior SS ranks. Therefore, the intimate secrets of Salon Kitty were undoubtedly transmitted to Nebe by his hand-picked girls, and from Nebe to his regular contact in the Abwehr, Colonel Oster.*

General Remarks

From the preceding evidence alone, we must conclude that in 1940–1941 almost everyone was receiving and reading a substantial proportion of the secret communications of almost everyone else. Specifically, each of the six major powers was reading those of at least two of the other five.† This startling fact—startling at least

---

* Arthur Nebe was a highly competent professional policeman. As chief of the Criminal Police (KRIPOS) in Berlin since 1933 he (and his entire organization) had been brought into the SS in 1939 as chief of Amt V (civil crimes) of the Reich Security Main Office (RSHA). He was executed in 1945 for his part in the 20 July bomb plot. Contrary to most accounts, Nebe was not a belated anti-Nazi, nor was he ambiguous in his activities. He courageously remained at his detested death watch in the SS only at the urgent and repeated request of von Schlabrendorff, who recently disclosed Nebe's role as forming with Canaris and Army Judge Advocate General Carl Sack the "shield of the resistance." See Schlabrendorff (1965), 70, 75, 137, 167–176. See also Hans Bernd Gisevius, *Wo ist Nebe?* (Zürich: Droemer, 1966).

† See Table 6.1, where 20 of the 30 possible cross-tabulation cells linking the six major powers are at least partly filled.

to anyone who reads only diplomatic and political textbooks—emerges from even this hasty survey of sources. Furthermore, as this topic is one of the more closely concealed areas in national security, certainly much of what was accomplished in this field even a third of a century ago is still deleted from otherwise declassified materials. Consequently, the full extent of interceptions of intelligence in 1940–1941 is still publicly unknowable. Nevertheless, enough is now known to warrant two conclusions. First, few secret communications remained secret. Second and more important, the ineffective security procedures in most countries failed even to warn that codes and messages and personnel had been compromised, giving a dangerously unwarranted confidence in the continued secrecy of one's own communications.[121]

Although this section has shown that secure communications in 1940–1941 were seldom more than a dangerous delusion of either overconfident cryptographers or inadequately briefed military or foreign office executives, two questions remain. Were there *any* fully secure communications? (The matrix in Table 6.1 begs the question by leaving open all cases where no specific and positive evidence of interception and reading exists.) How true of other periods was this relatively open communications situation of 1940–1941? While this last question is not relevant to the argument on the diffusion of information about BARBAROSSA, it deserves a brief cautionary discussion lest any reader attempt to apply the findings of this study to other times. In any event, both questions can best be answered simultaneously by a précis of the development of the only unbreakable or holocryptic system known, the "one-time" system.

The only cryptograms that can never be solved are those whose key contains no systematic pattern, no repetition. The only way that this condition—a condition demanded by mathematical theory—can be met is by a key that is purely random.[122]

The one-time system was seemingly invented in 1918 by a brilliant thirty-six-year-old American Signal Corps cryptologist, Major Joseph O. Mauborgne. Because the system was developed in conjunction with Gilbert S. Vernam of A.T.&T., whose teletype-writer keytape machine was patented in 1919, this fundamental concept in cryptology soon became public knowledge. German Foreign Office cryptographers had introduced it in their work by 1923 in the form of "one-time" pads. The Soviet Foreign Commissariat first used one-time pads in 1930. The GRU had even managed sometime before 1940 to get one-time pads to its chief field agents: Sorge, Rado, and the Rote Kapelle. I presume one-time systems were also used at that time by the NKVD, but no evidence came to public view until after 1954 in the ciphers used by such Soviet agents as Gregory Liolios in Greece, Colonel "Rudolph Abel" in the United States, and Molody-"Lonsdale" in Britain. The British also presumably had one-time pads before the war. The French Maquis first began to use one-time pads, supplied by British S.O.E. intelligence, in 1943. The U.S. Army itself did not get around to adopting its own invention until about 1940—after its inventor, Mauborgne, then a major general, had become chief signal officer. OSS sometimes used IBM-generated one-time pads during World War II. The smug U.S. State Department succumbed only in 1944.[123]

If the technique of producing unbreakable ciphers was so widely known by World War II, why was it not in general use by the time of BARBAROSSA? There are two reasons. First, one-time systems are necessarily more expensive and cumbersome than any of the next most secure systems. Statistical theory requires that the enciphering key be at least as long as the cumulative length of all the messages sent; and communications technology further multiplies the length of the key. Thus, even today, it is normal practice to limit the use of one-time systems to cases where the message traffic is light or where maximum secrecy is desired. Apparently, only the Soviet intelligence services had adopted one-time systems for all but their minor codes and ciphers by 1941. Second, the diffusion of one-time systems was vigorously resisted by entrenched intelligence chiefs, who simply would not admit that their pet systems were insecure. This was a general problem, but the most egregious example was the U.S. State Department, whose antiquated codes had been read by almost everyone from World War I until 1944, when their codes were modernized only because a naval cryptologist was detailed to head State's new Division of Cryptography.[124]

Although none of the one-time systems used during World War II were broken, they were not truly holocryptic because they all violated the one mandatory condition—randomness. It is not widely known that the tables of so-called random numbers published in physics and statistics handbooks through the 1950s were not, in fact, random, albeit their periodicity was rather long. No lists of numbers can be random if generated by such statistically biased, periodic methods as drawing numbers from hats, throwing dice, tossing Eindhoven hexagonal bars, twirling disks (or roulette wheels), or programming electronic computers. No mechanical or even electrical process can generate truly random numbers, and no random (or stochastic) process was then confidently known to physical scientists. However, two truly stochastic processes are now thought to exist: the decay of a radioactive element, and thermal noise. Both processes are now used to generate random numbers.[125]

Today, anyone with $50,000 can acquire commercially complete, unbreakable, radioactively generated, one-time tape, on-line communication systems. These can be bought in Zug, Switzerland, from Crypto, Aktiengesellschaft, headed by Boris Hagelin, Jr., whose 140,000 primitive M–209 machines had monopolized America's middle-level crytographic communications during World War II. Crypto A.G. now services some sixty governments and a few large private industrial and financial firms.[126]

Thus since World War II the unbreakable one-time pad and tape systems have become the rule rather than the exception in all major and most minor diplomatic, intelligence, and military services. Even the joint Russo-American "hot line" is secured by one-time tape. We must therefore conclude that few major communications can any longer be solved by cryptanalysts. But the user and the historian should remember that cryptanalysis is only one means for acquiring the secret communications of others.

In sum, it appears that it is sheer happenstance that the BARBA-
ROSSA planning period of 1940–1941 coincided with a brief period
when the cryptanalysts had far oustripped the cryptographers.

International Intelligence Liaisons

Traditionally, the most secret activity of intelligence organizations is their official mutual liaisons. It is more difficult to obtain
reliable public information on this one topic than on cryptology
or even on deception operations. That is because such liaison is
politically sensitive[127] and not merely technologically so, as with
cryptology or diplomatically as with deception. Thus the realities
of domestic bureaucratic policies often make it easier to exchange
information with foreign intelligence services than with domestic
rivals. Yet even here the picture for early 1941 is reasonably clear.
In general, all intelligence services had at least intermittent official contacts with most other foreign services. These contacts were
mainly concerned with preliminary peace negotiations and occurred with increasing frequency throughout the period 1938–
1945.

Furthermore, most intelligence services also had permanent liaison arrangements with some of their competitors. These contacts
were of the following types. First, there was formal liaison among
allies. Such contacts characteristically involved the sharing of intelligence about mutual enemies, training in certain operational
or communications techniques, and even occasional collaboration
on specific operations. Beginning in 1940 this type developed in
unprecedentedly close form only between British intelligence on
the one hand and the United States[128] and the governments-in-
exile in London on the other. In 1942 the Soviet NKGB also
opened liaison with the British S.O.E. and the American OSS,
and later there was some low-level liaison between Soviet naval
intelligence and the American ONI, but these relations never
grew close because of inherent reluctance by the three governments.[129] Second, liaison was made between a belligerent and a
neutral or between two neutrals in which the sole purpose was a
straightforward swapping of intelligence. As we have seen, Swe-

den and Switzerland were the most active centers for this, involving Russian, British, American, German, Italian, Japanese, Swiss, Czech, Polish, Vatican, and undoubtedly other intelligence services in most of their possible bilateral combinations. Typical of this type was the intelligence clearinghouse in Stockholm operated by Japanese Military Attaché Onodera and to which Soviet intelligence was linked. The most spectacular example was the Soviet GRU network in Switzerland operated by Alexander Rado. Third, informal liaisons were initiated by one intelligence service with another and intended for leaking information in a specific direction. The preeminent practitioner of this one-way art was Colonel Oster of the Abwehr, who regularly passed German strategic plans to both Western intelligence services and the Vatican.

Not only did such international liaison cooperation among intelligence services exist in 1940–1941 but, as shown in Chapters 3–5, it accounted for some of the diffusion of BARBAROSSA warnings.

In wartime, Truth is so precious that she should always be attended by a bodyguard of lies.
—Churchill at Tehran, 30 November 1943

All military and political intelligence systems receive vast numbers of pieces of information.* Usually, only a small proportion of this great bulk is relevant to any single current problem such as predicting whether an attack is planned by one country against another. Even the small proportion of relevant information is seldom both complete and accurate. Most is a jumble of information that is accurate but incomplete or from a dubious source, unintentionally distorted or misleading, well-intentioned but wholly wrong, or deliberately intended to deceive. The task of the strategic information analyst is to construct a mosaic of these separate pieces, picking the accurate scraps, correcting the distorted bits, and discarding the false ones. This eternal labor of the intelligencer is made Herculean when the information system is flooded with disinformation (information intended to deceive), particularly when that disinformation is fed in as part of a systematic deception campaign.

This chapter will describe the types of misleading and deceptive information that perturbed the correct evaluation of intelligence on BARBAROSSA.

German Deception Operations

The fundamental principle of the magician's art [is] misdirection.
—Blackstone the Magician

Having decided to initiate war, the leader faces a dilemma: how to mobilize and deploy his martial means without sacrificing surprise, much less drawing a preemptive attack. The pedestrian

---

* Some examples of the volume of monitoring traffic: During World War I, French intelligence intercepted over 100,000,000 words of German radiograms. In the 1960s the translated foreign press and radio monitoring reports published daily for the major powers were:
U.S.A.: 150,000 words (CIA's *FBIS Daily Report*)
USSR: 80,000 words ("Red TASS")
Britain: 40,000 words (B.B.C. monitoring reports)
See Kahn (1967), 300, and Whaley (1964), 8.

textbookish answer is "security." But, as BARBAROSSA shows, it can be most unrealistic to expect conventional passive security measures to guard against ample disclosure of secrets. Only the most naïve, preoccupied, witless, incompetent, or unlucky enemy will remain unwarned. But the cunning leader can interject one special type of counterespionage activity that will enhance his chances of gaining surprise. That is stratagem—a coordinated campaign of deception to mislead the victim's analysis.

Deception has, of course, been used by occasional clever leaders in politics and war since antiquity. But evidently the Germans were the first to institutionalize it when late in World War I the Great General Staff created a Disinformation Service, which contributed to the occasional and rather crude German deception operations in that war. In the 1920s surprise and deception were preserved in German military doctrine and training by General von Seeckt, and by the mid-1930s the Abwehr had restored the specific organizational machinery for deception. This machinery was the D Group (Gruppe III-D), one of the half dozen main divisions in Colonel von Bentivegni's military security section (Abteilung III). Group D (subdivided into two geographic desks) was responsible for developing deception operations in coordination with the Army, Navy, and Air Force general staffs and for providing disinformation suitable for dissemination by the Abwehr's counterespionage (III-F) and other services. Its functions, although less centralized, were similar to the later British "Double-Cross Committee." However, the broad guidelines of strategic deception planning were centered in Hitler's personal military staff, the OKW, specifically in the operations staff (WFSt) under Jodl and in the latter's plans section (Abteilung L), under Warlimont during the BARBAROSSA planning. The Abwehr mounted rather primitive but more or less successful deception operations in connection with the Spanish Civil War in 1936, the take-over of Austria in early 1938, and the pressure on Czechoslovakia later that year. Finally, since at least as early as 1940, deception was made standard procedure in the OKW *Timetable* coordinating each of Hitler's surprise attacks. Thus, during the BARBAROSSA buildup, deception was a practiced, institutionalized, and routine part of Hitler's strategic planning. Indeed, these ruses of war were generally initiated by the Führer himself.[1]

Thus Hitler would devise the broad outline and even specify the main themes of each strategic deception operation, leaving it to his personal military staff (usually Keitel or Jodl) to coordinate the detailed planning and directives with the appropriate segments of the military, propaganda, and foreign affairs bureaucracy.

Hitler, with his intelligence and propaganda chiefs, wisely anticipated that the many highly visible preparations for BARBAROSSA would not go unnoticed. They also understood that enemy intelligence services and leaders could easily interpret these as signaling the intended invasion. Conventional security procedures were deemed inadequate.* Consequently, the Germans very deliberately launched what they themselves termed the "greatest deception operation in the history of war" [2] to mislead their enemies about the very intention to invade Russia, as well as to conceal the time, direction, and strength of the blow.

The deception campaign was conducted from 31 July 1940 until the invasion on 22 June 1941. During that period the Germans launched four distinguishable deception themes. These themes overlapped in time, were mutually supporting, and were well calculated to fit the preconceptions of their enemies at each stage of the developing operation.

The subsequent chapters will show the almost complete success achieved in Russia (and Britain, the United States, Japan, and other countries). For the present I shall just describe the themes used in the deception plan.

Invasion of Britain

The first deception theme launched by the Germans was that their military buildup on the eastern frontier (Operation AUFBAU OST) was merely part of the preparations for the widely heralded

---

* Nor, contrary to widespread belief, does conventional passive security ever offer a high probability of concealment of large military operations, as demonstrated in my general study of 167 military operations from 1914 through 1968. See Whaley (1969*b*).

invasion of Britain (Operation SEA LION). Originally conceived by Hitler himself and ordered into effect by him on 31 July 1940, this theme was maintained all the way through to B-day itself.[3]

A variety of plausible arguments was advanced in connection with this cover story. For example, it was explained as a training maneuver, held well out of range of British bombers and reconnaissance aircraft.[4]

Indeed, throughout early 1941 the Wehrmacht units in the east were not organized for attack: most lay well back, with only the original negligible force screening the frontier itself; they were widely dispersed and, in fact, engaged in training programs; leave was generously apportioned; and no more senior headquarters than that of Günther von Kluge's Fourth Army in Warsaw was east of the German border.[5] The posture was that of a peacetime army, but a "peacetime" army fully mobilized and quartered within striking distance of Russia.

On 15 February the OKW generated a special twist in this deception theme by touting BARBAROSSA to the *Russians* as itself a "deception diversion" to mislead the *British* about SEA LION. That rare double bluff was sustained until at least as late as 5 June.[6]

Then, on 24 April, von Brauchitsch ordered a major deception operation—*Fall* HAIFISCH (Operation SHARK)—to involve military activities from Scandinavia to Brittany.[7] A series of "secret" notices were sent in early May to the German military attachés in Moscow, Berne, Tokyo, and six other embassies, lying that the rumors of war were false and that some eight German divisions would soon be withdrawn from the Russian border.[8] Clearly, this widely distributed false information was expected to leak to Soviet intelligence.

Propaganda Minister Goebbels, privy to BARBAROSSA by June, contributed his personal bit of fakery. He wrote an article "disclosing" that the invasion of *England* was imminent. It was published on 13 June under his own name in the *Völkischer Beobachter* and ostentatiously withdrawn by the police as soon as copies were known to have reached the foreign press correspondents. Delighting in his own cleverness, Goebbels then even placed himself in simulated disgrace to complete the masquerade. This brief public "disgrace" was accepted by the foreign press corps as the final proof that the article did represent a genuine "leak." [9]

As absurd as this cover story has seemed in retrospect to historians, the "big lie" that BARBAROSSA was SEA LION not only apparently worked against the Russians but—suitably modified— almost completely deceived British intelligence until 1942, nearly a year and a half after Hitler had, in fact, abandoned his intention to invade Britain.[10]

Defense against Russia

On 6 September 1940 Hitler added a second major deception theme when he directed the Abwehr to mask the eastward troop transfers as a contingency shield against any hostile Russian moves, particularly into the Balkans, specifying that this cover story be fed to the "Russian intelligence service." Subsequently, on 18 December, Hitler further specified that BARBAROSSA planning and deployments be explained to subordinate German commanders as mere contingency planning and "precautionary measures" in case Russia should choose to become more hostile. This plausible lie was kept afloat until at least as late as 4 June 1941.[11]

By 19 March 1941 this cover story was modified slightly to present the eastern deployments as a "defensive measure" in response to the then apparent *Russian* buildup. That specific lie was maintained at least as late as 5 June. Moreover, during April and May the Germans introduced the momentarily appropriate theme that the Wehrmacht's eastern deployment formed a "rear cover" for their then current Balkan invasion.[12]

In accord with this cover story, relevant OKW orders often carried a preamble explaining their purpose as purely defensive in case of a possible Russian attack.[13] Since this tale was believed at Army Group staff level, it should not be surprising that Russian intelligence also credited it.

Buildup against Balkans

When, during April and May 1941, the Wehrmacht's blitzkrieg thrust through the Balkans, that operation was made to do double duty as cover for BARBAROSSA. Thus, on 3 February 1941, Hitler added the planned invasion of Greece to the BARBAROSSA camouflage list.[14] And on 12 May, after the Greek enterprise had been liquidated, Crete was substituted on the list.[15]

Impending Ultimatum

Sometime shortly before 17 May 1941 the Reich Foreign Ministry invented (or at least first utilized) the cover story that German actions were determined by Russian conduct. This crucial lie was picked up by the OKW on 25 May and further propagated by them.[16]

This became the main and most crucial set of rumors during the final weeks before the invasion. Because I have been unable to establish conclusively the official inspiration of most of these particular rumors, I have discussed them in the following section on rumor.

Other Aspects

The Gestapo's intelligence service (the SD) had a major part in these deception operations. In addition to its partially successful efforts to cut Russian intelligence off from sources of authentic information, the SD contrived to pass them considerable misleading information prepared by the Wehrmacht, including material about renewed preparations for SEA LION.[17]

The German psychological warfare factories also busily contributed to the mass of rumors that were circulating in early 1941 about German plots and troop movements in the Mediterranean. Many of these themes—German "tourists" controlling the French air and naval bases in Morocco in February; 6,000 German troops in Morocco in March; 60,000 German troops massing in Spain in May to attack Gibraltar and Morocco—simply vanished with the invasion of Russia on 22 June. These and similar baseless tales were widely credited, for example, by the British and American Economic Warfare boards, the British ambassador in Washington, the American consul-general in Algiers, the British embassy in Lisbon, and the Foreign Office in London. Such rumors were effective not only in diverting attention from Eastern Europe but also simply in placing a great strain—and embarrassment—on all other intelligence and diplomatic services, as Robert Murphy has so well described.[18]

This elaborate rumor campaign was orchestrated at least in Spain by the German press attaché in Madrid, Hans Lazar, who simultaneously was playing out a private game by disclosing BARBAROSSA to Polish intelligence.[19]

An odd smoke screen, which evidently originated in early 1941 with Nazi propagandists, was the letters from German soldiers to their families. They bore faked Russian postmarks and contained false descriptions of Wehrmacht operations in conjunction with the Russians.[20]

A major part of Hitler's effort to lull Russian suspicions was the maintenance of normal economic and diplomatic ties. In this case, "normal" meant those intimate commercial negotiations and deliveries flowing from the Nazi-Soviet Pact of August 1939. This relationship involved the exchange of strategic goods, mainly Russian raw materials (such as oil and grain) for German machine tools, prototype weapons, and other military-industrial manufactures, as well as negotiations over minor delineations of frontiers.[21] For example, on 30 March 1940 Hitler ordered that the deliveries of war materials to Russia receive top priority, over that of the Wehrmacht itself, which he knew to be on the eve of its assaults on Denmark, Norway, Holland, Belgium, and France.[22] However, on 14 August, following the conquest of France, Hitler specified that punctual deliveries to the Russians would continue only to spring 1941. Göring conveyed this order to General Georg Thomas, chief of the OKW's Economic and Armaments Branch and himself one of the conspirators against Hitler, adding that thereafter "we would have no further interest in completely satisfying the Russian demands."[23] It is odd that the interests of logistic efficiency were allowed to take precedence over BARBAROSSA security, which would have required that the first order canceling deliveries would have been the accomplished fact of the invasion itself. As it happened, as seen in Chapters 3 to 5, the Russians did receive some of their war warnings through security leaks about these reallocations in German industry.

Rumors

The flying rumours gathr'd as they roll'd,
Scarce any tale was sooner heard than told;
And all who told it added something new,
And all who heard it made enlargements too.

—Pope, "The Temple of Fame"

Among the more dissonant bits of noise in the BARBAROSSA information system were the very many rumors about the state of Russo-German relations. These circulated widely and with increasing intensity in military, diplomatic, and press circles through the world, particularly during the spring of 1941.

In general, we can profitably distinguish three types of BARBAROSSA rumor on the basis of their source: authentic information posing as rumor, misleading information spread as part of the deliberate German deception campaign, and plausible speculation.

First, many of the bits of information then labeled rumors—with all that word popularly implies about low credibility—subsequently proved to be authentic warnings. The latter have been included in the chapters on warnings, although many were not fully credited at the time. It is curious how such a great volume of authentic information often became eroded from hard and often verifiable fact to discredited rumor. Moreover, this transformation seldom required more than one or two intermediary "tellers." This breakdown in communication is remarkable, given the prevailing circumstances: (a) tellers and listeners were political sophisticates fully integrated in elite circles, (b) the information was highly salient to both tellers and listeners, (c) the teller was sincerely trying to warn or inform his listener, and (d) the original source was an authentic document or briefing. Two mechanisms seem to be at work here, each serving to transmute fact into rumor and each essentially involving credibility as assessed by the listener. In the one case it is the credibility of the teller himself that is questioned; in the other, the credibility of his information.*

The four possible combinations of credibilities of source and of information can be illustrated by one example: the BARBAROSSA plan obtained by Sam Woods and passed by Sumner Welles to the Russians. (1) Both source and information were adjudged credible by the U.S. State Department (Hull, Welles, and Long), FBI Director Hoover, and President Roosevelt. They had the original text of the document and were able to verify the credentials of Woods and, more important, those of his informants. (2) The source was deemed credible but the information was seemingly somewhat discounted by the British (the prime minister and his intelligence community). At least, they made no noticeable use of it. The reason for this apparent discounting may be that the Americans chose to conceal the full history, thereby not fully satisfying any doubts that British intelligence may have had. (3) Both source and information were seemingly discredited by the Russians. Furthermore, they apparently treated all similar warnings from the British, Polish, and Czechoslovak intelligence services and governments with similar distrust. The Russians did so because they very rightly suspected the political motives behind such free information. Unfortunately, a "halo effect" carried over from the suspect source to the detriment of the authentic information. (4) Theoretically, there could have been a combination in which the source was not credited but the information was accepted. This situation could possibly have arisen had the U.S. State Department been willing to risk compromising Woods's clandestine channel into the Nazi hierarchy by sharing full knowledge of it with the Russians. Then the Russians could have inde-

* I am struck by the failure of the patterns of rumors found in this study to match the model of rumor developed by either experimental psychologists such as Gordon W. Allport and Leo Postman or clinical psychologists such as Carl Jung. The most relevant model seems to be the sociological one epitomized by Shibutani. See Tamotsu Shibutani, *Improvised News: A Sociological Study of Rumor* (Indianapolis: Bobbs-Merrill, 1966).

pendently verified the authenticity of the information but kept their correct belief that the source was deliberately provocative. The second source of rumor was disinformation. Some of the more widely credited rumors are now known to have been wholly false ones deliberately implanted by the Germans. These have already been discussed in the preceding section on German "deception operations." It remains only to point out that this was a large, well-organized campaign that pumped a considerable volume of misleading information into the channels that were being assiduously monitored by the foreign intelligence services.*

At a private meeting in 1942, Werner Wächter, a senior official in the Propaganda Ministry and a regular member of Goebbels's morning conferences disclosed Goebbels's BARBAROSSA rumor technique. Because it was "the age of whispering propaganda," Wächter explained, the invasion preparations were accompanied by so many rumors, "all of which were equally credible, so that in the end there wasn't a bugger left who had any idea of what was really up." [24] Consider only the contradictory confusion of dates of a predicted invasion flowing through the rumor mills. Valentin Berezhkov, the first secretary of the Soviet embassy in Berlin, recalls that the rumors reaching the embassy from March on gave dates of 6 April, 20 April, 18 May, and—correctly—22 June, all Sundays. Berezhkov now realizes that these were, in good cry-wolf fashion, designed "evidently to put us off the track." [25]

The third source of rumor was speculation. Undoubtedly, many of the rumors concerning the state of Russo-German relations and the impending war were spontaneous. Even the outer rings of the diplomatic, military, and journalistic circles were aware that something was afoot between Russia and Germany. Given a salient mystery it may be expected that much plausible speculation will occur. Once launched, most speculation soon loses its original

---

* While—except for Goebbels's efforts—no detailed account of how the Germans went about this exists, one possible model is the contemporary British S.O.E. and P.W.E. rumormongering, whose concerted, systematic word-of-mouth campaigns are described by Walker (1957), 163–178. For Goebbels see Whaley (1969b), A294–A295. For German rumoring techniques see also Hoare (1947), 90–91.

label and begins circulating as factual rumor—mere noise distracting and confusing the public, intelligence analysts, and foreign-policy makers.

The rest of this section will present a few of the more interesting examples of this third type of rumor, the "spontaneous" ones. They are, however, presented with the caveat that the main one is a previously unidentified example of German disinformation.

Rumors of a possible German attack on Russia began circulating in Berlin itself in August 1940. These were officially and emphatically denied.[26] However, their locus, timing, and some specific details suggest they were authentic indiscretions.

One odd rumor attached itself to some of the authentic leaks about BARBAROSSA. This version asserted that the German General Staff, not Hitler, had originally urged the attack on Russia, doing so on strategic grounds.[27] * If, as reported, these specific leaks came from OKW quarters itself, I presume they were from some junior and late arrival on the OKW staff who mistook Field-Marshal Keitel's obsequious, wholehearted acquiescence in Hitler's scheme for a rational appraisal that a preemptive strike was needed.

One of the more fantastic rumors was an announcement by the government-controlled radio in Rome in May 1941. Radio Rome asserted that a Russo-German military alliance had already been signed. This led to a flurry of denials: publicly by Berlin, privately by the Germans to Japan and by the Russians to Britain.[28] Some rumors of this type, namely, those implying that Russo-German negotiations were still possible, were deliberately spread by the German authorities to lull Russian suspicions by implying that Germany had certain negotiable conditions. Thus Ribbentrop is said to be the source of the "news" floated in Berlin from

* This curious theory even infused much of the early postwar histories of the Nazi-Wehrmacht relationship and beclouded the vindictive prosecution case at the Nürnberg war crimes trials. The subsequent efforts, mainly by German writers, to slough off all "guilt" onto Hitler represent a wrong but understandable reaction to the earlier uninformed theory. Only recently has a balanced account, based on close reading of all sources, emerged. See, for example, O'Neill (1966).

late May on that Stalin was arriving in an armored train for talks in Berlin or Königsberg.[29] These rumors were passed promptly and directly to the Soviet TASS news bureau chief in Berlin, Filippov, by Herr Schneider, the editor of the *National Zeitung*.[30] Similarly, on 11 June, no less than the puppet chief of the SA ("Brownshirts"), Gruppenführer Viktor Lutze, categorically assured Giuseppe Renzetti (the Italian consul-general in Berlin and former president of the Italian Chamber of Commerce) that Stalin was due momentarily in Berlin to reach accord with Hitler.[31] Considering the high level of the source and the lateness of the date, I presume this must have become an officially disseminated rumor, even if it did not begin as such.[32] Indeed, one scholar flatly asserts that the rumors about an imminent visit by Stalin originated in Goebbels's Propaganda Ministry and were deliberately spread with the aid of Nazi party officials.[33]

One set of rumors concerned the various specific "conditions" that Hitler was said to be demanding of Stalin. A major alleged demand was to permit greater German control over the grain-producing Ukraine.[34] At least one variant of this rumor—that Germany was demanding a 99-year lease of the Ukraine—was deliberately designed in the Propaganda Ministry and circulated for them by the Nazi party organization.[35]

Whatever their origin—whether spontaneous or officially inspired—this set of rumors was made the key part of the Germans' coordinated deception campaign in the last fortnight before invasion. This explains Göring's clever lie in mid-June to the indiscreet Swede, Dahlerus (warning 73). Göring knew that Dahlerus would promptly pass along the story that the Russians were about to receive an ultimatum demanding demobilization and German control of the Ukraine and the Baku oil fields.

Another rumor had German troops already marching through the Ukraine, on some unspecified and therefore sinister mission to the Turkish (*sic*) frontier.[36] A more specific version placed these troops in Tiflis, awaiting the arrival of German petroleum engineers.[37]

Early and continuing press reports of indicators of a possible

Russo-German war appeared in the *Neue Zürcher Zeitung* from July 1940 on. This internationally respected Swiss newspaper competently collated and reported the rumors of German deployments and other invasion indicators, drawing mainly on Swiss, Turkish, and Finnish sources.[38] An unusually perceptive and increasingly accurate series of dispatches had also been appearing in the *Chicago Daily News* from as early as November 1940. They originated with that paper's own stable of foreign correspondents: John T. Whitaker (Rome and, later, Lisbon), William H. Stoneman (London), and Wallace R. Deuel (Berlin). In November 1940 it reported the shaky state of Russo-German "friendship"; about Christmas, the huge German deployments; on 4 June 1941, a categorical prediction of the German invasion; then a prediction that it would come that month; and, finally, on 10 June, the remarkable disclosure that no Russian concessions could delay it; that is, there would be no German ultimatum.[39]

Foreign press coverage from Berlin was particularly difficult, despite the availability of leaks and the high visibility of mobilization, because of the swift retribution by the German press censors and police for any unwelcome publication. For example, Ralph Barnes of the *New York Herald Tribune* was expelled in June 1940 for writing of deteriorating Russo-German relations.[40] And Reto Caratsch, the well-informed Berlin correspondent for the *Neue Zürcher Zeitung,* was expelled the next month for his dispatch mentioning German disquiet about the Soviet occupation of Bessarabia.[41] A similar situation existed in Moscow, where on 5 June 1941 the then pro-Soviet correspondent John Scott was ordered expelled for some superb speculative articles he had published in the *London News Chronicle.*[42]

The *Manchester Guardian* on 31 May 1941 published an article on Anglo-Russian relations from Sir Bernard Pares, the distinguished Russian expert. After discussing the problem of Poland, Sir Bernard reminded his readers of Hitler's greedy desire for *Lebensraum* in the Ukraine, self-proclaimed in *Mein Kampf*. He concluded: "Meanwhile Hitler has his Quisling ready. Skoropadski, already tested in the German exploitation of the Ukraine in 1918, is training Ukrainian troops for the great invasion." [43] An altogether strange warning. Was it perhaps an inspired piece directed mainly to the readers in Moscow rather than Manchester or London? If so, it was an ignorant blunder of British intelligence, for *Hetman* Skoropadski had long been a joke with Hitler and all his entourage except the dreaming Rosenberg. The only actively supported Ukrainians in Germany were the two OUN factions headed respectively by Mel'nyk and Bandera. And even those two groups were to be used (by the Abwehr) only for sabotage and guerrilla warfare. Political administration was always planned as an all-German business. [44] Soviet intelligence, which had deeply penetrated these émigré groups, presumably knew the actual state of affairs. Consequently, Pares's article would only discredit British intelligence in the eyes of Moscow and reinforce the Russian suspicion that the British were mere provocateurs.

In the first week of June the British reportedly decided to leak a more or less general public warning of BARBAROSSA. It has been alleged that on 5 June (or thereabouts) Foreign Secretary Eden took the occasion of one of his intermittent briefings of selected American correspondents to disclose that Germany might invade Russia sometime in the second half of the month and that the British and U.S. governments had already warned Stalin. Furthermore, Eden disclosed to the Americans—including Drew Middleton of Associated Press—such supporting details as the number of Wehrmacht infantry, panzer, and aviation units redeployed to the East. He even disclosed that much of this intelligence had come from British agents throughout Central and Eastern Europe. Eden concluded by serving tea to the rather startled journalists. Middleton immediately reported to his competent Associated Press London bureau chief, Robert Bunnelle, who decided that this was the first hard news in the previously contradictory flood of rumors. Finding Eden's authority and specificity of details convincing guarantee against a British propaganda trap, Bunnelle released Middleton's story on the AP wire. [45] However, the AP version that finally emerged from the New York City editorial desk as a "roundup" datelined Ankara was so thoroughly mixed with other rumors of Russo-German tension as to be reduced to their level.[46]

The Soviet elite was quite aware of the rumors circulating in the foreign press. Not only was it standard practice for the Russian leaders to receive confidential monitoring reports prepared by TASS and their other information-intelligence services;[47] but in this case the Soviet press itself took particular care to voice immediate and emphatic denials.[48] Such denials were surely intended to reassure the German press monitors rather than the Soviet public. However, this publicity had two unanticipated side effects. First, it overly lulled both the Soviet public and, more important, middle-level officials who might otherwise have taken some alert measures. Second, it raised an embarrassing question about the omniscience of Bolshevik leadership after the attack broke.

The official, public Soviet denials of some specific rumors, coupled with silence on others, look very much like a deliberate Russian effort at tacit negotiation with Germany. If true it would be interesting empirical proof of the most consequential type of pitfall in "tacit bargaining." [49] That is, here presumably was a case where the Russians falsely interpreted the rumors as German "trial balloons" and pathetically deceived themselves that they had succeeded in opening an informal channel of negotiation. For example, the vituperative tone of *Pravda*'s denial of a story in the largest Finnish newspaper, *Helsingin Sanomat,* that any piece of Russian soil had been yielded up to German demands indicated in advance of the expected formal set of demands that territorial claims on the Ukraine were to be excluded from the agenda.[50] Conversely, the absent or weaker denials of the equally widely circulated rumors about economic concessions or German supervision of Soviet industry, agriculture, or transportation implied that they were suitable topics for negotiation or even an ultimatum. Even stronger evidence is that the Russians reciprocated the German denials of all *general* rumors of deterioration in Russo-German relations and then at the last minute even explicitly sought through diplomacy to elicit Hitler's supposed demands. To have done these two things shows that the Russians did indeed view some of those rumors as authentic signals about points of negotiation.

A more systematic analysis of all the recorded rumors would undoubtedly help round out the picture of information flow that has emerged from my study. Such an analysis would show their sources and channels of flow and would assess their effects on intelligence, diplomatic, military, press, and public audiences. Moreover, it might enable us to track some of them to their sources, permitting a judgment about whether they were inadvertent leaks, calculated disinformation, or spontaneous noise. However, this type of detailed analysis will be left off with a mere listing of the known published sources. Inspection of the following bibliographic checklist (Table 7.1) of these rumors will at least show their wide geographic appearance and the availability of raw data.

Table 7.1   Published References to Rumors of a Russo-German War, Early 1941

Primary Circulation	Reference
International	*DGFP*, 12 (1962), 1027
	FRUS: 1941, 1 (1958), 753; 4 (1956), 933
	Middleton (1964), 56
	Nekrich (1968), 184–188
	New York Times Index for 1940 and 1941
	Times (London), 1940 and 1941
Britain (London)	Bryant (1957), 191
	Gripenberg (1965), 175–176, 180–181
	Raczynski (1962), 89
	Sheean (1943), 321, 325–326
Finland (Helsinki)	Upton (1964), 261, 268, 271, 27 6–277
	Krosby (1968*a*), 157
France (Vichy)	Leahy (1950), 30, 71
Germany (generally)	Ernst Kris and Hans Speier, *German Radio Propaganda* (London: Oxford University Press, 1944), pp. 302–305

Table 7.1   Published References to Rumors of a Russo-German War, Early 1941
(continued)

Primary Circulation	Reference
Germany (Berlin)	Aguirre (1944), 207, 215, 236 Alfieri (1955), 120 Andreas-Friedrich (1947), 63–65, 67–68 Berezhkov (1966*b*), in Bialer (1969), 213 Bojano (1944), 206 *DGFP*, 12 (1962), 788, 827, 926–927, 1043 Flannery (1942), 272–273, 361 Fredborg (1944), 4, 25–28 *FRUS: 1941*, 1 (1958), 134–135, 138–142, 148, 150, 151, 153, and ibid., 4 (1956), 931 Goerlitz (1963), 27 Hassell (1947), 198 Huss (1942), 255–278 Lochner (1942*a*), 4 Smith (1942), 66–69 Simoni (1946), 220–242 Weizsäcker (1951), 241
Germany (Vienna)	*FRUS: 1941*, 1 (1958), 141n
Germany (army)	Blumentritt (1952), 96–97 Erich Kern, *Dance of Death* (London: Collins, 1951), pp. 13–14 *TWC* (1951), 10: 1050
Germany (Sachsenhausen Concentration Camp)	Captain S. Payne Best, *The Venlo Incident* (London: Hutchinson, [1949]), pp. 100–102
Italy (Rome)	*FRUS: 1941*, 1 (1958), 168, 170, for the Rome radio announcement of May 1941 that a Russo-German military alliance had been signed Whitaker (1943), 304
Japan (Tokyo)	*DGFP*, 12 (1962), 967–969 Newman (1942), 301 Newman (1967), 129 Tōgō (1965), 50 Tolischus (1943), 92–93, 118, 133, 137–139

Table 7.1   Published References to Rumors of a Russo-German War, Early 1941 (continued)

Primary Circulation	Reference
Poland (Warsaw underground)	Stypulkowski (1951), 52
Portugal (Lisbon)	Listowel (1952), 94–95, 97 Middleton (1946), 134 Middleton (1964), 55 Whitaker (1943), 303, 305
Rumania (Bucharest)	*FRUS: 1941*, 1 (1958), 139, 320–321, 753 Scott (1942), 139, 140
Russia (generally)	Caldwell (1942), 20, naïvely alleges lack of rumors among populace because government did not disseminate them Leonhard (1958), 88, 106–112, for rumors in Moscow among students and German Communist émigrés
Russia (Leningrad)	Salisbury (1969), 3–130
Russia (Moscow diplomatic and press corps)	Bojano (1944), 207 Cassidy (1943), 14–15 *DGFP*, 11 (1960), 941–943 *FRUS: 1941*, 1 (1958), 132–134, 144, 754; and ibid., 4 (1956), 940 Gafencu (1945), 206 Hilger and Meyer (1953), 324–325, 327–329 Scott (1942), 189–190, 250
Sweden (Stockholm)	Aguirre (1944), 254, 258 Krosby (1968a), 157 *New York Times*, 10 June 1941, p. 6
Switzerland (Zürich)	Hohenberg (1964), 340
Turkey (Ankara)	Brock (1942), 294–304 *FRUS: 1941*, 3 (1959), 850 Papen (1953), 479

Then came all the king's wise men: but they could not read the writing, nor make known to the king the interpretation thereof.

—Daniel 5:8

This chapter examines the manner in which the Russian intelligence services and leaders processed and used the vast, amorphous conglomeration of often contradictory raw intelligence impinging on their senses.

I have already described numerous bits of information concerning BARBAROSSA that were flowing out of Germany to foreign intelligence, diplomatic, and journalistic circles. Although only some of these messages are known to have reached a destination inside the Kremlin, it is likely most did. Indeed, for those that did not, we should assume that there were at least as many comparable ones that did, but which we merely have not yet identified. This assumption is reasonable for two reasons:

First, there are clearly some gaps remaining in the record of warnings. Many memoirs and diaries await publication. Only since Khrushchev's de-Stalinizing speech of 1956 have the Russians been cautiously disclosing bits of relevant information, and even that source has virtually dried up since the end of the "thaw" in 1966. And some inhibitions about full disclosure remain on the British and even the American side. However, quite enough is now publicly known to confidently outline the subject.

Second, as we have seen, BARBAROSSA planning proceeded in an environment of nearly unrestrained exchange of information. It almost seems as if no one could keep a secret, and everybody was reading everyone else's private "mail"; and the Soviet intelligence services in 1940–1941 were among the more adept at intercepting and reading others' messages.

The Soviet Intelligence System and Its Perceptions

There are lots of things that happen even here in Russia which our Secret Service do not necessarily tell me about.

—Stalin, to Churchill, 1944 [1]

The cold war image of the Soviet intelligence system as "the net that covers the world" [2] is quite correct—as far as it goes. It has been the world's largest and most extended secret intelligence service ever since the 1920s, its agent networks or *apparats* reaching into every country and into most national political and military organizations. It is vast, expensive, and supplies the Soviet decision makers with a huge volume of information. However, this still rather common image of Soviet intelligence implies two false conclusions: that it is efficient and that it is monolithic. In general, the Soviet intelligence system has proved both inefficient and highly fragmented.[3] These two important characteristics held specifically true in the period preceding BARBAROSSA.

The inherent inefficiencies of the Soviet intelligence system were multiplied by its bureaucratic fragmentation. Like the German, British, and American systems of the time, Soviet intelligence was split among several organizations. Popular myth, now slowly dissipating before newly emerging official and academic publications, sees centralized intelligence everywhere—from the legendary British Secret Service (actually a collective term), through the German Gestapo (another collective term) and the U.S. Central Intelligence Agency (a post–World War II phenomenon), to the Soviet's so-called Secret Police. In fact, with the single exception of the Polish intelligence service, which was centralized in the late 1930s, central intelligence has only *begun* to materialize since World War II.[4] The first effort in that direction was American, with their founding of the Central Intelligence Agency in 1947; but even the CIA has met with vigorous competition from the more recently founded but equally large though more discreet Defense Intelligence Agency (DIA). The second effort was Russian, when in 1947 they briefly experimented with combining military intelligence (GRU) with the Foreign [Intelligence] Administration (INU) of the Ministry of State Security (MGB) under the new Committee of Information (KI). However, the GRU reverted to the Defense Ministry the next year, and the KI itself was totally abolished in 1951. The British have made the third and most recent effort to move toward a central intelligence concept, with their creation in 1964 of a Director-General of Intelligence, who at least sits above the separate service intelligence directors if not the Security Service

(M.I.5) and the Secret Intelligence Service (M.I.6). Despite these efforts, no country even today has achieved centralized intelligence; and the situation in 1940–1941 was, for all countries, one of great and highly competitive fragmentation.

In early 1941 the Soviet intelligence community comprised two major services and several minor ones. The major ones, which are described in more detail in the following pages, were the NKGB (or state security) and the GRU (military intelligence). The minor ones included specialized intelligence services attached to the Commissariats of Navy, Foreign Affairs, and Foreign Trade. In addition, the Comintern had its own intelligence service, the OMS (Otdelenie Mezhdunarodnoi Svyazi, "Section for International Liaison"). Although once ubiquitous, the OMS had been rendered moribund by the Great Purge of 1937–1938.[5]

State Security (NKGB) and Internal Affairs (NKVD)

The paramount Soviet intelligence service is the state security institution, the so-called Secret Police. Founded in 1917, just six weeks after the October Revolution, it inherited the monstrous tradition (and much of the junior personnel) of the Tsar's infamous Okhrana. Whether called Cheka, GPU, OGPU, NKVD, NKGB, MVD, MGB, or, since 1954, KGB, it has remained the basic coercive instrument of the regime.[6]

Twice purged in the late 1930s, the NKVD emerged in 1938 under the iron hand of Lavrenti Beriya as the loyal and feared tool of Stalinist absolutism. It was all-seeing inside Russia, yet half-blinded as an instrument for foreign intelligence; but, then, its sole reason for being was internal control.

Still, even internal security required some counterintelligence to monitor, penetrate, and subvert the antiregime exile movements and the institutions of surrounding hostile governments. Accordingly, the Bolshevik State Security incorporated a specialized bureau for foreign intelligence. Originally called the Fourteenth ("Orientalists") Section, in 1922 it was renamed the Foreign Division (Inostranny Otdel, or INO).

The INO had been part of the Main Administration of State

Security (GUGB) of the People's Commissariat of Internal Affairs (NKVD) from 1934 until 3 February 1941. At that point, that is, four and a half months before the German invasion, the GUGB was split off from the NKVD to form its own separate commissariat, the People's Commissariat of State Security (NKGB). Simultaneously, the INO was itself elevated from a "division" to an "administration" to become the INU (Inostrannoye Upravleniye, or Foreign Administration), a designation it has kept ever since.

Thus, on the eve of BARBAROSSA, both the NKVD and the NKGB existed as separate commissariats. The NKVD, under Commissar L. P. Beriya, retained immediate jurisdiction over such security functions as the prisons, labor camps, highways, fire protection, migration, and—relevant to BARBAROSSA—the Border Guards. The NKGB, under Beriya's loyal protégé Commissar V. N. Merkulov, received all the traditional intelligence and covert operation functions, including foreign intelligence and espionage (INU), counterintelligence (KRU), foreign political assassination (OO, later "Smersh"), diversion and terror (Fourth Administration), supervision of Soviet diplomats and other officials abroad (First Administration), and the secret political police (SPU). At this time the deputy commissar was that rapidly rising star Ivan Serov.

As we have seen, both the NKGB intelligence networks abroad and the NKVD Border Guards were collecting many indications of BARBAROSSA and forwarding them to Moscow. Moreover, we now know that many of these were passed directly to Stalin and Molotov.[7] But what if any interpretations did the NKGB or NKVD transmit with their reports? Unfortunately, we have no direct evidence bearing on this point. However, we do know Beriya's general attitude; and since Merkulov was his protégé, we may presume Merkulov's was the same. Beriya's view was consistent throughout: nothing must be done to "provoke" the Germans; and he personally countermanded his subordinates' independent orders for the Anti-Aircraft Command to fire on the Luftwaffe reconnaissance flights or for the Border Guards to occupy forward positions.[8] Thus it is likely that the NKGB and NKVD reports sent to Stalin hedged the warnings by stressing Beriya's belief that they were mere "provocations."

Military Intelligence (GRU)

The Soviet organization receiving most of the BARBAROSSA warnings was military intelligence, the GRU.[9] Attached directly to the General Staff, the GRU (Glavnoye Razvedovatelnoye Upravleniye, "Main Intelligence Administration") exercised centralized direction of the intelligence operations of the Soviet ground and air services.[10]

The GRU, since its founding in 1918, has been the most professional of all Soviet intelligence services. Its relatively high professional standards, competence, and efficiency in intelligence have been a direct result of two factors. First, the GRU was the only Soviet intelligence institution that in fact devoted the bulk of its effort to intelligence, and it was the only one whose middle-level staff and field agents largely escaped the terrible sickle of the Great Purge. As a consequence, the GRU was the only Soviet intelligence agency to enter the 1940s relatively free of the professionally incompetent Communist party hacks who then inundated the slaughtered ranks of the Foreign Commissariat, the Comintern, the TASS news agency, and even the dreaded NKVD itself. By 1940/41 only the GRU could still tolerate (and protect) such brilliant and eccentric agents as Leopold Trepper, Richard Sorge, Alexander Rado, and Rudolf Rössler.

During the period in question, the GRU was headed by Lieutenant-General Filipp Ivanovich Golikov. He had held this key position since mid-July 1940. Golikov has recently (1964) described the GRU role at the time:

The first warnings came from the Soviet military intelligence much earlier than [the Welles-Umansky message of] March 1941. The Intelligence Directorate carried out enormous work in the collection and analysis of information, through various channels, about the intentions of Hitler's Germany . . . against the Soviet state. Along with the collection and analysis of extensive agent data, the Intelligence Directorate exhaustively studied international information, the foreign press, the comments of public opinion, the military-political and military-technical literature of Germany and other countries, etc.[11]

There is no question that the GRU was a somewhat industrious and efficient harvester of raw data. But what of its powers of analysis and evaluation? It is highly suspicious that until 1966 none of the GRU defenders or the attackers of Stalin ever publicly mentioned the specific *form* in which intelligence was transmitted to Stalin. They implied by their silence that Stalin was receiving raw, unevaluated data and that its misinterpretation was wholly his fault. However, the seemingly authentic smuggled verbatim report of a closed meeting in 1966 of the Division of History of the Great Patriotic War of the Institute of Marxism-Leninism gives our first insight.[12] In the very lively discussion at the Institute, Stalinist Professor G. A. Deborin noted:

Golikov did not so much inform the government as lie to it. His reports were in many cases completely untrue. They were always in two parts: in the first part he reported information which he classified as *"from reliable sources"*; here, for example, he included everything that supported the forecast of Germany's invading Great Britain. In the second part of his communications he reported information *"from doubtful sources"*: for example, information from the spy Richard Sorge about the date on which Germany would attack the USSR. One must expand the criticism of the personality cult and say that certain people composed their reports in such a way as to please Stalin, at the expense of truth.[13]

Anfilov, an anti-Stalinist official with the Soviet Army Staff, added:

Golikov and Kuznetsov appear as heroes in their own speeches and memoirs. The truth is that Golikov gave Stalin a report dealing with plan Barbarossa, but with the comment that it was a fake by *agents provocateurs* who wanted to push the USSR into war with Germany.[14]

Dachichev, another anti-Stalinist from the Army Staff, interjected that "Golikov was a criminal not only because he wrote his reports so as to please Stalin, but also because he got our best counter-espionage agents abroad arrested." [15] Finally, Gnedin (or, perhaps, Gnedich), an anti-Stalinist former member in Stalin's own Secretariat at the time, elaborated:

It is quite true that Golikov was a *"misinformer."* But that is not the point. All the "reliable" parts of Golikov's regular reports appeared in one form or another in our official press. Stalin, however, on principle was only interested in the information classed by Golikov as "doubtful." Stalin knew everything, and his policy was to take no measures. Golikov is responsible for the repression which fell upon the [GRU] cadres; but he is not responsible for the fact that no defense measures were taken. . . .[16]

These very critical assessments of Golikov have now been fully substantiated by Marshal Zhukov. His testimony is singularly valuable on two grounds. First, as chief of staff, he was Golikov's nominal boss and did indeed receive *some* of the GRU intelligence reports, although Golikov often reported directly to Stalin. Second, Zhukov's political power position was always outside the Stalinist camp. Consequently, his memoirs are both informed and non-Stalinist in bias. But they did not appear until 1969, and they do bear unmistakable signs of bowing to the then officially required policy that rejected the earlier freedom under Khrushchev to register strong criticism of Stalin. In any case, Zhukov, after summarizing the several accurate and detailed warnings given by Golikov in his report submitted to Stalin on 20 March 1941, comments: "However, the conclusions drawn from the information cited in the report actually nullified its importance." Zhukov then damns Golikov out of his own mouth by quoting Golikov's conclusions directly:

1. On the basis of all the statements cited above . . . I [Golikov] consider that the most probable time operations will begin against the USSR is after victory over England or the conclusion of an honorable peace treaty with her.
2. Rumours and documents to the effect that war against the USSR is inevitable this spring should be regarded as misinformation coming from the English or perhaps even the German intelligence service.[17]

Thus we find that Golikov, as chief of the GRU, was not only impeaching his own best sources but had totally succumbed to the German deception operations.

Naval Intelligence

From 1940, when it became independent of the GRU, through the war, naval intelligence was a small, separate organization reporting directly to the commissar of the Navy, Admiral Nikolai Kuznetsov.[18]

Despite its organizational independence, Soviet naval intelligence did not serve Stalin any better or, indeed, any differently than the GRU. Like the GRU, naval intelligence acquired many authentic warnings and transmitted at least some of them to Stalin. And, like the GRU's Golikov, Admiral Kuznetsov has pointed with pride to these excellent warnings. However, again like Golikov, Kuznetsov's claim has been exposed as a sham. Anfilov first raised this question at the closed meeting at the Institute of Marxism-Leninism in 1966.[19] Then, in 1969, Zhukov proved it by quoting Kuznetsov's hitherto suppressed conclusions presented to Stalin in his prideful "warning" memorandum of 6 May 1941: "I [Kuznetsov] consider that this information is false and was specially sent through this channel so that it would get to our government and the Germans could see how the USSR would react." [20]

The Foreign Commissariat

The People's Commissariat of Foreign Affairs (Narkomindel) did not have an intelligence bureau of its own. That function had been absorbed by the regular state security organization when, after the Revolution, the Narkomindel was created from the ruins of the tsarist Ministry of Foreign Affairs. Nevertheless, like all foreign offices, the Narkomindel still had the essential function of *reporting* international political developments.[21]

Although Stalin personally set Soviet foreign policy, its supervision and management were delegated to two of his loyal cronies: Zhdanov and Molotov, both full members of the Politburo, the governing body of the Communist party.

Andrei A. Zhdanov was also one of the four secretaries (Stalin was General-Secretary) of the immensely powerful Secretariat of the Communist party's Central Committee. Zhdanov's special responsibility as secretary was the supervision of foreign policy. In addition, he was a member of both the government's Supreme Military Council and Supreme Naval Council. In these various capacities Zhdanov had received many party, foreign office, military and

naval intelligence indications of BARBAROSSA by February. Yet he
told Admiral Kuznetsov that month that he believed Germany incapable of fighting on two fronts and therefore thought an attack
improbable. He interpreted the German violations of Soviet air
space and military buildup on the Soviet border to be mere precautionary measures on Hitler's part or, at most, a means of putting
psychological pressure on the Soviet Union.[22]

Vyacheslav M. Molotov, in his capacity as foreign commissar, was
merely the general manager of the machinery of Soviet diplomacy
and its senior messenger boy. Even so, this vantage point—as well
as that on the Politburo—gave Molotov full access to the diplomatic reporting system. Yet as late as 14 or 15 June, when Admiral
Kuznetsov tried to discuss the numerous warnings received by
naval intelligence, Zhdanov brushed him aside, remarking: "Only
a fool would attack us." [23]

Stalin

Stalin sought absolute power and clearly recognized the power that
information confers. Accordingly, he acted as his own central intelligence analyst, monopolizing the final collation, evaluation, and
interpretation of intelligence from the separate agencies. Thus
Golikov was directly responsible only to Stalin and submitted few
reports to the chief of staff (Zhukov) or to the commissar of defense
(Timoshenko), who were consequently somewhat in the dark about
the extent and quality of warnings about German intentions.[24]

All intelligence reports—at least those of the GRU and, presumably, the NKGB—were carried forward to Stalin (and Molotov) by
Comrade Gnedin (or Gnedich), who was apparently on the staff of
Stalin's personal secretariat. Gnedin held this position for two
years, including the period immediately preceding the German invasion.[25] Although almost nothing has been revealed about the
workings of this crucial secretariat, headed by the sinister A. N.
Poskrebyshev, it does not seem to have had any evaluative function.
Nevertheless, because it was the master conduit or channel linking
Stalin to the rest of his communication system, Poskrebyshev was
in a unique "gatekeeper" position to edit selectively the reports
and people reaching the top.[26]

Numerous "inside" accounts of the real perceptions of the top Soviet leadership preceding BARBAROSSA have appeared.[27] These comprise a few contemporary reactions intended to influence foreign leaders or local juniors, some after-the-fact statements offered in justification by those responsible, and many recent reinterpretations of these perceptions by Stalin's successors. All such sources must be taken as biased or even as deliberately misleading. Nevertheless, they are all consistent with four tentative conclusions:

1. that Stalin clearly recognized the *threat* of a German attack;

2. that while he did not realize—at least not until the previous day, if then—that B-day had been set for 22 June, he did not rule out an imminent German attack;

3. that, in any case, any German attack would definitely be preceded by an ultimatum that would give him the initiative at the last moment; and

4. that he would then hope to yield sufficient concessions to buy peace until mid-1942, when he believed the Red Army would be ready to defend itself.

Even if we concede to Stalin a perception that a German attack was forthcoming, it is almost certain that he expected a final forewarning to come in the form of a German ultimatum. If so, it was not at all an unreasonable interpretation of the course of events and the available signals. It is only by hindsight that we know Hitler had privately decided otherwise sometime in 1940. Indeed, as late as 15 June 1941, Ribbentrop himself lied to both Ciano and the Hungarians that final demands would be presented by the end of the month and would precede any final decision on war or peace.[28] This assessment was also almost universal among those few senior German officials who were not privy to BARBAROSSA. For example, Ambassador Schulenburg and his counselor of embassy, Gustav Hilger, held to this view until they were notified otherwise by a confidential agent on 14 June.[29] This was also the unexceptional view of the British, the Americans, and the Swedish envoy to Berlin (discussed in the following section). We must assume that this virtual agreement among foreign intelligence and policy elites—including the German—was known to Stalin, and it is reasonable to presume that he found this mass of informed consensus quite convincing.

There can be no question that the Bolsheviks and Nazis believed each other to be unreconcilable enemies, determined on nothing less than the eradication of the other. However, they did not specify the deadline for this supposedly inevitable outcome. Moreover, the Russian Bolsheviks had always believed it possible for the Soviet Union to make certain temporary accommodations with Germany, and many German officials shared this view. Hence throughout the 1920s and early 1930s, the Red Army and the incipient German army, the Reichswehr, conspired to circumvent the international efforts to keep them both militarily weak. At the same time, the Comintern and the German authorities were free to wage civil war, both sides tacitly accepting the Bolshevik fiction of the independence of the Comintern from Soviet government control. When Hitler came to power in 1933, he quickly severed the hitherto mutually profitable military collaboration.[30] While Stalin sought to keep open an option to restore liaison, he recognized as surely as Hitler that such accommodations could be only temporary.* Indeed, the final rapprochement represented by the Nazi-Soviet Pact of 1939 was still in full effect on the day Hitler attacked. (See Chapter 2.)

The Soviet leadership was as fully aware as the Germans of Hitler's programmatic statements regarding Russia as revealed in *Mein Kampf* in the mid-twenties. Thus, as early as 1935 and again in 1936, Molotov publicly quoted and attacked that specific portion of Hitler's program.[31] It is certain that the Bolsheviks recognized the sincerity of the Führer's aggressive intentions.

---

* The only knowledgeable insider to argue on the basis of evidence that Stalin was blind to Hitler's recalcitrance was General Walter Krivitsky, the defected chief *Rezident* of the GRU in Western Europe. But, like GRU Colonel Penkovsky after him, Krivitsky mistook a specific option or contingency for set policy. Stalin (and Khrushchev) was more flexible than these middle-level officers recognized. See W. G. Krivitsky, *In Stalin's Secret Service* (New York: Harper, 1939), pp. 1–25.

Soviet Expectations

'Pon my word, Watson, you are coming along wonderfully. We have really done very well indeed. It is true that you have missed everything of importance, but you have hit upon the method.
—Sherlock Holmes, in "A Case of Identity" (1891)

It is not known when or how Stalin first perceived that his carefully nurtured pact with Hitler was about to be unilaterally dissolved. However, the fragmentary evidence gives tentative answers to both these questions. The earliest clear indication dates from 16 April 1941. We have already seen that a substantial body of intelligence, leaks, and rumors of the German buildup had accumulated by that date. Soviet intelligence was at least as aware of these indications as any other national intelligence system, but we do not know what assessment they made of them. The evidence suggests that the inherent ambiguity of the available signals combined with deliberate German disinformation to minimize the Russians' perception of threat. (See Chapter 9.)

There are unquestionable indications that by mid-spring 1941 the Soviet authorities were sufficiently apprehensive that they began to alert some lower echelons of the Communist party, secret police, and military to the possibility of war. They were able to do this on such a selective basis, avoiding the indiscriminate publicity of the mass media, by limiting these warnings to the channel of their well-developed oral agitation-propaganda network.[32] However, only a small number of persons were evidently reached by this means, and the thin evidence suggests that it was done on an uncharacteristically spotty basis, suggesting that no clear policy line had been decided on in the Kremlin. For example, postwar interviews with a dozen or so defected Soviet officers ranging in rank from lieutenant to general failed to find any who recalled that their agitprop meetings had given any warning of a possible German invasion.[33] Nevertheless, some officers were forewarned at meetings.

The earliest such briefings that have been alleged are those said to have been made by Communist party officials at factory meetings in Moscow during the first fortnight in March 1941. On these occasions the officials were said to have alluded to possible Russo-German conflict.[34] Next, on 16 April, General Klokov, the deputy chief of the Political Division of the Lenin Military Air Academy in Moscow, arrived fresh from a meeting of the Main Political Directorate of the Army primed with the following message that he delivered to an open meeting of the academy's council and faculty:

The position at present is that war may break out at any moment between the U.S.S.R. and Germany. . . . It is essential that we should not be caught unawares. . . . The Germans are already concentrating their troops on our Western frontiers. . . . They are carrying out systematic reconnaissance flights across our borders.[35]

It seems plausible that this new cautionary line arose in immediate response to Hitler's impulsive invasion of Russia's Balkan ally, Yugoslavia, ten days before. This is confirmed by Wolfgang Leonhard, who was then a young German Communist student in the political emigration in Moscow. He recalls that some time about early May his class of fellow Comintern students was addressed by Walter Ulbricht at the headquarters of MOPR, the International Organization for Aid to Militants of the Revolution. Ulbricht made the startling announcement that the class character of the war might change in mid-course. He explained to his astonished audience:

This fact is particularly important in connection with the attack by Germany and Italy on Yugoslavia and Greece. There are certain factors to be noted, especially in the case of Yugoslavia, which point to the possibility that one might speak in some respects of a justified defensive war on the part of these two peoples against foreign attack.[36]

But, then, on 3 June the Army Supreme Military Council—chaired by Marshal Timoshenko—was convened to vote on a draft directive instructing the army's political commissars to stress the imminent danger of war. Georgi M. Malenkov sharply attacked this draft, arguing that "The document is formulated in primitive terms, as though we were going to war tomorrow." Stalin supported Malenkov's view, and the instructions were not issued.[37]

The direct consequence of this policy was to reduce the state of readiness throughout all subordinate army headquarters. Moreover, it strongly discouraged the upward reporting of operational intelligence about the German border deployment from the frontier army and NKVD Border Guard units. For example, MVD Lieutenant-Colonel Grigori Burlutski, who was then an army junior lieutenant on the Rumanian border, recalls that the intelligence collected by his unit and the local NKGB undercover agents was deplored as indications of cowardice and panic in the face of enemy provocation; and at least two senior officers in Burlutski's unit were dismissed for persisting to report German preparations.[38] Similarly, the commander of the Western Special Military District (headquartered at Minsk), General of the Army Dmitri Pavlov, when faced with these warnings took steps to prevent any "alarmist" from answering any German "provocations" with fire. And to the reports received the night of the twenty-first, he merely commented, "Seems rubbish to me," and refused to leave the officer's club. The actual attack report was dismissed by him the next morning with the remark, "Can't fathom it—some sort of devilish trick."[39]

Only the Red Navy managed to maintain a fairly consistent policy of alert. This is primarily to the credit of the Navy's Commissar Admiral Kuznetsov and chief naval political commissar Ivan Rogov. They were puzzled by the discrepancy between the increasing warnings and rumors of war and the bland tone of the Soviet press, but they decided on their own to encourage naval officers and political commissars to stress vigilance and the fact that Germany was the probable enemy. This line was consistently pushed throughout the Navy during June. For example, on 14 June, when Vice-Admiral I. I. Azarov finished briefing the personnel of the cruiser *Krasny Kavkaz* on the German threat, he explained away the sharp contrast between his statements and TASS's denunciation of the war rumors as mere provocation, which had appeared in that morning's *Pravda,* by stating that the TASS communiqué was intended only for foreign consumption.[40]

Perhaps the earliest and most stunning clue to Stalin's recognition of Hitler's threat was the revival of the Mosfilm production of *Aleksandr Nevsky*. This blatantly patriotic and savagely anti-Nazi and anti-German film had been explicitly commissioned by the Kremlin and directed by Eisenstein, who was closely supervised by D. I. Vasiliev to ensure political correctness. It had originally been released in late 1938. Then, with the signing of the Nazi-Soviet Pact in August 1939, it was deemed too provocative and promptly withdrawn along with all other anti-Nazi propaganda; and Eisenstein was made to join the new German-Soviet "cultural" program.[41] Now, in March 1941, *Aleksandr Nevsky* was revived at a special Kremlin performance and awarded a Stalin Prize. Although the screening was private, it was publicly reported in *Pravda* and *Izvestiya*.[42] Finally, early in May, Eisenstein gave *Life* correspondents Erskine Caldwell and Margaret Bourke-White a private showing and remarked cryptically: "We think that it will not be much longer before *Alexander Nevsky* will be shown in public cinema theatres again." He was right. *Nevsky* was back in general release by 28 June, six days after the invasion.[43]

The earliest indication directly from Stalin himself was in his ambiguous telephone conversation with Ilya Ehrenburg on 24 April 1941. Ehrenburg instantly interpreted Stalin's permission to publish his long-suppressed, openly anti-Nazi novel, *The Fall of Paris,* as proof that Stalin knew war to be imminent.[44] *

During the May Day parade in Red Square, the most important item in the display of Soviet military might and political solidarity was the quiet but very public unveiling of Maxim Litvinov. He had been unexpectedly invited to join Stalin and the other top officials on the reviewing platform of the Lenin Mausoleum.[45] Litvinov too had been politically embalmed. His resignation as foreign commissar on 3 May 1939 symbolized the failure of the anti-Fascist policy of "collective security" that he had championed with fervent consistency. His replacement by Molotov introduced the new isolationist policy of nervous rear-guard-action appeasement of a now

* Ehrenburg's analysis was truly "kremlinological" since it was not based on any intimate personal or "inside" knowledge of Stalin. This was the only time he ever spoke with the Vozhd.

unleashed Hitler that culminated in August in the Nazi-Soviet
Pact. Litvinov was not shot but simply placed in reserve. The nadir
of his career was reached on 20 February 1941, when he was publicly dropped from membership in the Communist Party Central
Committee—another act of appeasing Hitler. Thus, while his sudden reappearance was not commented on in the Soviet press, his
physical presence alone was mute proof of some new line of thought
in the Kremlin.*

Sometime around early May, while temporarily back in Moscow
for consultations, the Soviet ambassador to Vichy France, Alexander Bogomolov, spoke to French Ambassador Gaston Bergery. He
made the significant remark that Russia would welcome good commercial relations with Germany but would have no part of any
New Order in which Germany would be prime beneficiary and
Russia would be merely one of the exploited. Bogomolov added
that Russia would forcibly resist such integration into Germany's
New Order. Bogomolov's remarks were undoubtedly intended for
German ears as a "trial balloon." Although I have no direct evidence, the pro-Nazi Bergery probably did pass this word to his
German counterpart. (He did discuss it with Japanese Ambassador
Tatekawa and even telegraphed a report to Charles Arsène-Henry,
the Vichy ambassador in Tokyo.)†

The Russians seemingly made systematic use of one most interesting ruse to communicate their intentions to the Germans. At least
this is the recent conclusion of Professor McSherry of Pennsylvania
State University. As noted earlier, the Soviet Union was the only
country in early 1941 whose secret enciphered diplomatic, intelligence, and senior-level military communications were totally se-

---

* During this period, from May 1939 to at least February 1941, Litvinov
continued to hold a post as chief of the Foreign Affairs Information Bureau in
the Communist Party Central Committee Secretariat. With almost all his
former colleagues executed or imprisoned, his experience was needed in this
political intelligence reporting post. See Pope (1943), 458.
† Bergery's telegram to Arsène-Henry was secretly leaked to U.S. Ambassador
Grew by the French counselor in Tokyo, Guy F. J. Fain. Grew promptly forwarded this information to U.S. Secretary of State Hull. See telegram, Grew
to Hull, 23 May 1941, as printed in *FRUS: 1941*, 1 (1958), 146–147.

cure from unauthorized interception *and* reading because they used the unbreakable "one-time" key system. There was one exception: the telegraph line from the Soviet Foreign Ministry to its consular offices in the Far East. These messages were being regularly intercepted in 1941 from at least as early as 6 March until at least into June by August Ponschab, the German consul in Harbin. (Presumably these messages were being passed to Herr Ponschab by the local Japanese authorities in Manchuria who controlled the telegraph lines.) These messages—obviously in a low-grade cipher —were then decrypted in the consulate and transmitted to the Wilhelmstrasse, specifically to State Secretary Weizsäcker, who was seemingly quite convinced of their significance because he kept them in his personal "Russia" file. However, Professor McSherry has shown by a preliminary analysis that it is likely that the Russians knew of this leak (indeed, perhaps created it) and deliberately used this channel to pass a mixture of trial balloons and disinformation. In any case, the themes contained in these particular messages conveyed precisely the signals the Russians *wanted* the Germans to get. Thus from early March through May they stressed the sincerity of Soviet adherence to the Nazi-Soviet Pact, the satisfactory progress of negotiations with Germany, and a hands-off policy in the Balkans. They gave priority to "the destruction of the English Empire" but also warned Germany that the Soviets were prepared to "protect their interests" if pushed too far.[46]

On 15 May Molotov told the Japanese ambassador that the rumors of an impending German attack on Russia were entirely unfounded "British and American propaganda," and their relations were, in fact, "excellent." At least this is what Ambassador Tatekawa reported to U.S. Ambassador Steinhardt the following evening.[47]

On 5 June "President" Kalinin, the chairman of the Presidium of the Supreme Soviet, was alleged to have asserted in a speech at the Political-Military Academy that: "The Germans are preparing to attack us, but we are ready. The sooner they come, the better: we will wring their necks." [48]

It is apparent that Stalin by 13 June recognized that his relations with Hitler had reached a desperate state. That evening Molotov presented German Ambassador Schulenburg with the advance text of the famed TASS communiqué broadcast later that night (at 7 P.M.) and published the next morning in the Soviet central press. This very curious document is worth repeating in its entirety.

Even before the arrival of Sir Stafford Cripps, English ambassador to the USSR, in London, but in particular after his arrival, rumours began to appear in the English and generally in the foreign press about the 'proximity of war between the Soviet Union and Germany'.

According to these rumours, first, Germany has presented to Russia demands of a territorial and economic character, and negotiations are now being conducted between Germany and the Soviet Union for the conclusion of a new and closer agreement between the two countries. The rumours state, secondly, that the USSR has rejected the demands, as a result of which Germany has begun to concentrate troops on its frontier with the USSR in preparation for an attack on the USSR; and, thirdly, that the Soviet Union in its turn has begun to step up preparations for war with Germany, and is also concentrating troops on its western frontiers.

Although these rumours are obviously absurd, responsible circles in Moscow have just the same considered it necessary in view of the constant repetition of these propaganda rumours spread by forces hostile to the Soviet Union and Germany, forces interested in the further expansion and spreading of the war, to authorize Tass to state that they are clumsy fabrications.

Tass states that: 1. Germany has not presented any demands to the USSR, nor has it asked for any new and closer agreement. Thus there could be no question of any negotiations on this subject.

2. According to Soviet data Germany, like the USSR, is also strictly observing the stipulations of the Soviet-German non-aggression pact, and therefore, in the opinion of Soviet circles, rumours of Germany's intention to break the pact and open an attack on the USSR are devoid of all foundation; the recent transfer of German troops, freed from operations in the Balkans, to the eastern and north-eastern regions of Germany is, it must be assumed, connected with other reasons which have no bearing on Soviet-German relations;

3. The USSR, consistently with its policy of peace, has observed and intends to observe the provisions of the Soviet-German non-aggression pact, and therefore rumours that the USSR is preparing for war with Germany are lies and provocations;

4. The sole purpose of the summer call-up of the Red Army reserves and of the forthcoming exercises is the training of the re-

serves and the testing of the railway system which, as is known, takes place each year. To interpret these measures as hostile to Germany is, to say the least, absurd.[49]

This desperate but carefully drafted TASS release indicates that the official Soviet position (specifically, Stalin's) was still a delusion just seven days before disaster. It reveals, among many things, the persisting belief that these rumors were a British provocation (confusing need with action); a clear recognition of urgency (while mistaking Hitler's inexorably approaching B-Tag for a ripening occasion to open negotiations); and a pointed implication that economic or even territorial demands were not categorically excluded from negotiations.[50]

The Germans made no response to this TASS approach. They did not even deign to reprint it in their press, although its importance—if not its significance—was recognized by the leading international news media. Furthermore, the Press Section of the German Foreign Ministry declined all questions about the TASS communiqué at its press conferences. Thus the Russians were left in suspense, without the reassurance they had, I presume, sought to provoke. Indeed, the absence of a German response probably increased the sense of threat. Thus, when six days after the German attack, the Vice-Chief of the just-created Soviet Information Bureau (Sovinformburo), Solomon Lozovsky, summoned the Moscow foreign press corps to its first wartime briefing, he asserted that the Soviet government had been warned that Germany was to become an enemy by virtue of the fact that the controlled German press had not published the conciliatory TASS communiqué.[51]

Churchill's first wartime visit to Moscow ended on 15/16 August 1942 with a six-hour private midnight dinner in Stalin's apartment. There Stalin told the Prime Minister some of the circumstances surrounding the signing of the Russo-German Pact back in August 1939. Stalin asserted that he knew Hitler would eventually attack and, as Russia was then quite unprepared to resist, he had signed the pact (and joined in the attack on Poland) to gain needed time.[52] This seems to have been Stalin's undeviating strategy until it was overtaken by Hitler's decisive act of 22 June. The earliest verification of this is found in American Ambassador Steinhardt's report to Hull on 5 May: "I have learned from a reliable source that Stalin recently made the statement to a Soviet official that he did not expect an attack by or war with Germany this year and that he anticipated 'satisfactory' negotiations with Germany." [53]

On 5 May 1941, Stalin delivered a forty-minute address at a Kremlin reception for the combined graduating classes of military academy officers. His theme was, "We must be prepared to deal with any surprises," and he discussed the changes in the Red Army's organization and equipment that had been taken to meet the lessons of modern war. Beyond these bare facts as reported in *Pravda* the next day, nothing official has ever appeared on just what Stalin did take forty minutes to say. But there are a number of secondhand and thirdhand reports that, while often contradictory, indicate that Stalin probably included the following significant points.

1. The title phrase, "be prepared for any surprises," meant that the situation was most serious, and a German attack in the near future should be recognized as distinctly possible, if unlikely.

2. Although the Red Army was now a "new army . . . equipped . . . with modern weapons," the Wehrmacht was still "the best army both in *matériel* and organization"—but not invincible. The Red Army still needed reequipping and, particularly, training and political indoctrination.

3. Soviet diplomacy would strive to forestall any German attack until at least the fall, when weather would rule it out.

4. If such a diplomatic effort succeeded, then, *almost inevitably*, war would break out in 1942, either by a German invasion or a Soviet preemption.[54]

At least some members of the NKVD had concluded by May that war was only a month off. This was certainly true of one NKVD captain in the department handling surveillance of the foreign diplomatic corps in Moscow. On 22 May he confidentially disclosed

his conclusions to one of his former *mozhno* ("permitted girls"),*
Nora Korzhenkova, the twenty-two-year-old daughter of a recently
purged senior NKVD official. However, it is not clear whether the
captain had been warned through official channels or had merely
inferred it from such quite visible facts as the intensive Soviet
troop deployments and his own call-up scheduled for 23 May.[55]

On Saturday, 21 June at 9:30 P.M., Ambassador Schulenburg
called on Molotov at the Kremlin in accord with the latter's unexpected summons. Molotov stated:

There were a number of indications that the German Government
was dissatisfied with the Soviet Government. Rumors were even
current that a war was impending between Germany and the
Soviet Union. They found sustenance in the fact that there was
no reaction whatsoever on the part of Germany to the Tass report
of June 13. . . . The Soviet Government was unable to understand the reasons for Germany's dissatisfaction. . . . [I] would
appreciate it if [Schulenburg] could tell [me] what had brought
about the present situation in German-Russian relations.

Schulenburg replied with great embarrassment that he could not
answer, because he "lacked the pertinent information." [56] Molotov's desperate and obsequious attempt to induce the Germans
to name their demands was simply irrelevant.

In an embarrassed radio broadcast on 3 July, Stalin implied that
the Germans had achieved total surprise but, incidentally, suggested his own innocent gullibility in the face of duplicity by
stating:

The fact of the matter is that the troops of Germany, as a country
at war, were already fully mobilized . . . and in a state of complete readiness, only awaiting the signal to move into action,
whereas Soviet troops had still to effect mobilization and move up
to the frontiers. Of no little importance in this respect is the fact
that Fascist Germany suddenly and treacherously violated the non-
aggression pact. . . .[57]

Five days later, he told Cripps that the Red Army was still suffering
from the element of surprise.[58] And, on 31 July, Stalin admitted his

---

* Women allowed by the NKVD to provide secretarial, housekeeping, and
other services to foreigners in the USSR in return for acting as NKVD informers.

surprise in even more explicit terms to President Roosevelt's personal envoy, Harry Hopkins, saying "he himself believed that Hitler would not strike." Visibly shaken, Stalin confessed pathetically: "Once we trusted this man." He also volunteered the information that he not only had not intended a preemptive attack but "had no intention of doing anything but be straightforward in his dealing with Germany." These were private admissions, only Litvinov being present as interpreter. The impression of total gullibility is quite credible because Hopkins himself failed to recognize the significance of Stalin's remarks, publishing what he intended to be a glowing picture of a stalwart wartime leader.[59]

Some time in the fall of 1941, in Washington, Walter Duranty asked Ambassador Umansky if he had been as surprised by the suddenness of the attack as the Moscow foreign press corps, including Duranty himself. Umansky replied: "I certainly was, although I knew that the clouds were darkening." Duranty pressed on to ask if there had been an ultimatum or, at least, grumbling about Russian supplies. Umansky elaborated: "To the best of my knowledge, none. The attack was made without warning, in Hitler's own treacherous manner." [60]

Maxim Litvinov soon added his public testimony, contradicting both Stalin's public speeches and Stalin's private discussion with Harry Hopkins, at which the no-doubt-shocked Litvinov had been interpreter. He had always been one of the more independently minded Bolsheviks. Now, restored by Stalin to office—and life itself—from the limbo of the Great Purge, Litvinov proved remarkably independent in speech as well. On 13 December 1941, six days after arriving in Washington to take up his new post as ambassador to the United States, Litvinov told reporters:

My government did receive warnings as to the treacherous intentions of Hitler with regard to the Soviet Union, but it did not take them seriously and this not because it believed in the sacredness of Hitler's signature, or did not believe him capable of violating the treaties he signed, and the oft-repeated solemn promises he made, but because it considered that it would have been madness on his part to undertake war in the east against such a powerful land as ours, before finishing off his war in the west.[61]

These are brave and quite credible words from the one senior Soviet official who had no direct responsibility for the Hitler-Stalin nonaggression pact or the events leading to BARBAROSSA.

Stalin explicitly admitted the extent of his surprise in his Order of the Day on 23 February 1942, if we can accept at face value a belated, public exposition:

> The Germans now no longer have the military advantage they possessed during the first months of the war as a result of their treacherous and sudden attack. . . . This removes the inequality in fighting conditions created by the suddenness of the German fascist attack. Now the outcome of the war will be decided not by such a fortuitous element as surprise, but by permanently operating factors. . . .[62]

Later in the war (probably in October 1943) Stalin told Eden that Russia had risked antagonizing Hitler by giving open diplomatic support to Yugoslavia on 5 April 1941 because he was "fairly sure by then" that Hitler would attack Russia anyway. Eden seriously doubted this belated explanation, finding it inconsistent with Stalin's statements and actions at the time.[63] Eden conveniently forgets the considerable body of data showing Stalin to have pursued a flexible two-handed policy, coupling outright appeasement on some issues with desperate stands and efforts on others. Soviet policy toward Yugoslavia was a clear instance of the latter.

Members of the Soviet embassy in Tokyo admitted to John Scott only days after the German invasion that Soviet public policy vis-à-vis Germany was largely motivated by an effort to avoid provocation. Scott, a pro-Soviet American free-lance journalist, had been expelled from Moscow on 10 June for a series of prescient articles about the deteriorating Russo-German relationship that he had published in the British press. (See Chapter 7.) These diplomats told Scott by way of apology for his expulsion: "You must understand the situation, Mr. Scott. The things you said in your articles were true enough, but we were trying in every way to avoid provoking Germany. It was obvious that we could not allow correspondents to write that sort of thing without taking some measures." [64] The implication that the Russians had shared Scott's belief that Stalin's policy was to appease Hitler while girding for war is quite plausible. However, it should be noted that Scott's informants were possibly the very men who had been directly receiving Richard Sorge's detailed intelligence reports on BARBA-ROSSA from the German embassy. (Sorge's main contact at the Soviet embassy was then Viktor Zaitsev, the second secretary and GRU "legal" *Rezident.*) Thus their views may have been only personal convictions based on Sorge's compelling evidence and not necessarily views shared by Moscow.

On 15 May Molotov reportedly told the Japanese ambassador to Moscow, General Tatekawa, that the rumors of a German attack were a mere provocation of "British and American propaganda," entirely fantastic in view of the "excellent" Russo-German relations.[65]

Two years after the war the ill-fated Nikolai Voznesensky, deputy premier and chief of the State Planning Commission, admitted that the economic plan in effect at the moment of the invasion had envisioned that the third quarter of 1941 would be "a relatively peaceful period." [66]

Soviet Decisions

It is useful for the counter-revolution to call us to battle now, but we must not yield to the provocation, we must show a maximal revolutionary reserve.

—Stalin, Speech at the Petrograd Party Conference, 16 July 1917

We do nothing without our Comrade Stalin.

—Molotov, 5 April 1941

No single Soviet decision was based on a unitary interpretation of the incoming intelligence. No one ordered a general "Red Alert." Nor had such a single order been prepared, much less a rapid centralized bureaucratic procedure for its dissemination. Soviet interpretations of Germany's intentions, plans, and action both changed with time and varied with individual Russians. Not only did Stalin make more than one "decision," but his subordinates each took individual decisions ranging from no action to full alert affecting their own local or service commands. This section will summarize the actual decisions and measures taken inside the Soviet Union to meet a possible military onslaught. They will be seen to be fragmentary, decentralized, spastic, and inadequate.

One clear proof of surprise of timing is if crisis catches the key officials pursuing daily bureaucratic or personal routines. And weekend crises tend to catch political and military bureaucracies at their least responsive, as Hitler and, later, the Japanese found. Casual normality characterized most Russian leaders on the night of 21/22 June 1941. Only the Red Navy was on a full standby alert. Zhdanov, party boss of Leningrad and Stalin's righthand man, was vacationing at Sochi on the Black Sea, where he had gone two days before.[67] Most senior military officials had left their Moscow offices at the normal 6 P.M. dinner time. Only a few, such as Navy Commissar Kuznetsov, People's Commissar for Defense Timoshenko, and Chief of Staff Zhukov, alerted by last-minute omens, remained at their desks.[68] Thousands of Red Army officers were, like Zhdanov, vacationing at Black Sea resorts.[69] The Soviet diplomatic corps abroad was similarly taken unawares. The ambassador in Berlin, Dekanozov, had ordered a staff picnic outing for the morning of the attack;[70] and the ambassador to Rome, Nikolai Gorelkin, was off bathing at a resort with his staff and gave an impression of complete surprise to his colleagues in the diplomatic corps.[71] Yet these were the very men—Kremlin chiefs, military commanders, and overseas diplomats—upon whom Russia depended for evaluation of the last-minute evidence warning against strategic surprise, for urgent decisions, or for a responsive national defense.

Another significant measure of the degree of strategic surprise visited on the Kremlin was the abject failure of the Comintern to anticipate the forthcoming reverse in Russo-German relations. With one possible exception, the various national Communist parties did nothing to prepare themselves for any imminent change in international relations. They acted as if the Russo-German non-aggression pact of 1939 rather than Munich had brought peace in their time. No warnings or contingency instructions were sent out from Moscow.[72] Indeed, seemingly the only warning and instructions were those sent *to* Moscow and locally carried out by the independent-minded Yugoslav Communists under Tito.[73] Stalin's personal responsibility for the Comintern's unreadiness is clear, for he had exercised virtually total mastery over the Comintern policy and apparatus since 1938. Furthermore, the critical year of 1941 found the Comintern stripped by Stalin of not only its own centralized intelligence service, the OMS,[74] but even two entire parties, the Polish and Korean Communist parties, which had simply been abolished in 1938. That the Communist parties in Germany, Czechoslovakia, Japan, Britain, France, and the United States did not change their *public* policy is understandable as part of Stalin's appeasement and fear of provocation of Hitler; but their failure to prepare for crises unnecessarily weakened them for their forthcoming role in the resistance movements and as lobbyists for their Kremlin masters.

Although the Comintern took no special steps to meet the German threat, the top leaders in Moscow evidently shared Stalin's uneasiness. We have seen earlier in this chapter that Walter Ulbricht, the German Communist party leader in Moscow, had passed veiled warnings to cadres. Moreover, the story circulated in Moscow that Dmitry Manuilsky, the second secretary of the Comintern, had declared as early as the end of March that "a war with Nazi Germany could now scarcely be avoided." [75]

As the evidence of the approaching crisis accumulated in the Kremlin, Stalin grew more cautious, but in a peculiarly self-defeating way. He clearly determined to avoid any actions he believed might *provoke* a German attack. This faulty judgment is the only "rational" explanation for the almost total tactical surprise that overtook the local Red Army units on the morning of 22 June.[76] Stalin's efforts at hardheaded bargaining between Russo-German equals had foundered with Molotov's mission to Berlin in November 1940, and his last gratuitous slap at Hitler was the signing of the Soviet-Yugoslav treaty of friendship on the eve of the Nazi invasion of the Balkans. Thereafter, Stalin's policy was largely one of appeasement—some unilateral concessions and an expressed willingness to negotiate, both coupled with avoiding provocations.

Stalin was understandably reluctant to make unilateral concessions to Germany and thereby weaken his position in what he presumed would be the upcoming Russo-German negotiations. Nevertheless, he did signal his willingness to be conciliatory by making a series of mild unilateral concessions. Thus between 9 May and 2 June the Soviet Union publicly and officially severed diplomatic relations with Yugoslavia, Norway, Belgium, and Greece. These actions were taken without any pressure from Germany.[77] Also, on 30 May, Stalin personally offered the Finns 20,000 tons of grain, which were promptly delivered.[78]

The Soviet attitude toward "provocations" is both important and strange. For the ideologically trained Bolshevik, *provokatsia* is an omnipresent potential tool of his enemy, and he has been virtually conditioned to respond to it according to two rules: never provoke an enemy and never be provoked by him. To do otherwise means that the good Communist has abdicated control over the thrust of history and handed the initiative to hostile forces.[79] In the four or five months before BARBAROSSA-*Tag,* the Soviet leaders perceived two distinct types of provocation, one being the warnings from their implacable Anglo-American capitalist foe and the other from their temporary German "Fascist" ally.

Given their strong preconceptions regarding provocation, it is not surprising that the Russians viewed the Anglo-American warnings with grave suspicion. Stalin was quite right to recognize that any warnings from that quarter not only would not be disinterested but might well conceal a calculated provocation. He presumably understood that the very survival of beleaguered Britain urgently depended on German arms becoming engaged elsewhere and that Russia was the only power left in Europe that could supply this diversion. Moreover, as seen in Chapters 3–5, the Anglo-American warnings—although based on hard intelligence—were so degraded in transmission to the Russians as to be little more than unsubstantiated assertions; and some, such as Lord Casey's (warning no. 36), were patently absurd. In general, the previous studies of BARBAROSSA have overly stressed the warnings from Britain and the United States. First, they were not particularly credible, although Soviet intelligence was remiss in not attempting to verify more closely some of the more circumstantial ones. Second, Soviet intelligence was already well provided with its own warning signs and signals.

More serious in its effects was Stalin's ill-considered effort to avoid rising to the bait of what he imagined to be *German* provocations. It is frankly quite difficult for me to understand precisely by what mechanism such provocations could operate. I can only suppose that, as the initial Soviet war directives imply, he unrealistically presumed that the German intention could be a limited attack for narrowly limited geographic and political objectives.

There had been a rather steady Russian troop buildup in its western zone ever since the 1939 Polish crisis (see Table 3.2). Furthermore, an actual state of emergency had been declared in the Russian western zone by 10 April 1941, apparently in response to the suddenly increased threat of general war accompanying the German attack on the Balkans.[80] And we have already noted (warning 5) that Stalin had responded to Luftwaffe reconnaissance sorties with some by the Red Air Force. But the state of Russian readiness did not at all keep pace with the German timetable.

More or less normal conditions prevailed on the Russian side of the frontier until midnight of 21/22 June when the Red Army and Navy issued orders for a state of combat alert to defend against an imminent German attack.[81] Of course, given the creaking, ponderous bureaucratic machinery available, only the most senior commands and a handful of local units were reached in the two or three desperate hours remaining between peace and war. For most units, their first warning of the attack was delivered by German bombers, strafers, artillery barrage, or infantry assault. In some cases, counterfire was withheld because the local commanders mistook these all-out assaults for local accidents or probes, which they were forbidden to respond to.[82]

The first operational order of the Red Army command was not issued until 0715 Moscow time, three hours after the attack. Even then, its vague, defensive tone implies a continuing hope of avoiding general war. Thus, while it ordered the Red Army to repel all enemy forces on Russian soil, it directed that "unless given special authorization ground troops will not cross the frontier." Similarly, while the Red Air Force was ordered to mount air strikes, they were to be limited "to a depth of 100–150 kilometers into German territory," and it was explicitly directed that "there will be no raids on the territory of Finland and Rumania without specific orders." [83] But Khrushchev exaggerated in stating:

Moscow issued the order that the German fire was not to be returned . . . because Stalin, despite evident facts, thought that the war had not yet started, that this was only a provocative action on the part of several undisciplined sections of the German Army, and that our reaction might serve as a reason for the Germans to begin the war.[84]

At most, it would be fair to conclude that Stalin and Molotov may have falsely believed that the war might still be kept somewhat limited, specifically regarding the participation of Rumania and Finland.

BARBAROSSA gives a rare view of the immediate psychopathological effect of strategic surprise on both its perpetrator and its recipient. Hitler was elated, "spiritually free," "happy to be relieved of these mental agonies." [85] Stalin, conversely, had a nervous breakdown. The purportedly omniscient Vozhd was immediately precipitated into a paralyzed failure of nerve, if we can believe the recent rewriting of Soviet history by Premier Khrushchev, Ambassador Maisky, and Admiral Kuznetsov.* Stalin was gradually induced to resume active leadership only by several terrified members of his drifting, decapitated Politburo. On 3 July he finally broadcast— but with most uncharacteristic agitation, hesitation, and emotion—

---

* Indeed, Stalin was so withdrawn at this time that it was widely thought he was away from Moscow, at his Black Sea retreat. See, for example, Markoff (1950), 175. However, Zhukov's eyewitness account conclusively places Stalin in his Kremlin office during the evening and night of 21/22 June.

to his "Comrades! Citizens! Brothers and Sisters! . . . , my dear friends!" [86] However, Stalin was sufficiently recovered by 8 July to grant Ambassador Cripps an hour-long interview to receive and discuss a message from Churchill.[87] On the nineteenth he took over the Defense Commissariat. And, at last, on 9 August he became commander in chief of the Soviet armed forces.[88] His élan restored, Stalin had again taken command.

9 The Uncertain Trumpet

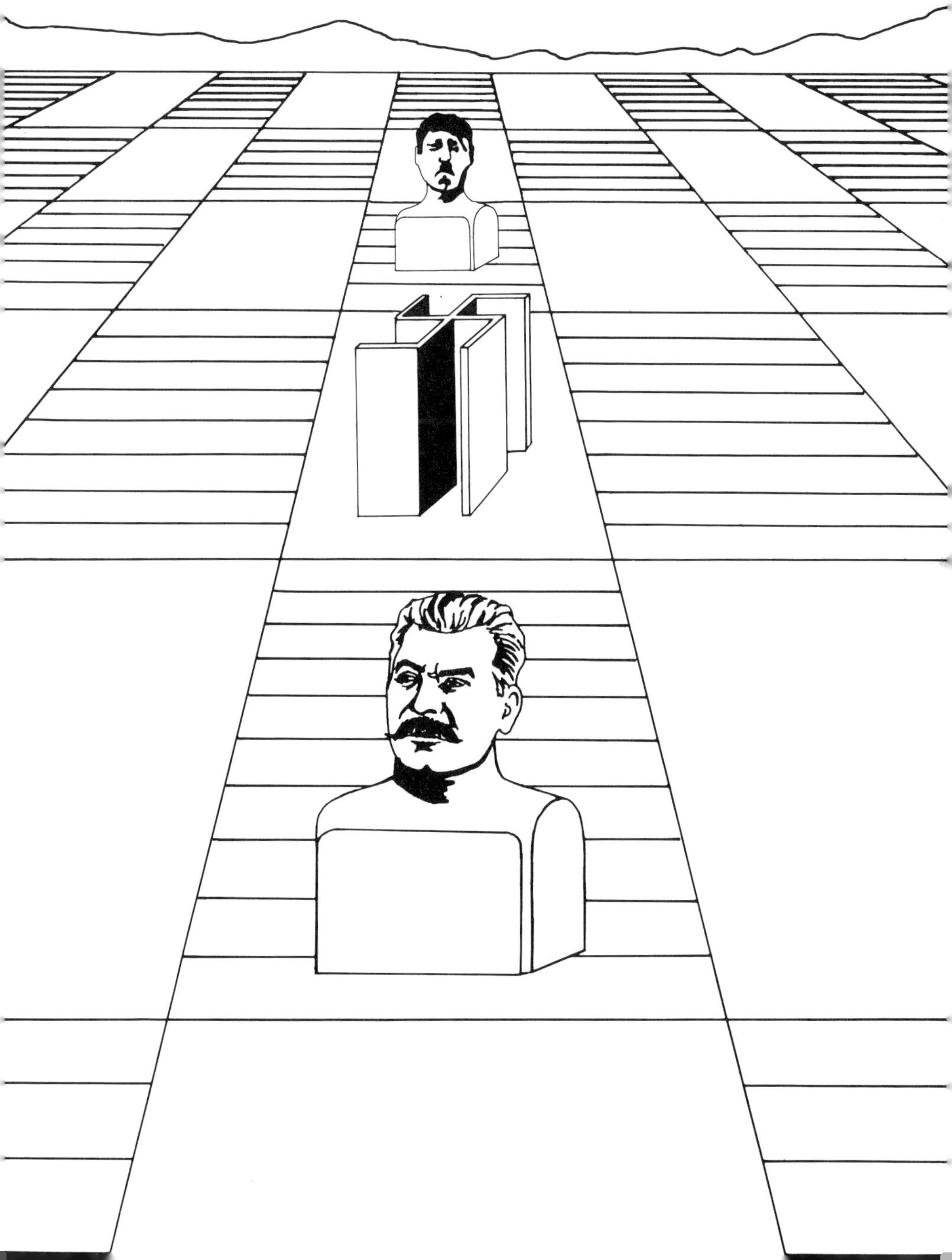

If the trumpet give an uncertain sound,
who shall prepare himself to the battle.

−Corinthians 14 :8

So far this book has scanned the evidence on BARBAROSSA, Hitler's plan to crush Bolshevik Russia. Specifically, the chapters have covered: Hitler's decisions about the attack. The authentic information, the misinformation, and the disinformation about German intentions and plans that flowed into foreign intelligence, diplomatic, and journalistic channels. The German efforts to conceal their intentions from hostile powers and the intended victim. The faulty Soviet interpretations of this hotch-potch of information. And, finally, the inappropriate Soviet decisions and responses.

This chapter sorts out the evidence, unravels the web of deception, and suggests a theory of surprise. After presenting the alternative interpretations that could have been derived from the evidence, it tests these against the actual forecasts made by the various intelligence, diplomatic, and information analysts of other nations. The book concludes by telling how Hitler achieved complete surprise over Stalin, subverting even the authentic warnings passed to the Soviet leader, and places Hitler's successful plan in a wider context of strategic information.

The Alternatives

An intelligence hypothesis may become your hobby-horse on which you will ride straight into a self-made trap.

−Stalin, c. 1936 [1]

The most distrustful persons are often the biggest dupes.

−Cardinal de Retz, 17th century

Given *all* the information available about BARBAROSSA at the time, any proper intelligence service could be expected to formulate several rough sets of plausible hypotheses. My analysis takes as proven that Hitler did, in fact, perceive the Soviet Union as a political and, potentially, military antagonist. The analysis concedes that the military balance between Germany and Russia was sufficiently close that either could at least contemplate initiating war.

The critical hypotheses concerning Hitler's *intent* toward the Soviet Union are: *

I: *Unilateral war hypothesis*—Hitler intends to attack Russia, regardless of Russia's diplomatic or military anticipations.

II: *Ultimatum hypothesis*—Hitler intends to attack, *if* Russia does not meet conditions of a forthcoming ultimatum.

III: *Bluff hypothesis*—Hitler does not intend war, but will use military demonstration as a bluff to obtain further Russian concessions.

IV: *Contingency hypothesis*—Hitler does not intend war, merely protects frontier while pursuing SEA LION.

V: *Preventive war hypothesis*—Hitler, expecting a Soviet attack, intends to strike first.

The first hypothesis (I) states that Hitler intended to attack regardless of Soviet military or political countermoves. In retrospect, this was the actuality. However, it was accepted at the time only by those national leaders who had some realistic appreciation of Hitler's peculiar style of action. This is the only interpretation that makes rational sense of Churchill's sudden wholehearted grasp of the movement of events back in April 1941.

As seen, Stalin finally opted for the "ultimatum" hypothesis (II). Nor was he alone in this choice. It was also accepted by the perceptive American ambassador, Steinhardt, and the *New York Times*. Indeed, it may well be that this particular hypothesis best fits the potpourri of *then available* data comprising the list of warnings in Chapters 3–5. It is easy to select from that body of data at least as impressive a set of clues pointing to the "ultimatum" hypothesis as to the "unilateral" attack-no-matter-what hypothesis. Curiously, the "ultimatum" hypothesis may not have *originated* as one of the German's deliberate cover stories. It may have been a spontaneously generated rumor, albeit one soon picked up and effectively exploited by the Germans. In either case, it proved more effective than any of the other calculated disinformation. For example, the

---

* Other important sets of contingent hypotheses that could also be studied systematically would concern the details of Hitler's specific plan of operations and his timetable. Both sets assume hypotheses I, II, and V.

Swedish minister to Germany, Arvid Richert, reportedly learned that the Germans, having abandoned their projected invasion of Britain, decided to confront Russia in May with the alternatives of full Axis alliance (and parts of Finland and Iran) or a blitzkrieg. Richert also learned that the plans for the latter "contingency" were completed and the necessary deployments already under way. (See warning 21.)

The hypothesis (III) that Hitler did not intend war at all, but did make a massive military demonstration along the Soviet frontier solely as a bluff to exact economic and perhaps other concessions, is interesting.[2] It was, in fact, Eden's initial interpretation. A corollary of this "bluff" hypothesis is that the various security leaks of "Directive No. 21" and nearly all other parts of the authentic BARBAROSSA plans and activities *could* be interpreted as part of a deliberate German disinformation operation, albeit an almost unprecedentedly gigantic and persistent one.* Indeed, the only earlier operation of comparable magnitude that comes to mind is Stalin's own elaborate forgery of the Great Purge. By his own public testimony following the German attack, Stalin proves he was quite capable of projecting his own suspicious nature and intricately conspiratorial operations onto Hitler, thus lending plausibility to the notion that he could have believed Hitler capable of such a gargantuan hoax. To accept this hypothesis requires that we must, I think, assume that Stalin was insane—a paranoid psychotic. Despite the temptation to do so, the evidence and judgment of historians make this at best a still moot assumption. Moreover, this hypothesis does not account for the clearly desperate last-minute efforts of Soviet diplomats in Berlin and Moscow to elicit supposed "terms" from the Germans, implying that *they* at least were operating to the last on the basis of the "ultimatum" hypothesis (II).

* Of the approximately 70 cases of strategic deception operations that occurred in connection with general war during the period 1914–1968, BARBAROSSA takes second place in magnitude and comprehensiveness only to the BODYGUARD-FORTITUDE ruse played successfully by the Allies to dissimulate the Normandy landing site for the Cross-Channel invasion in 1944. See Whaley (1969b).

That the "bluff" hypothesis indeed balances on the edge of insanity is seen by the nature of the "two" authors who upheld it even after the fact. The "first" was the pseudonymous "Colonel Kalinov," who attributed this view to Ambassador Dekanozov (warning 45). Although Kalinov's testimony on this point was accepted by at least one authority,[3] the self-styled defector from the Soviet General Staff and his absurd book are hoaxes, long exposed as complete fabrications of the postwar group of forgers in Paris headed by Grigory Bessedovsky. (Faced with evidence of his forgeries, Bessedovsky admitted with admirable frankness: "I write books for idiots.")[4] The "second" author also turns out to have been Bessedovsky (or one of his stable of "ghosts"), writing as Stalin's nonexistent nephew, "Budu Svanidze." In this version the "bluff" hypothesis is attributed specifically to Poskrebyshev and, by implication, to Stalin. The pseudo-Svanidze "overheard" Stalin's first words on learning of the German attack: "Hitler fooled us. I didn't think he was going to attack now. We did all we could to avoid war." [5]

The "contingency" hypothesis (IV) assumes that Hitler did not intend to attack Russia, at least not until England was defeated, but sought only a defensive reinforcement of his eastern frontier in case Stalin decided to attack.[6] This hypothesis was, we now know, part of Hitler's deliberately inculcated deception operation to lull the Russians and entice the Finns. It certainly deceived British intelligence.

Most absurd of all is the "preventive war" hypothesis (V). It views BARBAROSSA as a narrowly won race against time in which a peaceful Hitler happily got off the first shot at an aggressive Stalin who was about to dishonor their pact. While it is true that one could have fabricated a plausible case for this hypothesis by a biased selection among the signals flowing into Germany in early 1941, Hitler himself clearly did not believe it at the time. He did, however, cleverly mention this view as justification to two or three of his wavering generals such as Göring and Keitel. He also expounded it at great length to General Antonescu of Rumania. Finally, he used this argument in his pep talk to his assembled BARBAROSSA commanders eight days before B-day. Furthermore, he may even have come to believe it himself after the fact,[7] as did Keitel and some other apologists. Thus the "preventive war" hypothesis was a myth used before BARBAROSSA to goad the cautious and, afterward, to rationalize the Hitler-OKW blunder.[8]

In sum, Stalin was too certain of his command of the threads of diplomatic-political-military intrigue. His policy toward Hitler was one of sheer appeasement. True, he was not so deluded as Chamberlain to believe that his prostitution was buying peace in his time. He thought only to buy peace until the next year, when he expected the Red Army would have rebuilt to the unassailable state from which he had himself reduced it by the Great Purge. Unwilling to entirely abandon his preconceived policy of appeasement, Stalin was partly deafened to the authentic signals of doom and preferred listening to the soothing misinformation and disinformation that allowed him a false sense of mastery over the approaching catastrophe.

The subtle intrigues of Stalin were simply an inappropriate response to Hitler's child-like, single-minded desire to attack regardless of anything Stalin would do. Stalin erred in attributing to his opponent his own complex yet basically rational view of Russo-German relations. The Soviet intelligence services had delivered the true signals in abundance and with speed, but these were unavailing given Stalin's faulty hypotheses about the probable course of German action.

The Forecasts

The ability to foresee is the strongest sign of Stalin's genius.
                                        —Major-General Fomichenko, 1945

We have seen the criticism—often abusive, seldom sympathetic, and never systematically analytic—leveled against Stalin's lack of foresight or, at least, against the fact that BARBAROSSA achieved almost total strategic and tactical surprise. I have acknowledged that Stalin's perception was indeed the wrong one. But I have also argued that the available data—all the data—did suggest several alternative interpretations to the one dictated by hindsight.

A brief survey of the contemporary interpretations of the same set of warnings by other intelligence services and other policy makers gives two important facts and one major conclusion. First, the strategic surprise visited upon Stalin was not his alone. Aside from *some* of the Germans, only a handful of the world's many intelligence chiefs, national policy makers, or press pundits unambiguously foresaw the denouement. Second, while the onset of BARBAROSSA became more apparent in both its nature and its timing as the signals rapidly accumulated, the original preconceptions were slow to fall away, so not until the last few days before the attack did the correct intelligence evaluations begin to prevail. Otherwise, the only individuals that *early on* foresaw the outcome—if we can trust their ex post facto recollections—were Churchill, Cavendish-Bentinck, Beneš, and, perhaps, Roosevelt and his senior officials at the State Department and Pope Pius XII. Finally, as a consequence of the two prior facts, we can state an important conclusion that contradicts a widely held view of BARBAROSSA. The great failure of strategic intelligence that it represents should not, as heretofore, be dismissed as the "final fatuity" of a paranoid national leader nor attributed to the Byzantine workings of a totalitarian intelligence system. The great failure was, with few exceptions, a general failure. It holds a sober lesson for all intelligence services and national policy makers.

The United States of America

The American foreign policy leaders were the first to correctly assess that Hitler's intention was, indeed, to attack Russia in the summer of 1941. They had reached this conclusion in February. At least this is the postinvasion claim by Secretary of State Hull and his undersecretary, Welles. Some skepticism about their prideful assertion is warranted by their proven misrecall of most of the verifiable circumstances such as dates and recollected conversations. Moreover, Hull had certainly retreated to a somewhat skeptical position by 9 June, despite the continuing flow of confirmation.[9] Perhaps the mists of German deception had begun to settle in Foggy Bottom.

In any case Hull and Welles, armed with Sam Woods's documents, apparently won President Roosevelt to the "attack" view in late February. This was easily done, as the president had long believed that Hitler would eventually attack Russia. As early as 4 July 1939 Roosevelt had asked Soviet Ambassador Umansky to caution Stalin that, if he aligned himself with Hitler, Hitler would attack Russia as soon as he had conquered France.[10]

But most senior U.S. officials remained unconvinced.[11] For example, the astute Ambassador Steinhardt wired from Moscow on 12 June his continued belief that Stalin would yield to the expected German ultimatum.[12] Similarly, the rather politically naïve secretary of war, Henry Stimson, confided to his diary on 17 June that in the face of "gigantic" German pressure for concessions, "At present, from all the dispatches, it seems nip and tuck whether Russia will fight or surrender. Of course, I think the chances are she will surrender." [13]

Similarly, the Polish ambassador in Washington—himself alerted to the possibility of a German attack—recalled that the materialization of BARBAROSSA on 22 June "was unexpected in Washington, to say the least." [14] This surprise extended to even such senior members of official Washington as Secretary of Interior Ickes.[15]

Opinion was divided even in the superbly informed American embassy in Berlin. On the one hand, as we have seen, the commercial attaché, Woods, and the military attachés were reportedly convinced of the attack. On the other, First Secretary George Kennan frankly recalls that he was slow "to draw the necessary conclusions" from the accumulating evidence, so that 22 June dawned as a partial surprise for him.[16]

Britain

British intelligence had long known of the Wehrmacht's eastward deployment and other warning signals of BARBAROSSA. However, official British opinion remained fragmented in its interpretations of the data until the very week of the event.

Sir Stafford Cripps was a stiff and stuffy extreme left-wing member of the Labour party, and his appointment as His Majesty's ambassador to Moscow introduced a man of quite eccentric opinions into the British Foreign Office. He was out of step on most points, including his firm conviction that war was inevitable between Germany and Russia. He expressed this view privately as early as June 1940 while between airplanes in Sofia en route to his new ambassadorial post in Moscow.[17]

Prime Minister Churchill proudly claimed to have been the first to assess correctly both Hitler's intention and his timing. Although priority should probably go to President Beneš and perhaps even to the U.S. State Department, Churchill's claim is quite true so far as British military, diplomatic, and intelligence services are concerned. Indeed, I suspect—although Churchill was perhaps for once too modest to suggest it—that it may well have been the pressure of his vocal conviction in this matter that eventually swung his own Joint Chiefs of Staff and Joint Intelligence Committee to this position. Furthermore, Churchill's own claim is authentic and not a result of his notoriously intermittent memory. There is some documentary evidence of this: as early as the previous June he had written to the prime minister of the Union of South Africa: "If Hitler fails to beat us here, he will probably recoil eastward. Indeed, he may do this even without trying invasion, to find employment for his Army, and take the edge off the winter strain upon him." [18] And this prediction was followed up within a fortnight by a similar prediction to the head of his Ministry of Aircraft Production, Lord Beaverbrook, calling for the development of a British strategic bomber force: "Should he [Hitler] be repulsed here or not try invasion, he will recoil eastward, and we have nothing to stop him. But there is one thing that will bring him back and bring him down, and that is an absolutely devastating, exterminating attack by very heavy bombers from this country upon the Nazi homeland." [19]

That Churchill stuck to this belief is evidenced by five subsequent expressions of it. First, there was his analysis of 30 March 1941 to Eden,[20] followed up during April by his too cryptic warning to Stalin (warning 28). Next, on 15 June 1941 the "Former Naval Person" cabled President Roosevelt: "From every source at my disposal, including some most trustworthy, it looks as if a vast German onslaught on Russia was [sic] imminent. Not only are the main German armies deployed from Finland to Rumania, but the final arrivals of air and armoured forces are being completed. . . ." [21] Then, five days later, on Friday, 20 June, Churchill holed up at Chequers for the weekend to prepare a public broadcast for Saturday dealing with the event that he now believed would occur in "a matter of days, or it might be hours." On unguided impulse he decided to defer the speech until Sunday night, the twenty-second, when he "thought all would be clear." [22] Finally, on Saturday evening, during dinner at Chequers he told his guests that "a German attack on Russia was now certain." [23] With his expectations fulfilled the next morning, Churchill broadcast his forthright welcome of Bolshevik Russia to the common fight.[24]

But Churchill's widely publicized prescience has obscured the generally fumbling wisdom of the bulk of the British intelligence, military, and diplomatic communities. For a more balanced view of British capabilities in coping with strategic intelligence let us now survey these other key organizations and individuals.

Long-range forecasting of German plans had been assigned to an experimental interservice body created in late November 1940 as a subcommittee of the Joint Intelligence Committee (J.I.C.) of the powerful Chiefs of Staff (I.G.S.) Committee. Cutely christened F.O.E.S. (Future Operations Enemy Section), this four-man group of middle-rank officials was imaginatively assigned to a role-playing simulation of the German General Staff (OKH). Using the same intelligence as the Joint Planning Staff, F.O.E.S. assumed that the German military would do its best "to avoid a war on two fronts and that consequently there would be no violation of the German-Soviet agreement, so long as Britain stood on her feet." [25] An accurate appraisal of the cautious thinking of the professional German military leaders, but one that overlooked the governing fact that it was not the General Staff but Hitler whom they should have been anticipating. Hitler had, of course, already vetoed these considerations. Given F.O.E.S.'s basic misorientation, it was small loss when it was dissolved in February or March.[26]

F.O.E.S. was superseded in March 1941 by the Advanced Planning Enemy Section. Despite its even less felicitous acronym, A.P.E.S. proved a more effective evaluator of strategic intelligence, particularly regarding the accumulating clues of German intentions toward Russia.[27] Much of this credit is due Mr. Victor Cavendish-Bentinck, the Foreign Office's representative on and chairman of the Joint Intelligence Committee (J.I.C.), A.P.E.S.'s senior body. Cavendish-Bentinck later rather vaguely recalled:

Early in 1941, I think March or the end of February, I noticed reports from Poland that the Germans were increasing the length of the runways of the airfields in Poland and reinforcing these runways. It occurred to me that this was not being done for the benefit of Lufthansa! A little later we received reports that the Germans were beginning to subsidize again anti-Bolshevik organizations in the Caucasus [Ukraine?]. These two pointers led me to suggest to my colleagues on the JIC that [APES] . . . be directed to prepare a report on the possibility of a German attack on the Soviet Union.[28]

Accordingly, A.P.E.S. soon turned in a comprehensive analysis "predicting that the Germans intended to attack the Russians in the near future." However, this appreciation was ill-received by Cavendish-Bentinck's colleagues on the J.I.C., the J.I.C. Secretary telling him that A.P.E.S. had gone "mad" and giving his boss a look of sheer contempt when Cavendish-Bentinck disclosed that he had himself commissioned the study.[29]

Subsequently, sometime in early May, A.P.E.S. daringly and on its own initiative forecast the German invasion of Russia for between 20 and 25 June. However, as Captain Stuart Paton, the Royal Navy's member, recalls: "The Directors of Intelligence [sitting ex officio on the J.I.C.] and the Chiefs of Staff thought we were all mad and we all nearly landed in the loony bin." [30] And Cavendish-Bentinck confirms that "it took a little time to convince the Chiefs of Staff that the Germans intended to go for the Russians." [31]

Foreign Minister Eden first interpreted the huge German

buildup in the East as only a demonstration force intended to blackmail the Russians into further concessions. Later, however, he gradually began to suspect the truth: Hitler simply intended to seize what he wanted from Russia, eliminating Stalin as the middle man. This was still Eden's somewhat uncertain view as late as 11 June, when he communicated it to American Chargé d'Affaires Herschel V. Johnson.[32]

The Ministry of Economic Warfare on 28 May produced a brilliantly argued memorandum on the economic trade-offs to Germany of invasion versus greater control of the Russian economy. However, the memorandum clearly showed how deeply committed M.E.W. was to the "ultimatum" thesis.[33]

The Chiefs of the Imperial General Staff on 31 May had swung around to agree with Churchill that Hitler intended war, but they still expected that an ultimatum would precede any attack.[34]

However, the Joint Intelligence Committee did not concur with Churchill's view until ten days before the German invasion. Indeed, it had taken them until 10 June to recognize that war itself was imminent, but even then only if the Russians did not accede to an ultimatum. Prior to that time the J.I.C. had been wedded to the hypothesis that the German maneuverings were merely a military demonstration to frighten the Russians into new concessions. The J.I.C. reasoned that Hitler was not prepared to take on Russia in 1941; Britain *must* come first.[35]

The director of Military Intelligence (and ex officio member of the J.I.C.), Major-General Francis Davidson, had circulated an appreciation at the end of March stating in response to the crop of rumors: "we have no grounds for believing an attack on Russia is imminent."[36]

As early as 13 March 1941, the commander in chief Home Forces, General Sir Alan Brooke, noted in his diary: "The rumour season is beginning to accentuate itself. Where are the Germans going to push next? I would not be surprised to see a thrust into Russia. In many ways this is far the most promising line of action."[37]

On 6 June a special meeting of the psychological warfare department (S.O.1, later P.W.E.) was convened at its eccentric premises at Woburn Abbey to be notified for the first time of BARBAROSSA. Mr. Reginald Leeper, the special chief of the department—and concurrently chief of the Political Intelligence Department of the Foreign Office—announced from the chair:

Gentlemen, I have obtained permission from the Prime Minister to reveal to you a piece of secret information which has been known to Mr. Churchill and the Chiefs of Staff for several weeks, but has until now been denied any wider circulation. He has authorized me to impart to you—and to you only—in order that we may concert as early as possible our plans for the situation which we shall be facing shortly. Briefly, the information is that Hitler and his Wehrmacht are about to attack Soviet Russia. German armies have been secretly assembling on what I suppose will soon be called the Eastern Front. The actual invasion is expected to take place around the middle of June. The estimate of the Joint Intelligence Committee at their meeting yesterday was that June the 22nd is the most likely date. . . .[38]

Forewarned by Churchill's stretching of the J.I.C. estimate, S.O.1 began planning its "black" and "white" propaganda campaigns; but it seemingly did not launch them until after the invasion.

If the British intelligence community was slow to evaluate the mass of incoming evidence, it was even slower to circulate its evidence and conclusions within the "establishment." Having informed the S.O.1 "black" propagandists and the foreign (or at least American) press corps, the intelligencers neglected to coordinate with the Ministry of Information, as witness the preattack befuddlement of Harold Nicolson, the principal private secretary and protégé of Information Minister Duff Cooper. The Information Ministry's Planning Committee did not bother considering what policies or actions to take in event of a Russo-German war until 18 June; and even then Nicolson deemed such a development "very unlikely indeed." [39] * If the British—with their rare

---

* Oddly this represented a retreat from Nicolson's earlier correct intuition on 29 March, when his diary (p. 155) noted that "Rab Butler [the Parliamentary Under-Secretary of State for Foreign Affairs] agrees with me that as the Germans have come up against a difficult problem in their invasion of this country and in their invasion of the Balkans, they may strike suddenly at

talent for crosscutting clogged bureaucratic channels with interlocking committees and caste-based informal communications—
could barely cope with the intelligence on BARBAROSSA, they reveal
an unseemly hypocrisy in deriding the barely inferior Soviet efforts.

The British press was also caught by surprise, although it had
been monitoring the many public rumors and even reporting some
of them. Moreover, the editors and their military and foreign affairs correspondents enjoyed the special confidence of Government
in the frequent, detailed, and frank though off-the-record briefings by officials.[40] Nevertheless, they were content to substitute
impressionistic bias and mindless skepticism for intelligent analysis, and accordingly wrote the whole bit off as rumor. Even the
staunch editor of *The Times,* Geoffrey Dawson, was slow to be
alerted. Not until 11 June does his private diary acknowledge even
the "great German concentration on the Soviet frontier." Then,
on the nineteenth, he mentions without comment that his luncheon guest, Deputy Prime Minister Attlee, had said that he had
been convinced by Cripps of the "imminence of a Russo-German
war." Finally, on the twentieth, Dawson recorded only that "The
symptoms of a German-Russian war [are] slightly stronger." [41]

In general, British foresight on BARBAROSSA can be summarized as
slow, vacillating, and quite fragmented despite access to information even more detailed and accurate than that received by the
Russians. The gradual appreciation of Hitler's intent seems to have
originated with Churchill and been forced by him upon a slowly
yielding bureaucracy. Even sixteen years after the event, the senior
official British war historian was unable to entirely shake off the
"ultimatum" hypothesis.[42]

Vichy France

The Vichy French leaders also chose the "ultimatum" hypothesis.
Their ambassador to Moscow, Gaston Bergery, arrived newly appointed in early May 1941, fresh from Berlin where high officials
assured him that a peaceful settlement was being sought for the

---

Russia. Everybody else regards this idea as fantastic, but I am not so sure."
Note that Nicolson was unaware that his view was shared by the prime
minister.

German demands for major economic, political, and military concessions. And at least by early June Admiral Darlan had accepted
this view in his multihatted capacity as premier, vice-president,
foreign minister, and interior minister (see warning 55).

However, the Vichy military intelligence services (the Deuxième
Bureau of Lieutenant-Colonel Baril, the Fifth Bureau of Colonel
Rivet, and Air Intelligence under Lieutenant-Colonel Ronin) were
evidently satisfied that Hitler did intend war, at least if we can
credit their ex post facto claims (see warning 59).[43]

Czechoslovak Government-in-Exile

A particularly prescient reading of the events of 1941 was made
by Dr. Eduard Beneš, then president of the Czechoslovak government-in-exile in London. Even before the Nazi-Soviet Pact in 1939,
he believed on ideological grounds in the inevitability of war between Russia and Germany, and in 1940 he became convinced
that it would occur before Hitler's settlement with Britain.[44]

In early 1941, by March, Beneš had become convinced by the
detailed information from his own excellent military intelligence
service that the already expected war would be Hitler's—not Stalin's—decision and that it was imminent.[45] Like Churchill, but
independently of him, Beneš recognized that Hitler was capable
of such irrationality.

Polish Government-in-Exile

The effective Polish underground intelligence service managed to
keep its government-in-exile in London quite well-informed of the
deteriorating state of Russo-German relations, of the Wehrmacht's
intensive buildup along the Soviet frontier, and finally even of the
approximate B-day. Yet both the underground and the London
officers were divided in their interpretation of the portents. Some
believed war imminent; others thought there would be no final
break. Mikolajczyk, a leading figure in the London group, had the
uncommon intellectual and moral honesty to recall that as late as
June:

The thought of a war between Russia and Germany was alien to
me. I felt that there was essentially no difference between the twin
invaders. In talks with the press in Canada [during his trip there

with Premier Sikorski in April 1941] I predicted that the two would not fight. I based my belief also on the idea that Hitler's mind, however warped, could never prompt him to blunder into fighting Russia without first annihilating the west.[46]

This incorrect view was shared by Premier Sikorski. On 23 May he circulated a memorandum that, drawing on Polish intelligence sources, argued that a genuine community of interest bound Germany to Russia. While Sikorski did not rule out a German attack for the spring of 1942, he firmly held that such a conflict in 1941 "does not seem to enter into consideration." [47]

Subsequently, the evidence pointing to BARBAROSSA accumulated to a point that two days before the invasion Premier Sikorski felt warranted in reversing his previous views and warned the Americans that the attack was set for 22 June (see warning 76).

The Vatican

As we have seen (warning 40), Pope Pius XII was one of the very few world leaders who had not been surprised by the advent of BARBAROSSA. The anti-Nazi leaders of the Abwehr had been supplying him with a steady stream of top-level strategic intelligence since late 1939. He had personally long known and trusted several of the German figures involved in this strange liaison: Admiral Canaris, Dr. Müller, and General Beck. Moreover, the accuracy of their previous warnings of Hitler's invasions of Scandinavia and the Low Countries had led Pius to fully credit the accuracy of their information. Consequently, he entertained no doubts when the Abwehr warned him of the imminence of BARBAROSSA.

Italy

Although Mussolini and Foreign Minister Ciano were not formally notified by Hitler of BARBAROSSA until the very moment of its launching, they had correctly perceived the ominous decline in Russo-German relations. By mid-June Count Ciano had come to believe that Hitler had decided to attack. (See Chapter 6.)

Moreover, as early as 14 May the Italian chief of Military Intelligence (SIM), General Cesare Amè, had concluded not only that the Germans were firmly decided on an invasion of Russia but that it was scheduled for 15 June. His conclusion was based on information recently acquired in Budapest.[48] Although the specific source is not identified, the nature of the details indicates a high-level leak and not a mere inference from such visible manifestations as train-watching. Indeed, his source was probably his liaison with the Hungarian Army Staff, which had already been unofficially warned by General Halder. (See Chapter 6.)

The Italian diplomatic service was a bit slower in reading the signs. Ambassador Alfieri and First Secretary Lanza in Berlin did not recognize until late April that matters had reached a serious turn, but as late as 9 May Alfieri was reporting these signs to Rome as merely part of a war of nerves.[49] The ambassador in Moscow, Augusto Rosso, had not firmly concluded until 10 June that Germany was contemplating an attack on Russia,[50] and even then he was taken quite by surprise by the timing.[51]

Japan

We have seen that the Japanese intelligence and diplomatic services had acquired excellent clues of the imminent German assault on Russia. Ambassador Ōshima in Berlin reached this conclusion on 18 May (warning 69). Yet the Japanese leaders were simply incapable of readjusting their preconceptions to accept the possibility of such a war. For the Japanese Supreme Staff, Ambassador Tatekawa in Moscow, and Foreign Minister Matsuoka, "Wishful thinking carried the day in the form of a conclusion that the whole thing was nothing more than a German maneuver designed to camouflage an intention to invade England."[52] Thus the senior Japanese leaders gullibly swallowed the main German deception plan. Indeed, even to the limited extent that Matsuoka eventually recognized the possibility of war he slid into the easy trap of the "ultimatum" hypothesis. At the joint Cabinet–High Command Liaison Conference of 7 June he concluded: "Since Germany will need a pretext when she declares war on the Soviet Union, she is expected to impose conditions first and then go to war."[53] War Minister Tōjō concurred, as apparently did the Chiefs of Staff of the Army and Navy.

The day after the German thrust into Russia shattered Matsuoka's dream-world foreign policy he uttered with audacious bluff: "Something must be wrong with the brains of those who are surprised." [54] Whatever its effect on the Japanese public, for Matsuoka's colleagues his remark was rank dissimulation; and it did not save him from swift removal as foreign minister.

It is ironic that Ambassador Ōshima's radiograms were heeded not in Tokyo but in Washington, where, as already described, they were being eagerly read by the State Department and Chiefs of Staff.

Germany

Even some of the German elite opted for wrong hypotheses. They, more than any, knew Hitler's dictum that a two-front war had brought German defeat in the Great War. And they remembered the mutually profitable Reichswehr–Red Army collaboration on rearmament during the 1920s and early 1930s. But they also perceived Bolshevik Russia as their mortal enemy. Thus it is understandable that individually they opted initially for any one of the available hypotheses except the perverse one chosen by their Führer. It was only after each was brought into the BARBAROSSA planning that he understood Hitler's true intention. For propaganda purposes, the insiders encouraged a theory of preventive war planning. But only one senior German believed this unquestioningly, despite his intimate knowledge of BARBAROSSA. This was Hitler's self-styled "loyal shield bearer," Field-Marshal Keitel, who with his incredible fawning amorality viewed BARBAROSSA as a *Präventiv-Angriff*. He stubbornly and mistakenly argued to a deaf posterity from his Spandau cell that, "The Soviet Union was methodically preparing for an attack on us; and their preparations along the whole front line were exposed by our own attack on 22nd June 1941." [55]

"The Wayward Press"

The international and major independent national news media are, in a practical sense, intelligence services; and they are so used by most persons regardless of their station in the polity or their access to conventional intelligence sources. Indeed, the "prestige" newspapers are known to draw readers from a far higher proportion of senior government officials than of the literate adult citizenry in general. This is true even in authoritarian states such as the Soviet Union, where a controlled press serves not merely to propagandize the general public but also as a conduit for disclosing policy and selected information to the middle-level government and party officers who can read "between the lines" to get at these hidden messages.[56]

International news media resemble professional intelligence services in both function and structure. They ferret out, collect, collate, evaluate, analyze, summarize, and report vast quantities of information; and they do so with an organization comprising correspondents in the field with their networks of local stringers and contacts, all heading up in research and library staffs, editors, and commentators in the home office. All these journalistic functional and organizational categories find their almost exact analogues in intelligence services, with little more than an occasional change of parochial cant such as "agent" for "stringer" or "analyst" for "commentator." The news media also resemble professional intelligence services in that they seldom succeed in predicting events. Neither excel in the Delphic art or the new science of futurology.*

In the case of BARBAROSSA, the news media proved a particularly inadequate instrument for prediction. At best they can be credited with more or less complete reporting of the more obvious signs of strain in Russo-German relations. This was true of the Reuters, Associated Press, and United Press wire services and of such newspapers as the *Times* (London), the *Neue Zürcher Zeitung,* the *New York Times,* the *New York Herald Tribune,* the *Chicago Daily News,* and the *Washington Post.*

* Among the notably few exceptions in which the international press has served to fully forewarn its readers of secret operations was the Bay of Pigs in 1961. Then an unusually alert U.S. and foreign press corps was able to penetrate that operation with ease because the U.S. agencies concerned had contented themselves (perhaps, as Ernst Halperin has suggested, by design) with shoddy cover and deception work. See Whaley (1969*b*), Case A65.

In the week before the invasion the Luce weekly magazines, *Life* and *Time,* had reported only "crisis" in Russo-German relations, stressing the "ultimatum" hypothesis. However, *Life* executive editor Wilson Hicks had a strong enough hunch of possible war to send Margaret Bourke-White and her husband Erskine Caldwell over to Russia the previous month. And *Time*'s editors kept a four-color dummy cover of Stalin and Timoshenko on hand just in case. The scrapping on 22 June of 800,000 covers of Emir Abdullah of Transjordan and the substitution of the Stalin-Timoshenko one became the fastest color-printing job in magazine history. In other words, the mass media proved as confused as official institutions at forecasting BARBAROSSA.

Typical of the best and worst BARBAROSSA forecasting is the *New York Times.* During the week before the attack it gave its readers a kaleidoscopic array of inconsistent dispatches, commentaries, and editorials. In accuracy they ranged from the tocsin sounded from the Ankara listening post by C. L. Sulzberger and Ray Brock, through a mishmash of reports and rumors hedged with rhetorical cautionary qualifiers but no evidence that simple verification had been sought, to yes-maybe-no editorials and commentaries. In general, readers were being sold the "ultimatum" hypothesis, although at least one report unwittingly pushed the German deception cover scheme that the Wehrmacht's activities along the Russian border were a feint to mask its imminent invasion of Britain.[58] On Saturday, 21 June, the newspaper's military commentator, Hanson W. Baldwin, was in Tennessee covering Army war games and polishing his column for the approaching Sunday edition. His crystal ball was quite flawed—the piece concluded that the European war was deadlocked and that Germany would never attack Russia. His story had just been filed through Western Union when Baldwin learned, shortly after 10:45 P.M., of the NBC bulletin announcing the attack. Although the frantic journalist was unable to get through to the home office, an alert editor there managed to save embarrassment all around by substituting an innocuous reserve Baldwin piece, tactfully datelining it "Washington, June 21."[59]

The Art of Surprise

Gentlemen, I notice that there are always three courses open to the enemy, and that he usually takes the fourth.
—The Elder von Moltke

While each of the five hypotheses (or intelligence "appreciations" or "estimates") of BARBAROSSA examined here had at least some measure of plausibility and each was credited in varying degrees by at least some insiders, two deserve closer attention: the "unilateral attack" hypothesis because it was the correct one, and the "ultimatum" hypothesis because it was the one increasingly credited in the Kremlin as the time for effective countermeasures ran out. Indeed, of all the plausible solutions, the "ultimatum" hypothesis best fits the information then available to Soviet intelligence. It is "best" in the sense that it takes into account or explains more of the relevant data, that is, both the genuine and the false signals, than any of the other solutions, including the correct one.

Consequently, if we are to be fair to Stalin we must concede, according to the principle of Occam's Razor, that he had made the most logically elegant estimate of the available evidence. Moreover, Stalin was in distinguished company, the ultimatum ruse having been swallowed whole by the following (with the last known date in 1941 of their holding that mistaken view):

Swedish ambassador to Berlin (Richert)	March
British ambassador to Moscow (Cripps)	27 April
Italian ambassador to Berlin (Alfieri)	9 May
Vichy French ambassador to Moscow (Bergery)	early May
British Ministry of Economic Warfare	28 May
British Chiefs of Staff (Dill and others)	31 May
British Foreign Office Permanent Under-Secretary (Cadogan)	2 June
Japanese foreign minister (Matsuoka)	7 June
Finnish minister to Stockholm	9 June
British Joint Intelligence Committee (except Cavendish-Bentinck)	10 June
U.S. ambassador to Moscow (Steinhardt)	12 June

Turkish foreign minister (Saracoglu)	12 June
U.S. military attaché in London (Lee)	13 June
Vichy French deputy premier (Darlan)	14 June
U.S. secretary of war (Stimson)	17 June
U.S. undersecretary of state (Welles)	18 June
Soviet foreign minister (Molotov)	19 June
The New York Times	21 June

At the point when the five hypotheses were formulated, about four months into my research, I had a second insight (see Chapter 1) that shifted the research to its final level of analysis. I suddenly realized that the Wohlstetter model was a quite inappropriate representation of BARBAROSSA surprise. Stalin (and almost everyone else) had been surprised not because the warnings were *ambiguous* but precisely because German intelligence had managed to *reduce* their ambiguity. In short, surprise had been inflicted by the deliberately false signals and not by the ambiguous signals, much less the distracting noise.*

What Hitler had done was not to make Stalin merely uncertain and therefore indecisive. His cunning "ultimatum" stratagem served to eliminate ambiguity, making Stalin quite certain, very decisive, *and wrong*. Stalin was misled into expecting an ultimatum before any attack, thereby giving him the option of conceding or preempting. Stalin's false expectation was the direct effect of Hitler's campaign to manipulate his victim's information, preconceptions, conclusions, and decisions. By the judicious transmission of disinformation, he masked not only the timing and direction of his attack but also his very intention to attack.

But what of Churchill and the very few other statesmen, diplomats, journalists, or intelligencers who did at least correctly guess Hitler's *intention* to attack Russia. By being able to discard the false preconception that Hitler would never be so rash as to send the German Army to fight on a second major front, they were able

---

* I gratefully acknowledge the help of Dr. William R. Harris for pointing the way out of "noise" and my initially somewhat narrow concept of "disinformation" and directing my attention to "deception" as a broad concept that applies to other cases of strategic surprise.

to see the authentic warnings in a fresh light. However, they were puzzled that Stalin (and many of their own experts) failed to believe their warnings, for they did not understand *how* Hitler was masking his unqualified decision to attack.

If Hitler's actual deception plan had been suspected, the evidence could have been reassessed and everyone, including Stalin, would at least have sought new information to verify it. But the art of deception was very imperfectly understood outside Germany at that time. It was not until later in the war that first the British, and then the Americans, and finally the Russians began to organize their own strategic deception operations. Then it was Germany's turn repeatedly to fall victim to deception.*

The contemporary intelligencers, like the later historians (see my introductory remarks in the Bibliography), failed to solve the mystery of BARBAROSSA despite having been given *two* chances by an unintentionally generous Hitler. He had not only perpetrated the very subtle "ultimatum" ruse, but he also carried out the more obvious SEA LION "contingency" hoax. When SEA LION, Hitler's plan to invade Britain, became the initial cover story for BARBAROSSA, the contemporary intelligence services could have accidentally stumbled upon the solution to BARBAROSSA by recognizing or even suspecting the deceptive nature of SEA LION. Again neglecting to systematically explore the possibility of an underlying deception operation, the experts failed.

The case study of BARBAROSSA was finished. However, I had ended not with the expected replication of the Wohlstetter paradigm but with a new model of strategic surprise.†

* See Whaley (1969*b*), Sefton Delmer, *The Counterfeit Spy* (New York: Harper & Row, 1971); Ladislas Farago, *The Game of the Foxes* (New York: McKay, 1971); and J. C. Masterman, *The Double-Cross System* (New Haven: Yale University Press, 1972).

† Obviously, the two models are not mutually exclusive. Each covers different subsets of surprise. Nor are they logically exhaustive—other causes of surprise can be imagined. For example, in the absence of any *warnings,* as with the dropping of the A-bomb on Hiroshima in 1945; or in the complete absence of any *expectations,* as in the hypothetical possibility of invasion from outer space before H. G. Wells alerted our imaginations to the concept, however scientifically improbable.

The Wohlstetter thesis, as noted earlier, states: "To understand the fact of surprise [attack] it is necessary to examine the characteristics of the noise as well as the signals that [only] after the event are clearly seen to herald the attack." The flaw in this model is that it treats deliberate disinformation as part of the ambient background "noise." And noise is defined in her model as one of the sources of distraction and confusion that make the interpretation of the authentic warning signals ambiguous. Consequently, Wohlstetter pigeonholes disinformation together with the relevant but mistaken information and the entirely irrelevant information flowing into and confusing and distracting intelligence systems. However, the purpose of disinformation is to reduce ambiguity, confusion, and uncertainty by making its victim more certain and wrong. Thus disinformation is best considered a special type of signal—a false signal in contrast to authentic signals.* This weakness in the Wohlstetter model is a direct consequence of the common practice of social scientists to borrow the models of the natural sciences and apply them too hastily to human affairs. In this case, Wohlstetter has adapted to a problem of human communications the "signal/noise" concept invented by Claude Shannon at the Bell Telephone Laboratory in 1948 as a key part of his mathematical Theory of Communication of electronic information.[60]

By tying deception (disinformation) to noise, Wohlstetter not only misinterpreted BARBAROSSA as a case of ambiguity analogous to her classic Pearl Harbor surprise attack case[61] but was even led to disregard the very significant elements of Japanese deception planning in the Pearl Harbor case itself.[62] Wohlstetter's is the most influential and widely applied model developed until now for understanding surprise. It is a useful tool for this purpose, but only in cases where deception is not practiced.

Strategic surprise is the hobgoblin of all intelligence services. Intelligencers find too comfortable refuge in attributing the frequent

---

* Dr. William R. Harris suggests, however, that a three-part model is required, one comprising separate categories for "signals," "sprignals," and "noise." Memorandum, Harris to Whaley, 4 September 1967. The useful neologism "sprignals" (that is, spurious signal) was coined by Dr. Harris.

costly surprises of their enemies to structural or procedural flaws
in the information system[63] or, when justifying their own embarrassing surprises, to the "inherent" ambiguity of information.[64]

Lawrence of Arabia once remarked that "deceptions . . . for the
ordinary general were just witty hors d'oeuvres before battle."
Colonel Lawrence could with equal justice have extended his criticism to the "ordinary" intelligencer or historian who does not
understand how a well-calculated and systematic deception plan
can be the key to strategic surprise.

Appendix A:
A Chronology of Deceit: German Documents on Deception
Planning

This appendix opens with the first English-language publication
of the OKW's "Guidelines for Deception of the Enemy," the key
BARBAROSSA deception planning document.

The appendix concludes with an annotated list of the sixty-seven
known German documents on their deception planning in connection with BARBAROSSA. Ordered chronologically, this set of documents provides a unique record of a deliberately designed and
carefully coordinated plan to achieve strategic surprise. For complete translations, critical discussions, content analyses, and more
detailed source and reference citations, see Whaley (1969c).

Translation of Document 12

TOP MILITARY SECRET
[stamp]

The Führer's Headquarters
15 February 1941

High Command of the Armed Forces [OKW]
No.44 142/41 Top Military Secret/Senior Officers Only
WFSt/Abt. L (I Op.)

MATTER FOR CHIEFS! [stamp]	15 *copies*
THROUGH OFFICER ONLY! [stamp]	9th copy

Reference: OKW/WFSt/Abt.L No.22048/40
Top Military Secret/Senior Officers
Only of 3 February 1940

Guidelines for Deception of the Enemy

A) 1) *The aim* of the deception is *to conceal* the preparations of
Operation BARBAROSSA. This essential goal is the guiding

principle for all the measures aimed at keeping the enemy misinformed. It is a matter of maintaining uncertainty about our intentions during the first period, that is, until the middle of April. In the ensuing second period the misdirecting measures meant for BARBAROSSA itself must not be seen as any more than misdirection and *diversion for the invasion of England.*

2) *Guidelines* applied to misleading intelligence and other measures are:

a) *during the 1st period:*
Strengthening the existing impression of a coming *invasion* of England. Enclosed are instructions about new means of attack and transportation.
Exaggeration of the significance of the *secondary operation* (MARITA), SUNFLOWER, the Xth Flying Corps, and the forces engaged therein. *Reason for the troop movements connected with* BARBAROSSA are to be presented as an exchange operation between the West, the [German] Homeland, and the East, as a concentration of reserve units for Operation MARITA, and in the final analysis as defensive rear cover against Russia.

b) *during the 2nd period*
the *troop movement for* BARBAROSSA *is to be seen as the greatest deception operation in the history of war,* intended as a cover-up for the final preparations for the invasion of England.
This measure is made possible by the fact that the first surprise attack against England would be carried out with relatively weak forces, thanks to the strongest concentration of the new [German] combat methods and in recognition of the superiority of the English fleet. As a consequence, the bulk of the German forces could be chiefly engaged in the deception undertakings. The deployment against England, however, will be initiated simultaneously with the surprise attack.

B) *Execution of the Deception:*

  I) *Intelligence Service* (under the guidance of the Chief of the Abwehr [Admiral Canaris]): Efficient use of the general policy of going only through the channels established by the Chief of the Abwehr.

  The latter channels infiltrate false intelligence among the routine information of our own attachés in neutral countries and the neutral attachés in Berlin. The pattern will be a mosaic picture, determined by this general policy. In order to bring the actual measures, especially the troop movements, of the High Commands into agreement with the intelligence service and to make full use of suggestions, the OKW/WFSt/Abt. L will hold a briefing on the general guidelines for the time periods depending on the situation, in coordination with the High Commands and the Abwehr. During the first briefing it will be established, among others:

  a) how long the intended transport movements are to be interpreted as normal West-to Homeland-to East commutings,

  b) which westbound transports could be used in counter-espionage for the deception "invasion" [of England] (for example, concentration of camouflaged new weapons).

  c) if and how to disseminate the intelligence that the Navy and Luftwaffe were held back according to plan and because of bad weather conditions, in order to spare their forces for the main attack.

  d) how to prepare the Codeword ALBION (see below) preliminary operations.

II) *Measures of the High Commands:*

  1) In spite of the further relaxation of the preparation for SEA LION, everything should be done to maintain the impression that the landing in England is being prepared, although in a new form, although the troops stationed

there would be withdrawn at a later date. Even the troops deployed in the East are to be kept as long as possible under the impression that this was simply conceived as a deception, that is, as defensive rear cover for the forthcoming blow against England.

2) The Army High Command is requested to check if measures connected with BARBAROSSA, such as introduction of the full capacity timetable, leave cancellation, etc., could be synchronized with the beginning of MARITA.

3) Particular significance for the deception is attached to intelligence about the airborne forces, pointing to their use against England (assignment of English interpreters, newly printed English maps, and the like). The Luftwaffe High Command is requested to make the appropriate arrangements in cooperation with the Abwehr.

4) The stronger the troop concentration in the East, the harder the attempts to foster uncertainty about our plans. In addition the plan for the sudden "closing" of certain areas around the Channel and in Norway is to be prepared by the Army High Command in cooperation with the Abwehr. (Codeword for its initiation: ALBION.) In doing so it is less a question of carrying out this blockade in minute detail by engaging a great concentration of forces, but much more to create great effect through the appropriate measures. In this manner an impression should be created that surprises are in store for the British Isles, as well as by using other measures, for example, the disposition of instruments that would look to the enemy like hitherto unknown "rocket batteries."

The more the preparations for BARBAROSSA stand out, the more difficult it will be to maintain a successful deception. However the utmost must be done to keep to these guidelines to ensure the secrecy of the operation.

Suggestions and proposals of the participating service are desired.

Chief of the High Command of the Armed Forces
Keitel
Field-Marshal

[illegible signature]
Captain

Comment: This was the basic German order concerning deception for BARBAROSSA. It was introduced at the Nürnberg trials as Document 875–PS but not published at that time. The deception plan was updated by document 42, below.
Sources: Krummacher and Lange (1970), 554–557, for complete German text. A microfilm of the original document is in the National Archives, Washington, D.C., Microcopy Series T–77, Roll 792. Italics are as in original. This English translation by Mrs. Rodica Saidman was revised by me (unfortunately before I was able to see the original document).

References: Weinberg (1954), 149n6, 189; Hillgruber (1965), 460; document 13 below; *TWC* (1951), 10:1029, for testimony of Warlimont in June–July 1948 at Nürnberg; Zhukov (1971), 224; and "Sovetskie organy" (1965), 23.

The Documents

No.	Date	Title, Description, and Source
1	31 July 1940	OKH *War Diary* entry. Notes by Halder of conference with Hitler who expressed view that "Should Russia . . . be smashed, then England's last hope is extinguished." Decides Russia "must be disposed of" in "spring 1941." Notes need to "camouflage" oper-

ation by feigning operations against Spain, North Africa, and Britain.

Sources: Halder, 2 (1963), 46–50, for German text; *DGFP,* 10 (1957), 370–374, for English translation.

2   Aug. 1940   Memorandum, Raeder to Assmann, dated 30 Jan. 1944.

In this remarkable paper, Raeder, the head of the German Navy acknowledges the deception practiced on him (and others) by Hitler in August 1940. Moreover, this memorandum verifies the suspicion that the notion of using SEA LION as the cover for the initial BARBAROSSA deployments did indeed originate with Hitler.

Sources: *TMWC,* 34 (1949), 276–282, for German text; *NCA* (1946), 6:887–892, for garbled English tr.

3   6 Sept. 1940   "Guidance for the Intelligince Service," WFSt/Abt.L, No.33264.40.

On the need to conceal from Russia the preparations for "an offensive in the East." Specifies various plausible cover stories.

Sources: *TMWC,* 27 (1948), 72–73, for German text; Weinberg (1954), 176–177, for English tr.

4   Nov. 1940   Affidavit dated 20 Nov. 1945 of General Ernst Köstring to U.S. Army interrogator.

Recollections of the former German military attaché to Moscow about his instructions from General von Tippelskirch that the cover story to the Russians about eastward deployments was only safety from British air attacks.

Source: *NCA* (1946), 5:734–735, for English tr.

5   9 Dec. 1940   OKM/Skl Naval *War Diary* entry.

Notes that SEA LION is to be maintained as a deception measure until the beginning of the Russian campaign.

Reference: Klee (1958), 226, for passing mention of this unpublished passage.

6   18 Dec. 1940   "Directive No.21: Operation BARBAROSSA."

Hitler's key directive ordering the Wehrmacht to "be prepared to crush Soviet Russia *in a quick campaign* (Operation BARBAROSSA) even before the conclusion of the war against England." Stresses that all orders to subordinates should pretend that they are "precautionary measures" to guard against any renewed Russian hostility.

Source: Walther Hubatsch, ed., *Hitler's Weisungen für die Kriegführung 1939–1945* (Frankfurt: Bernard und Graefe, 1962), pp. 84–92, for German text.

7   22 Jan. 1941   Draft "Deployment Directive BARBAROSSA," OKH/I, No.050/41.

Stresses need for secrecy and mentions the "precautionary measures" cover story.

Source: *TWC,* 10 (1951), 960–964, for a nearly complete English tr.

8   3 Feb. 1941   "Conference on Operation BARBAROSSA and SUNFLOWER," WFSt, No.44089/41.

Hitler directs that "The strategic con-

centration for BARBAROSSA will be camouflaged as a feint for SEA LION" and MARITA
(the invasion of Greece).

Sources: *TMWC,* 26 (1947), 391–399, for
German text; *NCA* (1946), 3:626–633,
for English tr.

9   4 Feb. 1941   "Report of the Commander-in-Chief,
Navy, to the Führer on the Afternoon of
4 February 1941," Skl I Op 112/41.

Hitler specifies to Raeder that the Navy
must maintain its present level of activities against Britain, since "SEA LION must
be maintained as a deception."

Source: *Fuehrer Conferences,* 1 (1947),
5–11, for English tr.

10   5 Feb. 1941   "Deployment Directive BARBAROSSA,"
Army Group C, Ia 8/41.

Stresses secrecy and cover stories.

Source: *TWC,* 10 (1951), 970–973, for
almost complete English tr.

11   6 Feb. 1941   "Directive No. 23: Guidelines for the
Conduct of the War Against the English
War Economy," OKW/WFSt/Abt.L (IL
Op), No.44095/41.

Hitler directs that "Until . . . BARBA-
ROSSA we should strive to step up . . .
naval operations [against England] . . .
to simulate the appearance of an attack
on the British Isles impending this year."

Sources: Hubatsch (1962), 100–103, for
German text; *DGFP,* 12 (1962), 42–44,
for English tr., omitting only the distribution list.

12   15 Feb. 1941   "Guidelines for Deception of the Enemy," OKW, No.44142/41.

Issued by Keitel, this is the most detailed early BARBAROSSA deception planning document.

Sources: Krummacher and Lange (1970), 554–557, for German text. See previous section for my English tr.

13   18 Feb. 1941   OKM/Skl Naval *War Diary* entry.

A summary of doc. 12.

Sources: *TMWC,* 34 (1949), 217–218, for German text; *NCA* (1946), 6:847–848, for partial English tr.

14   18 Feb. 1941   "Special Activity Report," Army Group Command C, Ia No.31/41.

Specifies that "for reasons of camouflage" no problems connected with BARBAROSSA preparations will be mentioned in the Army Headquarters' regular "Activity Report." Deception by omission.

Source: *TWC,* 10 (1951), 964–965, for partial English tr.

15   19 Feb. 1941   OKM/Skl Naval *War Diary* entry.

Specifies cover story to be used with junior naval headquarters.

Sources: *TMWC,* 34 (1949), 220, for German text; *NCA* (1946), 6:849, for a very poor English tr.

16   Mar. 1941   Deposition of General Franz von Bentivegni given to his Soviet interrogators on 28 Dec. 1945.

Recollections by the Chief of Abwehr III of Canaris's instructions on security and disinformation operations.

Source: *TMWC,* 7 (1947), 270, for a fragmentary English tr.

17   9 Mar. 1941   Chief OKW, WFSt/Abt.L (IV/Qu) No.00400/41.

Summarizes document 12 for the benefit

of Herr Todt, the chief of military construction.

Source: *NCA* (1946), 1:803, for English tr.

18   11 Mar. 1941   OKW/WFSt/L *War Diary* entry.

The Abwehr's military attaché section is ordered to direct a disinformation campaign against the Soviet military attaché in Berlin, Maj.-Gen. V. I. Tupikov.

Source: Jacobsen, 1 (1965), 352, for German text.

19   12 Mar. 1941   OKW, WFSt/Abt.L (I Op) No.44277/41.

Orders continued simulated preinvasion activities against Britain as camouflage for BARBAROSSA.

Reference: Wheatley (1958), 98, for mention of this unpublished doc.

20   12 Mar. 1941   "Deployment Directive BARBAROSSA," Panzer Group 3, Section Ia, No.25/41.

Pretends deployments in the East are a "precautionary measure" in the event "Russia should change her present attitude towards Germany." Stresses security and camouflage.

Source: *TWC*, 10 (1951), 976–978, for English tr.

21   13 Mar. 1941   Memorandum by Dr. Karl Ritter, Foreign Ministry, Pol I M 653.

On problems of security in dealing with the Russian officials of the German-Russian boundary commission working on the German side of the frontier.

Sources: *Das nationalsozialistische Deutschland und die Sowjetunion, 1939–1941* (Washington, D.C.: Department of State, 1948), pp. 313–314; *DGFP*, 12 (1962), 289–290, for English tr.

22	13 Mar. 1941	OKW/WFSt/L *War Diary* entry.

On OKW-Foreign Ministry-Abwehr collaboration in disinformation campaign against the Russian military attaché in Tokyo by using the German naval attaché there.

Source: Jacobsen, 1 (1965), 356.

23	18 Mar. 1941	Memorandum, Dr. Ernst Woermann, Director, Political Department, Foreign Ministry.

On the design of a pretext to interfere with the free movement in the border area by Russian members of the German-Russian border commissions.

Source: *DGFP*, 12 (1962), 317–318, for English tr.

24	19 Mar. 1941	OKH, General Staff of the Army, Operations Section, No.465/41.

Directs Army Group B to construct defensive fortifications along Russian border to make it seem the German buildup is only a response to the Russian buildup. Soviet intelligence is to be helped to discover these fortifications through spreading rumors and permitting Russian air reconnaissance.

Source: Weinberg (1954), 178–179, for English tr.

25	21 Mar. 1941	Memorandum, "Conference at the OKH Operations Department."

Col. Heusinger and Gen. Greiffenberg discuss doc. 24 and stress need for speed in final deployments to avoid "premature . . . demasking of the secret operation," BARBAROSSA.

Source: *CAGH* (1961), 42–44, and 131, for English tr. and partial German text.

26   22 Mar. 1941   Army Group C *Activity Report* entry.
                            Summarizes doc. 24.
                            Source: *TWC,* 10 (1951), 966, for English
                            tr.

27   26 Mar. 1941   OKW, WFSt/Abt.L (I Op), No.44349/41.
                            Directs the German military com-
                            mander in the Netherlands to maintain
                            the threat of imminent invasion of Brit-
                            ain. Various specific local ruses are au-
                            thorized.
                            Source: Jacobsen, 1 (1965), 1007, for Ger-
                            man text.

28   28 Mar. 1941   Letter, Woermann to Schulenburg.
                            Veiled discussion of the border commis-
                            sion problem.
                            Source: *DGFP,* 12 (1962), 404, for Eng-
                            lish tr.

29   22 Apr. 1941   Army Group North *War Diary* entry.
                            To conceal the buildup at the Russian
                            frontier of Army Group C, the com-
                            mander (Leeb) will stay in Munich. The
                            advanced headquarters has the cover
                            name "Sector Staff East Prussia."
                            Source: *TWC* (1951), 10:967, for partial
                            English tr.

30   22 Apr. 1941   OKM/Skl, B No. 1st Naval War Staff,
                            No.00501/41.
                            In its comments to OKW Operations
                            Staff, the Navy discusses problems of
                            maintaining successful deception.
                            Source: *TWC* (1951), 10:981–982, for
                            English tr.

31   23 Apr. 1941   OKH directive from Brauchitsch.
                            Orders HARPOON SOUTH, deception activ-
                            ities in Norway to imply a continuation
                            of SEA LION.
                            Reference: Wheatley (1958), 98, for pass-

		ing mention of this unpublished directive.
32	24 Apr. 1941	"Instruction for the Preparation of Operation SHARK," OKH, Brauchitsch.

On SHARK, a major deception operation in the English Channel area to simulate SEA LION.

Reference: Wheatley (1958), 98, for mention of this unpublished document.

| 33 | 24 Apr. 1941 | Telegram, No.34112/110, Naval Attaché in Moscow (Baumbach) to OKM. |

Mentions Baumbach's endeavors to counteract the "manifestly absurd" rumors of war current in Moscow.

Sources: *NDS* (1948), 369, for German text; *DGFP*, 12 (1962), 632, for English tr.

| 34 | 28 Apr. 1941 | OKW, WFSt, No.44594/41. |

Briefing notes on how to conceal BARBAROSSA from Finns.

Source: *TWC* (1951), 10:982–984, for English tr.

| 35 | 30 Apr. 1941 | "Conference with Chief L," memorandum of OKW conversation between Tippelskirch and Warlimont. |

"The Führer has decided: BARBAROSSA to begin 22 June." But Germany's allies are to be told that their participation is needed only as rear cover along the Eastern Front during the buildup for the "projected German assault in the West."

Source: *TMWC*, 26 (1947), 399–401, for German text.

| 36 | 1 May 1941 | OKW, No.44638/41. |

On cover story (see doc. 35) to be given Finland, Hungary, and Rumania.

Sources: Hubatsch (1962), 91–92, for

German text; *DGFP*, 12 (1962), 685–686,
for English tr., but omitting distribution
list.

| 37 | 1 May 1941 | OKM directive. |

An order for deception Operation
SHARK (see doc. 32).
Reference: Wheatley (1958), 98, for passing mention of this unpublished document.

| 38 | 3 May 1941 | Telegram No.878, Foreign Ministry Po- |

litical Department to German Embassy
in Moscow.

In reply to doc. 33, the OKW says all
rumors of a Russo-German war are probably a British attempt "to poison the
wells." German military buildup near
Russian border is only "rear cover for
the Balkan operations."
Sources: *NDS* (1948), 374–375, for German text; *DGFP*, 12 (1962), 698–699, for
English tr.

| 39 | 6 May 1941 | OKH, Gen. St. d. H., Op. Abt. Ia, |

No.810/41.

Further specifications for deception operations SHARK and HARPOON to simulate
SEA LION.
Reference: Klee (1958), 226, for citation
of this unpublished document.

| 40 | 10 May 1941 | Army Group North *War Diary* entry. |

Refers to order about local camouflage
to prevent Russian detection.
Source: *TWC* (1951), 10:968, for English
tr.

| 41 | 11 May 1941 | "Combat Directive," Panzer Group 4. |

On tactical deception measures to keep
Russians "in the dark as to the time of

our attack and as to the direction of the push of the Panzer Group."

Source: *TWC* (1951), 10:988–989, for partial English tr.

42 12 May 1941 "Deception of the Enemy," OKW, WFSt/Abt.L (I Op), No.44699/41.

Updates doc. 12. Intensifies simulation of invasion of Britain, stressing the "rear cover" and "feint assembly of forces in the East" themes. False orders to be issued to military and civil authorities. The invasion of Crete (Operation MER-CURY) to be used in slogan: "Crete was the general try-out for the landing in Britain!" Additional steps for the "political" deception of Russia are urged.

Source: *NCA* (1946), 3:635–636, for English tr., complete except for distribution list.

43 12 May 1941 Memorandum, Ritter (Foreign Ministry) of conversation with Jodl (OKW).

Says discussions with Finns on military cooperation should conceal BARBAROSSA and stresses instead the need for German-Finnish defense in case the *Russians* should originate a conflict.

Source: *DGFP*, 12 (1962), 787, for English tr.

44 17 May 1941 Sector Staff East Prussia [Army Group C], Ia/Engineers, 415/41.

On local camouflage measures near Russian frontier.

Source: *TWC* (1951), 10:989–990, for English tr.

45 17 May 1941 Foreign Ministry, State Secretary, No.340.

Memorandum of discussions with the

Japanese and Swedish ambassadors in which State Secretary Weizsäcker stressed that the German buildup was only in defensive reply to the Russian buildup and that the future of German-Russian relations "depended on Stalin's conduct." Sources: *NDS* (1948), 384, for German text; *DGFP*, 12 (1962), 844, for English tr.

46   19 May 1941   OKW/Armed Forces Operations Staff, Department National Defense (IV Qu), No.44560/41.

On special security measures in connection with BARBAROSSA.
Source: *TWC* (1951), 10:990–994, for incomplete English tr.

47   20 May 1941   "Assembly Order for the Attack," Fortress Staff Allenstein [cover name for Army Group North], Sec. Ia, No.95/41.

On tactical security and deception measures to mask the initial invasion assault.
Source: *TWC* (1951), 10:995–996, for partial English tr.

48   22 May 1941   "Conference with Finland," OKW/-WFSt/L (I Op) II Ang., No.44638/41.

On presenting BARBAROSSA to the Finns as merely a defensive contingency.
Source: *TWC* (1951), 10:998–1000, for English tr.

49   22 May 1941   "Conference of the Commander-in-Chief, Navy, with the Führer at the Berghof."

Admiral Raeder reports and Hitler agrees the Russians must be given a plausible cover story to mask the stoppage of supplies to Russia.

Source: *Fuehrer Conferences,* 1 (1947), 62–67, for English tr.

50   24 May 1941   Minute by Woermann for the Foreign Minister.

Instructions for the delay of negotiations with the Russians.

Source: *DGFP,* 12 (1962), 871, for English tr.

51   25 May 1941   OKW/WFSt/Abt.L (I Op), No.44794/41.

The protocol of the OKW-Finnish discussions that day. Stressed to Finns the defensive nature of the German buildup. Germany might launch a preventive war if Russia does not reach a political accommodation with Germany. Tactical deception measures were discussed.

Source: *DGFP,* 12 (1962), 879–885, for English tr.

52   29 May 1941   "Protective Measures against the Population," AOK 17 Ic, No.266/41.

A report by 17th Army headquarters dealing with deception on BARBAROSSA.

Reference: Weinberg (1954), 149, 193, for passing references to this unpublished document.

53   4 June 1941   "Order for the preparation of the deployment BARBAROSSA," Corps Headquarters, XXX Army Corps, Sec. Ia, No.075–41.

Shows that subordinate headquarters were deceived into believing that BARBAROSSA was only a "precaution." Stresses secrecy in the German buildup.

Source: *TWC* (1951), 10:1000–1002, for partial English tr.

54   5 June 1941   "Guidance to OKH bureaus for their dis-

cussions with the Commanders of the Western Front."

In these briefing notes used by Halder, Operation SHARK is discussed as deceptive cover for BARBAROSSA.

Source: Halder, 2 (1963), 479–480.

55   5 June 1941   OKW/WFSt/Abt.L (I Op), No.44842/41, with enclosed "Timetable BARBAROSSA."

Gives the detailed military and deception schedule from 1 June on.

Sources: *TMWC*, 34 (1949), 228–239, for German text; *NCA* (1946), 6:857–867, for English tr.

56   5 June 1941   Verbal instructions of Goebbels at his staff conference, as recalled by Moritz von Schirmeister at the Nürnberg war crimes trial on 29 June 1946.

Reports Goebbels's lie to his own staff that the invasion of Britain was imminent and his ordering a renewed propaganda campaign against Britain.

Source: *TMWC*, 17 (1948), 252, for verbatim English transcript of testimony.

57   12 June 1941   OKM file on Russo-German relations, excerpt.

Mentions a naval directive to prevent the departure of German merchant ships for Russian ports by a false pretext.

Sources: *TMWC*, 34 (1949), 708, for German text; *NCA* (1946), 6:1000, for English tr.

58   12 June 1941   OKH *War Diary* entry.

Recommendations on communications deception by creating false radio traffic in Hungary and Rumania.

Source: Halder, 1 (1963), 453.

59	c.13 June 1941	Memorandum, OKW. On Operation SHARK II. References: Jacobsen, 1 (1965), 415, and Halder, 2 (1963), 450, for passing references to this unpublished document.
60	13 June 1941	Goebbels, "Crete as an Example." Goebbels's published article pretending that the invasion of Crete foreshadows the imminent invasion of Britain. Source: *Völkischer Beobachter,* 13 June 1941.
61	13 June 1941	"Offensive action against enemy submarines in Operation BARBAROSSA," Skl. B. Nr. I. Skl., I. Op, 00969/41. Request to OKW/WFSt/L for security guidance. Sources: *TMWC,* 34 (1949), 226–227, for German text; *NCA* (1946), 6:855–856, for complete but faulty English tr.
62	15 June 1941	"Offensive action against enemy submarines in the Baltic Sea," OKW/WFSt/Abt.L (I Op), No.44986/41. Keitel, in reply to doc. 61, states reason for attacking Russian submarine patrols is to be that they were "believed to be . . . British." Sources: *TMWC,* 34 (1949), 227–228, for German text; *NCA* (1946), 6:856–857, for English tr.
63	15 June 1941	"Planning for BARBAROSSA," OKM/Skl Naval *War Diary* entry. Further consideration of the Russian submarine problem (see docs. 61 and 62). Source: *NCA* (1946), 6:854, for English tr.
64	19 June 1941	Army Group North *War Diary* entry.

On need to avoid war scare by exercising more constraint in civil defense measures in the East.

Source: *TWC* (1951), 10:969, for English tr.

65	21 June 1941	"New Directive for Guidance in Conversation," Foreign Ministry (Bruns).

Gives Foreign Minister Ribbentrop's cover story that he cannot negotiate with the Russians because he is out of Berlin for the day.

Source: *DGFP,* 12 (1962), 1059, for English tr.

66	21 June 1941	"Second Directive for Guidance in Conversation," Foreign Ministry.

Reinforces the cover story in doc. 65.

Source: *DGFP,* 12 (1962), 1059, for English tr.

67	7 Aug. 1941	OKW directive.

Order canceling deception operations SHARK and HARPOON.

Reference: Hillgruber (1965), 460, and Halder, 3 (1964), 109, for citation of this unpublished directive.

German Officials Formally Notified of BARBAROSSA

Note: The names of persons involved in anti-Nazi conspiracies by 22 June 1941 are preceded by an asterisk (*).

Date	Knower	Current Assignment	Number of New Knowers	Cumulative Total (Approximate)
Spring 1940	Adolf Hitler	Führer and CinC Wehrmacht	1	1
c. Spring	Col. Rudolf Schmundt	Chief Adjutant to Führer	1	2
2 June	Col.-Gen. Gerd von Rundstedt Lt.-Gen. Georg von Sodenstern	CG, Army Group A (later South) CofS, Army Group A (later South)	2	4
c. 1 July	Gen. Walther von Brauchitsch	CinC, OKH	1	5
2	*Col.-Gen. Franz Halder	CofS, OKH	1	6
3	Lt.-Col. Eberhard Kinzel	Chief, Eastern Intelligence Department (FHO), OKH	1	7
3	Col. Hans von Greiffenberg	Chief, Ops. Div., OKH	1	8
29	Field-Marshal Wilhelm Keitel	Chief, OKW	1	9
29	Maj.-Gen. Alfred Jodl	Chief, Ops. Staff (WFSt), OKW	1	10
29	Lt.-Col. Adolf Heusinger	First Deputy Chief, Ops. Div., OKH	1	11
29	Maj.-Gen. Erich Marcks	CofS, 18th Army (breveted to OKH)	1	12
29	Col. Walter Warlimont Lt.-Col. Bernhard von Lossberg Capt. Wolfgang Junge Maj. Baron Sigismund von Falkenstein	Chief, L, WFSt, OKW Army / Navy / Luftwaffe } representative with L, WFSt, OKW	4	16
31	Cmdr. Karl Jesko von Puttkamer	Naval Adjutant, OKW	1	17

Date	Knower	Current Assignment	Number of New Knowers	Cumulative Total (Approximate)
by August	*Adm. Wilhelm Canaris	Chief, Abwehr, OKW	1	18
by August	*Col. Franz von Bentivegni	Chief, Section II (security), Abwehr, OKW	1	19
by August	*Col. Hans Piekenbrock	Chief, Section I (intelligence), Abwehr, OKW	1	20
c. 1 Aug.	Ministerialrat Helmuth Greiner	War Diarist of L, WFSt, OKW	1	21
9 Aug.	Reichsmarschall Hermann Göring	CinC, OKL	1	22
c. 9	Lt. Dr. Wilhelm Scheidt	War Diarist of WFSt, OKW	1	23
14	*Inf.-Gen. Georg Thomas	Chief, Wi Rü Amt, OKW	1	24
3 Sept.	Lt.-Gen. Friedrich Paulus	Deputy Chief, OKH	1	25
3	Cav.-Gen. Ernst Köstring	Military Attaché in Moscow	1	26
6	*Col. Hans Oster	CofS, Abwehr, OKW	1	27
Oct.	Lt.-Col. Theodor Rowehl	Luftwaffe photoreconnaissance staff officer	1	28
by 7 Oct.	Maj.-Gen. Hoffmann von Waldau	Chief, Operations Section, OKL	1	29
Nov.	*Maj.-Gen. Eduard Wagner	Chief, Supply and Adm. Div. (i.e., Quartermaster General), OKH	1	30
c. Nov.	{Field-Marshal Wilhelm von Leeb / Field-Marshal Fedor von Bock	CG, Army Group C (later North) / CG, Army Group B (later Center)	2	32
c. Nov.	Lt.-Gen. Kurt Brennecke	CofS, Army Group C	1	33
29 Nov.	Maj.-Gen. Kurt von Tippelskirch	Chief, OQu IV (Foreign Armies Section), OKH	6+	39+

13 Dec.

Anonymous }	Assistants to Tippelskirch	
Anonymous }		
Lt.-Gen. Rudolf Gercke	Chief, Transportation Dept., OKH	
*Gen. Erich Fellgiebel	Chief, Communications (WNV), OKH	
Lt. Gen. (Luftwaffe) Rudolf Bogatsch	OKL liaison officer with OKH	26
Inf.-Gen. Hans von Salmuth	CofS, Army Group B	
Cav.-Gen. Eberhard von Mackensen	CofS, 12th Army	
Lt.-Gen. Eugen Müller	General Officer Specially Employed, OKH	
Lt.-Gen. Karl Hilpert	CofS, Army Group D	
Maj.-Gen. Rudolf Konrad	OKH Liaison Officer to OKL	
Maj.-Gen. Walter Buhle	Chief, Organization Dept., OKH	
Naval Capt. Loycke	OKM liaison with OKH	
Col. Richter	CofS, 7th Army	
Col. Edgar Röhricht	CofS, 1st Army	
Col. Erich Buschenhagen	CofS, German forces in Norway	
Col. Otto Wöhler	CofS, 17th Army	
Col. Wilhelm Hasse	CofS, 18th Army	
Col. von Witzleben	CofS, 2nd Army	
Col. Weckmann	CofS, 9th Army	
Col. Günther Blumentritt	CofS, 4th Army	
Col. Rolf Wuthmann	CofS, 16th Army	
Col. Heim	CofS, 6th Army	
Col. Bäntsch	Department head, Quartermaster-General Dept., OKH	
Col. von Bernuth	Ausb. Abt., OKH	
Col. Ulrich Liss	Chief, 3rd Dept., OKH	
Lt.-Col. von Ziehlberg	Chief, Central Dept., OKH	
Lt.-Col. Max Bork	Chief, Field Transportation Dept., OKH	
Maj. H. G. Schmidt von Altenstadt	Department head, OKH	
	Chief, Military Administration Dept., OKH	
Maj. Burkhart Müller-Hillebrand	Chief Adjutant (to Halder), OKH	
1st Lt. Nette	Staff Officer, OKH	65+

Date	Knower	Current Assignment	Number of New Knowers	Cumulative Total (Approximate)
13 Dec.	Col.-Gen. Johannes von Blaskowitz	CG, 1st Army	1	66+
18 Dec.	Obergruppenführer Reinhard Heydrich	Chief, RSHA, SS	1	67+
18 Dec.	Grand-Admiral Erich Raeder Adm. Otto Schniewind	CinC, OKM CofS, OKM	2+	69+
1 Jan. 1941	Reichsführer-SS Heinrich Himmler	Chief, SS	1	70+
c. 1 Jan.	Field-Marshal Albert Kesselring	Commander-designate, Air Fleet 2	1	71+
Jan.	Field-Marshal Günther von Kluge	CG, Fourth Army	2+	73+
Jan.	Col. Torsten Christ	Aide to Maj.-Gen. Hoffman von Waldau, Luftwaffe Operations Chief	1	74+
Jan.	Brigadeführer-SS [Maj.-Gen.] Walter Schellenberg	Head, Amt IVE (counterespionage), SD, SS	1	75+
13 Jan.	Field-Marshal Erhard Milch	Inspector-General, Luftwaffe	1	76+
mid-Jan.	Col. Josef Schmid	Chief, Intelligence Section, Luftwaffe	1	77+
c. Feb.	*Lt.-Col. Henning von Tresckow	GSO-1, Army Group B (Center)	1	78+
by Feb.	*Lt.-Col. Erwin von Lahousen	Chief, Section II (sabotage), Abwehr, OKW	1	80+
by Feb.	Lt.-Gen. Hermann Reinecke	Chief, General Armed Forces Dept. (AWA), OKW	1	81+
late Feb.	Maj.-Gen. Kurt von Österreich	Commander, POW Section, 20th Military District (Danzig)	20+	101+
	Over 20 others	Commanders of district POW sections		

Date	Name(s)	Position	No.	Ref.
28 Feb.	Col. Becht Lt.-Col. Witte Lt.-Col. Luther Lt.-Col. Gerhard Matzky Maj. Otto von Gusevius Maj. Hans von Payr Maj. Huch Capt. Emmerich Capt. Dr. Hamann	Staff, Wi Rü Amt, OKW	9	110+
by 10 Mar.	*Maj. Fabian von Schlabrendorff	Aide to Tresckow	1	111+
19 Mar.	Capt. Bernd von Brauchitsch	?Staff, Wi Rü Amt, OKW (or Göring's staff)	1	112+
20 Mar.	Col. Jansen	?Staff, Wi Rü Amt, OKW	1	113+
by 21 Mar.	Col. Rudolf Huenermann Ministerial Director Sarnow	Chief of Staff, Wi Rü Amt, OKW Staff, Quartermaster-General Dept., OKH	2	115+
27 Mar.	Lt.-Gen. (Luftwaffe)Karl Bodenschatz Lt.-Col. Walther Scherff Maj. Nicolaus von Below Maj. Eckhardt Julius Christians Lt.-Col. Sieverth Joachim von Ribbentrop Senior Counselor Walter Hewel Maj.-Gen. Enno von Rintelen	Aide to Göring? In military history section, OKW Luftwaffe adjutant in Führer HQ An aide to Jodl ? Foreign Minister Head, Personal Staff, Reich Foreign Minister Military Attaché in Rome	8	123+
30 Mar.	Briefing for c. 250 military staff members concerned		—	c. 250+
2 Apr.	Reichsleiter Alfred Rosenberg	Chief, Foreign Policy Office (APA), Nazi party	1	c. 251+
21 Apr.	*Ernst von Weizsäcker	State Secretary, Foreign Ministry	1	
by 29 Apr.	Lt.-Gen. (Air) Dr. Wilhelm Schubert	Staff, Wi Rü Amt, OKW	1	c. 252+

Date	Knower	Current Assignment	Number of New Knowers	Cumulative Total (Approximate)
by 29 Apr.	Capt. (Cavalry) Jonas	Staff, Wi Rü Amt, OKW	1	c. 253+
c. late Apr.	Walther Funk	Minister of Economics and President of Reichsbank	1	c. 254+
Apr.	Martin Bormann	Chief of Staff (Stabsleiter), Nazi party	1	c. 255+
16 May	Maj. Gaedke	Staff, Wi Rü Amt, OKW	1	c. 256+
c. 25 May	SS Gruppenführer Otto Ohlendorf	Leader Amt III (Domestic Security Service), RSHA, SS	1	c. 257+

Notes

Chapter 1

1. See the delightful essays in Robin W. Winks, ed., *The Historian as Detective: Essays on Evidence* (New York: Harper & Row, 1969).
2. Subsequently published as Whaley (1969*a*). Full references for sources abbreviated in the notes, for example, by author and year, will be found in the Bibliography.
3. I recall these as being Beloff, 2 (1949); Carell (1965); Churchill, 3 (1950); Clark (1965); D. Dallin (1955); Erickson (1962); Farago (1954); Farago (1961); Foote (1949); Hull (1948); Johnson (1964); Khrushchev (1965); Langer and Gleason (1953); Welles (1944); Werth (1964); and Willoughby (1952).
4. The only cases of careful scholarship were Beloff, 2 (1949); Erickson (1962); Langer and Gleason (1953); and Weinberg (1954).
5. Kalinov (1950).
6. Wohlstetter (1962).
7. Oskar Morgenstern, *The Question of National Defense* (New York: Random House, 1959), p. 226n. Wohlstetter's study, patently and explicitly free of any revelations from classified sources, had been suppressed for political reasons.
8. Wohlstetter (1962), 3.
9. Wohlstetter posits her tentative claim of generalization on pp. 398–401 of her book.
10. The only replication is Johan Jörgen Holst, "Surprise, Signals and Reaction: The Attack on Norway, April 9th, 1940—Some Observations," *Cooperation and Conflict,* 1966, no. 1, pp. 31–45.
11. A point overlooked by the only three books—all recent ones—that make an effort at all comparable to mine at collating all warnings: Nekrich (1968), Salisbury (1969), and Bialer (1969).

Chapter 2

1. Adolf Hitler, *Mein Kampf* (1939), 950–951; see also Laqueur (1965).
2. Hitler had first raised this question with his senior military commanders in 1934. See O'Neill (1966), iv, 40–41. For relevant remarks by Hitler to his personal adjutant, Colonel Rudolf Schmundt, see Freiden and Richardson (1956), 39, and *TMWC* (1947), 7:158–160.
3. Ribbentrop (1954), 146.
4. The detailed scenario for Paulus's *Kriegspiel* is given in Goerlitz (1963), 99–120. Paulus later thought the two-day exercise was played in mid-December. Professor Goerlitz accepts this date uncritically. Actually, the game was played in three phases, beginning on 29 November and 3 and 7 December. See Blau (1955), 19–20, and Halder, 2 (1963), 201, 205, 217, which pinpoint these dates.
5. Warlimont (1964), 111–114; see also Halder, 2 (1963), 49–50, entry for 31 August 1940, and NCA (1946), 5:740.
6. The term first appears on 1 August 1940 in Helmut Greiner's OKW/L diary. See Jacobsen, 1 (1965), 5, and 6, 16.
7. For this commonly overlooked chapter in the history of Nazism see Laqueur (1965), 64–68.

8. OTTO was completed on 10 May 1941. See Pottgiesser (1960), 21–26. See also Halder, 2 (1963), 133, 208, 210, 214, 216, 224, 381. Judging from Halder's OKH diary, codename OTTO was in use from 11 October 1940 to 25 April 1941.

9. As closely argued and impressively documented by Weinberg (1954), 116–117, 128–129, 138–139.

10. Schmidt (1951), 209–220. See also eyewitness recollections of Ribbentrop (1954), 148–150, 154–155; Hilger and Meyer (1953), 291, 321–325; and Weizsäcker (1951), 245–246. For the details of Molotov's visit see Weinberg (1954), 140–144.

11. Or so Ribbentrop (1954), 152, recalled in 1946.

12. DGFP, 12 (1962), 373. See also the Halder (1947) diary for 27 March.

13. Jacobsen, 1 (1965), 213.

14. Ibid., 226, and Halder, 2 (1963), 224.

15. Jacobsen, 1 (1965), 233, 265; see also Halder, 2 (1963), 248.

16. Ernst Kantorowicz, Frederick the Second, 1194–1250 (London: Constable, 1931), p. 688.

17. See Reuben Ainsztein, "How Hitler Died: The Soviet Version," International Affairs (London), vol. 43, no. 2 (April 1967), pp. 307–318, and Lev Bezymenski, The Death of Adolf Hitler: Unknown Documents from Soviet Archives (London: Michael Joseph, 1968).

18. For the designation B-Tag, see Jacobsen, 1 (1965), 365, and The Case Against General Heusinger (1961), 49, 50, 137, 138. This last source, valuable only for its publication of hitherto unpublished OKH documents captured by the Russians, is hereafter cited as CAGH.

19. For the specific plans and schedule for the attack on Russia see Weinberg (1954), 106–173. See also Higgins (1966); Blau (1955); Wheeler-Bennett (1961), 509–513; Carell (1965); Shirer (1960), 793–852; Churchill, 3 (1950), 361; Seth (1964); Eden (1965), 185, 220, 229–230; Ansel (1960), 135, 172–189, 295–296. The reader is cautioned that except for Weinberg's monograph all these works are quite defective, even in their mere recitation of the documentary evidence. The early book by Blau (1955) is useful but undocumented. The only instances of careful scholarship found are the early but still essential works by Langer and Gleason (1953); Weinberg (1954); and the more recent book by Higgins (1966).

20. NCA (1946), 6: 857–867, gives the complete translated text of OKW document no. 44842/41, "Timetable BARBAROSSA," dated 6 June 1941. The history of "Timetable BARBAROSSA" is given by Warlimont (1964), 147. For a derivative OKH summary dated 10 June see CAGH (1961), 50, 138.

21. Halder, 2 (1963), 456, entry for 14 June 1941.

22. Warlimont (1964), 147, 605–606; Goerlitz (1963), 107; and Halder, 2 (1963), 455. The agenda and list of those invited are in NCA (1946), 6:909–911.

23. NCA (1946), 6:1001.

24. Weizsäcker (1951), 225. See also DGFP, 12 (1962), 1050, 1059, 1061–1063.

25. Jacobsen, 1 (1965), 408. DORTMUND is the first entry for 21 June in the OKH diary of Halder, 2 (1963), 450.

26. Jacobsen, 1 (1965), 409. For the special Luftwaffe schedule see Bekker (1968), 217–218.

27. On the Russian unpreparedness see particularly Erickson (1962a), 565–627, and Werth (1964), 131–167.

Chapter 3

1. Churchill, 2 (1949), 135–136. Some writers such as Shirer (1960), 795, mistakenly presume that Churchill's letter was delivered prior to Cripps's audience. This error probably results from the circumstance that no mention was made of the meeting itself until leaked by the B.B.C. on 17 July. See *New York Times*, 18 July 1940, p. 13.

2. *DGFP*, 10 (1957), 207–208.

3. Ibid.

4. See also Paulus in Goerlitz (1963), 121–122.

5. See, for example, Huss (1942), 271–274, for observations by the International News Service (INS) correspondent in Berlin.

6. For example, see the OSS memoir, Peter Tompkins, *A Spy in Rome* (New York: Simon and Schuster, 1962), pp. 90–91.

7. *DGFP*, 11 (1960), 941–943, citing a report dated 26 November 1940 from the Turkish ambassador in Moscow, Ali Haydar Aktay, intercepted by the German ambassador in Ankara.

8. Noel-Baker (1955), 210–217, and Petrov and Petrov (1956), 204–205. Much later, in 1946, Enbom was transferred to the direction of the GRU. See also *FRUS: 1941*, 1 (1958), 33.

9. Mannerheim (1954), 397, 404.

10. Huss (1942), 274.

11. Erickson (1962a), 574, 586; Raymond L. Garthoff, *Soviet Military Doctrine* (Glencoe, Ill.: The Free Press, 1953), p. 434; Petrov and Petrov (1956), 94; and Fedyuninsky (1961), 5–6.

12. Carell (1965), 47, 57. Unfortunately Paul "Carell" (Dr. Paul Karl Schmidt) does not cite a source for this highly interesting piece of evidence.

13. On the Wehrmacht's mobilization for BARBAROSSA, see Weinberg (1954), 118–119.

14. Huss (1942), 271–273.

15. Ibid., 255–258. See also *FRUS: 1941*, 1 (1958), 141n, and ibid., 4 (1956), 940.

16. Huss (1942), 258, and Bor-Kormorowski (1951), 57.

17. *CAGH* (1961), 44.

18. Lonsdale (1965), 25–30.

19. Huss (1942), 270. As matters turned out, the Germans had taken 2,053,000 prisoners by 1 November and 3,600,000 by 28 February 1942. See *NCA* (1946), 3:127.

20. A. Dallin (1957), 409–411, 412n3.

21. *TMWC* (1947), 7:175, 363–364, citing the Soviet interrogation of Lieutenant-Colonel Kurt von Österreich, a former POW district chief.

22. Blumentritt's recollections in Frieden and Richardson (1956), 42.

23. On German intelligence on and in Russia see Reile (1963); Höhne and Zolling (1971), chap. 1; Jong (1956), 125–133, 235–240; Leverkuehn (1954), 115–183 and throughout; Schellenberg (1956), 23–28, 130, 132–133, 136–146, 190–207, 233, 261–276, 373–375; Gouzenko (1948), 64, 65, 74–75; and *TMWC* (1947), 7:270–273.

24. Greiner (1951), 312–313.

25. Carell (1965), 59–61.

26. Halder, 2 (1963), 308, entry for 11 March 1941, and Jong (1956), 236.

27. Halder, 2 (1963), 448, diary entry for 7 June 1941.

28. Carell (1965), 59–61; *TMWC* (1947), 7:402–403; and Blau (1955), 42.

29. For example, Jong (1956), 237. For the actual Rowehl bases see Eyermann, 2 (1963), 44.

30. *NSR* (1948), 328, and reprinted in *DGFP*, 12 (1962), 602–603; and for the German responses, ibid., 822, 841. As too often elsewhere, Shirer (1960), 841, misinterprets (and misdates) this document.

31. *DGFP*, 12 (1962), 1061–1063, 1071–1072.

32. *New York Times*, 29 June 1941, p. 18.

33. *TWC* (1949), 12:1268. See also Weinberg (1954), 165. Although this and related detailed top secret OKW and Abwehr "special reports" to the Foreign Ministry on border violations are presumably true, Warlimont (1964), 148, recently revealed that they were only written around June, being predated in many instances in order to fabricate a case for preventive war. Although no totals are given, the number of Russian overflights between 11 and 19 April 1941 was more than 14. Hitler also mentioned such overflights to Rumanian head of state Antonescu at their meeting on 11 June 1941. *DGFP*, 12 (1962), 1004.

34. *New York Times*, 23 June 1941, p. 10.

35. Constance Babington-Smith, *Air Spy: The Story of Photo Intelligence in World War II* (New York: Harper & Brothers, 1957), pp. 6–12, 22–25, 73, 187. British photoreconnaissance missions were apparently first flown over Poland and East Prussia only in 1943, using the new high-performance plywood Mosquito bombers.

36. Ample documentation exists, but the two most detailed summaries are Soviet: "Sovetskie organy" (1965), 20–39, Nekrich (1968), 53–54, 76–82, 164–166 (of Petrov [1968] translation). See also the accounts by Jong (1956); Leverkuehn (1954); and Schellenberg (1956), 158, 205–206.

37. *IVOVSS*, 1 (1960), 478, as cited by Nekrich (1968), 165.

38. Nekrich (1968), 164.

39. See Appendix A, doc. 6.

40. "Sovetsky organy" (1965), 17 (of translation), citing archives of the USSR Ministry of Defense, no. 7272, d. 1, 1. 75.

41. Berezhkov (1966a), no. 1, p. 11, and in Bialer (1969), 212.

42. Colvin (1951), 91, 138, based on his postwar interview with Madame J—— at her new home in England. Her relationship with Canaris was verified to

Colvin by a former Polish diplomat. Colvin is a sober journalist who worked closely with the British S.I.S. in the late 1930s and early 1940s.
43. Werth (1964), 119–120.
44. Cripps's view—but not the warning—is confirmed by Gafencu (1945), 135, 198, where, however, Cripps's return to Moscow is incorrectly dated 7 March 1941. In fact, he returned to Moscow on 28 February. See also *FRUS: 1941*, 3 (1959), 833, and Eden, 2 (1965), 240.
45. Duranty (1941), 185–186.
46. "Sovetskie organy" (1965), 27.
47. Zhukov (1971), 228–229. This report is incorrectly identified by Höhne (1971), 236 as originating with the Soviet military attaché in Berlin. The anachronistic use of Petrograd for Leningrad shows that, whatever its source, it was not drafted by a Soviet citizen.
48. I am indebted to Professor William E. Griffith of M.I.T., a friend of Woods, for disclosing the name and role of Respondik.
49. Long (1966), 182–184, and Hull, 2 (1948), 967–168. Slightly garbled versions are in Farago (1961), 121–123, and Shirer (1960), 842–843.
50. Long (1966), 183n.
51. A reference by Roosevelt to other material from Woods is in a letter to Hull dated 3 March 1941. In this Roosevelt refers to a lengthy copy of a German report on raw material needs and the Soviet fulfillment of these. See Roosevelt (1950), 1130–1131. The original intercepted German report, dated Berlin 24 January 1941, is now missing from the U.S. files. See Langer and Gleason (1953), 340–341.
52. Hull (1948), 968; Long (1966), 184; and Welles (1944), 171. Langer and Gleason (1953), 336–337, 341–342, recognize the serious discrepancies among the recollections of Hull and Welles and the surviving archival records but only partly succeed in resolving them. Long gives the needed evidence.
53. The texts of the Hull telegram of the first, Steinhardt's reply of the third, and Hull's rejoinder of the fourth are in *FRUS: 1941*, 1 (1958), 712–714.
54. Hull (1948), 968–969, and Welles (1944), 170–171. The original U.S. memos of the Welles-Umansky meeting of 1 March are lost. The initial publication of this story—apparently as a "leak" from the White House itself—was in an article by Forrest Davis and Ernest K. Lindley in the *Ladies Home Journal* for July 1942, reprinted in Davis and Lindley (1942), 175–176, 241. This garbled version incorrectly states that Umansky was given the 22 June date but took the news casually. It also charged that Umansky had immediately conveyed Welles's warning to the German ambassador in Washington, an allegation flatly denied by Umansky from Moscow. See also D. Dallin (1942), 332–333. Umansky's actual disclosure and public denial are discussed in warning 15. The lost papers are reportedly among Welles's effects.
55. The assertion (by Davis and Lindley, and by others following them) that the Soviet government had formally asked that the 20 March meeting be held so that Welles could "repeat" the warning is borne out neither by these authors' own sources nor by the other relevant surviving documents. See

FRUS: 1941, 1 (1958), 723, and *Peace and War* (1943), 638, for Welles's memo of conversation of 20 March 1941.

56. *FRUS: 1941,* 1 (1958), 723n.

57. Hull's statement about lack of any later response is not strictly accurate. On 22 March, during his next talk with Welles, Umansky vaguely indicated that his government had become more apprehensive about German designs upon them. See ibid., 4 (1956), 112–113.

58. *DGFP,* 12 (1962), 221–227.

59. "Sovetskie organy" (1965), 17. See also Nekrich (1968), 84, who, though entirely on the basis of Schmidt's transcript in *DGFP,* 12 (1962), 221–227, perceives Göring's remarks to have embodied such "very transparent hints" that Antonescu could have had no "doubts about the approaching war with the USSR."

60. A general historical and analytic study of this office is given in Alfred Vagts, *The Military Attaché* (Princeton: Princeton University Press, 1967).

61. See warning 7.

62. Zhukov (1971), 229.

63. Ibid.

64. The most detailed account is by Farago (1967). Except for some errors inevitable in a work of this type and some highly questionable extrapolations of data from earlier periods, this is an excellent book. Reviewers have grossly underrated it, perhaps because they were biased by the slap-dash character of some of his numerous earlier books on intelligence, by his rather eccentric career, or merely by the obvious pun on his name. Other accounts are in Kahn (1967), 26–27, 507–508, and Wohlstetter (1962), 177–178.

65. The complete text as translated in *DGFP,* 12 (1962), 661.

66. For details of its interception see Farago (1967), 191. Farago is seemingly wrong in dating the interception to the twenty-ninth, probably because he overlooks the Berlin-Washington time difference.

67. *PHA* (1946), 3:1861, as translated by the U.S. Navy's Op-20-GZ section on 6 May 1941. A slightly different version is given by Farago (1967), 191.

68. For the Japanese security investigation and findings see *PHA* (1946), vol. 3, p. 1203, vol. 4, pp. 1859–1863, vol. 5, pp. 2069–2070; Farago (1967), 192–194, 197–199; Tōgō (1956), 61, 167–169; Kahn (1967), 26–27; and Wohlstetter (1962), 178.

69. For the American security investigation and findings see Farago (1967), 194–195, 200–201; Kahn (1967), 24–28; and *PHA* (1946), 3:1130–1133, 1208–1210, 1369–1370, and 11:5475. See also Wohlstetter (1962), 176–179.

70. Farago (1967), 195–196, 412. Farago's information on these BARBAROSSA intercepts comes from the index of translations and memoranda kept by Captain Laurence Safford, the then chief of Op-20-G.

71. Farago (1967), 196–197. This is the only published allegation of Welles's disclosure of "Magic" to the Russians. Farago's charge is entirely "based on interviews and correspondence with sources who wish to remain anonymous." While this is hardly conclusive and such deplorable anonymous denunciations must be suspect, the charge fits the circumstantial evidence to such a

degree that I accept it as the best-fitting hypothesis. The leak did occur, and Welles had the best opportunity and the strongest motive to perpetrate it.
72. Ibid., 197.
73. Farago (1967) missed this contemporary evidence that partly confirms his version.
74. Forrest Davis and Ernest K. Lindley, "How War Came," *Ladies' Home Journal*, July 1942, pp. 109–110, as cited by D. Dallin (1942), 332–333.
75. "1941 Report to Nazis Denied by Oumansky," *New York Times*, 6 July 1942, p. 6.
76. See Davis and Lindley (1942), 175–176, 241.
77. Mowrer (1968), 321. Mowrer was working in Washington, D.C., at that time.
78. On the Polish underground intelligence and its communications see Bor-Komorowski (1951), 56–62; Mikolajczyk (1948), 8, 11; and Listowel (1952), 77–80.
79. Bor-Komorowski (1951), 56–57.
80. Ibid., 57–58.
81. Ibid., 58, and Churchill, 3 (1950), 390, who dates these reports only "since March, 1941" and does not acknowledge the earlier ones. See also Ciechanowski (1947), 24, who states this intelligence was "promptly passed to the Allied Governments."
82. Bor-Komorowski (1951), 58.
83. Ibid., 58, 62, and Ciechanowski (1947), 24.
84. Bor-Komorowski (1951), 63–64.
85. Whitwell (1966), 187–189.
86. Weinberg (1954), 160. On Skorniakov see also D. Dallin (1955), 133.
87. "Sovetskie organy" (1965), 27, citing the archives of the Ministry of Defense, no. 4551, d. 2, 1. 79.
88. As reported in telegram, Steinhardt to Hull, 24 March 1941, printed in *FRUS: 1941,* 1 (1958), 133–134.
89. See previously cited telegram from Steinhardt. The memoirs of Assarsson (1963) should be checked to see if they give any relevant details.
90. On Wennerström see H. K. Ronblöm, *The Spy Without a Country* (New York: Coward-McCann, 1965), pp. 45–49, and Thomas Whiteside, *An Agent in Place* (New York: Viking, 1966), pp. 8–12.
91. Warlimont (1964), 160–171. For general discussions of the order see Reitlinger (1960), 66–86, and A. Dallin (1957), 30–34.
92. Hassel (1947), 189. Von Hassel learned the details from Oster on 8 April at Colonel-General Ludwig Beck's home. See also Schlabrendorff (1947), 33, and Higgins (1966), 101–102.
93. Ritter (1958), 213–214.
94. Manstein (1958), 179–180.
95. Telegram from Steinhardt to Hull, 6 April 1941, in *FRUS: 1941,* 1 (1958), 302. This information had been given Steinhardt in person that very afternoon by Gavrilović. A similar verbal report was subsequently given by Gavrilović to Alexander Werth (1964), 121. Although signed at 1:30 A.M. on

6 April 1941, the published treaty was predated one day, probably only as a clerical oversight, although most commentators unwarrantedly presume a devious Russian motive to avoid gratuitously insulting the Germans who invaded Yugoslavia four hours later, at 5:30 A.M. Central European Time. See, for example, Cassidy (1943), 10–11. In a later retelling, Gavrilović is made to quote Molotov [sic] as saying: "We are ready." See *FRUS: 1941*, 1 (1958), 315, citing the memorandum by the first secretary of the U.S. embassy in Turkey, on an informal conversation with Gavrilović in Ankara on 16 June. The USSR broke relations with the Yugoslav government on 8 May, but Gavrilović did not leave Moscow until 3 June, going directly to Turkey.
96. Cassidy (1943), 10. In part confirmed by Hoptner (1962), 278–280, who quotes Gavrilović to the effect that Vyshinsky frankly admitted to him that the *Russians* had been listening in.

Chapter 4

1. Although the British parachuted in additional transmitters later in the war, the Czechoslovak underground intelligence service was substantially reduced in effectiveness by the German purge following the assassination of SS intelligence chief Heydrich in 1942. Specifically, the Germans' enhanced security measures cut the link between the German General Staff and Czechoslovak intelligence. For the émigré Czech military intelligence see Beneš (1954), 41n, 70–71, 84, 85, 102, 136, 137, 138, 143, 146, 149–150, 158n, and Wiener (1969).
2. On Czechoslovak intelligence liaisons with the British and Yugoslavs, see Beneš (1954), 150, 152, 158n.
3. Or so recalls William Phillips, the head of the American OSS London office about August 1942, when he was told this by Beneš. See Phillips (1952), 336.
4. Beneš (1954), 149–150, 153–154, 164n.
5. Ibid., 150, where "March" is given incorrectly, as is clear from remarks on pp. 149 and 153 as well as from the reference to the ongoing Yugoslav campaign. Moreover, the April date is what he told Phillips (1952), 336, the following year.
6. Beneš (1954), 150–151. As partially verified by Phillips (1952), 336.
7. Beneš (1954), 150–151. Churchill makes no reference in his memoirs to this meeting, much less to Beneš's disclosure. Arnold verifies details of the meeting but does not mention this topic as having been raised. H. H. Arnold, *Global Mission* (New York: Harper, 1949), pp. 231–232. However, *Saturday Evening Post* correspondent Vincent Sheean confirms the essence of Beneš's version of prior intelligence: that Beneš learned Hitler's intention in late February and knew his deployments and plans in April. See Sheean (1943), 331–332.
8. Beneš (1954). Soviet Ambassador Maisky (1968), 169, confirms only that Beneš "disposed of very valuable information about the situation in Germany and Central Europe, which he willingly shared with us."

9. On Czech liaison with the Russian intelligence see Beneš (54), 146, 164n. Colonel Pika was hanged by the Czechoslovak Communist government in 1949 for his alleged spying in Moscow for British intelligence while serving as Czechoslovak military attaché during World War II. His case was being reopened by the Dubček regime in 1968, just before the Soviet invasion. For Pika see Sir Robert Bruce Lockhart, *Friends, Foes and Foreigners* (London: Putnam, 1957), pp. 133–139.

10. Kurt Glaser, *Czecho-Slovakia: A Critical History* (Caldwell, Idaho: Caxton, 1961), pp. 71, 260.

11. Beneš (1954), 154.

12. For Paul Thummel, see Wiener (1969), 25ff., 61–69, 174. I understand that a biography, titled *Agent A-54*, was published in Czechoslovakia in the early 1960s. Thummel's role in BARBAROSSA has been confirmed to me by Dr. Ladislav Bittman, a former deputy chief of Department D[isinformation] of the Czechoslovak Interior Ministry.

13. In general, see Bailey (1960), and A. Dallin (1957).

14. Höhne (1971), 52–53.

15. A. Dallin (1957), 117–118. An inaccurate account of these two is Guenther Reinhardt, "Hitler Aide—Stalin Spy," *Plain Talk*, vol. 3, no. 11 (August 1949), pp. 24–28.

16. Drożdżyński and Zaborowski (1960), 75–79, 165–166.

17. See Chapter 6; A. Dallin (1957), 118; and Armstrong (1963), 75.

18. Flannery (1942), 239.

19. One also meets the incorrect dates of 1, 3, 5, 6, 7, and 11 March for the Hitler-Paul meeting. Some Yugoslav sources also accept an apocryphal visit on 18 March. Even Churchill, 3 (1950), 356, errs in giving this 18 March date. The official German Foreign Office records are *DGFP*, 12 (1962), 218–219, 230–233. The 4 March date is independently confirmed by the OKW/L war diary. See Jacobsen, 1 (1965), 344. Furthermore, the error of these other dates is clear from a check of Hitler's itinerary and activities such as that compiled by Hillgruber (1965), app. B–7.

20. Woodward, 1 (1970), 604, 609, and Eden (1965), 220, 265. See also *FRUS: 1941*, 1 (1958), 315, and Fotitch (1948), 58–59. Eden's unlikely tale is also conveniently accepted by Dedijer (1953), 134. The ultimate source of this leak, if such there was, is not disclosed. Although Prince Paul discussed this secret meeting later that month (20 March) with friend and prominent anti-Hitler conspirator, Ulrich von Hassell, he did not disclose BARBAROSSA to the German resistance. Hassell (1947), 175–178. Similarly, though Prince Paul saw U.S. Ambassador Lane and discussed his visit with Hitler, he apparently did not mention any such matter to him. The Overseas News Agency (ONA) Balkan correspondent, Leigh White, had the same story in Belgrade around 10 March from "a Serbian friend . . . who worked for British Intelligence." Leigh White, *The Long Balkan Night* (New York: Scribner's, 1944), pp. 175–176.

21. *FRUS: 1941, 2* (1959), 973.

22. Officially, Donovan was designated "Unofficial Observer of the Secretary of the Navy of the United States." See Hyde (1962), 45–46, and Corey Ford, *Donovan of OSS* (Boston: Little, Brown, 1970), pp. 102–103.

23. This is the belief of the SD's southeast European affairs officer, Wilhelm Hoettl (1953), 134, who also asserts that Simović had close liaison with British and Russian intelligence.

24. Memorandum of conversation of 16 June by Robert F. Kelley, the first secretary of the U.S. embassy in Turkey, in *FRUS: 1941,* 1 (1958), 312–315. For MacMurray's telegram to Hull of 22 June, see ibid., 3 (1959), 870–871.

25. See *DGFP,* 12 (1962), 231n.

26. As repeated in his memoirs (1965), and Woodward, 1 (1970), 604–605. Among historians, only McSherry, 1 (1970), 299–300, rejects this story as improbable.

27. "Sovetskie organy" (1965), 27, and Nekrich (1968), 180.

28. L. I. Pankratov, interview in *Trud,* 19 December 1967, pp. 1–3, as translated in *FBIS* (USSR), 10 January 1968.

29. Ibid.

30. Nekrich (1968), 179. There is no anachronism because the British, as noted, had received their information in late March.

31. Deborin and Telpukhovsky (1967), 133.

32. Churchill, 3 (1950), 352–369. See also Eden, 2 (1965), 324–325. Additional material on the views of the various segments of the British intelligence community is in Gwyer (1964), 82–84.

33. Gwyer (1964), 83. More briefly cited in Churchill, 3 (1950), 356.

34. Gwyer (1964), 83.

35. Churchill, 3 (1950), 358. Khrushchev in his "secret" speech also acknowledged Churchill's message; see Khrushchev in Wolfe (1957), 166.

36. But see Werth (1964), 276–277, for Cripps's version given to correspondent Werth in the summer of 1941. In defending himself, Cripps only demonstrates the gulf in understanding that existed between himself and Churchill. See also *FRUS: 1941,* 1 (1958), 164–165.

37. Churchill, 3 (1950), 358–361. Tactfully, Eden, in his otherwise detailed memoirs, makes no mention of this particular awkward incident. This sorry tale is recounted in detail in Woodward, 1 (1970), 604–607.

38. Churchill, 4 (1950), 493. Beaverbrook returned to London on 10 October and promptly reported to Churchill and Eden, apparently mentioning Stalin's query at that time. See Eden (1965), 278.

39. Churchill, 4 (1950), 493.

40. Zhukov (1971), 224.

41. *NSR* (1948); *NCA* (1946), 6:997; and reprinted in *DGFP,* 12 (1962), 632.

42. *DGFP,* 12 (1962), 721.

43. These meetings in 1941 were on 16 April and 2, 5, 10, and 13 June according to Eden, 2 (1965), 238, 265–269. The extraordinary meeting of 13 June is described in *FRUS: 1941,* 1 (1958), 170–172. Curiously, Maisky (1968) does not mention these early warnings from Eden but, as described below,

only later ones from Cadogan and Cripps. But Soviet historian Nekrich (1968), 193, freely summarizes and cites the *FRUS* document.

44. Werth (1964), 277.

45. Sweet-Escott (1965), 51, 84.

46. Summarized in *FRUS: 1941*, 1 (1958), 141n.

47. Langer and Gleason (1953), 527n.

48. See Weizsäcker (1951), 253.

49. Whaley (1969*a*), and Höhne (1971), 35–39.

50. The best studies of Trepper and his network are D. Dallin (1955); Perrault (1969); and Höhne (1971).

51. Perrault (1969), 45.

52. D. Dallin (1955), 132–136; Schellenberg (1956), 139–140; and W. G. Krivitsky, *In Stalin's Secret Service* (New York and London: Harper, 1939), 214, 216.

53. Ege's testimony before U.S. Congress, Senate, Judiciary Committee, Internal Security Subcommittee, *Interlocking Subversion in Government Departments: Hearing*, 83rd Congress, 1st session, 28, 29 October 1953, pt. 15, pp. 1005–1006.

54. Berezhkov (1966*a*), 10–11.

55. As quoted by Khrushchev in Wolfe (1957), 166, 168. Both ellipses as in original text. Vorontsov was neither a "Captain" nor the "military attaché" as the text of Khrushchev's speech has it, and as all subsequent Western commentators except Salisbury (1969), 65, have uncritically accepted. Vorontsov is authoritatively identified by Berezhkov (1966), in Bialer (1969), 213, and Kuznetsov (1967), no. 2, 99–100.

56. Lonsdale (1965), 28–30.

57. Casey (1962), 67.

58. Dozens of books and articles have been written on Sorge's GRU network in Tokyo. However, only two are comprehensive scholarly efforts. The best is a work of private scholarship: Johnson (1964). An almost equally competent study—and more detailed on BARBAROSSA—is Deakin and Storry (1966). The often cited study personally directed by General MacArthur's chief of intelligence is so cluttered with ignorant howlers that it must be used only as a supplementary source. See Willoughby (1952). The most detailed Soviet biography is Kolesnikov (1965).

59. V. Chernyavsky, ["Richard Sorge's Exploit"], *Pravda*, 6 November 1964, p. 6; Kolesnikov (1965), 167–168; and "Sovetskie organy" (1965), 27. The published portion of the Nazi Foreign Ministry's communications to Tokyo does not bear this out. On the contrary, the messages bearing on Russo-Soviet relations suggest that the Tokyo embassy was kept much longer in the dark. Although B-day was indeed then still set for May as Kolesnikov's biography states, the *Pravda* version gave "the latter half of June." Although this slip is probably only an honest blunder, it is suggestive of forgery. Deakin and Storry (1966), 230, seem to be unaware of these discrepancies.

60. Deakin and Storry (1966), 228–229. See also Johnson (1964), 155–156.

This may be the information alluded to in a Soviet article by Mayevsky (1964), 4.

61. Deakin and Storry (1966), 229, and Johnson (1964), 156.

62. See Herbert von Dirksen, *Moscow, Tokyo, London* (Norman: University of Oklahoma Press, 1952), pp. 121–122.

63. Deakin and Storry (1966), 230. See also Johnson (1964), 156; and Willoughby (1952), 105. A much garbled version of this message (misdated 12 May) is in the distorted Sorge biography by a former acquaintance in Tokyo, the German embassy third secretary, Hans-Otto Meissner, *The Man With Three Faces* (New York: Rinehart, 1956), pp. 198–200.

64. Chernyavsky (1964), 6. This article in *Pravda* gives the date of transmission as 15 May 1941. However, *Sovetskaya Rossiya*, 5–6 September 1964, gives the transmission date as 15 June 1941. I prefer the latter since it fits the evidence better, particularly the chronology. Deakin and Storry (1966), 230, 362, chose the *Pravda* date, presumably because it is the more authoritative (and more closely proofread) source. See also Mayevsky (1964), 4, and Kolesnikov (1965), 169–171.

65. Deakin and Storry (1966), 231, and Johnson (1964), 156.

66. See Deakin and Storry (1966), 230, and Johnson (1964), 156, 167.

67. This story, as eyewitnessed by its recipient, was first given in Newman (1942), 301–303. Only recently has Newman revealed the name of his informant: Voukelitch. See Newman (1967), 129–136.

68. For example, see Deakin and Storry (1966), 229, and Willoughby (1952), 191–193.

69. For Voukelitch's role in the Sorge net see, particularly, Deakin and Storry (1966), index; Johnson (1964), index; and Willoughby (1952), throughout.

70. See Johnson (1964), 143.

71. Duranty was so self-impressed by this phrase that he repeated it in an article for the English-language edition of the leading Tokyo daily newspaper, *Asahi Shimbun*.

72. Newman (1967), 132, and Newman (1942), 296–297.

73. This rumor is credulously reported by Huss (1942), 64, and Kleist (1950), 241. It is not supported by even the most salacious gossip of Soviet defectors.

74. Salisbury (1969), 48n.

75. Deborin and Telpukhovsky (1967), 136.

76. The most detailed and carefully researched account of this ultrasecret Abwehr-papal intelligence liaison is that of Deutsch (1968), 108–148, 331–352. See also Colvin (1951), 112–113, and Schellenberg (1956), 348–351.

77. Deutsch (1968), 351, based on an interview in 1966 with Father Leiber.

78. Ibid., 351, based on the pope's private remarks in 1946 to Undersecretary of State Monsignor Domenico Tardini, as minuted by the latter and discovered in the Vatican archives in 1966.

79. Memorandum of Pol I M/Abwehr III, 12 July 1941, as reprinted in Saul Friedländer, *Pius XII and the Third Reich: A Documentation* (New York: Knopf, 1966), p. 75.

80. As reported on 24 June by the German ambassador to the Vatican, Diego

von Bergen, to the German Foreign Ministry. His telegram is reprinted in ibid., 76. The point is also implicit in Deutsch (1968), 351.

81. Colvin (1951), 138, citing his postwar interview with Müller.

82. Ibid., 139.

83. The transcripts of Kirkpatrick's interrogations are available as Nürnberg trial documents M–117, M–118, and M–119. See *TMWC* (1947), 7:138–143. See also Kirkpatrick (1959), 180.

84. Churchill, 3 (1950), 52, 55; Eden, 2 (1965), 256–257; Langer and Gleason (1953), 528–529; and Shirer (1960), 838.

85. Delmer (1962), 52–60.

86. Wrench (1955), 442.

87. Leasor (1962), 75. One piece of seemingly fabricated quotation is in Frischauer (1951), 229. He quotes Hitler (without citing a source) as having announced Hess's flight to his cronies at the Berghof on 10 May by stating Hess "says in his letter that he is trying to make peace, but will not disclose my plans to attack Russia. . . ."

88. Leasor (1962), 39–43, 205.

89. See Chapter 6.

90. Schellenberg (1956), 186, 187.

91. Papen (1953), 553.

92. Clark (1965), 40. Scott (1942), 260, says "Churchill relayed [Hess's] information to . . . Maisky late in May." Walter Duranty (1941), 197, also believed at the time that Hess had told the British and that Churchill had passed the disclosure on to the Russians.

93. Schacht (1956), 373–374.

94. Alfieri (1955), 257.

95. Root, 1 (1945), 631–638.

96. Leasor (1962), 179–180, and Eden (1965), 257.

97. Deakin and Storry (1966), 229. See also Fischer (1946), 34, where a parallel theory is alleged by Fischer to have emerged during a conversation he had with Eden late in July 1941. Eden's own memoirs do not support Fischer on this point, although Eden is writing with the hindsight of the postwar biographies of Hess.

98. Flannery (1942), 273, 274, goes so far as to connect it with Sir Stafford Cripps's return to London, overlooking that this latter event did not occur until a full month later, on 11 June (having been recalled on the sixth). Scott (1942), 260, makes the same point.

99. *NCA,* "Opinion and Judgment" (1947), 112.

100. Leasor (1962), 70, 81, 203, 208, 211–212.

101. Ibid., 69.

102. *NCA,* "Opinion and Judgment" (1947), 178–180.

103. *FRUS: 1941,* 4 (1956), 971. Inexplicably, Langer and Gleason (1953), 527n, refer to a U.S. Chungking embassy telegram of 12 May asserting that Chiang's information was that the invasion would occur in six weeks. No message of that date or content is referred to in the published sources. See also Tong (1950), p. 157.

104. Schellenberg (1956), 135, 257–260. Such unsupported assertions by SS-Sturmbannführer Schellenberg should always be taken with caution. That the Chinese ambassador in London did have private access to British cabinet secrets in 1940 is dramatically confirmed by Sir Stafford Cripps's diary entry of 20 May 1940. See Colin Cooke, *The Life of Richard Stafford Cripps* (London: Hodder & Stoughton, 1957), p. 266.

105. Whitaker (1943), 305. Quo replaced Wang Chung-hui as Nationalist foreign minister in late June.

106. Telegram, dated 11 June 1941, Polish Foreign Minister Zaleski to the Polish minister in Japan, as translated and embodied in a telegram dated 13 June 1941 from Grew to Hull, in *FRUS: 1941*, 4 (1956), 975–976. This document was secretly passed to Grew by the Polish minister. Schacht (1956), 373, in his autobiography admits only to having learned of BARBAROSSA the previous April.

107. Boelcke (1966), 752.

108. Riess (1948), 208.

109. Various accounts are given in Boelcke (1966), 752; *TMWC* (1948), 17: 253; Riess (1948), 208; Huss (1942), 123–146, 273; Smith (1942), 68, 228–229; Fredborg (1944), 4, 28; Lochner (1942a), 318–319; Flannery (1942), 338; *New York Times*, 9 August 1941, p. 3, 29 June 1942, p. 6, 24 August 1942, p. 2, 8 September 1942, p. 4; Walter Hagemann, *Publizistik im Dritten Reich* (Hamburg: Hansischer Gildenverlag, 1948), p. 324; and Ernest K. Bramsted, *Goebbels and National Socialist Propaganda, 1925–1945* ([East Lansing]: Michigan State University Press, 1965), p. 244n. A completely garbled account appears in Manvell and Fraenkel (1960), 149, 291n. Brief mention of Bömer's fate is made by Bojano (1944), 176.

110. Filippov (1966), as cited in Salisbury (1969), 61.

111. *NCA* (1946), 1:809–814. The complete text is in ibid., 3:811–816. See also ibid., 3:908–911, and 5:378.

112. Reitlinger (1960), 62, and *NCA* (1946), 3:832–833. Thomas had been coordinating economic policies with Göring as early as 20 March. See *NCA* (1946), 3: 808–811.

113. Namely, Reitlinger (1960), 62–63, who characterizes Kalinov, with insufficient caution, as "perhaps suspect."

114. Kalinov (1950), 32–33.

115. See the biography of Kowalewski (under the pseudonym of Colonel Peter Nart) by his postwar friend and collaborator Countess Listowel (1952). Additional biographical information is in Colvin (1951), 167–173; Herbert O. Yardley, *The American Black Chamber* (Indianapolis: Bobbs-Merrill, 1931), pp. 279–281; and Kahn (1967), 357, 579.

116. Listowell (1952), 140.

117. For background on Hans Lazar see ibid., 76, 83–86, 135–137, 233–235; Raczynski (1962), 123; Hamilton (1943), 242; and Hoare (1947), 37–38, 89–91, 97, 197–199.

118. Listowel (1952), 83–87.

119. Ibid., 87, 92–97.

120. Ibid., 97, apparently quoting Kowalewski's diary.

121. Ibid.

122. Lochner (1942*a*), 4.

123. For Lochner's contacts with German resistance groups see Lochner (1942*b*), 216–236; Lochner (1956), 287, 294–295; Hans Rothfels, *The German Opposition to Hitler* (Hinsdale, Ill.: Henry Regnery, 1948), 71n, 133–134; and Wheeler-Bennett (1953), 551–552.

124. Lochner (1942*b*), 1.

125. Ibid.

126. Ibid., 4.

127. Letter dated 25 August 1939, G. Ogilvie-Forbes to Ivone Kirkpatrick (then assistant head of the Foreign Office Central Office), in *DBFP*, 7 (1954), 257–260. Years later Lochner (1956), 187–188, misrecalled that the L–3 document had not reached him until "some days" after 27 August 1939.

128. Letter dated 27 August 1939, G. Ogilvie-Forbes to Ivone Kirkpatrick, in *DBFP*, 7 (1954), 316–317.

129. W. Byford-Jones, *Berlin Twilight* (London: Hutchinson, 1946), pp. 174, 176–177, as acknowledged by Lochner (1956), 287–288.

130. *Vollmacht*, 1 (1960), 381.

131. Ritter (1954), 488.

132. A biographical sketch of Maass and his part in the German resistance is given in Annedore Leber, *Das Gewissen Entscheidet* (Berlin: Mosaik, 1957), pp. 64–66, with photograph.

133. Ritter (1954), 488.

134. Alton Frye, *Nazi Germany and the American Hemisphere* (New Haven: Yale University Press, 1967), index.

135. Lochner (1942*a*); see also Lochner (1942*b*), 147.

136. Lochner (1942*a*). Curiously, he makes no mention in his later book (1942*b*) of passing this intelligence to the Russians.

137. Theodore E. Kruglak, *The Two Faces of Tass* (Minneapolis: University of Minnesota Press, 1962), and Barton Whaley, "Soviet Foreign Correspondents," draft (Cambridge, Mass.: M.I.T., Center for International Studies, 1967).

138. As quoted by Khrushchev in Wolfe (1957), 168. Ellipses as in Khrushchev's original text.

139. Dedijer (1953), 147.

140. Ribbentrop (1954), 157–158.

141. Weizsäcker (1951), 253–254.

142. On those later occasions his contacts were with the redoubtable Madame Kollontay, the Soviet ambassador in Stockholm. Ribbentrop's intermediary was Peter Kleist. See Deakin (1962), 244, 260n, 760. For an uncritically skeptical expression about the very fact of the 1943 negotiations see Shirer (1960), 1017n. Furthermore, some discreet channels were available to Ribbentrop in Sweden throughout early 1941 in conjunction with his abortive contacts with the British. See Weizsäcker (1951), 251.

143. Berezhkov (1966*a*), 11.

144. *TMWC* (1948), 13:159–160, and 18:238–239, and ibid. (1947), 26:580–584 (for Nürnberg document 1031–PS [equals Exhibit USA–844]), which is a memorandum of Funk's conversation of 28 May 1941).

145. For Operation (*Aktion*) BERNHARD see Hoettl (1953), 85–87; Schellenberg (1956), 367–369; Wilhelm Höttl, *Hitler's Paper Weapon* (London: Hart-Davis, 1955); Anthony Pirie, *Operation Bernhard* (New York: Morrow, 1962); and Elyesa Bazna, *I Was Cicero* (London: Deutsch, 1962). The SD did not develop passable forgeries of U.S. dollar bills until 1945. See also Murray Teigh Bloom, *Money of Their Own* (New York: Scribner's, 1957), pp. 234–267.

146. Schellenberg (1956), 367.

147. Kelly (1952), 275–276.

Chapter 5

1. Simoni (1946), 233. On Napoleon's timetable see David G. Chandler, *The Campaigns of Napoleon* (New York: Macmillan, 1966), pp. 739, 769–770, and General de Caulaincourt (1935), 45–46.

2. Kuznetsov (1967), no. 2, pp. 99–100.

3. "Discussion" (1967), 175.

4. Langer and Gleason (1953), 507. De Gaulle implies that their foreknowledge of BARBAROSSA explains Vichy's delay in negotiating the surrender of Syria. De Gaulle (1964), p. 187.

5. Langer (1947), 158.

6. See Leahy (1950), 30, 40, 71 for the rumors and p. 36 for the meeting, and *FRUS: 1941,* 2 (1959), 185–186, for an extract of his telegram of 4 June.

7. Weygand (1952), 335.

8. Scott (1942), 189.

9. Ibid., 241–242.

10. Farago (1954), 160.

11. D. Dallin (1955), 148, 243–245; Höhne (1971), 129; and Berezhkov (1966*a*), 11; and in Bialer (1969), 212. Indeed, in a later version utilizing Dallin, Farago (1961), 148–151, himself omits this story about an explicit warning.

12. "Sovetskie organy" (1965), 27. Also Pankratov (1967), 2, who confirms only that "On June data were made available on the concentration of some 4 million fascist troops at the Soviet-German border."

13. See Whaley (1969*a*).

14. Of the several books and many articles and chapters written on the Rado ring, perhaps only four can claim any substantial degree of accuracy. The best single general account is still the widely overlooked study by David Dallin (1955), 182–233. Second, there is the fine memoir by one of Rado's radio operators, Alexander Foote (1949). Third, a good piece of journalistic research on the later period of the network's operation is "Verräter im Führerhauptquartier: Sowjet-Spion Rudolf Rössler," *Der Spiegel* (16 January 1967), pp. 30–44. Finally, there is the account of Swiss intelligence in World War II by Kimche (1962).

15. D. Dallin (1955), 209, citing interview with Pünter as preserved in the

"D Papers," the late Professor Dallin's archive now deposited at Columbia University.

16. Ibid., 195, and 211, citing interview with Pünter in the Dallin "D Papers," pp. b484–b487. Foote (1949), 95 and 97, gives some independent confirmation.

17. For no reason that I can see, D. Dallin (1955), 211, dates this initial Rössler message to "about the end of April." The *Der Spiegel* article, "Verräter im Führerhauptquartier," also places it in April.

18. Foote (1949), 113, 114.

19. Ibid., 114, and p. 95, where he dates it "some two weeks" before 22 June. See also D. Dallin (1955), 195, 211, who claims Rössler had attributed the postponement to 22 June to a delay in preparations. Farago (1954), 159, citing Flicke, specifies 10 June. The *Der Spiegel* article dates this event to 16 June.

20. Foote (1949), 95, 113–115, 117, and D. Dallin (1955), 195–196, 202.

21. Foote (1949), 115.

22. GRU Sergeant Igor Gouzenko—later one of the major Soviet defectors —was himself processing much of the GRU radio traffic from Switzerland, particularly Berne, in 1942 and 1943. Gouzenko (1948), 108–109, 122.

23. See Whaley (1969a), chap. 3.

24. Flicke (1954), 47–61, as quoted by Farago (1954), 159–160. Later, Farago (1961), 135–137, "quotes" a slightly different version from the same source. This particular message is also uncritically accepted and partially quoted by both Kahn (1967), 659, and Wilhelm Ritter von Schramm, "Der Fall Rudolf Rössler," *Aus Politik und Zeit Geschichte,* 12 October 1966, p. 8.

25. See *NCA* (1946), 3:633, for text of the April directive; also my discussion in Chapter 2.

26. A number of authentic plaintexts exist. For example, 250 of these are in the David Dallin "D Papers" on deposit at Columbia University.

27. Accoce and Quet (1967). See my annotation in the Bibliography.

28. For example, Kahn (1967), 1084.

29. Accoce and Quet (1967), 15, 71–75.

30. For an adequate description of this "damage assessment" technique, see Thomas Whiteside, *An Agent in Place: The Wennerström Affair* (New York: Viking, 1966), pp. 141–150.

31. Muggeridge (1967), 21.

32. For example, Gert Buchheit, "Verräter im Hauptquartier," *Christ und Welt* (Stuttgart), 10 March 1967, p. 13, and Buchheit, "Entschlüsselung deutscher Geheimcodes," ibid., 25 August 1967, p. 6.

33. Malcolm Muggeridge, "Refractions in the Character of Kim Philby," *Esquire,* vol. 70, no. 3 (September 1968), p. 168.

34. A detailed history of the Vichy intelligence services in World War II is Stead (1959).

35. Pierre Nord [pseud. of Colonel Brouillard], *Mes camarades sont morts,* vol. 1 (Paris: Librairie des Champs Elysées, 1947), as cited by Stead (1959), 64.

36. Stead (1959), 64.

37. *Bulletin de l'Amicale des Anciens Membres des Services de Sécurité Militaire et des Réseaux T.R.,* no. 5, as cited by Stead (1959), 65.

38. Nekrich (1968), 168–170, quoting his interview with Susloparov on 11 February 1965.

39. Sevin (1963), 545; also 555. For a later estimate by de Sevin see warning 77.

40. Kahn (1967), 479–483, 644–645.

41. Ibid., 483, based on articles in the Swedish press that appeared in October–November 1964. Cripps was in Stockholm from 6 to 11 June 1941. See also *New York Times,* 10 June 1941, p. 6, and Woodward, 1 (1970), 620.

42. Boheman, 1 (1963), 154. This should be checked with the Moscow memoirs of Vilhelm Assarsson (1963), which I have not yet seen.

43. Boheman, 1 (1963), 154–155.

44. Wipert von Blücher, *Gestander zwischen Diktatur und Demokratie* (Wiesbaden: Limes, 1951), p. 224.

45. Hull (1948), 973, and *FRUS: 1941,* 1 (1958), 753–754. Shirer (1960), 843, incorrectly states that Steinhardt did pass Hull's information to Molotov but gives no source other than Hull's memoir, which is not explicit on this point. Hull's telegram on the ninth and Steinhardt's reply of the twelfth implicitly contradict Shirer.

46. Shirer (1960), 843n, citing the personal recollection of George F. Kennan, who was then first secretary of the U.S. embassy in Berlin.

47. Maisky (1968), 148–149; also Nekrich (1965), 193.

48. Maisky (1968), 149.

49. Simoni (1946), 237, *sub datum* 11 June 1941.

50. Ciano (1946), 351–352. Amè's own published account of his SIM discloses nothing of this nor, indeed, of much more than the changes in the SIM organizational chart. See Amè (1954).

51. Amè (1954), 193–199, and Schellenberg (1956), 354–355.

52. Hedin (1951), 134.

53. Ibid., 222.

54. Schellenberg (1956), 205–207. See also D. Dallin (1955), 134.

55. For the repatriation schedule see Ege (1953), 1006; Schellenberg (1956), 205–207; and Hilger and Meyer (1953), 337–338. But compare Papen (1953), 480.

56. I take this date from "Sovetskie organy" (1965), 27, which is probably based on original documents. Hilger and Meyer (1953), 334, imply the order was received some time around 14 June but base that date only on Hilger's often vague postwar memory.

57. Hilger and Meyer (1953), 334–336.

58. "Sovetskie organy" (1965), 27, and *IVOVSS,* 6 (1965), 135, as cited by Nekrich (1968), 180.

59. Hilger and Meyer (1953), 335–336.

60. Sherwood (1948), 299, citing an otherwise still unpublished telegram from Steinhardt in Moscow.

61. Simoni (1946), 236, 241, *sub data* 9 and 20 June 1941.

62. *FRUS: 1941,* 1 (1958), 755.

63. Appendix A, doc. 55.

64. Ibid., doc. 57.

65. Kuznetsov (1967), no. 2, p. 100, and in Bialer (1969), 191.

66. Panteleyev (1965), 36.

67. On Japanese intelligence operations in Poland see Schellenberg (1956), 125–135, and Whitwell (1966), 112, 211–214.

68. On Japanese intelligence operations in Sweden see Schellenberg (1956), 134–135, who incorrectly identifies Onodera as the Japanese ambassador. For other information based on a postwar interview with Onodera see John Toland, *The Last 100 Days* (New York: Random House, 1966), pp. 309–310, 611.

69. Leverkuehn (1954), 63–64.

70. Schmidt (1951), 224–225. Ribbentrop (1954), 158–159, largely confirms this. See also *DGFP*, 12 (1962), 376–383, 386–394, 405–409, 413–420, for. Dr. Schmidt's original rapportorial memorandum.

71. Schmidt (1951), 231. Recognizing its crucial implications, Dr. Schmidt translated this last sentence of Hitler's *twice* for Matsuoka's benefit. Ribbentrop (1954), 159, confirms this, but his faulty memory attributes Hitler's parting remark to himself. See also *DGFP*, 12 (1962), 453–458, 469–474, where these remarks are omitted from Schmidt's original memoranda. And, as ever, see Weinberg (1954), 156–157.

72. Weinberg (1954), 156, 157n; Weizsäcker (1951), 249–250; and Kordt (1950), 141.

73. Feis (1950), 187. Another paraphrase of this cable from Steinhardt, dated 15 or 16 April 1941, is in *FRUS: 1941*, 4 (1956), 952–953.

74. Shigemitsu (1958), 213, 217.

75. *DGFP*, 12 (1962), 788, 891–892, and *FRUS: 1941*, 4 (1956), 973.

76. Lu (1961), 174, citing the original telegram.

77. Ibid., 174, where, however, no source is cited.

78. An apochryphal story exists—credited by Nekrich (1968), 173, and others —that on 1 May 1941 Hitler told Ōshima of his intention to attack on 22 June. This story (for which no source is cited) adds that it was learned in Tokyo by Sorge's chief agent, Ozaki.

79. Ike (1967), 46–47, and Lu (1961), 174.

80. Ike (1967), 47, and Lu (1961), 175.

81. Langer and Gleason (1953), 532n.

82. Ike (1967), 47.

83. Ibid., 54, and Butow (1961), 212.

84. Ike (1967), 54–55.

85. Eden, 2 (1965), 311. Eden's more detailed version of this meeting as reported to the Americans that same day is in *FRUS: 1941*, 1 (1958), 170–172.

86. Quoted by McLachlan (1968), 243. This postwar recollection by Mr. Cavendish-Bentinck is admittedly vague, as he writes that the meeting took place "about June 10 or so." The occasion does, however, seem to fit the June 13 meeting.

87. Nekrich (1968), 193, citing *FRUS: 1941*, 1 (1958), 170–172.

88. Farago (1967), 196, 412.

89. Ibid., 201, 412. Farago's information is clearly limited to reading only

Captain Safford's index cards on these memorandums, although in his text he thinly pads out the mere dates and titles that apparently constituted all that was available to him. It is to be hoped that the original documents can be made available under the new Freedom of Information Act.

90. "Sovetskie organy" (1965), 27, citing the Central Archives of the Main Administration of Border Troops.

91. For Dahlerus see L. B. Napier, "An Interloper in Diplomacy," in his *Diplomatic Prelude, 1938–1939* (London: Macmillan, 1948), pp. 417–433, and Irving (1968), 24–25.

92. Woodward, 1 (1970), 620, 622–623.

93. Ibid., 620.

94. *IVOVSS*, 1 (1960), 479, and Tyulenev (1960), 138. Both as cited in Erickson (1962b), 110.

95. Fedyuninsky (1961), 10–12. Also cited by Nekrich (1968), 205; Bialer (1969), 241–242, 585–586; and Salisbury (1969), 15.

96. As quoted by Khrushchev in Wolfe (1957), 168.

97. Eden (1965), 269.

98. See Maisky (1968), 156, and warning 80.

99. Langer and Gleason (1953), 532n, citing a still unpublished letter from Biddle to Hull dated 20 June 1941.

100. McSherry, 2 (1970), 235; Krosby (1968a), 170, 175–176; and Upton (1964), 268–276.

101. See Salisbury (1969), 74n. Contrary to Salisbury, the Soviet minister to Finland was not then S. I. Zotov, who had been succeeded by Orlov on 24 April 1941.

102. *DGFP*, 12 (1962), 341, 433, 657–658, 864–866, 966–1006, and 1047–1049. See also Schmidt (1951), 233, and Ribbentrop (1954), 152.

103. Ribbentrop (1954), 151–152. The previous Hitler-Antonescu meetings were on 22 November 1940 and 14 January 1941. Ribbentrop's memory is off on the season. See also *TMWC* (1947), 7:162–164, where Antonescu misdates his third meeting with Hitler to May.

104. *FRUS: 1941*, 1 (1958), 315.

105. Papen (1953), 474.

106. Brock (1942), 290.

107. Ibid., 290–291.

108. Ibid., 291–295.

109. Ibid., 298–301. See also Ray Brock, "Nazi-Soviet Talks on Rift Reported," *New York Times*, 17 June 1941, p. 8, and Brock, "Reich-Soviet War Is Thought Nearer," ibid., 18 June 1941, p. 5. This last dispatch is noted by Nekrich (1968), 205–206. For the "peace feelers" see Papen (1953), 472, 477–478.

110. A biographical sketch of Wiitanen (1902–1961) is in *Vem och Vad? 1957* (Helsinki: Schildts, 1957), p. 606. He had been posted to Ankara from his position as chief of some (unspecified) bureau in the Finnish General Staff. It is very likely that he originally became witting on BARBAROSSA in Helsinki, and General Rohde merely kept him up to date. Perhaps he had become more discreet by the time of his posting as military attaché in Moscow in 1956.

111. Brock (1942), 295, 302–305.
112. Ibid., 302–303. See also C. L. Sulzberger, "Tension Increased," *New York Times*, 21 June 1941, p. 4. These dispatches from Sulzberger are noted by Nekrich (1965), 208, 209.
113. Brock (1942), 303–305. See also C. L. Sulzberger, "Big Armies Mass on 'Eastern Front,' " *New York Times*, 22 June 1941, p. E4.
114. In his 1969 memoirs, Sulzberger somewhat overplays his own prescience (pp. 142–143).
115. Sulzberger (1969), 143.
116. C. L. Sulzberger, "Tension Increased," *New York Times*, 21 June 1941, p. 4, and Sulzberger, "Big Armies Mass on 'Eastern Front,' " ibid., 22 June 1941, p. E4.
117. Maisky (1968), 156. For previous warnings from or through Cripps see warnings 1, 10, 28, 42, 60, 75.
118. Perrault (1969), 45.
119. Ibid., 45–46.
120. Ege (1953), 1006.
121. Zhukov (1971), 231–233, including the complete text of the alert directive.
122. Khrushchev in Wolfe (1957), 172, 174. See also Erickson (1962*a*), 586, and Salisbury (1969), 15n.
123. Leonhard (1958), 121–122.
124. *Pravda,* as quoted by Leonhard (1958), 122.
125. Nekrich (1968), 212.
126. Zhukov (1971), 234.
127. On the inadequacy of Soviet military communications, see ibid., 200–201.
128. Ibid., 236, and Fedyuninsky (1964), as quoted in Bialer (1969), 243.
129. Hilger and Meyer (1953), 336–337.

Chapter 6

1. Deutsch (1968), 32, quoting his interview with Halder on 19 June 1958.
2. On the German security arrangements see Schellenberg (1956), 99–100, 139–140, 193–197; Shirer (1960), 812, 842, 844, 845, 849; and *DGFP*, 11 (1960), 902. See also Charles R. Allen, Jr., *Heusinger of the Fourth Reich* (New York: Marzani & Munsell, 1963), p. 82, for a relevant comment in an otherwise hysterical book of propaganda against the German Federal Republic.
3. *TMWC* (1947), 7:270, for von Bentivegni's deposition of 8 January 1946.
4. See Blumentritt (1952), 78, 94–96.
5. Blau (1955), 1–3.
6. Goerlitz (1963), 24–27.
7. Bailey (1960); D. Dallin (1955), 158–161; A. Dallin (1957), 112; and Höhne (1971), 52–53.
8. Higgins (1966), 68, 81, and *TMWC* (1947), 9:342, 427. On Göring's reluctance see Frischauer (1951), 227–228, and *TMWC* (1947), 9:49–50, 130–132, 427–428.
9. Kesselring (1954), 87, 91–98.

10. Jacobsen (1965), 973.

11. *TMWC* (1947), 7:263, for the Russian interrogations of Piekenbrock and von Bentivegni.

12. Halder (1963), 224, 462–463. See also Appendix B.

13. Raeder (1960), 332–339; *NCA* (1946), 6:887–891; and Appendix A, doc. 2.

14. Warlimont (1964), 159. See also Reitlinger (1957), 161, and A. Dallin (1957), 27–30.

15. Schellenberg (1956), 138–139, and Higgins (1966), 101.

16. A. Dallin (1957), 42–43, 176.

17. See particularly Sefton Delmer, "The Secret Minutes of Dr. Goebbels," *Times Literary Supplement,* 9 November 1967, pp. 1063–1064.

18. A. Dallin (1957), 22–23.

19. Ibid., 17n, 24-26, 84, 108–109, and Reitlinger (1960), 134. See also *TMWC* (1947), 11: 116–117, 476–477, and *NCA* (1946), 3:674–701.

20. Warlimont (1964), 160, and Halder, 2 (1963), 335–337.

21. For example, *TWC* (1951), 10:1050.

22. A. Dallin (1957), 35–36.

23. Ribbentrop (1954), 152, and A. Dallin (1957), 40–42.

24. Weizsäcker (1951), 246–247. One of his informants was Walter Hewel, the Foreign Ministry's liaison officer with the OKW and an even closer intimate of Hitler than Ribbentrop.

25. Kleist (1950), 126.

26. Hilger and Meyer (1953), 336–337. However, Hilger (p. 334) recalls that on 14 June one of Schulenburg's "trusted collaborators" returned from Berlin to assure him verbally that the decision had, in fact, been made to attack "sometime around June 22nd."

27. See Appendix A, doc. 4. After the war Köstring misremembered the date of his meeting with Halder as falling "on about the 6th or 8th" of "August." See Hillgruber (1965), 228n; Halder, 2 (1963), 86; and *NCA* (1946), 5:734–735; also Blau (1955), 12, 18.

28. Papen (1953), 479. See also *DGFP*, 12 (1962), 1072–1073.

29. Guderian (1952), 142.

30. Manstein (1958), 171, 175, 178, 180.

31. Galland (1954), 59–61, 69–71.

32. Schacht (1956), 373.

33. Hassel (1947), 146, 149, 153, 159, 166, 174, 187, 188, 189, 195, 197–199, 202. Hassell's earliest relevant diary entry, *sub datum* 10 August 1940, could already knowledgeably record (p. 146) that: "It is characteristic of his [Hitler's] whole mentality that he already has his eyes fixed on an attack on Russia for the spring of 1941, in case he should not be completely successful against England." Hassell's last reference, *sub datum* 15 June 1941, notes: "the attack will most probably begin about June 22."

34. Schellenberg (1956), 139–140, 143, 197, and *NCA* (1946), 6:864.

35. For example, see comments by Kesselring (1954), 19–21, 31, 46–47.

36. A definitive reference is Seabury (1954).

37. Kesselring (1954), 91.

38. Higgins (1966), 104, 108–109; Goerlitz (1963), 30–32; [Erwin Rommel], *The Rommel Papers* (New York: Harcourt, Brace and Company, 1953), p. 119; and John Connell [pseud. of John Robertson], *Wavell* (London: Collins, 1964), pp. 426–427, 477.

39. Krosby (1968a), 96, 122–125, 157–159, 170–185; Upton (1964), 235–294; and McSherry, 2 (1970), 226–227, 234–235.

40. The definitive critique of the Paulus and Buschenhagen allegations is in Krosby (1968a), 125, 222, 227. See also Paulus in Goerlitz (1963), 122–123, and Buschenhagen in *TMWC*, 7 (1947), 161.

41. Gripenberg (1965), 175–176, 180–181.

42. Krosby (1968a), 182–185.

43. Goerlitz (1963), 123–126.

44. *DGFP*, 12 (1962), 341, 685, 1030, 1070, 1077–1078; also in *NSR* (1948), 364. The most detailed account is Macartney (1961), 17–22.

45. Ciano (1946), entry for 14 May 1941, and Macartney (1961), 18.

46. *TMWC* (1947), 7:335. See also Stephen D. Kertesz, *Diplomacy in a Whirlpool: Hungary Between Nazi Germany and Soviet Russia* (Notre Dame, Ind.: University of Notre Dame Press, 1953), p. 54. Kertesz seems to be the only scholar to note this evidence from the Nürnberg trials. Except for Macartney, the others overlook Hungary's prior knowledge.

47. This suspicion is shared by Macartney (1961), 17–18.

48. *TMWC* (1947), 7:331. However, I find no confirmation in Halder's diary.

49. Ibid., 331–335.

50. Ciano (1946), 364.

51. Nicholas Horthy, *Memoirs* (New York: Robert Speller, 1957), pp. 190–191, and Macartney (1961), 17, 25–32. Significantly, the modern Hungarian Communist historians who have zealously sought to prove Horthy's "war guilt" over other issues have failed to turn up documents that contradict him on these particular points. See *The Confidential Papers of Admiral Horthy* (Budapest: Corvina Press, 1965).

52. *DGFP*, 12 (1962), 341, 1059–1060. The fact of his visit to Otto in Bratislava (Pressburg) is confirmed by Halder, 2 (1963), 457.

53. *DGFP*, 12 (1962), 219. See also Feis (1950), 183–184, and *DGFP*, 12 (1962), 361–362.

54. Gafencu (1945), 308; also *FRUS: 1941*, 1 (1958), 132, 755.

55. *Füehrer Conferences* (1947), 27 December 1940.

56. *NSR* (1948), 346–357, and reprinted in *DGFP*, 12 (1962), 1066–1069. See also Schmidt (1951), 233, and Ciano (1946), 369. Mussolini's surprise is recalled by his widow, who was present at the receipt of this telephone call (which she incorrectly attributes to the German military attaché). Rachele Mussolini, in collaboration with Michael Chinigo, *My Life with Mussolini* (London: Hale, 1959), p. 111.

57. See Ciano (1948), 409, and Ciano (1946), 351–352, 361, 363, 364, 367, 368, 369.

58. Ciano (1948), 446, minutes of 15 June 1941. See also Ciano (1946), 367. No record of this conversation has been found in the Wilhelmstrasse's archives.

59. Ciano (1948), 446.
60. The Italian espionage services in Germany are described in Hoettl (1953), 221–222.
61. *DGFP*, 12 (1962), 924.
62. Ivone Kirkpatrick, *Mussolini* (New York: Hawthorn, 1964), pp. 478–480; Schmidt (1951), 199–200; and *DGFP*, 11 (1960), 411–422. Il Duce had himself deliberately concealed from Hitler the date of the attack on Greece because he was miffed at Hitler's secret move into Rumania. "This time I am going to pay him back in his own coin. He will find out from the newspapers that I have occupied Greece."
63. An almost uniquely sensitive discussion of this ethic by a former German resistance woman is Boveri (1963), 303–310.
64. Schlabrendorff (1965), 194–204.
65. See Appendix B. I am not certain that Fellgiebel joined the conspiracy *before* the attack on Russia. See Deutsch (1968), 198.
66. Exceptions are the recent comprehensive history of cryptanalysis by Kahn (1967) and the excellent account of German radio and telephone interception by Irving (1968).
67. Mario Toscano, *The History of Treaties and International Politics*, vol. 1 (Baltimore, Md.: Johns Hopkins Press, 1966), pp. 28–30, gives the only comprehensive summary of this problem. See also L. B. Namier, "Ciano's Early Diary," in his *Europe in Decay* (London: Macmillan, 1950), pp. 112–116; and Gordon A. Craig and Felix Gilbert, eds., *The Diplomats, 1919–1939* (Princeton: Princeton University Press, 1953), pp. 523–524.
68. Papen (1953), 482. According to Schellenberg (1956), 337, the British diplomatic code was finally broken around December 1943 after several weeks of intensive work on the materials taken by "Cicero" from the British embassy safe in Ankara. See also Colvin (1951), 74. German naval raiders had captured the British merchant ship signal codes in use until the beginning of 1941. Furthermore, until August 1940, they even had the British Admiralty ciphers, as officially disclosed by Captain S. W. Roskill (1954), 19, 267, 283. See also Captain Ellis M. Zacharais, *Secret Missions* (New York: Putnam's, 1946), pp. 86–88. For some German intercepts of Greek and Yugoslav messages from their Moscow embassies in July 1940 see *DGFP*, 10 (1967), 321n. The best single study is Irving (1968).
69. Foot (1966), 105–109, 312. See also Kahn (1967), 539. Later, in 1942, the Abwehr succeeded in capturing *all* British S.O.E. ciphers in Holland; and in 1943 the SD managed a similar coup among several of the S.O.E. teams in France.
70. Leahy (1950), 71.
71. Irving (1968), 41. This breakthrough was made possible by Tyler Kent, a young, witless Princetonian code clerk in Ambassador Joseph P. Kennedy's London embassy from October 1939 until his arrest on 18 May 1940. Throughout that period he provided German intelligence (through the Italian diplomatic pouch) with photocopies of over 1,500 embassy communications he had

decoded. With this data the Germans easily reconstructed the American diplomatic code. Released immediately after the end of the war after serving five years of a seven year sentence, Tyler returned to the United States as a hero of the ultraright patriots. See John Roy Carlson, *The Plotters* (New York: E. P. Dutton, 1946), pp. 32-34, 148, and Kahn (1967), 494-495.

72. *FRUS: 1941*, 3 (1959), 835, and Irving (1968), 17.

73. Hyde (1962), 106-108, and Hyde (1965), 123-157. See also Hull, 2 (1948), 927; *Sunday Times* (London), 11 November 1962; and *Time*, 20 December 1963, p. 17. Farago (1961), 162-163, implies that the Italian naval codes formed part of the extensive materials supplied the British by the Italian naval intelligence headquarters in Rome. While this is possible, it is neither probable nor substantiated.

74. Associated Press dispatch, "Quiet Canadian," 23 November 1966, as cited by Kahn (1967), 1058.

75. Bragadin (1957), 99-103.

76. Maugeri (1948), 39.

77. Papen (1953), 482; Ciano (1946), 356; and Alfieri (1955), 168-170. See also *DGFP*, 13 (1964), 660-662, 664, 733, for the apparently dissimulated German memorandum of the Ribbentrop-Alfieri exchange. Anfuso's postwar memoirs (1957) do not mention his part in the affair.

78. For Göring's Forschungsamt ("Research Office") and its "Braune Blätter" (brown sheets, derisively called "brown birds" by the Abwehr), see Irving (1968); Kahn (1967), 446-447, 450; and Deutsch (1968), 342-344.

79. Farago (1967), 189-190, 192, 198.

80. Ibid., 198.

81. Wohlstetter (1962), 75n, 172-173, 175; Butow (1961); and Farago (1967).

82. Telegram, German chargé d'affaires in the United States to German Foreign Ministry, 28 April 1941, as published in *DGFP*, 12 (1962), 661. This German agent has never been exposed. He appears to be the American State Department code clerk in Washington who as early as April 1940 was showing secret telegrams from the American ambassadors in London and Rome to a "reliable and tried confidential agent" of the German embassy in the United States. See *DGFP*, 9 (1956), 73. A possible clue is mentioned by ex-mail clerk in Berlin, William Russell (1941), 242, who describes an anonymous chief of the consular section who returned to Washington in 1940, bringing negligent security habits and odd connections with the Nazis.

83. See the two secret and urgent telegrams of Ponschab in Harbin to the Wilhelmstrasse dated between 6 May and 13 May 1941 in *DGFP*, 12 (1962), 250-251, 793. These intercepts were being forwarded from Harbin at least as early as 6 March 1941 and at least as late as June 1941. No fewer than 105 of these intercepts, covering only the two-month period May-June 1941, are preserved but almost forgotten in the German and U.S. national archives. It should today be easy to verify their authenticity from internal evidence alone. The standard intelligence procedure ("pre-content analysis") for authentication of such *series* of alleged intercepts is spelled out in Paul W. Blackstock,

Agents of Deceit (Chicago: Quadrangle Books, 1966), pp. 223–239. A recent analysis of some of these messages by McSherry (discussed later) suggests that they were deliberate leaks.

84. Kahn (1967), 650–671. See also Kahn, *Two Soviet Spy Ciphers* (Great Neck, N.Y., 1960); D. Dallin (1955), 151–181, 252–262; and Irving (1968), 17, 34.

85. Kahn (1967), 460, and Schellenberg (1956), 175, 179.

86. Constantine Fotitch, *The War We Lost* (New York: Viking, 1948), pp. 47–48; and Irving (1968), 17.

87. Irving (1968), 17, 41.

88. Amè (1954), 74–76.

89. Whitwell (1966), 113.

90. Muggeridge (1967), 21. The preliminary work toward solving these ciphers was supposedly done by the French military intelligence (Deuxième Bureau). See Gert Buchheit, "Entschlüsselung deutscher Geheimcodes," *Christ und Welt,* 25 August 1967, p. 6.

91. Farago (1967), 254, and Kahn (1967), 483–486.

92. Farago (1967), 253.

93. D. C. Watt, *Personalities and Policies: Studies in the Formulation of British Foreign Policy in the Twentieth Century* (London: Longmans, 1965), p. 200. See also Ciano (1946), 229, 239, and Farago (1971), 341. A brief account of Signor Costantini's activities, admitted belatedly in 1957 by Whitehall spokesmen, is "The Tactful Servant," *Time,* 9 December 1957, pp. 31–32.

94. Kirkpatrick (1959), 137.

95. On the Italian SIS see Maugeri (1948), for the memoirs of its wartime director.

96. Farago (1961), 158, and Maugeri (1948), 42–43.

97. Maugeri (1948), 40–41, and Farago (1961), 158–160.

98. Maugeri (1948), 43, 277–279, and Farago (1961), 160–163.

99. "Cicero" (the SD's codename for Elyesa Bazna, *alias* Diello) was "blown" only by the defection to the British of one of the Ankara Abwehr men, Erich Vermehren. See Papen (1953), 509–519; L. C. Moyzisch, *Operation Cicero* (London: Wingate, 1950); Elyesa Bazna, *I Was Cicero,* trans. Eric Nosbacher (New York: Harper & Row, 1962); Schellenberg (1956), 335–344; Leverkuehn (1954), 207; Seabury (1954), 130–131, 193n, 195n; and Shirer (1960), 1026. Security had never been Sir Hughe Knatchbull-Hugessen's forte. As British minister to the Baltic states in the mid-1930s, he had given the run of the legation in Riga to one of the footmen, a homosexual Balt, who was later discovered to be with the Gestapo. See Whitwell (1966), 73–74.

100. Gouzenko (1948), 112–115.

101. See *DGFP*, 12 (1962), 873, for von Papen's copy of Ambassador Aktay's report from Moscow dated 1 May 1941. This reached von Papen from his "Source X" on the fifteenth. He forwarded it on 24 May to his Foreign Ministry in Berlin, when it went full circle to Moscow to the German embassy there on 13 June, arriving on the sixteenth.

102. *DGFP*, 11 (1960), 980, 1085, and ibid., 12 (1962), 1042, 1049. Kobulov's

real position in Berlin as NKGB Chief *Rezident* is confirmed by Ege's testimony in the U.S. Senate. See Ege (1953), 1021, 1054, where his name is, however, incorrectly rendered "Kabulov" and "Kubalov." Kobulov and Dekanozov, his ambassador and fellow-Georgian, were trusted NKGB agents of Beriya and Stalin brevited to the foreign service. Both were purged and executed with Beriya in 1953, soon after Stalin's death. See D. Dallin (1955), 132–135, 234.

103. Or so it is stated by John Pearson in his not always well researched biography of Ian Fleming (1966), 99.

104. Pearson (1966), 105, who claims this raid became the model for Commander Ian Fleming of N.I.D. in forming No. 30 Assault Unit, which attempted similar missions against the Germans, Vichy French, and Italians from 1942 on. Pearson incorrectly ascribes the prototype raid, if such there was, to the SS and states the raiding party was headed by Otto Skorzeny who, in fact, was not transferred to this work until 1943. Charles Foley, *Commando Extraordinary* (London: Longmans, Green, 1954).

105. Hoptner (1962), 279.

106. Cassidy (1943), 10.

107. Schellenberg (1956), 176–177.

108. Colvin (1951), 74, quoting Richard Protze, Canaris's friend and former chief of Counter-Espionage (Abwehr III–F).

109. Irving (1968), 33.

110. Cianfarra (1944), 271–272.

111. Weinberg (1954), 92n.

112. Kahn (1967), 555–557; Farago (1971)), 585–590; and Irving (1968), 41–42.

113. Kahn (1967), 549–560.

114. *FRUS: 1941,* 5 (1956), 922, and *DGFP,* 12 (1962), 721.

115. See Hyde (1962), 79–87, 214.

116. Charles W. Thayer, *Diplomat* (New York: Harper, 1959), pp. 155–156, and Marshal Mannerheim, *Memoirs* (New York: E. P. Dutton, 1954), pp. 396–397, who says it was a *French* courier who was lost, perhaps confusing the courier's name, Henry Antheil, for his nationality.

117. Thayer (1959), 153–154. Thayer is quite vague on this point. He may be referring to the Anti-Comintern Pact in 1936 as discussed in Whaley (1969a).

118. Three books with the term *Industriespionage* in their titles appeared between 1930 and 1937. See Ladislas Farago, ed., *German Psychological Warfare* (New York: Putnam's, 1942), pp. 290–291.

119. Colvin (1951), 74.

120. Schellenberg (1956), 17–19; Kersten (1957), 95–96; and Dollmann (1967), 93, 159–160. Three colorful but seemingly inauthentic accounts are Gunther Peis, *The Man Who Started the War* (London: Odhams, 1960), pp. 149–154; Charles Wighton, *Heydrich* (Philadelphia: Chilton, 1962), pp. 94–95; and Anthony Pirie, *Operation Bernherd* (New York: Morrow, 1962), pp. 9–11, 17–18, 20.

121. For an excellent, personal account of the almost nonexistent security and intelligence of the U.S. State Department in the 1930s, 1940s, and 1950s, see Thayer (1959), 139–182. For the noteworthy neglect of security at the U.S.

embassy in Berlin in 1939–1940, see Russell (1941), 241–243. The British, German, Japanese, and Italian failings in this regard are already quite clear from the cases of interception cited.

122. For the invention and explanation of the "one-time" system see Kahn (1967), 398–400, 1044–1045. See also W[illiam] F. F[riedman], "Codes and Ciphers," in *Encyclopædia Britannica* (Chicago, 1954), vol. 6, p. 930.

123. On the diffusion of "one-time" systems see Kahn (1967), 401–403, 452, 492, 539, 650, 662–666, 714–716, 731.

124. Numerous examples are given in ibid.

125. Ibid., 433, 540. For the computer-generation and statistical biases of one of the largest and most sophisticated tables of random numbers see the RAND Corporation, *A Million Random Digits with 100,000 Normal Deviates* (Glencoe, Ill.: The Free Press, 1955), pp. xi–xvi.

126. Kahn (1967), 432–434, based on Crypto A.G. brochures and on interviews with Mr. Hagelin.

127. For an example see McLachlan (1968), 219.

128. See particularly ibid., 216–239; Hyde (1962); Sweet-Escott (1965), 126–153; Delmer (1962), 74; Pearson (1966); Farago (1967), 248–261; and Kelly (1952), 275.

129. See Whaley (1969a), 110, 118–119.

Chapter 7

1. For the history of German deception planning see Whaley (1969b). See also Mader (1970), 215, 446, and Henderson B. Braddick, *Germany, Czechoslovakia, and the 'Grand Alliance' in the May Crisis, 1938* (Denver: University of Denver, 1969), pp. 15, 37–40.

2. See Appendix A, docs. 12, 13.

3. See ibid., doc. 1–5, 8, 9, 11–13, 16, 17, 19, 27, 31, 32, 36, 37, 39, 42, 54–56, 59, 60.

4. Ibid., doc. 8.

5. Blumentritt (1952), 96–97. See also Appendix A, doc. 24.

6. Appendix A, docs. 12, 13, 17, 55.

7. Ibid., doc. 32; Wheatley (1958), 97–98; Klee (1958); and Ansel (1960), 305.

8. Appendix A, doc. 38.

9. See ibid., doc. 60.

10. This story, grossly overlooked by all British and American historians of SEA LION, is documented in Whaley (1969b).

11. See Appendix A, docs. 3, 6, 7, 10, 15, 16, 20, 42, 43, 53.

12. Ibid., docs. 24–26, 34, 36, 38, 42, 45, 48, 51, 55.

13. Blumentritt (1952), 96.

14. Appendix A, docs. 8, 12, 13.

15. Ibid., doc 42.

16. Ibid., docs. 45, 51.

17. Schellenberg (1956), 135, 143, 197, 202.

18. Murphy (1964), 84–85.

19. Hamilton (1943), 242. For Lazar's part in BARBAROSSA see warning 46.
20. Huss (1942), 267–270.
21. Summaries of the Soviet-German economic and frontier negotiations are in Toynbee (1958), 406–414, and *FRUS:1941,* 1 (1958), 116–155. A detailed account is given in McSherry, 1 (1970).
22. *NCA* (1946), 4:1082, and Shirer (1960), 667.
23. *NCA* (1946), 4:1082.
24. Boelcke (1970), 174.
25. Berezhkov (1966*a*), 11, and in Bialer (1969), 213.
26. Weizsäcker (1951), 241, and Huss (1942), 259.
27. For contemporary versions see Whitaker (1943), 301–304, and *New York Times,* 22 June 1941, p. E3.
28. *FRUS: 1941,* 1 (1958), 168, 170, and *DGFP,* 12 (1962), 788n. See also the *Times* (London), 6 June 1941, p. 3, for this rumor's persistence in Rome.
29. See Ernest K. Bramsted, *Goebbels and National Socialist Propaganda, 1925–1945* ([East Lansing]: Michigan State University Press, 1965), p. 244, apparently based in part on Ruth Andreas-Friedrich (1947), 67; also Simoni (1946), 232, 234, 236, 237, entries for 25 May, 7 June, 8 June, and 10 June 1941, and Hassell (1947), entry for 15 June 1941. The *New York Times,* 6 June 1941, p. 8, carried a rumor from Vichy that the meeting had already occurred.
30. Filippov (1966), in Salisbury (1969), 77n.
31. Simoni (1946), 237.
32. For a critique of an odd, false rumor that circulated *after* the war that Molotov had secretly visited Berlin in March 1941 to offer a military alliance see Beloff, 2 (1949), 365n–366n.
33. Boelcke (1970), 174.
34. Simoni (1946), 232, 236, entries for 28 May and 8 June 1941.
35. Boelcke (1970), 174.
36. Hassell (1947), 198, entry for 15 June 1941, and *DGFP,* 12 (1962), 788n. This rumor inspired the famous contemporary David Low cartoon, "Hi, Joe! I wonder if you'd do me a favor. . . ."
37. *FRUS: 1941,* 1 (1958), 753.
38. John Hohenberg, *Foreign Correspondence* (New York: Columbia University Press, 1964), p. 340. See also Wiskemann (1959), 72–74.
39. Whitaker (1943), 304, 305–306.
40. Huss (1942), 259–274.
41. Wiskemann (1959), 72–73.
42. Scott (1942), 251–257.
43. The article is reprinted in Raczynski (1962), 351–352. *Hetman* Pavel Skoropadski, a leading Ukrainian émigré leader, headed the 3,500 aged yet prestigious members of the Ukrainian Community (UH) organization in Germany until he was killed in an air raid at the end of the war. See Armstrong (1963), 27–29, 316n.
44. A. Dallin (1957), 114–119.
45. Middleton (1946) 135. See also Middleton (1964), 56–57. Since the de-

tails added by Middleton between his 1946 book and 1964 article coincide with those in Churchill's war memoirs, I suspect Middleton's memory may have been overstimulated by the latter. Certainly, there are many outright contradictions between his earlier and later recollections of the same events. I have found no independent confirmation of Eden's alleged briefing of American correspondents.

46. *Washington Post,* 6 June 1941, p. 2, and *New York Times,* 6 June 1941, p. 8.

47. For a monograph on the general mechanism of Soviet foreign press monitoring see Whaley (1964).

48. Leonhard (1958), 106–107, 108, 111.

49. On his theory of "tacit bargaining" see Thomas C. Schelling, *The Strategy of Conflict* (Cambridge, Mass.: Harvard University Press, 1963), pp. 53–80, and Thomas C. Schelling, *Arms and Influence* (New Haven: Yale University Press, 1966), pp. 131–141.

50. David Zaslavsky article in *Pravda,* 25 May 1941, as cited in Scott (1942), 250, and D. Dallin (1942), 372.

Chapter 8

1. Churchill, 3 (1950), 55, quoting from their conversation in Moscow in October 1944.

2. To cite only the title of a popular 1955 book on Soviet intelligence by E. H. Cookridge.

3. See Whaley (1969a), chap. 2.

4. See Harry Howe Ransom, *Central Intelligence and National Security* (Cambridge, Mass.: Harvard University Press, 1958).

5. The history of these several Soviet intelligence services is summarized in Whaley (1969a). See also Höhne (1971), 1–34.

6. The most detailed historical study is Simon Wolin and Robert M. Slusser, *The Soviet Secret Police* (New York: Praeger, 1957). See also Whaley (1969a), chap. 8.

7. "Sovetskie organy" (1965).

8. Salisbury (1969), 59, 71, 73.

9. No detailed or historical study of the GRU has ever been published. Meanwhile see Whaley (1969a), chap. 6.

10. Naval intelligence was detached from the GRU in 1940 and remained a separate service until after World War II, when it again, but briefly, was subordinated to the GRU. For Soviet naval intelligence see ibid., chap. 7.

11. Nekrich interview with Golikov on 25 September 1964, as quoted in Nekrich (1968), 181.

12. "Discussion" (1967), 173–180. See also Petrov (1968), 246–261.

13. "Discussion" (1967), 173.

14. Ibid., 175.

15. Ibid., 176.

16. Ibid., 177.

17. Zhukov (1971), 229.
18. Whaley (1969a), chap. 7.
19. "Discussion" (1967), 175.
20. Zhukov (1971), 229, quoting directly from Kuznetsov's original memorandum.
21. Whaley (1969a), chap. 9.
22. Kuznetsov (1965), in Bialer (1969), 190.
23. Ibid., 191.
24. Anfilov (of the Soviet Army Staff), reporting his conversation with Zhukov, in "Discussion" (1967), 175, and Zhukov (1971), 216, 228.
25. Gnedin, as quoted in "Discussion" (1967), 177.
26. For Stalin's secretariat see Whaley (1969a), 56, 65.
27. Most of these are conveniently summarized in Nekrich (1968), Salisbury (1969), and particularly Bialer (1969).
28. Ciano (1948), 446, minutes of 15 June 1941, and DGFP, 12 (1962), 1030.
29. Hilger and Meyer (1953), 328, 330, 334.
30. A useful introduction to the Reichswehr–Red Army collaboration and Weimar-Comintern conflict is Harvey Leonard Dyck, Weimar Germany and Soviet Russia, 1926–1933 (New York: Columbia University Press, 1966).
31. The relevant extract of Molotov's report of January 28, 1935 to the Seventh Soviet Congress is given in Degras (1953), 111–112. For the relevant portion of Molotov's report of 10 January 1936 to the Central Executive Committee, see ibid., 153–154.
32. For these agitprop techniques see Alex Inkeles, Public Opinion in Soviet Russia (Cambridge, Mass.: Harvard University Press, 1950), pp. 67–93.
33. Garthoff (1953), 435.
34. Telegram, Steinhardt to Hull, 17 March 1941, in FRUS: 1941, 1 (1958), 132–133.
35. Tokaev (1951), 34.
36. Leonhard (1958), 107–108.
37. IVOVSS (1965), 58, as translated by Salisbury (1969), 69. See also Survey, June 1967, which errs both in dating this discussion to 17 June and by having it be an argument between Malenkov and Kuznetsov.
38. Burlutski in Thayer (1954), 70.
39. Boldin (1961), 81–85.
40. Salisbury (1969), 68–69, 73–74.
41. Marie Seton, Sergei M. Eisenstein (New York: A. A. Wyn, 1952), pp. 379–388.
42. Pope (1943), 460. See also Seton (1952), 397–398, and Werth (1964), 120.
43. Bourke-White (1942), 30–31, 58.
44. Ehrenburg (1963), 274–275.
45. Pope (1943), 460. I have been unable to verify this assertion. Scott (1942) does not mention it, although he was present. Nor was it mentioned in the covering stories in either the Times (London) or the New York Times or in U.S. Ambassador Steinhardt's reports to the State Department.
46. McSherry, 2 (1970), 229, 296, 300–301.

47. Telegram, Steinhardt to Hull, 17 May 1941, as printed in *FRUS: 1941*, 1 (1958), 144.

48. As asserted in 1966 by Zastavenko of the Institute of Marxism-Leninism in "Discussion" (1967), 175. Zastavenko also attributed this view to the Politburo as a whole.

49. For the complete text as translated from *Izvestiya*, 14 June 1941, see Degras (1953), 489. See also *DGFP*, 12 (1962), 1027–1028, for the text as received by the German ambassador; and *FRUS: 1941*, 1 (1958), 148–149, for the version transmitted to Washington by the American ambassador. The slight differences among these versions seem due only to the whims of their translators and do not suggest any difference between the hand-delivered text of 13 June and the *Izvestiya* publication of 14 June.

50. For contemporary interpretations and reactions see Huss (1942), 275–277; D. Dallin (1942), 372–374; Cassidy (1943), 16–17; Gafencu (1945), 207–210; Simoni (1946), 239; Schuman (1946), 416–417; Churchill, 3 (1950), 365, 366, 367; Fedyuninsky (1961), 10; and Maisky (1968), 149. See also Weinberg (1954), 166–167.

51. Cassidy (1943), 17, 58–60. Cassidy covered this conference for AP. See also the UP dispatch in the *New York Times*, 29 June 1941, p. 18, reporting Lozovsky's press conference of 28 June.

52. These remarks are reported only in the paraphrase by General Sir Alan Brooke, then chief of the Imperial General Staff, from the notes of the interview by Churchill's interpreter, Major Arthur Birse. Brooke had accompanied Churchill to Moscow but was absent from this informal dinner. Indeed, only five persons were present: Stalin, Churchill, Molotov, and the two interpreters, Birse and Pavlov. In addition, a housekeeper, NKVD Major Aleksandra Nakashidze (a cousin of Beriya's wife), and Stalin's sixteen-year-old daughter, Svetlana, came in and out, and a belated appearance was made by Foreign Office Permanent Under-Secretary Sir Alexander Cadogan. See Bryant (1957), 383. Churchill, 4 (1950), 496–499, makes no mention of these remarks in his recollections of this prolonged conversation. Nor did he convey them to his personal physician on returning from the dinner. See Lord Moran, *Winston Churchill* (London: Constable, 1966), pp. 62–64. Nor do the memoirs of Major Birse reveal any more than the circumstances of the soirée. See A. H. Birse, *Memoirs of an Interpreter* (New York: Coward-McCann, 1967), p. 102. See also Svetlana Alliluyeva, *Twenty Letters to a Friend* (New York: Harper & Row, 1967), pp. 170–171.

53. *FRUS: 1941*, 1 (1958), 141.

54. The only published version of this speech consists of the few lines given by Zhukov (1971), 225–226. The only published firsthand comment is by Starinov (1964), in Bialer (1969), 223, who says Stalin greatly exaggerated the degree of Red Army readiness. Conflicting secondhand accounts are given by Werth (1964), 122–123; Hilger and Meyer (1953), 330; Scott (1942), 245–246; Bourke-White (1942), 31; Ribbentrop (1954), 155; Gafencu (1945), 194; and *DGFP*, 2 (1958), 964–965. I have relied mainly on Werth. See also the comment by Bialer (1969), 583–584.

55. Murray (1950), 203–204, 214.

56. For the text of Schulenburg's telegram informing Berlin of this meeting see *DGFP*, 12 (1962), 1071–1072. See also Hilger and Meyer (1953), 335–336, for additional recollections of the conversation, by Hilger, who was present.

57. The complete text of the official English translation is in Scott (1942), 354–360. The complete Russian text as published in *Pravda* on 3 July 1941 is republished in Stalin (1967), 1–10.

58. *FRUS: 1941*, 1 (1958), 179–180.

59. Sherwood (1948), 335, and Hopkins (1941), 14–15, 114–117. For Hopkins's own undated report of this meeting to Roosevelt see *FRUS: 1941*, 1 (1958), 805–813, particularly 808.

60. Duranty (1941), 188–189.

61. *New York Times*, 13 December 1941, p. 20, giving the complete text of Litvinov's prepared press conference statement. Louis Fischer (1946), 24, is the only commentator to note this major disclosure by Litvinov.

62. J. Stalin, *On the Great Patriotic War of the Soviet Union* (Moscow: Foreign Languages Publishing House, 1965), p. 45. The complete Russian text as originally published in *Pravda*, 23 February 1942, is republished in Stalin, 2 (1967), 36–44. This speech is misidentified as that of Stalin to the Moscow Soviet on 6 November 1941 by Garthoff (1953), 273–274.

63. Eden (1965), 238 and 301. Some internal evidence in Eden's account points to October 1943 as the occasion for Stalin's remark. Eden's five wartime meetings with Stalin occurred in December 1941 (Moscow), October–November 1943 (Moscow), November–December 1943 (Tehran), October 1944 (Moscow), and February 1945 (Yalta).

64. Scott (1942), 270.

65. *FRUS: 1941*, 4 (1956), 972.

66. Nikolai V. Voznesensky, *The Economy of the USSR during World War II* (Washington, D.C.: Public Affairs Press, 1948), p. 21. See also Khrushchev's remarks about the incomplete state of mobilization of industry on the eve of war in Wolfe (1957), 168, 170.

67. Zhdanov did not get back to his post until 27 June. See Salisbury (1969), 41, 145n.

68. Kuznetsov (1967), no. 3, 90, 91, who, however, wrongly supposed Timoshenko and Zhukov to have been out. See Zhukov (1971), 234–235.

69. According to a U.S. embassy clerk who saw them at Sochi. *FRUS: 1941*, 1 (1958), 177. See also Markoff (1950), 175.

70. Ege (1953). The Italian ambassador, Alfieri (1955), 137, confirms that Dekanozov was quite surprised by Ribbentrop's announcement of war.

71. Packard (1942), 208, citing what other diplomats close to the Russians told the foreign press corps at the time. This is confirmed by Ciano (1946), 369.

72. For the Comintern and Communist parties in general see Armstrong (1961), 118–121, 165–171. For the Czech Communist party see Beneš (1954), 143–144, 162–163, and Paul E. Zinner, *Communist Strategy and Tactics in Czechoslovakia, 1918–1948* (New York: Praeger, 1963), pp. 71–75. For the Polish Communists see Bor-Komorowski (1951), 46; and M. K. Dziewanowski,

The Communist Party of Poland (Cambridge, Mass.: Harvard University Press, 1959), pp. 160–161. For the French party see A. Rossi [pseud. of Angelo Tasca], *A Communist Party in Action* (New Haven: Yale University Press, 1949), pp. 100–105; and Alexander Werth, *France, 1940–1955* (New York: Holt, 1956), p. 195. For the U.S. party see Irving Howe and Lewis Coser, *The American Communist Party* (Boston: Beacon Press, 1957), pp. 395, 398, 405.

73. The evidence, pro and con, is presented in rather skeptical terms by Hamilton Fish Armstrong, *Tito and Goliath* (New York: Macmillan, 1951), pp. 11–17. See specifically Dedijer (1953), 147. See also Milorad M. Drachkovitch, "The Comintern and the Insurrectional Activity of the Communist Party of Yugoslavia in 1941–1942," in Milorad M. Drachkovitch and Branko Lazitch, eds., *The Comintern* (New York: Praeger, 1966).

74. On the OMS see Whaley (1969a), chap. 4.

75. Unfortunately Werth (1964), 120, cites no source for this important assertion.

76. Weinberg (1954), 167.

77. McSherry, 2 (1970), 223; also Cassidy (1943), 13–14.

78. McSherry, 2 (1970), 234; Upton (1964), 243; and *FRUS: 1941,* 1 (1958), 27–28.

79. The role of provocation in the operational code of the Russian Communist elite is documented and analyzed in detail in Nathan Leites, *A Study of Bolshevism* (Glencoe, Ill.: Free Press, 1953), pp. 46–47, 321–323.

80. *NCA* (1946), 6: 996–997, quoting entries of 10 April 1941 from the German OKM diary.

81. Erickson (1962a), 586–587, and Higgins (1966), 131.

82. Erickson (1962a), 587.

83. A. V. Karasev, *Leningradtsy v gody blokady, 1941–1943* (Moscow: Akademiya Nauk SSSR, Institut Istorii, 1959), pp. 32–33, which reproduces the complete text of this document from the Defense Ministry archives.

84. Khrushchev, in Wolfe (1957), 172.

85. Or so Hitler wrote on the eve of the attack in his letter to Mussolini and repeated on the afternoon of 22 June to the Italian ambassador. See *DGFP,* 12 (1962) 1066–1069, and Alfieri (1955), 142, 147.

86. For recollections and reports of the broadcast of 3 July 1941 see Ilya Ehrenburg, *The War: 1941–1945* (Cleveland and New York: World Publishing, 1964), pp. 10–11; *FRUS: 1941,* 1 (1958), 628; Cassidy (1943), 62–63; and Werth (1964), 162–167. For the text as originally published in *Pravda,* 3 July, see Joseph Stalin, *War Speeches . . .* (London: Hutchinson, 1946), p. 7, and Stalin, 2 (1967), 1–10.

87. Churchill, 3 (1950), 331.

88. For general discussions of Stalin's alleged breakdown and recovery see Salisbury (1969), 80, 133, 139–141, 216; Higgins (1966), 143–145; Carell (1965), 51–52; and Robert Payne, *The Rise and Fall of Stalin* (New York: Simon and Schuster, 1965), pp. 557–560. For Khrushchev's revelation in 1956 see Wolfe (1957), 176, 178. For Maisky's recollections see "Stalin Hid as Nazi Attack

Began, Ex-Envoy Recalls," *New York Times,* 7 January 1965, p. 2. For Kuznetsov's, see "Stalin's Absence as Nazis Attacked in 1941 Recalled," *New York Times,* 4 November 1965, p. 19. For contemporary Moscow rumors about Stalin's absence see Cassidy (1943), 56–57. But compare I. Deutscher, *Stalin: A Political Biography* (New York and London: Oxford University Press, 1949), pp. 461–464, and Zhukov (1971), 231–235. A definitive source might be Stalin's daughter, Svetlana; but her recent memoirs give no clue to her father's state of mind in June 1941.

Chapter 9

1. Quoted by Orlov (1963), 10.
2. The only study to examine the "demonstration" aspect is Kaufmann (1949–1950).
3. Namely, the then editor of *Foreign Affairs,* Hamilton Fish Armstrong, *Tito and Goliath* (New York: Macmillan, 1951), p. 11n.
4. Bertram D. Wolfe, "Adventures in Forged Sovietica," *New Leader,* vol. 38, nos. 30, 31, 32 (25 July, 1 August, 8 August 1955), and Paul W. Blackstock, *Agents of Deceit* (Chicago: Quadrangle, 1966), pp. 171–185.
5. Budu Svanidze [pseud. of G. Bessedovsky?], *My Uncle Joseph Stalin* (New York: Putnam's, 1953), p. 169. This profitable hoax deceived not only Waverley Root at the time but, more recently, Martin Ebon, *Svetlana* (New York: New American Library, 1967).
6. See Krummacher and Lange (1970), 442–447, for a critique of the "contingency" hypothesis.
7. Thus see Hitler's remarks during table talk at his "Wolfsschanze" field headquarters on 17 September 1941 in [Adolf Hitler], *Hitler's Secret Conversations, 1941–1944* (New York: Farrar, Straus and Young, 1953), p. 26.
8. Comprehensive critiques of the "preventive war" hypothesis are Laqueur (1965), 260–263; Busse (1961); Erickson (1962c), 178–183; Krummacher and Lange (1970), 447–453; and Warlimont (1964). See also Blumentritt (1952), 97, 98. For the Hitler-Antonescu conversation of 11 June 1941 see *DGFP,* 12 (1962), 1001–1006.
9. Telegram, Hull to Steinhardt, 9 June 1941, in *FRUS: 1941,* 1 (1958), 753.
10. On 18 July he instructed his former ambassador to Moscow, Davies, to try to pass this same warning to Stalin and Molotov. See Joseph E. Davies, *Mission to Moscow* (New York: Simon and Schuster, 1941), p. 450, diary entry for 18 July 1939. Roosevelt's talk with Umansky was on the occasion of the latter's farewell visit before taking home leave on 5 July 1939. The German chargé in Washington soon learned in part of Roosevelt's message to Umansky. See *DGFP,* 6 (1956), 1028. For some reason, the version forwarded on 4 August by Undersecretary Welles through Ambassador Steinhardt and delivered by him to Molotov on the sixteenth was quite watered down. See *FRUS: 1939,* 1 (1956), 293–294, 296–299.
11. Langer and Gleason (1953), 525–528.
12. *FRUS: 1941,* 1 (1958), 755.

13. Langer and Gleason (1953), 528. This oracular passage is tactfully omitted from McGeorge Bundy's rewrite of Stimson's diary.

14. Ciechanowski (1947), 24.

15. Ickes (1954), 548–549.

16. Kennan (1967), 130–132.

17. The occasion was a meeting with a leader of the Social Democratic wing of the Bulgarian Labor party, the only other person present—as interpreter—being Michael Padev, the Sofia correspondent of the *Times* (London). See Michael Padev, *Escape from the Balkans* (Indianapolis, Ind.: Bobbs-Merrill, 1943), p. 124.

18. Telegram, Churchill to Smuts, 27 June 1940, in Churchill, 2 (1949), 227–228.

19. Minute, Churchill to Beaverbrook, 8 July 1940, in Churchill, 2 (1949), 643.

20. Telegram, Churchill to Eden, 30 March 1941, in Eden (1965), 272.

21. In Churchill, 3 (1950), 369. The gaps—from 8 July 1940 to 30 March 1941 and from 22 April to 15 June 1941—among his three published flurries of conviction do, however, permit some skepticism about its consistency that can be definitively resolved only by further publication of official documents or private memoirs.

22. Ibid., 368–369.

23. Memorandum by Churchill's assistant private secretary, Mr. J. R. Colville, as published in ibid., 370–371. The dinner guests were U.S. Ambassador and Mrs. Winant, Foreign Secretary and Mrs. Eden, Secretary to the War Cabinet Sir Edward Bridges, and Mr. Colville. See Winant (1947), 203–204, and Eden (1965), 312.

24. The complete text of the broadcast, carried live over B.B.C. at 9 P.M., is in Churchill, *War Speeches*, 1 (1951), 450–454.

25. Kirkpatrick (1959), 154.

26. F.O.E.S. was constituted as follows:
Chairman: Admiral Sir Thomas Troubridge (Admiralty)
Members: Major-General P. J. Mackesy (Army)
        Air Commodore J. L. Vachell (R.A.F.)
        Mr. Ivone Kirkpatrick (Foreign Office) (until 3 February 1941)
Secretary: Donald McLachlan (N.I.D.—17z)
Incidentally, all except Mackesy had previously served together in Berlin. For F.O.E.S. see McLachlan (1968), 252–256; Kirkpatrick (1959), 153–155, who unaccountably calls it "Forward Operations Enemies"; Delmer (1962), 75, who calls it "Forward Operations Enemy"; Francis de Guingand, *Operation Victory* (London: Hodder and Stoughton, 1947), 112; and K. Strong (1969).

27. For A.P.E.S. see McLachlan (1969), 252, 256, and Butler, 2 (1957), 541, where it is called the "Axis Planning Section." Its only publicy identified member is Captain Stuart Paton, the naval representative. In spring 1942 it was renamed the Joint Intelligence Staff (J.I.S.).

28. McLachlan (1968), 242, quoting an unpublished postwar memorandum by Cavendish-Bentinck.

29. Ibid., 243, quoting Cavendish-Bentinck.

30. Ibid., 242.

31. Ibid., 243.

32. *FRUS: 1941*, 1 (1958), 168–169, gives a secondhand but contemporary summary of Eden's changing views. See also Eden (1965), 234–235, 263–269; Middleton (1946), 135; and Middleton (1964), 57.

33. Woodward, 1 (1970), 617–618.

34. Churchill, 3 (1950), 355–356, and Woodward, 1 (1970), 617n. This assessment of the I.G.S. view is partly confirmed by its director of Military Operations, Major-General Kennedy (1957), 128–130, 133. Indeed, both Kennedy and Field-Marshall Dill (the C.I.G.S.) were caught by surprise on 22 June.

35. Churchill, 3 (1950), 355–356, and Gwyer (1964), 82–83, both summarizing the J.I.C. paper, dated 23 May 1941, assessing Russo-German relations. See Woodward, 1 (1970), 619–620, for a detailed summary of the J.I.C. memorandum of 9 June.

36. Gwyer (1964), 82.

37. Bryant (1957), 191.

38. Delmer (1962), 62–63. Delmer, who was present, confirms (p. 47) that this was indeed S.O.1's first intimation of this overshadowing event.

39. Nicolson, 2 (1967), 172.

40. For the official British press briefing and "D-notice" system see D. C. Watt, "Foreign Affairs, the Public Interest and the Right to Know," *Political Quarterly*, vol. 34, no. 2 (March–April 1963), pp. 121–136.

41. Wrench (1955), 443.

42. Thus Butler, 2 (1957), 544.

43. See also Scott (1942), 241–242.

44. Beneš (1954), 78, 147.

45. Ibid., 78, 131–166. Beneš's post factum claim to have predicted BARBAROSSA is largely verified by Sheean (1943), 331–332.

46. Mikolajczyk (1948), 11. He was then the first deputy of the Polish Parliament-in-exile and an intimate of Premier Sikorski.

47. Gwyer (1964), 82–83.

48. Ciano (1946), 351–352, entry for 14 May 1941.

49. Simoni (1946), 220–223, 226, 231–242, and Alfieri (1955), 120, 138.

50. As confided by Rosso to Rumanian Ambassador Gafencu and reported by Gafencu to Steinhardt on 12 June. See *FRUS: 1941*, 1 (1958), 755.

51. Through some mix-up in Rome, Rosso did not even receive the belated Italian declaration of war to deliver to the Russians, only learning of it that afternoon from Vyshinsky! See Bojano (1944), 230–231.

52. Butow (1961), 208–212. See also Presseisen (1958), 301–303, and *FRUS: 1941*, 4 (1956), 272–273, for Tatekawa's remarks to Steinhardt on 27 May.

53. Ike (1967), 47, and Lu (1961), 175.

54. *New York Times*, 24 June 1941, p. 3, citing Matsuoka's statement to the Tokyo newspaper *Yomiuri*.

55. Keitel (1966), 121–124. Kesselring (1954), 93–94, also largely accepted this argument. Compare the more reasonable view of Manstein (1958), 181, and the devastating comments by Warlimont (1964).

56. The most recent study of this special use of authoritarian mass media is William E. Griffith, "Communist Esoteric Communications: *Explication de texte*" (Cambridge, Mass.: M.I.T., Center for International Studies, 1967).

57. Robert T. Elson, *Time Inc.: The Intimate History of a Publishing Enterprise, 1923–1941* (New York: Atheneum, 1968), pp. 475–476. See also Margaret Bourke-White, *Portrait of Myself* (New York: Simon and Schuster, 1963), pp. 174–175.

58. See *New York Times*, 16–22 June 1941.

59. Colonel Barney Oldfield, *Never a Shot in Anger* (New York: Duell, Sloan and Pearce, 1956), pp. 13–15, gives an eyewitness account of this episode. For the Baldwin column actually published, see Hanson W. Baldwin, "We Move Closer to a Showdown with Germany," *New York Times*, 22 June 1941, p. E3.

60. See Claude E. Shannon and Warren Weaver, *The Mathematical Theory of Communication* (Urbana: University of Illinois Press, 1949), and J. R. Pierce, *Symbols, Signals and Noise* (New York: Harper & Brothers, 1961).

61. Wohlstetter (1962), 398–401.

62. Whaley (1969b), case no. A30 ("Pearl Harbor").

63. For example, Kirkpatrick (1969), 73, 269–272; also the political scientist Bialer (1969), 579, and the historian Nekrich (1968).

64. Wohlstetter (1962) and, after her example, Kirkpatrick (1969), 267–281.

Bibliography on BARBAROSSA Planning

This bibliography attempts to list all the published books and articles that mention the planning of Operation BARBAROSSA and the diffusion of intelligence and rumor about the German plans. Consequently, it includes all the directly relevant works cited in this book. In addition, it lists a few works that I have not yet seen. All these unseen works, which have been cited elsewhere as containing relevant information, are explicitly identified as such in the annotation.

Many writers—political and military historians, journalists, intelligence buffs, and professional intelligencers—have studied BARBAROSSA intensively. Most of these men simply omit any reference to the element of deception. Many others make at least passing reference to some of the German deception operations. Yet none recognize the decisive part that Hitler's orchestrated deception campaign played in obtaining strategic surprise over Stalin.

Colonel E. Lèderrey, a prominent Swiss lecturer in military history, typifies most writers in confronting the German deception plan. His 232-page study of BARBAROSSA dismisses the deception aspect with one assertion (1955, p. 20): "By wishing to deceive Churchill and Stalin at the same time, Hitler failed to mislead either. The proof lies in the fact that the first named revealed to the second the preparations for an imminent attack on the U.S.S.R." Lèderrey fails to understand that warnings can be misinterpreted.

Several writers have made much of the warnings but, by overlooking the disinformation that accompanied them, do not understand *how* Stalin was surprised. This analytic failure applies even to the three writers, Nekrich (1968), Salisbury (1969), and Bialer (1969), who made the only detailed compilations of the warnings. These men are in thrall to the Wohlstetter theory of surprise as a consequence of ambiguous information. They probe deeply the evidence about Stalin's information, perceptions, and decisions but do not realize that these were being manipulated by Hitler. Bialer (1969, p. 579) even attributes Stalin's surprise to the theory that "Dictatorial governments are especially susceptible to certain hazards in the compilation and interpretation of intelligence." Bialer is unaware that the intelligence systems of democratic Britain, the United States, and others were as easily misled as the Russian system.

Even a professional intelligencer such as Lyman B. Kirkpatrick, Jr., a former senior CIA official, ascribes (1969, pp. 17–74) the BARBAROSSA surprise entirely to the "system" and Stalin's arrogant preconceptions, thereby also overlooking the intimate interaction between the dupe and the deceiver. The Soviet KGB did no better in its recently published analysis ("Sovetskie organy" [1965]) of the warnings and the surprise.

Only two recent studies have acknowledged the importance of the German deception campaign. Both are by Russians. Fomin (1966, p. 13) concludes that the German "misinformation policy . . . must be taken into account in studying the preparation of fascist aggression against the Soviet Union." And Marshal Zhukov, himself a moderately skilled practitioner of deception, notes

(1971, pp. 222–223) that the German disinformation that reached Stalin explains his "extreme caution" in preparing for an invasion. But, having found the key to the problem of surprise, neither Fomin nor Zhukov exploits it to full effect.

Like the world's intelligence services at the time, historians have *two* chances to solve the mystery of BARBAROSSA. Because SEA LION, Hitler's plan to invade Britain, was the main cover story for BARBAROSSA, the students of SEA LION could have stumbled upon the reason for Stalin's surprise. However, none of the SEA LION historians—Ansel, Fleming, Grinnell-Milne, Klee, or Wheatley—did so. Indeed, only one, the German historian Karl Klee, discovered that the later stage of SEA LION was a hoax, but he elaborated only on its effect in the West. This deception element of SEA LION was even missed by Ian's brother Peter Fleming, although he had been one of the top British deception planners in World War II.

Bibliographic Style

The annotation of the works in the Bibliography seeks no more than clarification of the titles, identification of the authors, and an occasional cautionary or explanatory note about the work's usefulness or relevance to BARBAROSSA.

The spelling, punctuation, and capitalization of authors' names, titles, and publication data follow the usage of the title pages of the works themselves, rather than being made to conform to the style manual of Procrustes. Thus we have Valentin Berezhkov *and* V. M. Berezhkov, Simon and Schuster *and* Harper & Row, and so on consistently through many seeming inconsistencies.

Accoce, Pierre (1928–), and Pierre Quet
A Man Called Lucy. New York: Coward-McCann, 1967.
First published in French in 1966. A thoroughly frustrating account by two French journalists of the Rado-Rössler GRU network in Switzerland during World War II. Much wild speculation is built on careless scrapings of the published record and some singularly unsuccessful interviews with uncommunicative survivors. Damning European press reviews forced the authors to admit that much of their data was mere imaginative fabrication. Poor journalism; incompetent historiography. Compare Foote (1949); D. Dallin (1955); Kimche (1962); and Höhne (1971).

Aguirre, José Antonio de (1904–1960)
Escape via Berlin. New York: The Macmillan Company, 1944.
Diary of the refugee president of the Basque government. A translation of the original 1940 Buenos Aires edition in Spanish.

Ainsztein, Reuben
"Stalin and June 22, 1941: Some New Soviet Views." *International Affairs* (London), vol. 42, no. 4 (October 1966), pp. 662–672.
A critical review of the then current Soviet discussions and disclosures about Stalin's expectations of BARBAROSSA.

Akhmedov, Ismail. See Ege, Ismail.

Aldus [pseud.]
"Il maresciallo Antonescu e la guerra control l'U.R.S.S." [Marshal Antonescu and the war with the U.S.S.R.]. *Rivista di Studi Politici Internazionali* (Florence), vol. 15, nos. 3/4 (July/December 1948), pp. 335–376.
Includes material on the Rumanian decision to join BARBAROSSA.

Alfieri, Dino (1886–)
Dictators Face to Face. New York: New York University Press, 1955.
Translation of the original Italian edition of 1948. Memoirs of a senior Fascist who, after breaking in as Minister of Propaganda and Ambassador to the Vatican, served as Ambassador in Berlin from 1940 to 1943.

Allen, Charles R., Jr.
Heusinger of the Fourth Reich. New York: Marzani & Munsell, 1963.
A flagrant piece of Communist propaganda against the German Federal Republic.

Amè, *Generale* Cesare
Guerra segreta in Italia, 1940–1943. Rome: Gherardo Casini, 1954.
Memoirs of the director of SIM (Italian military intelligence), 1940–1943. General Amè was a personal friend of his German counterpart, Admiral Canaris.

Anderle and Basler. See Busse, Hans

Anders, *General* Wladyslaw (1892–)
Hitler's Defeat in Russia. Chicago: Henry Regnery, 1953. Translation of the original Polish edition published in London in 1952. Part memoir, part history. Anders, an anti-Communist and patriotic Polish officer, commanded the Polish forces in Russia from late 1941 until 1942, when he led the main detachment out to join the British Middle East Command.

Andreas-Friedrich, Ruth [pseud. of Ruth Seitz] (1901–)
Berlin Underground, 1938–1945. New York: Henry Holt, 1947.
Memoirs—reconstructed as a "diary"—of an authentic, if minor, member of the anti-Nazi German underground.

Anfuso, Filippo (1901–1963)
Da Palazzo Venezia al lago di Garda, 1936–1945. 3rd rev. ed. Bologne: Cappelli, 1957.
The memoirs of Ciano's *chef de cabinet* (1938–1941). Anfuso was sentenced to death by the High Court of Justice in 1945 but acquitted in 1949 after a second trial. Originally published as *Du palais de Venise au lac de Garde* (Paris: Calmann-Levy, 1949).

Ansel, Walter
Hitler Confronts England. Durham, N.C.: Duke University Press, 1960.
One of the better efforts showing the effects of SEA LION on BARBAROSSA. See also Klee (1958); P. Fleming (1957); and Wheatley (1958). The author is a retired U.S. Navy Rear Admiral.

Armstrong, John A. (1922–)
The Politics of Totalitarianism: The Communist Party of the Soviet Union from 1934 to the Present. New York: Random House, 1961.
A carefully documented general history and analysis, drawing on many sources not usually used by Sovietologists.

Armstrong, John A.
Ukrainian Nationalism. 2nd ed. New York: Columbia University Press, 1963.
A scholarly study by one of the more careful American students of Soviet political history.

Assarsson, Vilhelm (1889–)
I skuggan av Stalin [In the shadow of Stalin]. Stockholm: Bonniers, 1963.
Moscow memoirs of the Swedish minister to Russia, 1940–1943. Not seen by me.

Assmann, Kurt (1883–)
Deutsche Schicksalsjahre: Historische Bilder aus dem zweiten Weltkreig und seiner Vorgeschichte. Wiesbaden: Eberhard Brockhaus, 1950.
A major memoir-cum-history of World War II by Admiral Assmann, a senior staff officer in the OKM. Chapter 7 ("Der Weg nach Stalingrad," pp. 197–229) received prior publication in an English translation by U.S. Naval Intelligence officer Captain R. E. Krause as "Stalin and Hitler, Part II: The Road to Stalingrad," *United States Naval Institute Proceedings,* vol. 75, no. 7 (July 1949), pp. 759–773.

The Attitude of the Soviet Government toward Finland after the Peace of Moscow. Helsinki, c. 1942.
This collection of documents is the Finnish Blue-White Book, no. 2, published during World War II to justify Finland's attack on Russia. It covers the period 13 March 1940–26 June 1941. Not seen by me.

Auswärtige Amt [the German Foreign Office]. See Documents on German Foreign Policy.

Avon, Earl of. See Eden, Anthony

Azarov, *Vice-Admiral* I[liya] I[lich] (1913–)
Osazhdennaya Odessa [Besieged Odessa]. Moscow: Voenizdat, 1962.
Memoirs of World War II. At the time of the German invasion the then Rear Admiral Azarov was chief of the Red Navy's Political Department. Two relevant passages, in English translation, are in Bialer (1969), 134, 259. A second edition appeared in 1966.

Bagramyan, *Marshal of the Soviet Union* I[van Khristoforovich] (1897–)
["The Difficult Summer" (in Russian)], *Literaturnaya gazeta,* 14 April 1965, pp. 1–2.
A complete English translation is in *CDSP,* vol. 17, no. 17 (19 May 1965), pp. 19–21. An interview by *Literaturnaya gazeta* Special Correspondent N. Mar with the Soviet Deputy Minister of Defense.

Bagramyan, *Marshal* I[van] Kh[ristoforovich]
"Zapiski nachalnika operativnogo otdela" [Memoirs of the Operations Section at the outbreak of war]. *Voenno-istorichesky zhurnal,* 1967, no. 3, pp. 52–68.

Until the German invasion, the then Colonel Bagramyan was Chief of Operations and Deputy Chief of Staff of the Kiev Military District. A condensed English translation of the article is in Bialer (1969), 244–254.

Bailey, Geoffrey [pseud.]
The Conspirators. New York: Harper & Brothers, 1960. A carefully researched British study of the battle of wits between Russian émigré organizations and Soviet Chekists during the 1920s and 1930s.

Bekker, Cajus [pseud. of Hans-Dieter Berenbrok] (1924–)
The Luftwaffe War Diaries. Garden City, N.Y.: Doubleday & Company, 1968. English translation of the original German edition, *Angriffshöhe 4000* (Hamburg: Stalling, 1964).

Beloff, Max (1913–)
The Foreign Policy of Soviet Russia, 1929–1942. 2 vols. London: Oxford University Press, 1949.
Vol. 2 ("1929–1941") includes the only thoroughly researched and documented account published before 1953 covering the BARBAROSSA diplomacy and intelligence. An excellent job for the time but now superseded.

Beneš, Eduard (1884–1948)
Memoirs of Dr Eduard Beneš: From Munich to New War and New Victory. Boston. Houghton Mifflin, [1954].
Translation of the original Czech edition of 1947. Dr. Beneš was president of Czechoslovakia, 1935–1938 and 1939–1948.

Berezhkov, Valentin [Mikhailovich] (1919–)
"On the Eve of Hitler's Invasion." *Atlas,* vol. 11, no. 1 (January 1966), pp. 10–15.
Cited as Berezhkov (1966a).
Translated from the author's memoir, "Na rubezhe mira i voinuy" [On the border of war and peace), *Novy Mir,* 1965, no. 7 (July), pp. 143–184. V. M. Berezhkov was First Secretary of the Soviet embassy in Berlin from late 1940 until the German invasion.

Berezhkov, V. M.
S diplomaticheskoi missiei v Berlin, 1940–1941 [With the diplomatic mission in Berlin, 1940–1941]. Moscow, 1966.
Cited as Berezhkov (1966b).
The key chapter (pp. 78–106), covering the indications of BARBAROSSA received at the Soviet embassy in Berlin, is also available in an abstracted English translation in Bialer (1969), 212–218. A complete German translation is also available (1967).

Bialer, Seweryn, ed.
Stalin and His Generals: Soviet Military Memoirs of World War II. New York: Pegasus, 1969.
An excellent collection of recent Soviet memoirs. For twenty-three pieces covering Soviet preparations for and warnings of war, see pp. 138–262.

Biryuzov, Marshal S. S. (1904–1964)
Kogda Gremeli Pushki [When cannons thunder]. Moscow: Voenizdat, 1961.
Memoirs of the Eastern Front from the German invasion until 1944. From
1939 to 1941 Biryuzov was commander of the 132nd Rifle Division on the
Moscow front. Not seen by me except for some pertinent excerpts in English
translation in Bialer (1969), 136–137, 238–240.

Blackstock, Paul W. (1913–   )
The Strategy of Subversion: Manipulating the Politics of Other Nations.
Chicago: Quadrangle Books, 1964.
The first scholarly survey of this subject. Responsible yet critical; informative
and informed. A much needed corrective to the Wise-Ross book on the CIA.
For a rare study of the role of intelligence in BARBAROSSA—albeit only from
the German side—see his Chapter 6 (pp. 142–157), "The German Campaign in
Russia: A Case Study in Ideological Crusades and Intelligence Estimates."

[Blau, George E.]
The German Campaign in Russia: Planning and Operations (1940–1942).
Washington [D.C.]: Department of the Army, 1955.
A quite incomplete early study by a professional military historian. Based
entirely on German documents, but they are not cited except in the general
bibliography.

Blumentritt, Guenther (c. 1893–   )
Von Rundstedt: The Soldier and the Man. London: Odhams Press, 1952.
A biography of Field-Marshal Gerd von Rundstedt (1875–1953) by one of his
former staff officers.

Blumentritt, General Günther
"Moscow," in Freiden and Richardson (1956), 35–86.
An account of the preparations for and first stages of BARBAROSSA, 1940–1941.
During that period Blumentritt was Chief of Staff of Field-Marshal von
Kluge's Fourth Army.

Boelcke, Willi A., ed. (1927–   )
*Kriegspropaganda, 1939–1941: Geheime Ministerkonferenzen im Reichspropa-
gandaministerium.* Stuttgart: Deutsche Verlags-Anstalt, 1966.
The collected minutes of Goebbels's so-called 11 A.M. Conference, the more or
less daily staff meetings of the twenty or so senior officials of the Propaganda
Ministry. Covers the period from 26 October 1939 through 31 May 1941. The
original minutes reposed, unused and unreported, in the East German State
Archives until they were secretly copied by one of the staff, Herr Boelcke, and
spirited by him to West Germany when he subsequently defected. Boelcke
now works in Stuttgart as a historian.

Boelcke, Willi A., ed.
The Secret Conferences of Dr. Goebbels: The Nazi Propaganda War, 1939–43.
New York: E. P. Dutton, 1970.
A slightly abridged translation of the original, "*Wollt Ihr den total en*

Krieg?": Die geheimen Goebbels-Konferenzen 1939–1943 (Stuttgart: Deutsche Verlags-Anstalt, 1967).

Bogomolov, A[leksandr] Y[efimovich] (1900–)
"Wartime Diplomatic Missions." *International Affairs* (Moscow), 1961, no. 6 (pp. 70–79), no. 7 (pp. 90–97), and no. 8 (pp. 69–76).
Memoirs of the Soviet diplomatic representative to Vichy France, initially (November 1940–March 1941) as Chargé d'Affaires and then (until the Nazi invasion of Russia in June) as Ambassador. Subsequently, until 1943, he served as Ambassador to the Allied governments-in-exile in London. Serial publication of this memoir was abruptly interrupted at the point at which he recounts the end of his mission to Vichy. I have not seen the last and, I presume, most relevant (no. 8), of the three published parts.

Boheman, Erik (1895–)
På Vakt [On duty]. 2 vols. Stockholm: P. A. Norstedt and Söners Förlag, 1963 and 1964.
Memoirs of a senior official of the Swedish Foreign Ministry. In 1941 he was its Secretary-General.

Bojano, Filippo (1896–)
In the Wake of the Goose-Step. London: Cassell, 1944.
Memoirs of an Italian foreign correspondent. He was in Moscow for the Stefani news agency from September 1940 to 31 May 1941. Translated by Gerald Griffin from the unpublished manuscript, "Per imitare il passo dell'oca."

Boldin, *Colonel-General* I[van] V[asilevich]
Stranitsuy zhizni [Pages from life].• Moscow: Voennoe izdatelstvo Ministerstva oboronuy Soyuza SSR, 1961.
A major Soviet military autobiography covering period from 1919 to 1955. Emphasizes the opening phase of the war when Boldin was a lieutenant-general serving as Deputy Commander of the Special Western Front under the soon to be executed Army General D. G. Pavlov.

Bor-Komorowski, T[adeusz] (1895–)
The Secret Army. London: Victor Gollancz, 1951.
World War II memoirs of General Komorowski (alias "Bor"), a leader of the Polish underground Home Army and its Commander in Chief, 1943–1944.

Bourke-White, Margaret (1906–1971)
Shooting the Russian War. New York: Simon and Schuster, 1942.
A memoir by the famous American photographer, who arrived in Moscow in May 1941. She and her husband, Erskine Caldwell, were there as a photo-correspondent team for *Life* magazine. See also Caldwell (1942).

Boveri, Margret (1900–)
Treason in the Twentieth Century. New York: G. P. Putnam's Sons, 1963.
Translation of Dr. Boveri's 2nd German edition of 1960. An excellent, popular survey using the case method. Includes one of the few frankly self-critical accounts of the German anti-Nazi underground by one of its survivors.

Bragadin, *Commander* Marc' Antonio (1906–   )
The Italian Navy in World War II. Annapolis, Md.: United States Naval Institute, 1957.
The author took the occasion of this translation to make major revisions of the original 1948 Italian edition. Includes some material on World War II codebreaking, pp. 13–14, 23, 98–103.

Brock, Ray (1913–1968)
Nor Any Victory. New York: Reynal & Hitchcock, 1942.

Bryant, Arthur (1899–   )
The Turn of the Tide: A History of the War Years based on the Diaries of Field-Marshal Lord Alanbrooke, Chief of the Imperial General Staff. Garden City, N.Y.: Doubleday, 1957.
General Sir Alan Brooke succeeded Dill as C.I.G.S. in late 1941, continuing until 1946.

Busse, Hans
"Die faschistische Lüge vom Präventivkrieg Hitlerdeutschlands gegen die UdSSR." In Alfred Anderle and Werner Basler, eds., *Juni 1941* (Berlin: Rütten & Loening, 1961), pp. 83–101.
A fully documented critique of the "preventive war" hypothesis used to justify BARBAROSSA. Busse is a lieutenant-colonel in the East German Army.

Butler, J. R. M. (editor) (1889–   )
Grand Strategy. Vols. I–III. London: Her Majesty's Stationery Office, 1956–1964.
The overview portion of the official British military history of World War II. The general editor, Professor (now Sir James) Butler, was in Military Intelligence during the war. Butler's own version of the prelude to BARBAROSSA is in vol. 2 (1957), pp. 533–546. For another version in vol. 3, pt. 1, see Gwyer (1964).

Butow, Robert J. C. (1924–   )
Tojo and the Coming of the War. Princeton: Princeton University Press, 1961.
A major scholarly study of political-military decision making.

Cadogan, *Sir* Alexander (1884–1969)
The Diaries of Sir Alexander Cadogan, O.M., 1938–1945. London: Cassell, 1971.

CAGH. See *Case Against General Heusinger.*

Caldwell, Erskine (1903–   )
All Out on the Road to Smolensk. New York: Duell, Sloan and Pearce, 1942.
A naïve eyewitness account of Russia in the weeks immediately before and after the German invasion. Caldwell and his wife, Margaret Bourke-White, had arrived in Moscow in May 1941 on a photo-correspondent assignment from *Life* magazine. See also Bourke-White (1942).

Carell, Paul [pseud. of Dr. Paul Karl Schmidt] (1911–   )
Hitler Moves East: 1941–1943. Boston: Little, Brown, 1965.
The original German edition, *Unternehmen* BARBAROSSA, appeared in 1963.

The most recent German history of the subject. A long, detailed, but un-documented study that hastily flits through the politically controversial planning period to get on with the war. One of the author's series of best-selling histories of Germany in World War II. Both his German and American publishers neglect to disclose that "Paul Carell" is a pseudonym masking Dr. Paul Karl Schmidt who was the notorious press chief in the Nazi foreign office.

Carroll, Wallace (1906–)
We're in This with Russia. Boston: Houghton Mifflin, 1942.
Memoirs of the United Press correspondent's visit to wartime Russia during July–November 1941. Includes some minor references to BARBAROSSA warnings on pp. 52–55, 144–145.

The Case Against General Heusinger: Documents illustrating the charges of the USSR against former Lieutenant-General Adolf Heusinger former Operations Chief of the Wehrmacht High Command. Chicago: Translation World Publishers, 1961.
Gross Soviet propaganda. Of value only because it includes the otherwise unpublished photostat texts and translations of several OKH documents, including some relevant to BARBAROSSA. See also Allen (1963).

Casey, Lord (1890–)
Personal Experience, 1939–1946. New York: McKay, 1962.
Memoirs of Richard Gardiner Casey. This Australian diplomat was his country's first diplomatic representative in the United States, where he served as Minister, 1940–1942. Created a Life Peer in 1960.

Cassidy, Henry C. (1910–)
Moscow Dateline, 1941–1943. Boston: Houghton Mifflin, 1943.
Memoirs of the author's tour as chief of the Associated Press bureau in Moscow.

de Caulaincourt, General [Armand] (1772–1827)
With Napoleon in Russia (New York: Morrow, 1935).
A diary of the Grand Armée by an officer on Napoleon's staff who had previously served as his Ambassador in Moscow. Enjoyed a sudden return to the best-seller lists of the German foreign office on the eve of BARBAROSSA.

CDSP. See *Current Digest of the Soviet Press*

Chernyavsky, V.
["Richard Sorge's Exploit"]. *Pravda,* 6 November 1964, p. 61.
A 650-word article in Russian. Available in condensed English translation in *CDSP,* vol. 14, no. 45, p. 13. V. G. Chernyavsky is a Soviet (and KGB?) expert on German and intelligence questions who is better known by his pen name, "V. Chernov."

Churchill, Winston S. (1874–1965)
The Second World War. Vols. 1–6. Boston: Houghton Mifflin, 1948–1953.

Churchill, Winston S.
The War Speeches. 3 vols. London: Cassell & Company, 1951–1952.
Compiled by Charles Eade.

Cianfarra, Camille M. (1907–1956)
The Vatican and the War. New York: E. P. Dutton, 1944.
A half-memoir, half-study of Italy during the period from 1935 to 1942 by the
Rome correspondent of the *New York Times.*

[Ciano, Galleazo] (1903–1944)
The Ciano Diaries, 1939–1943. Garden City, N.Y.: Doubleday, 1946.
Revealing diary of the then Italian Foreign Minister. Edited by Hugh Gibson
with an Introduction by Sumner Welles.

Ciano, *Count* Galeazzo
Ciano's Diplomatic Papers. London: Odhams Press, 1948.
Miscellaneous personal records covering the years 1936–1942. Edited by former
British S.I.S. officer, Malcolm Muggeridge.

Ciechanowski, Jan (1887–)
Defeat in Victory. Garden City, N.Y.: Doubleday, 1947.
Wartime memoirs by the able Czechoslovak Ambassador to Washington from
March 1941 to July 1945.

Clark, Alan (1928–)
Barbarossa: The Russian-German Conflict, 1941–45. New York: William
Morrow, 1965.
A recent British account by a former student of A. J. P. Taylor. A popular
history. Very weak on the planning phase and its intelligence aspect.

Colvin, Ian (1912–)
Chief of Intelligence. London: Victor Gollancz, 1951.
A valuable but inadequately documented biography of Abwehr chief Admiral
Canaris (1890–1945). Colvin is a prominent British journalist who worked
closely with British Foreign Office intelligence before World War II. During
the war he was with P.W.E. and Combined Operations Headquarters.

Cookridge, E. H. [pseud. of Edward Spiro] (1908–)
Inside S.O.E.: The Story of Special Operations in Western Europe 1940–45.
London: Arthur Barker, 1966.
An unofficial but adequate history, particularly when taken together with
Foot (1966). Mr. Spiro is a sensationalizing British political journalist who
specializes in Soviet and espionage affairs. A former British intelligence agent,
he spent some time in Dachau and Buchenwald.

Cooper, Duff (Viscount Norwich) (1890–1954)
Old Men Forget. London: Rupert Hart-Davis, 1953.
The autobiography of the British Minister of Information, May 1940–July
1941.

Current Digest of the Soviet Press. New York: The Joint Committee on
Slavic Studies. vol. I (1949)–vol. XX (1968) +.
Cited as *CDSP.*
A weekly translation and indexing journal formerly edited at Columbia Uni-
versity by Leo Gruliow.

Dallin, Alexander (1921–)
German Rule in Russia, 1941–1945: A Study in Occupation Policies. New York: St Martin's Press, 1957.
The definitive study. Expansion of a preliminary study completed in 1955 by Professor Dallin for the State Department's Office of Intelligence Research.

Dallin, David J. (1889–1962)
Soviet Russia's Foreign Policy: 1939–1942. New Haven: Yale University Press, 1942.

Dallin, David J.
Soviet Espionage. New Haven: Yale University Press, 1955.
The only scholarly historical survey of this recalcitrant subject. Professor Dallin gives much carefully documented detail on Soviet intelligence networks in Europe during World War II. Often fails to distinguish correctly between NKVD and GRU networks.

Dalton, Hugh (1887–1962)
The Fateful Years: Memoirs, 1931–1945. London: Frederick Muller, 1957.
Includes Dr. Dalton's controversial period as Minister of Economic Warfare, 1940–1942.

Davis, Forrest (1893–1962), and Ernest K. Lindley (1899–)
"How War Came." *Ladies' Home Journal,* vol. 59 (July and August 1942). Reprinted in the authors' *How War Came* (New York: Simon and Schuster, 1942).
Leaks U.S. material on BARBAROSSA warnings to Russians. Lindley was then Chief of *Newsweek*'s Washington Bureau.

Dawson, Raymond H. (1927–)
The Decision to Aid Russia, 1941: Foreign Policy and Domestic Politics. Chapel Hill: The University of North Carolina Press, 1959.
A carefully researched and documented monograph.

DBFP. See *Documents on British Foreign Policy.*

Deakin, F. W. (1913–)
The Brutal Friendship: Mussolini, Hitler and the Fall of Italian Fascism. New York: Harper & Row, 1962.
A study of the final years of the Rome-Berlin Axis by the Warden of St. Antony's College, Oxford, who served with S.O.E. in Italy at the end of World War II.

Deakin, F. W. (1913–), and G. R. Storry (1913–)
The Case of Richard Sorge. New York: Harper & Row, 1966.
Includes the most detailed and carefully researched account of Sorge's warnings about BARBAROSSA. Deakin served in Europe with S.O.E. during World War II. Storry is a Japanologist. Both are at St. Antony's College, Oxford.

Deborin, G. A., and B. S. Telpukhovsky
"V ideinom plenu u falsifikatorov istorii" [In the ideological captivity of the

falsifiers of history]. *Voprosy istorii KPSS* (Moscow), 1967, no. 9 (September 1967), pp. 127–140.
Available in complete English translation in *Soviet Military Translations, no.* 403 (Washington, D.C.: Joint Publications Research Service, 31 October 1967), pp. 17–37. Another complete English translation with a useful introduction is in Petrov (1968), 271–304. Professor Deborin, Doctor of Economic Sciences, is a senior associate of the Institute of Marxism-Leninism of the Central Committee of the CPSU. Major-General Telpukhovsky is also an associate of the same institute. Their article is the major public pro-Stalinist denunciation of the 1965 book by Nekrich that had been withdrawn from circulation only two months earlier.

Dedijer, Vladimir (1914–)
Tito. New York: Simon and Schuster, 1953.
An authorized biography by one of Tito's closest wartime comrades. The unique source for Tito's warning the Comintern of BARBAROSSA.

De Gaulle, Charles (1890–1970)
The Complete War Memoirs. New York: Simon and Schuster, 1964.

Degras, Jane (1905–) (editor)
Soviet Documents on Foreign Policy, 1917–1941. Vol. III. London: Oxford University Press, 1953.
A useful collection, mainly of official press releases and speeches.

Delmer, [Denis] Sefton (1904–)
Black Boomerang. London: Secker & Warburg, 1962. New York: The Viking Press, 1962.
The second volume of Delmer's autobiography, covering World War II. This noted Beaverbrook foreign correspondent directed P.W.E.'s wartime "black" radio propaganda operations against Nazi Germany.

Desroches, Alain
La campagne de russie d'Adolf Hitler (Juin 1941–Mai 1945). Paris: G. P. Maisonneuve et Larose, 1964.
A popular, thinly documented history.

Deutsch, Harold C. (1904–)
The Conspiracy Against Hitler in the Twilight War. Minneapolis: The University of Minnesota Press, 1968.
A carefully and critically researched study of the clandestine German opposition to Hitler in 1939–1940. The author was chief of the Research and Analysis Branch for the OSS in Paris and Germany, 1944–1945.

DGFP. See *Documents on German Foreign Policy.*

"Discussion of A. M. Nekrich's book 22 June 1941," as translated in *Survey,* no. 63 (April 1967), pp. 173–180.
Cited as "Discussion."
This sensational document purports to be a verbatim transcript of the closed formal meeting of 16 February 1966 of the Division of the Great Patriotic War of the Institute of Marxism-Leninism of the Central Committee of the

CPSU. The agenda was to discuss the controversial (1965) book by Nekrich. Ostensibly, the text was smuggled out of the Soviet Union in two versions. One version has appeared in *La Sinestra* (1 October 1966) in Italian, in *Le Nouvel Observateur* in French, in *Der Spiegel* in German, and in *Survey*. The second version is shorter, but it contains some additional and slightly different material. It has been published in (presumably the original) Russian in *Possev* (Stuttgart), January 1967. The translation in *Survey*, with the *Possev* variations noted in footnotes, has been reprinted with a useful introduction in Petrov (1968), 246–261.

Documents on British Foreign Policy, 1919–1939. Third Series. Vols. I–X. London: Her Majesty's Stationery Office, 1949–1961.
Cited as *DBFP*.

Documents on German Foreign Policy. Series D. Vols. X–XIII. Washington: U.S. Government Printing Office, 1957–1962.
Cited as *DGFP*.
Selected portions of the captured archives of the Reich Foreign Ministry.

Dollmann, Eugen (1900–   )
The Interpreter. London: Hutchinson, 1967.
Translation by J. Maxwell Brownjohn of the German edition of the same year. Memoirs. Dr. Dollmann was a sophisticated SS interpreter attached to the German embassy in Rome from 1937 to 1943.

Drożdżyński, Aleksander, and Jan Zaborowski
Oberländer: A Study in East German Politics. Poznan, Warsaw: Wydawnictwo Zachodnie, 1960.
A biography of Dr. Theodor Oberländer (1905–   ), a leading German specialist on East Europe. See chap. 5, "Oberländer's BARBAROSSA Plan," pp. 73–82.

Dulles, Allen Welsh (1893–1969)
Germany's Underground. New York: Macmillan, 1947.
An early but still useful account of the German anti-Hitler movement. Dulles was the OSS station chief for Germany, operating in Switzerland from November 1942 until the end of World War II. He went on to become Director of CIA (1953–1961).

Dulles, Allen [Welsh]
The Craft of Intelligence. New York: Harper & Row, 1963.
This authoritative account includes a chapter on deception operations (pp. 145–153).

Duranty, Walter (1884–1957)
The Kremlin and the People. New York: Reynal & Hitchcock, 1941.
An account by the long-time Moscow correspondent for the *New York Times*. Left to return to United States in early 1941.

[Eden, Anthony] (1897–   )
The Reckoning. London: Cassell, 1965.

The World War II memoirs of Anthony Eden, Foreign Minister from 1938 to 1945 and subsequently Prime Minister and Earl of Avon.

Ege, Ismail [new legal name of Ismail Akhmedov] (1904–)
See U.S. Congress. Senate. Judiciary Committee. Internal Security Subcommittee. *Interlocking Subversion in Government Departments: Hearings.* 83rd Congress, 1st session, 28 and 29 October 1953. Pt. 15, pp. 1001–1029, 1047–1067.
A Soviet defector's testimony about the GRU and BARBAROSSA in 1940–1941. Major Akhmedov was chief of the GRU 4th Section (foreign technical military intelligence) from September 1940 until late May 1941, when he was posted to Berlin with "cover" as "Georgi Petrovich Nikolayev" of TASS. In July 1941 he was repatriated and worked thenceforward in Ankara under cover as the Soviet embassy's "Press Attaché." In 1942 he defected and was granted asylum in Turkey. In 1950 received Turkish citizenship with the new name of Ismail Ege.

Ehrenburg, Ilya (1891–1967)
Eve of War, 1933–1941. London: MacGibbon & Kee, 1963.
Anti-Stalinist memoirs of the controversial Soviet journalist.

Erickson, John (1929–)
The Soviet High Command: A Military-Political History, 1918–1941. London: Macmillan, 1962.
Cited as Erickson (1962a).
The definitive study by a leading British authority on the Soviet Army. Contains a good survey of the early Soviet versions of the BARBAROSSA warnings.

Erickson, John
"The Red Army before June 1941." *St Antony's Papers,* no. 12 (1962), pp. 94–121.
Cited as Erickson (1962b).
On the lack of Soviet military preparation. Based mainly on *IVOVSS,* vol. I (1960), with new material from Tyulenev (1960).

Erickson, John
"1941." *Survey,* no. 44/45 (October 1962), pp. 178–183.
Cited as Erickson (1962c).
A damning critique of the "preventive" war hypothesis as resurrected in 1962 by Dr. Fabry in his book on the Hitler-Stalin pact.

Eyermann, Karl-Heinz
Luftspionage. 2 vols. Berlin: Deutscher Militärverlag, 1963.
Vol. 2 of this East German work includes much material on the so-called Rowehl Squadron.

Fabry, Philipp W.
Der Hitler-Stalin Pakt, 1939–1941: Ein Beitrag zur Methode sowjetischer Aussenpolitik. Darmstadt: Fundus, 1962.

Farago, Ladislas (1906–)
War of Wits: The Anatomy of Espionage and Intelligence. New York: Funk & Wagnalls, 1954.
A popular but adequately documented study. The author has been a well-known if not always scholarly intelligence buff since his somewhat loose affiliation with ONI during World War II.

Farago, Ladislas
Burn After Reading: The Espionage History of World War II. New York: Walker, 1961.
A popular and ill-documented account.

Farago, Ladislas
The Broken Seal: The Story of "Operation Magic" and the Pearl Harbor Disaster. New York: Random House, 1967.
A useful history of U.S. cryptanalysis through 1941. Much material on the parallel activities on the other side of the hill. An essential complement to Wohlstetter's *Pearl Harbor.* Must be used with caution, as his references are not as complete as they appear and Farago tends to treat those he has used in rather cavalier fashion.

Farago, Ladislas
The Game of the Foxes. New York: David McKay, 1971.
A detailed and generally accurate but undocumented account of German espionage in Britain and the United States in the 1930s and 1940s. One of the first books to recognize the role of deception in counterespionage.

Fedorov, G.
"Mera otvetstvennosti" [A measure of responsibility]. *Novyi mir,* 1966, no. 1 (January), pp. 260–263.
A praiseful review of Nekrich (1968) by Dr. Fedorov, a Soviet historian. A complete English translation is in Petrov (1968), 264–270.

Fedyuninsky, Army General I[van] I[vanovich] (1900–)
Podnyatuye po trevoge [Raised by the alarm]. Moscow: Voennoe izdatelstvo Ministerstva oboronuy SSSR, 1961. 2nd ed., 1964.
Soviet memoirs discussing preparations, warnings, surprise, and the course of the war. Fedyuninsky was a major-general commanding the 15th Infantry Corps at Kiev from April to August 1941 when transferred to Leningrad. Werth (1964) was the only Western writer to use this source until 1967. See also Bialer (1969), 240–243.

Feis, Herbert (1893–1972)
The Road to Pearl Harbor. Princeton: Princeton University Press, 1950.
The earliest competent study. Dr. Feis was the U.S. State Department's Adviser on International Economic Affairs, 1937–1943.

Filippov, I[van] F[ilippovich] (1912–)
Zapiski o "Tretiyem Reikhe" [Memoirs of the "Third Reich"]. Moscow: Mezhdunarodnuye otnosheniya, 1966.

Memoirs of Germany in the months before BARBAROSSA. During that period the author was chief of the TASS bureau in Berlin and, covertly, a senior NKGB officer. Subsequently assigned to the Foreign Ministry, he has since 1967 served as Soviet Ambassador to Luxembourg. The relevant sections have been cited by Salisbury (1969), 22–23, 25, 61, 77, 599.

Fischer, Louis (1896–1970)
The Great Challenge. New York: Duell, Sloan and Pearce, 1946.
A personal account of World War II diplomacy by a well-connected and most perceptive American political journalist.

Fischer, Louis
Russia's Road from Peace to War: Soviet Foreign Relations, 1917–1941. New York: Harper & Row, 1969.

Flannery, Harry W. (1900–)
Assignment to Berlin. New York: Alfred A. Knopf, 1942.
Memoir by William Shirer's successor as CBS correspondent in Berlin, 1940–1941.

Fleming, D. F. (1893–)
The Cold War and Its Origins, 1917–1960. 2 vols. Garden City, N.Y.: Doubleday, 1961.
In vol. I (pp. 106–134), Professor Fleming summarizes the road to BARBAROSSA. Unfortunately, only the more standard sources are used. A rather eccentric work.

Fleming, Peter (1907–1971)
Operation Sea Lion. New York: Simon and Schuster, 1957.
Because he worked in British secret service during World War II, it is not surprising that Ian Fleming's also famous older brother includes much of the intelligence side of Hitler's aborted invasion of Britain.

Flicke, Wilhelm F.
Agenten funken nach Moskau. Kreuzlingen: Neptun, 1954.
Not seen by me. Reportedly a semifictionalized account of the Rado-Rössler GRU network in Switzerland. Major Flicke was himself in charge of the OKW's Funk-Abwehr, assigned to track down the GRU's radio transmitters inside German occupied Europe and conduct the "Radio Game" against them.

Fomin, V. T.
"Iz istorii podgotovki nemetsko-fashistskoi aggressii protiv SSSR" [From the history of the preparation of German Fascist aggression against the USSR]. *Voprosy Istorii,* 1966, no. 8 (August), pp. 77–87.
A 5,000-word Soviet article specifically on the German deception campaign for BARBAROSSA. Professor Fomin, a Doctor of History, citing only published Western sources, gives the first analysis of this subject.

Foot, M. R. D. (1919–)
SOE in France. London: Her Majesty's Stationery Office, 1966.
An astonishing volume in the official British *History of the Second World War* series. To undo earlier misleading and sensationalized accounts of the

Special Operations Executive, special waiver of the Official Secrets rules was obtained and an Oxford historian assigned to produce this solid piece of scholarship.

Foote, Alexander (1905–1958)
Handbook for Spies. Garden City, N.Y.: Doubleday, 1949.
An authentic memoir and description of the Rado-Rössler network in Switzerland during World War II. Foote (not a pseudonym as claimed by some) was one of Rado's wireless operators and cutouts from around 1939 to 1943 when he was arrested for espionage by the Swiss police. Freed the next year he went to Moscow for interrogation and additional training. When sent on a mission to East Berlin in 1947 he promptly defected to the West and lived quietly in England. A second edition (London, 1962) deletes some of Foote's original material and interpolates new editorial material and text.

Foreign Relations of the United States: 1941. Vols. I, III, IV, Washington [D.C.]: U.S. Government Printing Office, 1958–1959.
Cited as *FRUS: 1941.*
The continuing official series of U.S. diplomatic documents.

Fotitch, Constantin [Konstantin Fotič] (1891–1959)
The War We Lost: Yugoslavia's Tragedy and the Failure of the West. New York: The Viking Press, 1948.
A colored, partisan account. From 1942 to 1945 Fotič was Ambassador in Washington for the Royal Yugoslav government-in-exile.

Fredborg, Arvid (1915–   )
Behind the Steel Wall: A Swedish Journalist in Berlin, 1941–1943. New York: The Viking Press, 1944.
Translation of the Swedish edition that appeared in 1943. Memoirs of the Berlin correspondent of the *Svenska Dagbladet.*

Freiden, Seymour, and William Richardson (editors)
The Fatal Decisions. New York: William Sloane Associates, 1956.
A collection of six studies of World War II German campaigns, each written by a former Wehrmacht general.

Frischauer, Willi (1906–   )
Goering. London: Odham's, 1951.
A poorly researched, inadequately documented biography of Reichsmarschall Hermann Göring (1893–1946) written by a knowledgeable German journalist who was a refugee in London during World War II.

FRUS. See *Foreign Relations of the United States.*

Fuehrer Conferences on Matters Dealing with the German Navy, 1941. 2 vols. Washington, D.C.: Navy Department, Office of Naval Intelligence, 1947.
Cited as *Fuehrer Conferences.*
Translation of the official war diary of the German Navy, the *Kriegstagebuch der Seekriegsleitung,* consisting of the memoranda of the conferences between Hitler and Grand Admiral Raeder, the Commander in Chief of the Navy. The simultaneous publication by the British Admiralty has the title *Fuehrer Con-*

ferences on Naval Affairs, 1939–1945 and was reprinted with that title in *Brassey's Naval Annual: 1948* (New York: Macmillan, 1948), pp. 25–496.

Gafencu, Grigore (1892–1957)
Prelude to the Russian Campaign: From the Moscow Pact (August 21st 1939) to the Opening of Hostilities in Russia (June 22nd 1941). London: F. Muller, 1945.
An excellent analysis—written in 1942—by one of the outstanding Rumanian diplomats of the time. After serving as Foreign Minister, he was posted as Ambassador to Moscow from 1940 until the breaking of relations in 1941.

Gallai, M. I.
"Pervyi boi muy vyigrali" [The first battle we won]. *Novyi mir*, 1966, no. 9 (September), pp. 3–50.
Memoirs of a Red Air Force officer who, on the eve of war, was a test pilot. A partial English translation is in Bialer (1969), 128–129, 260–262.

Galland, Adolf (1912–   )
The First and the Last. New York: Holt, 1954.
Translation of the original German edition of 1953. World War II memoirs of one of the Luftwaffe's top fighter aces. In early 1941 he was commanding general of a fighter unit in France.

Garthoff, Raymond L. (1929–   )
Soviet Military Doctrine. Glencoe: The Free Press, 1953.
A carefully documented study by the U.S. government's most prominent civilian expert on the subject. The earliest book to collate the references from the Russian side on warnings of BARBAROSSA.

German Campaign in Russia, The. See Blau, George E.

Geschichte des Zweiten Weltkrieges. Würzburg: A. G. Ploetz, 1960.
Cited as *GZW*.
A useful handbook of World War II compiled by a team of West German scholars including Prof. Dr. Percy Ernst Schramm.
Part II, pp. 811–852, gives a fairly accurate survey of the World War II intelligence services of thirteen countries, from Germany to China.

Giskes, H. J. (1896–   )
London Calling North Pole. London: William Kimber, 1953.
An account by Abwehr Lieutenant-Colonel Giskes of *Funkspiel* and other Abwehr operations in World War II. In 1940–1941 Giskes was Abwehr III C_2 in Paris.

[Goebbels, Dr. (Paul) Joseph] (1897–1945)
The Goebbels Diaries, 1942–1943. Garden City, N.Y.: Doubleday, 1948.
Edited, translated, annotated, and with an Introduction by Louis P. Lochner. Includes material on strategic deception operations conducted in 1942 by the Nazi Propaganda Minister. See also Semmler (1947), Boelcke (1966), and Boelcke (1970).

Goerlitz, Walter (1913–   )
Paulus and Stalingrad: A Life of Field-Marshal Friedrich Paulus with Notes, Correspondence and Documents from His Papers. New York: Citadel Press, 1963.
Translated from the original German edition of 1960. The standard biography-semibiography. One would have expected Professor Görlitz to have provided more detailed and accurate background information and to have more closely edited the Paulus papers.

Golovko, Arseni G[rigoryevich] (1906–1962)
With the Red Fleet. Edited and introduced by Sir Aubrey Mansergh. London: Putnam, 1965.
The World War II memoirs of the late Soviet admiral who commanded the Northern Fleet. This is a virtually complete translation, by Peter Broomfield, from the original Russian edition, *Vmeste s Flotom* (Moskva: Voenizdat, 1960).

Gouzenko, Igor [Sergeievich] (1915–   )
The Iron Curtain. New York: E. P. Dutton, 1948.
World War II memoirs of a former cipher clerk with the GRU, which he joined in 1942. One of the few inside accounts of Soviet military intelligence (GRU) in the period immediately following BARBAROSSA. Lieutenant Gouzenko defected in 1945 from his post as GRU cipher clerk in the Soviet embassy in Ottawa. He lives incognito in Canada.

Greiner, Helmuth (1892–1958)
Die Oberste Wehrmachtführung, 1939–1943. Weisbaden: Limes Verlag, 1951.
A history of the OKW by its official diarist during the early period of the war. The German preparations for BARBAROSSA are covered in the last chapter (pp. 288–392).

Greiner, Helmuth (1892–1958), and Percy Ernst Schramm (1894–   ) (editors)
Kriegstagebuch des Oberkommandos der Wehrmacht. Vol. I.
See Jacobsen, Hans-Adolf

Gripenberg, G. A. (1890–   )
Finland and the Great Powers: Memoirs of a Diplomat. Lincoln: University of Nebraska Press, 1965.
Translation of the original two-volume Finnish edition published in 1959–1960. The author was Finnish Minister in London from 1933 to July 1941.

Guderian, *General* Heinz (1888–1954)
Panzer Leader. New York: E. P. Dutton, 1952.
Memoirs of the leading German exponent of tank warfare. Immediately prior to BARBAROSSA he was Colonel-General commanding Panzer Group 2.

Gunzenhäuser, Max
Geschichte der geheimen Nachrichtendienst: (Spionage, Sabotage und Abwehr): Literatur Berichte und Bibliographie. Frankfurt-am-Main: Bernard und Graefe, 1968.
The second comprehensive bibliography of secret intelligence. An 80-page

introductory essay precedes some 400 pages of bibliography. Although a smaller effort than Harris (1968), it includes many items, particularly German ones, missed by the earlier work. Moreover, the two bibliographies complement one another as the Gunzenhäuser bibliography is organized chronologically and geographically while the Harris one is organized under 27 topics.

Gwyer, J. M. A.
Grand Strategy. Vol. III (June 1941–August 1942). Pt. I. London: Her Majesty's Stationery Office, 1964.
Includes (pp. 49–88) a spotty, but official, British version of the origins of BARBAROSSA.

GZW. See *Geschichte des Zweiten Weltkrieges.*

Hagen, Walter [pseud.]. See Hoettl, Wilhelm.

Halder, Franz (1884–)
Diary: Aug. 14, 1939–Sept. 24, 1942. 7 vols. Cyclostyled. N.p., 1947.
An English translation, edited by A. Lissance, of the war diary of the Chief of Staff of the OKH. Copies of this rare work are on deposit at the Widener Library (Harvard), the Hoover Library (Stanford), and the Imperial War Museum Library (London). See following work.

Halder, *Generaloberst* [Franz]
Kriegstagebuch. Edited by Hans-Adolf Jacobsen. 3 vols. Stuttgart: W. Kohlhammer, 1962–1964.
The best edition of Halder's diaries, superseding the U.S. English-language edition. The editor has greatly enhanced its value by including explanatory annotation and appending an index of names. BARBAROSSA is covered in vol. II: *Von der geplanten Landung in England bis zum Begin des Ostfeldzuges (1.7.1940–21.6.1941)*, published in 1963.

Hamilton, Thomas J. (1909–)
Appeasement's Child: The Franco Regime in Spain. New York: Alfred A. Knopf, 1943.
Memoir of his assignment in Spain as correspondent for the *New York Times,* 1939–1941.

Harris, William R. (1941–)
Intelligence and National Security: A Bibliography with Selected Annotations. Rev. ed. Multilithed. Cambridge, Mass.: Harvard University, Center for International Affairs, 1968.
With 838 pages covering several thousand books, articles, and papers, this is the most comprehensive bibliography of the subject publicly available. The author's 92-page introductory bibliographic essay is the only such guide into the labyrinthine literature of intelligence.

[Hassell, Ulrich von] (1881–1944)
The Von Hassel Diaries. Garden City, N.Y.: Doubleday, 1947.
Translation of the original posthumous diary published in Zürich in 1946. Introduction by Allen Welsh Dulles. The magnificent but foolhardy diary of one of the leading conspirators against Hitler. A career diplomat in political

retirement since 1938, von Hassell was executed for treason on 8 September 1944.

Hedin, Sven (1865–1952)
German Diary, 1935–1942. Dublin: Euphorion Books, 1951.
In preparing his diary for publication, the noted pro-Nazi Swedish explorer substantially edited and supplemented it.

Heikki, Jalanti
"La Finlande dans l'étan germano-soviétique, 13 mars 1940–26 juin 1941." Doctoral dissertation (Thèse en Lettres), University of Paris, 1965.
Not seen by me.

Higgins, Trumbull (1919–)
Hitler and Russia: The Third Reich in a Two-Front War, 1937–1943. New York: The Macmillan Company, 1966.
A study of BARBAROSSA. Although written as a popularized "trade" publication, it is a useful survey, concealing much careful research by its author. Dr. Higgins is a professional, academic historian.

Hilger, Gustav (1886–), [with] Alfred G. Meyer (1920–)
The Incompatible Allies: A Memoir-History of German-Soviet Relations, 1918–1941. New York: Macmillan, 1953.
Memoirs of an anti-Nazi diplomat. Dr. Hilger was Commercial Counselor in the German embassy in Moscow immediately preceding BARBAROSSA.

Hillgruber, Andreas (1925–)
Hitlers Strategie: Politik und Kriegführung 1940–1941. Frankfurt: Bernard & Graef Verlag für Wehrwesen, 1965.
A scholarly study.

Hillgruber, Andreas
"Japanische dokumente zu dem Gesprächte Hitlers und Ribbentrops mit Botschaften Oshima vom Februar bis Juni 1941." *Wehrwissenschaftliche Rundschau,* vol. 18 (1968), no. 6, pp. 312–336.
Not seen by me.

Hitler, Adolf (1889–1945)
Mein Kampf. New York: Reynal & Hitchcock, 1939.
An unabridged English translation of the original 1924 version of the aspiring dictator's point of view. Expresses clearly his intentions toward Russia.

Hoare, Rt. Hon. Sir Samuel (Viscount Templewood) (1880–1959)
Complacent Dictator. New York: Alfred A. Knopf, 1947.
Original British edition published in 1946 as *Ambassador on Special Mission.* World War II memoirs of H.M. Ambassador to Spain, 1940–1944. A former intelligencer, Sir Samuel Hoare (now Lord Templewood) had been S.I.S.'s man in St. Petersburg during World War I.

Hoettl, Wilhelm (1915–)
The Secret Front. London: Weidenfeld & Nicolson, 1953.
Translated by R. H. Stevens. Edited with an Introduction by Ian Colvin.

The original edition, *Die Geheime Front* (Zürich: Europa, 1950), appeared under the pseudonym of Walter Hagen. While the German edition was a strictly historical account of the SD, Dr. Höttl was prevailed upon to include some of his personal experiences in the English edition. A quite authentic account by a former SD man who worked mainly in Italy and the Balkans.

Hohenberg, John (1906–   )
Foreign Correspondence: The Great Reporters and Their Times. New York and London: Columbia University Press, 1964.
A patchy but welcome initial history of *American* foreign correspondents by a Columbia University Professor of Journalism.

Höhne, Heinz
Codeword: Direktor—The Story of the Red Orchestra. New York: Coward, McCann & Geoghegan, 1971.

Höhne, Heinz, and Hermann Zolling (–1971)
Pullach Intern. Hamburg: Hoffmann und Campe Verlag, 1971.
A biography of General Reinhard Gehlen. Available in an English translation as *Network* (London: Secker and Warburg, 1972) and *The General Was a Spy* (New York: Coward, McCann & Geoghegan, 1972).

Hopkins, Harry (1890–1946)
"The Inside Story of My Meeting with Stalin." *American Magazine,* vol. 132, no. 6 (December 1941), pp. 14–15, 114–117.
An account of the Stalin-Hopkins meeting of 31 July 1941.

Hoptner, J. B. (1911–   )
Yugoslavia in Crisis, 1934–1941. New York: Columbia University Press, 1962.
Although an academic study, this book is noteworthy because it recognizes the role of intelligence in international relations. Of special value because it is the only study to make use of the then unpublished diary of Colonel Vauhnik, the remarkable Yugoslav Military Attaché in Berlin until April 1941.
See Vauhnik (1967).

Hull, Cordell (1871–1955)
Memoirs. 2 vols. New York: The Macmillan Company, 1948.
The U.S. State Department and foreign policy as viewed by Roosevelt's Secretary of State.

Huss, Pierre J. (1903–1966)
The Foe We Face. Garden City, N.Y.: Doubleday, Doran, 1942.
Life in Nazi Germany as seen by an INS Berlin correspondent for the eight years preceding his timely leaving in November 1941.

Hyde, H. Montgomery (1907–   )
The Quiet Canadian: The Secret Service Story of Sir William Stephenson. London: Hamish Hamilton, 1962.
Foreword by David Bruce. The U.S. edition, containing some minor changes and additions, was published in 1963 as *Room 3603* with a Foreword by Ian Fleming.

Biography of Sir William Stephenson, the remarkable WWII Director of British Security Co-ordination (B.S.C.), based in New York City. This uniquely valuable study—by a B.S.C. alumnus—is the most indiscreet yet authentic study of the British secret services to slip past the guardians of the Official Secrets Acts.

Hyde, H. Montgomery
Cynthia. New York: Farrar, Straus and Giroux, 1965.
A sensationalized and thinly researched biography of Amy Thorpe, an American agent of the British S.I.S. and B.S.C. Captain Hyde, one of Britain's most prolific and wide-ranging nonfiction writers, was also with B.S.C. during World War II.

Ickes, Harold L. (1874–1952)
The Secret Diary. Vol. III. New York: Simon and Schuster, 1954.
The World War II portion of the diary of Roosevelt's cantankerous Secretary of the Interior.

Ike, Nobutaka (editor) (1916–   )
Japan's Decision for War: Records of the 1941 Policy Conferences. Stanford: Stanford University Press, 1967.
A useful translation and annotation of the Japanese Imperial and Liaison Conferences of 1941 that determined Japanese foreign policy at that time. Dr. Ike is an American political scientist.

Irving, David (editor) (1938–   )
Breach of Security: The German Secret Intelligence File on Events Leading to the Second World War. London: William Kimber, 1968.
Introduction by D. C. Watt. A detailed account and analysis of the German interception services in the 1930s and 1940s.

Ismay, *General Lord* (1887–1965)
Memoirs. New York: The Viking Press, 1960.
As the then Major-General Sir Hastings Ismay, he served from 1940 to 1945 as Deputy Secretary (Military) to the War Cabinet and as Churchill's personal chief-of-staff.

Istoriya Velikoi Otechestvennoi Voiny Sovetskogo Soyuza, 1941–1945 [History of the Great Fatherland War of the Soviet Union, 1941–1945]. Vols. I–VI. Moscow: Voennoe Izdatelstvo, Ministerstva Oborony Soyuza SSR, 1960–1965. Cited as *IVOVSS.*
The standard Soviet history of World War II. Vol. I (1960) covers the period up to 22 June 1941. Its last part (pp. 351–481) gives the events leading to the German invasion and is based mainly on previously unused state archives. Vol. II (1961) covers the period from June 1941 to November 1942, adding some new disclosures on the pre-invasion period.

Jacobsen, Hans Adolf (editor) (1925–   )
Kriegstagebuch des Oberkommandos der Wehrmacht (Wehrmachtführungsstab). Vol. I. Frankfurt am Main: Bernard & Graefe, 1965.

A carefully annotated edition of the official OKW/L diary that was kept prior to BARBAROSSA by Helmut Greiner.

Johnson, Chalmers (1931–)
An Instance of Treason: Ozaki Hotsumi and the Sorge Spy Ring. Stanford: Stanford University Press, 1964.
Professor Johnson demonstrates that the highest academic standards can sometimes be met without access to classified documents.

Jong, Louis de (1914–)
The German Fifth Column in the Second World War. Chicago: University of Chicago Press, 1956.
A carefully documented study of the myths and realities of the Nazi "Fifth Column." For its Russian aspect see pp. 125–133, 235–240.

Kahn, David (1930–)
The Codebreakers: The Story of Secret Writing. New York: Macmillan, 1967.
The most detailed history of cryptology. Remarkably detailed for a book about secrets. Fully documented. The author is a professional journalist and a distinguished amateur cryptologist.

Kalinov, *Colonel* Cyrille [Kyril] D. [pseud., probably of Victor Alexandrov]
Les Maréchaux soviétique vous parlent. . . . Paris: Libraire Stock, Delamain et Boutelleau, 1950.
This book is a sheer forgery, uttered by the Bessedovsky atelier in Paris and repeatedly exposed since 1951 by Boris Souverine, Bertram Wolfe, C. L. Sulzberger, and Paul Blackstock. The nonexistent "Kalinov" deceived the Zürich *Wochenzeitung* (in 1949), the Munich *Echo der Woche* (1949), the Paris *France-Soir* (1950), *The Reporter* magazine (1950), and such Russo-German experts as Erich Wollenberg (1950), Dr. Wilhelm Scheidt (1950), Colonel Lèderrey (1955), Gerald Reitlinger (1960), and Paul Carrell (1963) and received wider currency in German and Italian translations in 1950. "Kalinov" claimed to have been a colonel of the Soviet General Staff who, while in Berlin in 1949, defected to the West. (Blackstock errs in saying Bessedovsky had already used this pseudonym in 1947 for his *J'ai choisi la potence.* In fact, Bessedovsky had attributed that forgery to the turncoat General Vlassov.) His book is a mishmash of known fact and spurious anecdote. It purports to be a translation from a Russian manuscript. The "translators"—Victor Alexandrov Perry and Catherine Pérard—are, it is presumed, the real authors, particularly because Victor Alexandrov was under his own name a prolific fabricator of imaginative "memoirs."

Kaufmann, William W. (1918–)
"Case Barbarossa." Draft paper, declassified from RESTRICTED. Santa Monica, Calif.: The RAND Corporation, 1949–1950.
The only adequate account written before 1953. Written as one of a series of RAND case studies of the deployment of military force for "demonstration" purposes.

Kazakov, *General of the Army* M[ikhail] I[lich] (1901–   )
Nad Kartoi Bylikh Srazhenii. Moscow: Voenizdat, 1965.
Autobiography of a senior Soviet officer who on the eve of war was Chief of Staff of the Central Asian Military District. The key excerpts of pp. 56–71 are given in English translation in Bialer (1969), 139–145, 187–189.

Keegan, John (1934–   )
Barbarossa: Invasion of Russia 1941. New York: Ballantine Books, 1970.
A largely pictorial account of the war after B-day.

Keitel, *Field Marshal* [Wilhelm] (1882–1946)
Memoirs. New York: Stein and Day, 1966.
Self-serving memoirs of Hitler's OKW Chief (1938–1945) written in his Spandau death cell.

Kelly, *Sir* David (1891–1959)
The Ruling Few, or the Human Background in Diplomacy. London: Hollis & Carter, 1952.
Memoirs of a professional British diplomat who was H.M. Minister to Switzerland, 1940–1942. Knighted in 1942, he retired in 1951 following a three-year assignment as Ambassador to Moscow.

Kennan, George F. (1904–   )
Memoirs: 1925–1950. Boston: Little, Brown and Company, 1967.
A perceptive, often frank, autobiography of the distinguished former American diplomat. Focused more on the author's intellectual development than on his personal life. Kennan was First Secretary at the American embassy in Berlin from September 1939 until the German declaration of war on 11 December 1941.

Kennedy, *Major-General Sir* John (1893–1970)
The Business of War. London: Hutchinson, 1957.
World War II as viewed by Britain's Director of Military Operations from his appointment in October 1940. Edited from Kennedy's papers by Bernard Fergusson.

Kern, Erich [pseud. of Erich Kernmayr] (1906–   )
Dance of Death. London: Collins, 1951.
Memoirs of BARBAROSSA by a German noncommissioned officer. Original title: *Der grosse Rausch: Russlandfeldzug, 1941–1945* (Zürich: Thomas-Verlag, 1948).

Kersten, Felix (1898–1960)
The Kersten Memoirs, 1940–1945. New York: Macmillan, 1957.
Translated from the German edition of c. 1953. The social and political life of the Nazi leaders as viewed by Himmler's masseur. The Introduction by H. R. Trevor-Roper (and actions by Dutch and Swedish officials) established Dr. Kersten's anti-Nazi and humanitarian credentials and exposes Count Folke Bernadotte's fraudulently exaggerated claims as a peacemaker with Himmler.

Kesselring, Albert (1885–1960)
A Soldier's Record. New York: William Morrow, 1954.
Autobiography of a senior Luftwaffe general. Field-Marshal Kesselring was
released from prison and pardoned in 1952.

Khrushchev, Nikita (1894–1971)
"Secret Report to the Twentieth Congress (CPSU) . . . February 24–25,
1956." See Wolfe (1957).

Khvostov, V., A. Grylev
"Nakanune Velikoi Otechestvennoi Voinuy" [On the eve of the Great Patriotic
War]. *Kommunist,* 1968, no. 12 (August), pp. 56–71. English abstract in *Current Abstracts of the Soviet Press,* vol. 1, no. 4 (September 1968), pp. 3–4.
Writing in the leading Soviet Communist party theoretical journal, the
authors assert that the Kremlin did not simply ignore the many warnings of
BARBAROSSA.

Kimche, Jon (1909–)
Spying for Peace: General Guisan and Swiss Neutrality. 2nd ed. London:
Weidenfeld and Nicolson, 1962.
The 1st edition appeared in 1961. A competent piece of journalistic speculation on the interrelationship of Swiss, Russian, German, British, and American
intelligence services during World War II. The Swiss-born Kimche, the distinguished recently fired editor of the London *Jewish Observer and Middle
East Review,* was Military Correspondent for the *London Evening Standard*
during World War II.

Kirkpatrick, Ivone (1897–1964)
The Inner Circle. London: Macmillan, 1959.
Memoirs of a senior British career foreign officer.

Kirkpatrick, Lyman B., Jr.
Captains Without Eyes: Intelligence Failures in World War II. New York:
Macmillan, 1969.

Klee, Karl
*Das Unternehmen "Seelöwe." Die Geplante deutsche Landung in England,
1940.* Göttingen: Musterschmidt-Verlag, 1958.
The most comprehensive study of SEA LION. Klee is the only writer who has
seriously examined its use and final liquidation after 1940 (pp. 215–229). Consequently, he is the only author who is generally aware of SEA LION as a
deception operation for BARBAROSSA (pp. 224–227).

Kleist, Dr. Peter (1904–)
Zwischen Hitler und Stalin, 1939–1945. Bonn: Athenäum-Verlag, 1950.
The memoirs of Ribbentrop's Soviet expert. A severely abbreviated English
translation appeared in 1965 as *The European Tragedy.*

Kolesnikov, M[ikhail Sergeevich]
Takim buil Rikhard Zorge. Moscow: Voennoe Izdatelstvo Ministerstva
Oboronuy, 1965.

A detailed biography of Richard Sorge. Includes some new data on Sorge's BARBAROSSA messages.

Kordt, Erich (1903–)
Nicht aus den Akten. Stuttgart: Union Deutsche Verlagsgesellschaft, 1950.
A personal account of the Wilhelmstrasse from 1928 to 1945 by a German career diplomat.

Korhonen, Arvi (1890–1967)
Barbarossa-suunnitelma ja Suomi: jatkosodan synty. Porvoo and Helsinki: Werner Söderström, 1961.
An apologetic study of Finland's role in BARBAROSSA planning, by the late Professor of History at Helsinki University. Also available in Swedish translation as *Barbarossaplanen och Finland* (Tampere: Söderström, 1963). See the critical review by Marvin Rintala in *Journal of Central European Affairs,* 12 (1962), 115–116.

Krosby, H. Peter (1929–)
Finland, Germany, and the Soviet Union, 1940–1941: The Petsamo Dispute. Madison: The University of Wisconsin Press, 1968.
Cited as Krosby (1968*a*).

Krosby, H. Peter
Suomen valinta 1941. Helsinki: Kirjayhtymä, 1968.
Cited as Krosby (1968*b*).
A detailed study by an American scholar of Finnish-German political and military planning for BARBAROSSA. Not seen by me.

Krosby, H. Peter
"Finland and Operation Barbarossa: The Origins of Finnish-German Co-belligerency, 1940–1941."
Manuscript in progress by an Associate Professor in the Department of Scandinavian Studies at the University of Wisconsin. Not seen by me. See also Krosby (1968*b*).

Krummacher, F. A., and Helmut Lange
Krieg und Frieden: Geschichte der deutsch-sowjetischen Beziehunger: Von Brest-Litowsk zum Unternehmen Barbarossa. Munich: Bechtle, 1970.
See chap. 12 (pp. 422–457) and pp. 554–557.

Kuznetsov, N. G. (1902–)
"Before the War." *International Affairs,* 1966, nos. 5–12; 1967, nos. 1–4.
The serialization in English of Admiral Nikolai Kuznetsov's memoirs. These give the most detailed account of Kremlin and Soviet General Staff decision making on the eve of BARBAROSSA to emerge to date from Russia. Admiral Kuznetsov was People's Commissar of the Navy and Commander in Chief of the Navy from 1939 to 1945. The Russian edition is N. G. Kuznetsov, *Nakanune* (Moscow: Voenizdat, 1966).

Langer, William L. (1896–)
Our Vichy Gamble. New York: Knopf, 1947.

An early but still useful study of wartime relations between Washington and Vichy. Harvard Professor Langer was a senior OSS official in World War II.

Langer, William L. (1896–), and **S. Everett Gleason** (1905–)
The Undeclared War, 1940–1941. New York: Harper & Brothers, 1953.
A still superb early study. Its intensive use of then unpublished documents has not yet been entirely superseded by more recent publications. Professors Langer and Gleason were both OSS officials in World War II.

Laqueur, Walter (1921–)
Russia and Germany. London: Weidenfeld and Nicolson, 1965.
The best study of Hitler's attitudes and aspirations regarding Russia.

Leahy, *Fleet Admiral* William D. (1875–1959)
I Was There. New York: Whittlesley House, 1950.
World War II political-diplomatic memoirs of a retired naval officer. Fleet Admiral Leahy was U.S. Ambassador at Vichy, 1940–1942.

Leasor, James (1923–)
Rudolf Hess: The Uninvited Envoy. London: Allen & Unwin, 1962).
A popularized but fairly well researched biography. The American edition, by McGraw-Hill, is an indiscriminately mangled abridgment.

Lederrey, *Colonel* E. (1887–)
Germany's Defeat in the East: The Soviet Armies at War, 1941–1945. London: The War Office, 1955.

Leonhard, Wolfgang (1922–)
Child of the Revolution. Chicago: Henry Regnery, 1958.
Memoirs of a German Communist party official who later defected to the West. At the outbreak of the Russo-German war he was in exile in Moscow as a junior Comintern official.

Leverkuehn, Paul (1893–1960)
German Military Intelligence. London: Weidenfeld and Nicolson, 1954.
A valuable account of the Abwehr in World War II, although carefully censored by its British editor-translators, Major R. H. Stevens and Constantine FitzGibbon. The late Dr. Leverkuehn held senior Abwehr posts in Iran and Turkey during the war.

Liddell Hart, B. H. (1895–1970)
History of the Second World War. London: Cassell, 1970.
The section on BARBAROSSA draws almost entirely on Seaton (1970).

Listowel, [Judith] The Countess of (1904–)
Crusader in the Secret War. London: Christopher Johnson, 1952.
Biography of "Colonel Peter Nart," a thinly veiled pseudonym for Colonel Jan Kowalewski (b. 1892) of the Polish General Staff. An engineer-mathematician, he headed its cryptanalytic section from 1919 to 1922 and in 1923 advised the Japanese General Staff on revision of its cryptographic systems. He served as Polish Military Attaché in Moscow (1928–1933) and Bucharest (1933–1937). After the German invasion of Poland he fled to Portugal, where from late 1940

until 1944 he was the Polish Army's covert operations liaison officer. From 1944 until 1953 he was co-editor of Countess Listowel's anti-Soviet London émigré magazine, *East Europe and Soviet Russia.*

Lobachev, A. A.
Trudnymi dorogami [On difficult roads]. Moscow: Voenizdat, 1960.
Not seen by me, but quoted by Nekrich (1968), 198–199. The later Major-General Lobachev was apparently then (at the time of the German invasion) on the staff of Colonel-General M. P. Kirponos, commander of the Kiev Special Military District.

Lochner, Louis P. (1887–   )
"Hitler Postponed War in Poland For Week. . . ." *New York Times,* 6 June 1942, p. 4.
Cited as Lochner (1942*a*).
A congeries of journalistic vignettes by the then newly repatriated Pulitzer Prize–winning Associated Press Bureau Chief in Berlin from 1928 until his wartime internment four days after Pearl Harbor.

Lochner, Louis P.
What About Germany? New York: Dodd, Mead, 1942.
Cited as Lochner (1942*b*).
An account of Nazi Germany drawn, in part, from the exceptionally well-informed American journalist's position as Associated Press Bureau Chief in Berlin from 1928 until the German declaration of war on the United States.

Lochner, Louis P.
Always the Unexpected: A Book of Reminiscences. New York: Macmillan, 1956.

Long, Breckinridge (1881–1958)
The War Diary of Breckinridge Long. Lincoln: University of Nebraska Press, 1966.
This exceptionally informative posthumous diary of a U.S. Assistant Secretary of State, 1940–1944, was edited by Fred L. Israel.

Lonsdale, Gordon [pseud. of Konon Trofimovich Molody] (1924?–1970)
SPY: Twenty Years in Soviet Secret Service. New York: Hawthorne Books, 1965.
The KGB's curious response to the CIA's *The Penkovskiy Papers.* The often wildly mendacious memoirs of the authentic KGB agent who, arrested in Britain in 1961, was repatriated to Russia in 1964 in exchange for British agent Greville Wynne.

Lossberg, *General* **Bernhard von (1900–   )**
Im Wehrmachtführungstab: Bericht eines Generalstabsoffiziers. Hamburg: Nölke, 1950.
The second edition of the memoirs of the Army representative on the OKW. Not seen by me.

Lu, David J. (1928–)
*From the Marco Polo Bridge to Pearl Harbor: Japan's Entry into World War
II.* Washington, D.C.: Public Affairs Press, 1961.
A carefully researched monograph, based on the author's doctoral dissertation.
Foreword by Herbert Feis. Dr. Lu is a Formosa-born naturalized American.

Luttichau, Charles von
"The Road to Moscow—The Campaign in Russia, 1941." Washington, D.C.:
Department of the Army, Office of the Chief of Military History, n.d.
Not seen by me.

Macartney, C. A. (1895–)
October Fifteenth: A History of Modern Hungary, 1929–1945. Pt. II. 2nd ed.
Edinburgh: At the University Press, 1961.
The first edition of Pt. II appeared in 1957. The standard, intensively re-
searched and referenced history of the subject. The author, an Oxford don
since 1936, was with the British Foreign Office's Research Department during
World War II.

McLachlan, Donald (1908–1971)
Room 39: A Study of Naval Intelligence. New York: Atheneum, 1968.

McSherry, James E.
Stalin, Hitler, and Europe. Vol. 2: *The Imbalance of Power, 1939–1941.* Cleve-
land and New York: World Publishing Company, 1970.
The latest and best diplomatic history of the eve of the Russo-German war.

Mader, Julius, ed. (1928–)
Hitlers Spionagegenerale sagen aus. Berlin: Verlag der Nation, 1970.

Maisky, *Academician* I[van] M. (1884–)
"Dni Ispuytany: Iz vospominanii posla." *Novy mir,* 1964, no. 12 (December),
pp. 160–194.
A chapter in the memoirs of the period immediately following the German invasion. By the wartime Soviet Ambassador to Britain. Critical of Stalin's failure
to anticipate BARBAROSSA. Summarized in the *New York Times,* 7 January
1965, p. 2. See also Maisky (1968).

Maisky, Ivan
Memoirs of a Soviet Diplomat: The War, 1939–1943. New York: Charles
Scribner's Sons, 1968.
Translation of the original *Vospominaniya sovetskogo posla* (Moscow:
"Nauka," 1965). Typically, the 1971 edition deletes all the references to
Stalin's surprise, unpreparedness, and inattention to warnings of BARBAROSSA.

Malinovsky, *Marshal* R[odion] (1898–1967)
["The twentieth anniversary of the start of the Great Patriotic War"]. *Voenno-
istoricheskey zhurnal,* 1961, no. 6, pp. 6–7.

Mannerheim, *Marshal* [Carl Gustav] (1867–1951)
Memoirs. New York: E. P. Dutton, 1954.

Manstein, *Field-Marshal* **Erich von (1887–)**
Lost Victories. Chicago: Henry Regnery, 1958.
Infantry-General Manstein was commanding a Wehrmacht corps at the outbreak of BARBAROSSA.

Manvell, Roger (1909–), and Heinrich Fraenkel (1887–)
Dr. Goebbels. New York: Simon and Schuster, 1960.
A popular biography of Paul Joseph Goebbels (1897–1945), Hitler's Minister of Propaganda.

Markoff, *Gen.* **Alexei [pseud.]**
"How Russia Almost Lost the War." *Saturday Evening Post,* vol. 222, no. 46 (13 May 1950), pp. 31, 175–178.
On 22 June 1941, General Markoff commanded a wing of long-range bombers of the Red Air Force. Soon shot down and captured by the Germans. Although he did not collaborate with his captors, he elected to remain in the West following his liberation by Allied troops.

Martin, Bernd
Deutschland und Japan im Zweiten Weltkrieg: Vom Angriff auf Pearl Harbor bis zur deutschen Kapitulation. Göttingen: Musterschmidt-Verlag, 1969.

Mashbir, Sidney Forrester (1891–)
I Was an American Spy. New York: Vantage Press, 1953.
Superpatriotic memoirs of an eccentric, innovative, persistent engineer and U.S. Army intelligence pioneer. Includes some material on MacArthur's deception operations. Also notes (p. 55) that Brigadier General Bonner F. Fellers, while serving in Egypt as U.S. Military Attaché, had predicted that Hitler would attack Russia and that Russia would hold.

Maslov, *Col.* **P.**
"Literatura o voennuykh deistviyakh leton 1941 goda" [The literature of the military operations in the summer of 1941]. *Voenno-istorichesky zhurnal,* 1966, no. 9 (September), pp. 87–95.
A useful Soviet survey of the literature with some valuable references to the lack of Russian material and psychological preparation for the German invasion. A complete English translation is in JPRS, *Soviet Military Translations,* no. 351 (Washington, D.C.: 8 November 1966), pp. 38–58.

Matt, Alphons
Zwischen allen Fronten: Der Zweite Weltkrieg aus der Sicht des Büros Ha. Frauenfeld: Verlag Huber, 1969.
An important monograph on Bureau Ha, the Swiss special intelligence service directed by Captain Hans Hausamann. Includes much material on the warnings of BARBAROSSA received by the bureau. Received too late to incorporate in the text.

Maugeri, *Admiral* **Franco (1898–)**
From the Ashes of Disgrace. New York: Reynal & Hitchcock, 1948.
Autobiography of the wartime Chief of Italian Naval Intelligence from May 1941 to Italy's surrender. Written with the assistance of its editor, Victor

Rosen, this book is not a translation. The anti-Fascist Admiral Maugeri was appointed Chief of the General Staff in 1947.

Mayevsky, Viktor (1921–)
["Comrade Richard Sorge"]. *Pravda,* 4 September 1964, p. 4.
An 1800-word biographical sketch by a prominent *Pravda* commentator on international affairs. A complete English translation is in *CDSP,* vol. 17, no. 36, pp. 10–11.

Mengin, Robert (1907–)
No Laurels for de Gaulle. New York: Farrar, Straus and Giroux, 1966.
World War II memoirs of an anti-Vichy anti-Gaulist journalist who worked in P.W.E. in England.

Middleton, Drew (1913–)
Our Share of Night: A Personal Narrative of the War Years. New York: Viking Press, 1946.
World War II memoirs of the noted Associated Press foreign correspondent.

Middleton, Drew
"Everyone Knew But Stalin." In David Brown and W. Richard Bruner, eds., *I Can Tell It Now* (New York: E. P. Dutton, 1964), pp. 54–59.
Warnings of BARBAROSSA acquired by Middleton while he was the Associated Press London Bureau correspondent, 1939–1941.

Mikolajczyk, Stanislaw (1901–1966)
The Rape of Poland: Pattern of Soviet Aggression. New York: McGraw-Hill, 1948.
A memoir and account by General Sikorski's successor in 1943 as Polish Prime Minister. He had been Minister of Interior, 1941–1943.

Molody, Konon. See Lonsdale, Gordon [pseud.]

Mowrer, Edgar Ansel (1892–)
Triumph and Turmoil: A Personal History of Our Times. New York: Weybright and Talley, 1968.
Memoirs of a leading American foreign correspondent.

Muggeridge, Malcolm (1903–)
"The 'Lucy' Spy Mystery." *Observer,* 8 January 1967, p. 21.
Some controversial opinions and some new information on Alexander Foot, who was Muggeridge's postwar friend. Also some intriguing speculation on British wartime cryptanalysis vis-à-vis BARBAROSSA.

Murphy, Robert (1894–)
Diplomat Among Warriors. Garden City, N.Y.: Doubleday, 1964.
Autobiography of a senior American diplomat.

Murray, Nora [Korzhenkova] (1919–)
I Spied for Stalin. London: Odhams Press, 1950.
Autobiography of the daughter of V. S. Korzhenko, one of the top NKVD chiefs purged in 1939. In 1942 Miss Korzhenkova married John Murray, a

British businessman-diplomat who was her assignment as a *mozhno* girl, and immediately emigrated to Britain.

Nazi Conspiracy and Aggression. 8 vols. and 2 supplementary vols. Washington, D.C.: U.S. Government Printing Office, 1946.
Cited as *NCA*.
An important collection of the more damning German documents entered in evidence by the British and U.S. prosecutors before the Nürnberg Tribunal. Poorly organized for research purposes. Many documents are given only in extract. Translations are often inferior.

Nazi-Soviet Relations, 1939–1941: Documents from the Archives of the German Foreign Office. Washington, D.C.: U.S. Department of State, 1948.
Cited as *NSR*.
Cold war propaganda by documentation. A famous case of misrepresenting the timing and course of Russia's part in the Nazi-Soviet Pact by selective cutting of authentic captured documents. Now entirely superseded by the better texts and far more complete coverage by the U.S.-British-French *Documents on German Foreign Policy* series (*DGFP*), which see.

NCA. See *Nazi Conspiracy and Aggression.*

Nekrich, A[leksandr] M[oiseevich]
1941, 22 Iyunya [1941: 22 June]. Moscow: Nauka Publishing House, 1965.
A complete English translation is in Petrov (1968), 31–245, and it is this version that I cite and quote as "Nekrich (1968)."
The manuscript, delivered to the press on April Fool's Day, 1965, was approved for printing on 27 August in an edition of 50,000 copies.
Nekrich, a former senior Soviet historian, drew heavily—but uncritically—on published Western sources in this study of the events leading to the German invasion and of Stalin's failure to predict the war, much less to prepare an adequate defense.
This major contribution to de-Stalinization, initially acclaimed, quickly became the subject of very harsh attack in the Soviet press, culminating in the book's suppression and the author's expulsion from the Communist party (CPSU) in July 1967. See also "Discussion" (1966), Deborin and Telpukhovsky (1967), and Petrov (1968).

Newman, Joseph
Goodbye Japan. New York: L. B. Fischer, 1942.
Memoirs of Japan from the late 1930s to October 1941. The author was a staff member of the *Japan Advertiser* until around the beginning of 1941 when he became the Tokyo correspondent for the *New York Herald Tribune.*

Newman, Joseph
"A Spy—for the *Herald Tribune.*" In David Brown and W. Richard Bruner, eds., *How I Got That Story: By Members of the Overseas Press Club of America* (New York: E. P. Dutton, 1967), pp. 129–136.
A specially commissioned piece on the disclosures about BARBAROSSA freely given the American correspondents in Tokyo since early May by Sorge's

agent, the *Havas* correspondent in Tokyo, Branko de Voukelitch. A more detailed version than the preceding.

Nicholson, Leslie Arthur. See Whitwell, John.

Nicolson, Harold (1886–1968)
Diaries and Letters. Vol. II. New York: Atheneum, 1967.
Memoirs of World War II by the then Parliamentary Secretary to the Minister of Information (May 1940–July 1941), a Governor of the B.B.C. (July 1941–1946), and a Member of Parliament (1935–1945).

Noel-Baker, Francis (1920–)
The Spy Web. New York: The Vanguard Press, 1955.
One of the better cold war exposés of Soviet espionage, as one might expect from the precocious son of Philip Noel-Baker and despite its humorless Introduction by Herbert A. Philbrick. Mr. Noel-Baker was a junior S.O.E. officer with the Free Greek Forces in the Middle East. In 1945 he became a Member of Parliament.

NSR. See *Nazi-Soviet Relations, 1939–1941.*

OKW/L war diary. See Jacobsen, I (1965).

O'Neill, Robert J.
The German Army and the Nazi Party, 1933–1939. London: Cassell, 1966.
An excellent history. Foreword by Sir Basil Liddell Hart.

Packard, Reynolds (1903–), and Eleanor Packard (1905–1972)
Balcony Empire: Fascist Italy at War. New York: Oxford University Press, 1942.
A memoir of their stint in Rome by the United Press husband-wife correspondent team.

Pankratov, L. I.
[Interview]. *Trud* (Moscow), 17 December 1967, pp. 1–3.
For complete text in English translation see FBIS, *Daily Report: USSR and East Europe,* 10 January 1968.

Panteleyev, Yu[ri] A[leksandrovich] (1901–)
Morskoi Front [The sea front]. Moscow: Voenizdat, 1965.
World War II memoirs of Vice-Admiral Panteleyev who on the eve of war was on the staff of Admiral Tributs, the Commander in Chief of the Baltic Fleet. A valuable source on Soviet fleet readiness for war. Substantial use of it has been made by Salisbury (1969).

Papen, Franz von (1879–1969)
Memoirs. New York: E. P. Dutton, 1953.
Acid and somewhat frank account by the former Reich Chancellor (1932) and Ambassador to Ankara (1939–1944). Acquitted at Nürnberg, he was sentenced by a German court in 1947 to eight years' hard labor but freed in 1949.

Paulus, E.
"Die Entwicklung der Planung des Russlandfeldzuges 1940/41." Ph.D. dissertation. Bonn, 1956. [Not seen by me.]

Paulus, Friedrich (1890–1957). See Goerlitz.

Peace and War: United States Foreign Policy, 1931–1941. Washington [D.C.]: Department of State, 1943.

Pearson, John (1930–   )
The Life of Ian Fleming. New York: McGraw-Hill, 1966.
A popular biography of Ian Fleming (1908–1964) by a former associate, trained historian, and professional journalist. The least carefully researched portion concerns Fleming's wartime activities as Personal Assistant to the Director of Naval Intelligence. Some of these events are questionable and others simply wrong.

Perrault, Gilles [pseud. of Jacques Peyroles] (1931–   )
The Red Orchestra. New York: Simon and Schuster, 1969.
A detailed but sometimes inaccurate study by a French journalist of the "Rote Kapelle," the GRU network in Western Europe. Translation of the original French edition, *L'Orchestre rouge* (Paris: Fayard, 1967).

Petrov, Vladimir (1907–   ), and Evdokia Petrov
Empire of Fear. New York: Frederick A. Praeger, 1956.
Despite its popularized cold war purpose, this book remains one of the few excellent memoirs of NKVD defectors.

Petrov, Vladimir [*editor*] (1915–   )
"June 22, 1941": Soviet Historians and the German Invasion. Columbia: University of South Carolina Press, 1968.
A noteworthy innovation in university press publishing in which the editor and his publishers imply on the title page, dust jacket, by its format, and in their advertising "flyers" that this 322-page book is authored "By Vladimir Petrov." It is in fact a (quite valuable) collection of reprints edited, translated (in part), and with a short (30-page) introduction (misleadingly called a "Prologue") by Professor Petrov, a former Soviet slave laborer.
The 214-page center-piece of this curious collection is a complete translation (by Petrov) of the suppressed and quite rare Soviet study of the events leading to the invasion, written in 1965 by A. M. Nekrich, which see.

PHA. See U.S. Congress, *Pearl Harbor Attack.* . . .

Philippi, Alfred (1903–   ), and Ferdinand Heim
Der Feldzug gegen Sowjetrussland, 1941 bis 1945. Stuttgart: W. Kohlhammer Verlag, 1962.
Includes a detailed summary of BARBAROSSA planning (pp. 19–53) written by Philippi. The complete absence of scholarly apparatus makes this work useful only as a popular textbook.

Phillips, William (1878–   )
Ventures in Diplomacy. Boston: The Beacon Press, 1952.
Informal memoirs of the U.S. Ambassador to Italy from September 1936 to 11 December 1941. In 1942 he became head of the OSS London office. He preceded David Bruce.

Plocher, *Generalleutnant* Hermann (1901–   )
The German Air Force Versus Russia, 1941. [Maxwell AFB, Alabama:] Air University, Aerospace Studies Institute, USAF Historical Division, July 1965. The first two chapters provide the most detailed account of the Luftwaffe's place in BARBAROSSA planning. Completed in 1953 for the USAF Historical Division's German Air Force Historical Project but not published until twelve years later as USAF Historical Studies No. 153. Throughout 1940 and 1941 Lieutenant-Colonel Plocher was Chief of Staff of the Fifth Air Corps. From 1957 until his retirement in 1961 he served in the West German Air Force.

Pope, Arthur Upham (1881–1969)
Maxim Litvinov. New York: L. B. Fischer, 1943.
This uncritical biography of Litvinov (1876–1951) barely avoids outright sycophancy only because Litvinov was truly such a remarkable Soviet official. (Pope reserves his full adulation for Stalin.) Based, in part, on Pope's interviews with Litvinov in Washington during the war. Litvinov was Foreign Commissar (1930–1939), Chief of the Foreign Affairs Information Bureau of the Central Committee Secretariat (1939–February 1941), and Ambassador to the U.S. (October 1941–1943).

Pottgiesser, Hans
Die Deutsche Reichsbahn im Ostfeldzug, 1939–1944. Neckargemünd: Kurt Vowinckel Verlag, 1960.
A detailed monograph on the part played by the German railway system in the Polish and Russian campaigns.

Presseisen, Ernst L. (1928–   )
Germany and Japan: A Study in Totalitarian Diplomacy, 1933–1941. The Hague: Martinus Nijhoff, 1958.
A detailed study by a naturalized American historian.

Presseisen, Ernst L.
"Prelude to 'BARBAROSSA': Germany and the Balkans, 1940–1941." *Journal of Modern History*, vol. 32, no. 4 (September 1960), pp. 359–370.

Raczynski, *Count* Edward (1891–   )
In Allied London. London: Weidenfeld and Nicolson, 1962.
World War II memoirs of the Polish Ambassador to London from 1934 to 1945.

Raeder, *Grand Admiral* Erich (1876–1960)
My Life. Annapolis: U.S. Naval Institute, 1960.
The self-justifying memoirs of Hitler's top seadog, completed in 1957 following his 10 years' imprisonment at Spandau. Translated from the original German edition.

Reile, Oscar
Geheime Ostfront: Die deutsche Abwehr im Osten, 1921–1945. Munich: Verlag Welsermühl, 1963.

Reitlinger, Gerald (1900–)
The SS. New York: Viking, 1957.
A scholarly study by a British historian.

Reitlinger, Gerald
The House Built on Sand: The Conflicts of German Policy in Russia, 1939–1945. London: Weidenfeld and Nicolson, 1960.
An often keenly perceptive analysis.

[Ribbentrop, Joachim von] (1893–1946).
The Ribbentrop Memoirs. London: Weidenfeld and Nicolson, 1954.
An English translation of the original German edition published posthumously in 1953. Written in desperate self-justification from his Spandau cell, it is quite tendentious. Written without access to documents, it is also filled with anachronisms.

Riess, Curt (1902–)
Joseph Goebbels. Garden City, N.Y.: Doubleday, 1948.

Ritter, Gerhard (1888–1967)
Carl Goerdeler und die deutsche Widerstandsbewegung. Stuttgart: Deutsche Verlags-Anstalt, 1954.
Also available in a condensed English translation: *The German Resistance: Carl Goerdeler's Struggle Against Tyranny* (New York: Frederick A. Praeger, 1958).

Robertson, E. M. (1923–)
"Barbarossa: The Origins and Development of Hitler's Plan to Attack Russia."
An unpublished official British monograph written by Mr. Robertson of the Enemy Documents Section, and based on the German archives seized at the end of World War II. Extensively used by Butler, 2 (1957) in preparing his volume of the official British war history series. Not seen by me. Submitted in 1956 as a thesis at Oxford University, where a typescript is available.

Rondière, Pierre
Et le monde retrint son souffle: Stalin et le 22 Juin 1941. Paris: Presses de la Cité, 1967.
Not seen by me.

[Roosevelt, Franklin D.] (1882–1945)
F.D.R.: His Personal Letters, 1928–1945. New York: Duell, Sloan and Pearce, 1950.

Root, Waverly (1903–)
The Secret History of the War. 2 vols. New York: Charles Scribner's Sons, 1945.
An eccentric history by an American journalist who is perennially credulous of unverified "inside" stories.

Roskill, *Captain* S. W. (1903–)
The War at Sea. Vol. 1. London: Her Majesty's Stationery Office, 1954.
A volume in the official British World War II history series. After serving during the war as commanding officer of a light cruiser, Captain Roskill became Deputy Director of Naval Intelligence, 1946–1948.

Russell, William (1915–)
Berlin Embassy. New York: E. P. Dutton, 1941.

Rybalko, *Captain First Rank* N. G.
"V pervyi den voiny na Chernom More" [On the first day of war in the Black Sea]. *Voenno-istorichesky zhurnal,* 1963, no. 6 (June), pp. 63–66.
A memoir of 21–22 June 1941 as viewed by the then duty officer of the Soviet Black Sea Fleet's headquarters in Sevastopol. An almost complete English translation is in Bialer (1969), 255–258. See also Salisbury (1969), 34–36.

Salisbury, Harrison E. (1908–)
The 900 Days: The Siege of Leningrad. New York: Harper & Row, 1969.
An excellent, knowledgeable account, based mainly on Soviet interviews, memoirs, and histories.

Sandalov, *Colonel-General* L[eonid] M[ikhailovich] (1900–)
Perezhitoye [My experiences]. Moscow: Voenizdat, 1961.
Memoirs. Sandalov was serving in the Brest-Litovsk area on the eve of the German invasion as Chief of Staff of the 4th Army (A. A. Korobkov, commanding). Extensively quoted and cited by Nekrich (1968), 194, 197, 203, 213.

Schacht, Hjalmar Horace Greeley (1877–1970)
Confessions of "The Old Wizard". Boston: Houghton Mifflin, 1956.
Originally published in 1953 as *75 Jahres meines Lebens.* A rather frank autobiography by Hitler's financial expert who turned against him after 1939. Subsequently he served as a Minister without Portfolio until his arrest by the Gestapo in 1944.

Schellenberg, Walter (1910–1952)
The Labyrinth. New York: Harper, 1956.
Translated by Louis Hagen. Introduction by Alan Bullock. Originally published in Britain as *The Schellenberg Memoirs* (London: Deutsch, 1956).
The authentic but sometimes dissimulative revelations of the precocious senior SS intelligence officer who served as Heydrich's deputy from 1934 until the latter's assassination in 1942.

Schlabrendorff, Fabian von (1907–)
They Almost Killed Hitler. New York: Macmillan, 1947.
An account of the anti-Nazi underground by its most important survivor.

Schlabrendorff, Fabian von
The Secret War Against Hitler. New York: Pitman Publishing Company, 1965.
An expanded version of the preceding. Foreword by John J. McCloy.

Schmidt, Dr. Paul Karl. See Carell, Paul

Schmidt, Dr. Paul [Otto], (1899–1970)
Hitler's Interpreter. New York: Macmillan, 1951.
An English translation of the original German edition of 1950. Dr. Schmidt was Chief Interpreter of the German Foreign Office from 1943 to 1945. As an accomplished linguist (with a record 300-words-per-minute stenographic skill) he was present as interpreter and rapporteur at almost all major diplomatic moments of Ribbentrop or Hitler.

Schulze-Holthus, [Bernhard] (c. 1895–   )
Daybreak in Iran: A Story of the German Intelligence Service. London: Staples Press, 1954.
Translation by Mervyn Saville of *Frührot in Iran.* Paul Weymar is credited as editor-collaborator in the writing of this memoir. Dr. Schulze-Holthus was a major in Abwehr I when posted in Tabriz with cover as Vice-Consul there from May to August 1941, when put to flight by the Anglo-Soviet occupation of Iran.

Schuman, Frederick L. (1904–   )
Soviet Politics: At Home and Abroad. New York: Alfred A. Knopf, 1946.
An early study by an American political scientist. Professor Schuman's book is a model of uncritical acclaim for Stalinism.

Scott, John (1912–   )
Duel for Europe: Stalin versus Hitler. Boston: Houghton Mifflin, 1942.
A remarkably prescient account of Russo-German relations by the son of Scott Nearing. He was a free-lance journalist in Moscow until his expulsion in early June 1941.

Seabury, Paul (1923–   )
The Wilhelmstrasse: A Study of German Diplomats under the Nazi Regime. Berkeley: University of California Press, 1954.
A scholarly, historical account.

Seaton, Albert
The Russo-German War, 1941–1945. New York: Praeger Publishers, 1970.
This is the most recent and best general military history of the war. The author, a British lieutenant-colonel, devotes the first hundred pages to the prewar buildup.

Seitz, Ruth (1901–   ). See Andreas-Friedrich, Ruth.

Semmler, Rudolf (1913–   )
Goebbels: The Man Next to Hitler. London: Westhouse, 1947.
Not seen by me. The author's name is, correctly, spelled Semler. Dr. Semler was Goebbels's personal press officer from January 1941 on.

Seth, Ronald (1911–   )
Operation Barbarossa: The Battle for Moscow. London: Anthony Bland, 1964.
An inadequately researched study. The overprolific author was a wartime British S.O.E. agent.

Sevin, X. de
"Souvenirs de Roumanie (1939–1941)." *Revue des Deux Mondes,* 15 October 1963, pp. 545–562.
Memoirs of the rumors and reports of the approaching German invasion of Russia as seen from Bucharest by the Vichy French Air Attaché there from October 1938 to July 1941.

Sheean, Vincent (1899–)
Between the Thunder and the Sun. New York: Random House, 1943.
A memoir by the noted American foreign correspondent, then with the *Saturday Evening Post.*

Sherwood, Robert E. (1896–1955)
Roosevelt and Hopkins. New York: Harper, 1948.
A joint biography by a close collaborator.

Shigemitsu, Mamoru (1887–1957)
Japan and Her Destiny. New York: E. P. Dutton, 1958.
A complete translation of the Japanese edition first published in 1952. An account of Japanese foreign policy from 1931 to 1945 by the distinguished diplomat and one-time "Class A War Criminal."

Shirer, William L. (1904–)
The Rise and Fall of the Third Reich: A History of Nazi Germany. New York: Simon and Schuster, 1960.
The comprehensive but rather carelessly researched best-seller. The author was CBS Berlin correspondent in the late 1930s.

Shtemenko, *General of the Army* S. M. (1907–)
The Soviet General Staff at War, 1941–1945. Moscow: Progress Publishers, 1970.
A translation of the original Russian edition. General Sergei Shtemenko presents a most curious and unconvincing apologia for "the Party and Government" by simply denying their unreadiness for BARBAROSSA. This lack of candor is inexcusable because Shtemenko's later service (1956–1957) as director of the GRU would have given him access to superb data.

Simoni, Leonardo [pseud. of Michele Lanza]
Berlino: Ambasciata d'Italia, 1939–1943. Rome: Migliaresi Editore in Roma, 1946.
Signor Lanza was First Secretary of the Italian embassy in Berlin, 1939–1943. Although formatted as a diary, this book is at most a heavily reconstructed one, interpolating entire texts of regular diplomatic correspondence.

Smith, Howard K. (1914–)
Last Train from Berlin. New York: Knopf, 1942.
A memoir of the author's tour as CBS junior correspondent in Berlin, 1939–1941.

"Sovetskie organy gosudarstvennoi bezopasnosti v gody velikoi otechestvennoi voiny" [Soviet state security organs in the years of the Great Patriotic War].

Voprosy Istorii, 1965, no. 5 (May), pp. 20–39, with summary in English on pp. 219–220.
An anonymous article on the role of NKVD-NKGB intelligence and counter-intelligence in World War II. Published in the leading Soviet historical journal. Clearly written for the KGB, probably by a KGB researcher or committee. Based on a wide range of sources, including archives of the KGB, the Soviet Defense Ministry, the Nürnberg Tribunal records, and the diaries of the OKW, OKH, Ciano, and other Soviet and published Western sources. The intelligence picture in the period of deteriorating Russo-German relations from 1939 to 22 June 1941 is covered in documented detail on pp. 20–29. Describes more than a dozen specific warnings and indications of BARBAROSSA, including some warnings and several details not published elsewhere. This major reference (for which I thank Dr. William R. Harris) makes its most important and original contribution by its emphatically stressed claim that many of the warnings were obtained by the NKGB and passed directly to "Stalin and Molotov." The article is clumsily slanted to show that the NKGB (i.e., KGB) was blameless in the surprise visited by BARBAROSSA. However, to make its point—by collating an array of specific warnings—it is ironic that the KGB had to draw heavily on GRU intelligence coups (and the GRU section of the Defense Ministry archives), although the author is careful in his text to credit by name only the NKGB and its patriotic "Chekists."

Speer, Albert (1905–)
Inside the Third Reich. New York: Macmillan, 1971.

Stalin, I. V. (1879–1953).
Works. Vol. 2 (XV). Stanford: Stanford University, The Hoover Institution, 1967.
An American collection in the original Russian of works omitted from the official Soviet series discontinued after Stalin's death with only 13 volumes covering his works through January 1934.

Starinov, I[lya] G[rigorievich] (1899–)
Minu Zhdut Svoyego Chasa [Mines await their hour]. Moscow: Voenizdat, 1964.
Memoirs of a Soviet mining and guerrilla warfare officer from his service in Spain in 1936–1937 through the first month of the Great Fatherland War when he was a colonel in the Army Engineer Training Department of the Main Military Engineering Directorate. Not seen by me, except in the extensive excerpts translated in Bialer (1969), 65–79, 161–166, 221–227, 236–238, 456–457.

Stead, Philip John
Second Bureau. London: Evans Brothers, 1959.
An adulatory history of Vichy French intelligence in World War II.

Stowe, Leland (1899–)
"Russian Fear of Hitler Told; Sure Attack if British Hold." *Chicago Daily*

News, c. 2 March 1941; reprinted in *8 Uncensored Articles by Leland Stowe* (Chicago: Appreciate America, Inc., 1941), pp. 8–10.
A most prescient journalistic "backgrounder."

Strawson, John
Hitler's Battles for Europe. New York: Charles Scribner's Sons, 1971.
A brief, inconsequential military history.

Strong, Anna Louise (1885–1970)
The Soviets Expected It. New York: Dial Press, 1941.
A model of apologia by a perpetual dupe.

Strong, *Major-General Sir* Kenneth (1900–   )
Intelligence at the Top: Recollections of an Intelligence Officer. Garden City, N.Y.: Doubleday, 1969.
Memoirs of the recently retired Director-General of Intelligence of the British Ministry of Defense. From September 1939 until February 1941 the then Major Strong headed M.I.14, German Section of British Military Intelligence. However, the outbreak of the Russo-German conflict found Strong serving as a battalion commander in Scotland.

Stypulkowski, Z[bigniew] (1904–   )
Invitation to Moscow. London: Thames and Hudson, 1951.
Memoir of a former Polish parliamentarian who served in the Polish resistance during World War II. Preface by H. R. Trevor-Roper.

Sulzberger, C[yrus] L. (1912–   )
"Big Armies Mass on 'Eastern Front.' " The *New York Times,* 22 June 1941, p. E4.
A "situationer" datelined "Ankara, 21 June," although Sulzberger's voice transmission from Radio Ankara began at 0117 on the 22nd. Marred by its credulous stress on the "ultimatum" hypothesis.

Sulzberger, C[yrus] L.
A Long Row of Candles: Memoirs and Diaries, 1934–1954.
New York: Macmillan Co., 1969.

Sweet-Escott, Bickham
Baker Street Irregular. London: Methuen, 1965.
A superb account and memoir of the British S.O.E. in World War II by one of its middle-level staff officers.

Teske, Hermann (1902–   )
General Ernst Köstring. Frankfurt am Main: Mittler, 1966.
A biography of the German military attaché in Moscow (1936–1941). Not seen by me.

Thayer, Charles W. (1910–1969)
Hands Across the Caviar. Philadelphia & New York: J. B. Lippincott Company, 1952.
A memoir of the OSS and U.S. State Department in and after World War II. For some aspects of BARBAROSSA see pp. 67–69, 190–191.

Thayer, Charles W.
"MVD Man's Declaration of Independence." *Life*, vol. 37, no. 1 (5 July 1954), pp. 69–80.
The story—based on Thayer's week-long interview of MVD Lieutenant-Colonel Grigori Stepanovich Burlutski (b. 1917) who defected to the West in June 1953 and was "surfaced" in June 1954. On 22 June 1941 Burlutski was a Red Army junior lieutenant on the Rumanian frontier. Thayer was a career U.S. FSO who had been on loan to OSS, 1944–1945.

Thayer, Charles W.
Diplomat. New York: Harper & Brothers, 1959.
A study of diplomacy by an American FSO from 1934 until his premature resignation in 1953, dictated by the pressures of McCarthyism.

Tippelskirch, Kurt von (–†)
Geschichte des Zweiten Weltkriegs. 2nd ed. Bonn: Athenäum-Verlag, 1956.
Includes a detailed but undocumented account of BARBAROSSA by the author, a former German general who served on the Russian Front. Indeed, he was Chief of OKH intelligence (OQu IV) during the planning stage.

TMWC. See *Trial of the Major War Criminals.* . . .

Tōgō Shigenori (1882–1950)
The Cause of Japan. New York: Simon and Schuster, 1956.
Translated from the original 1952 Japanese edition. The author served as Ambassador in Moscow (1938–August 1940) and twice as Foreign Minister (October 1941–August 1942 and April–August 1945).

Tokaev, *Colonel* G. A. (1909–)
Stalin Means War. London: George Weidenfeld & Nicolson, 1951.
Memoirs of a Red Army Engineer Lieutenant-Colonel. Grigori Tokaev was a Lecturer at the Zhukovsky Military Air Academy in Moscow at the outbreak of war. He defected to Britain in early 1948 from his post in East Berlin. The authenticity of Tokaev and his account is vouched for by Sir David Kelly, H.M. Ambassador to Moscow, 1949–1951. Nevertheless, the author is often quite wrong in his irrepressible speculations.

Tolischus, Otto D. (1890–1967)
Tokyo Record. New York: Reynal & Hitchcock, 1943.
Memoirs of the Tokyo correspondent for the *New York Times.*

Tong, Hollington K. (1887–1971)
Dateline: China; The Beginnings of China's Press Relations with the World. New York: Rockport Press, 1950.
Dr. "Holly" Tong was Vice-Minister of Information of the Republic of China, 1937–1945. Includes (p. 157) brief reference to Generalissimo Chiang Kai-shek's prior intelligence on BARBAROSSA that he passed to the U.S. Ambassador.

Toynbee, Arnold (1899–), and Veronica M. Toynbee (editors)
The Initial Triumph of the Axis. London: Oxford University Press, 1958.
A volume in the authoritative series, "Survey of International Affairs, 1939–

1946," produced under the auspices of the Royal Institute of International Affairs. For BARBAROSSA, see Part VI ("The Breach between Germany and the Soviet Union," pp. 364–440). That particular section was rewritten by Professor Toynbee, using recently available materials, on the basis of the original draft that had been prepared "several years" earlier by Mr. F. Ashton-Gwatkin, a former official of the Foreign Office.

Trial of the Major War Criminals before the International Military Tribunal, Nuremberg, 14 November 1945–1 October 1946. 42 vols. Nuremberg: International Military Tribunal, 1947–1949.
Cited as *TMWC.*
The official published record of the "War Crimes Trial" of the principal German war leaders.

Trials of War Criminals before the Nuernberg Military Tribunals. 15 vols. Nuernberg: Nuernberg Military Tribunals, 1951.
Cited as *TWC.*
The published portion of the proceedings and documents in the 12 trials of minor German "war criminals" held between 1946 and 1949.

Tyulenev, *Army General* I[van] V[ladimirovich] (1892–)
Cherez tri voiny [Through three wars]. Moscow: Voenizdat, 1960.
Memoirs of a senior Soviet soldier. On 22 June 1941 Tyulenev was a colonel-general commanding the Moscow Military District. Not seen by me, but extensively quoted by Erickson (1962*b*), Nekrich (1965), and particularly Bialer (1969), 200–203.

Upton, Anthony F.
Finland in Crisis, 1940–1941. London: Faber & Faber, 1964.
The most careful and critical study by a non-Finnish scholar. Confirms the fact that, for reasons of state, Finnish scholars as well as officials are less than frank in disclosing Finland's prior knowledge of—and, perhaps, active collaboration in—BARBAROSSA planning.

U.S. Congress
Pearl Harbor Attack: Hearings before the Joint Committee on the Investigation of the Pearl Harbor Attack. 79th Congress, 1st session. 39 vols. Washington, D.C.: Government Printing Office, 1946.
Cited as *PHA.*
The official record of the testimony, evidence, and findings of the 1945–1946 Pearl Harbor review. Contains a wealth of material on intercepts and intelligence organizations.

Vauhnik, Vladimir (1896–1955)
Memoiren eines Militärattachés. Buenos Aires: Editorial Palabra Eslovena, 1967.
Also published in a Slovene edition: *Nevidna fronta: spomini* (Buenos Aires: Svobodna Slovenija, 1965).
Valuable memoirs of the Yugoslav military attaché in Berlin from November 1938 until his arrest in April 1941. Colonel Vauhnik was one of the most

successful intelligencers of the time. After World War II Vauhnik emigrated to Argentina, where he died in 1955.

Velikaya Otechestvennaya Voina Sovetskogo Soyuza, 1941–1945 [The Great Fatherland War of the Soviet Union, 1941–1945]. Moscow, 1965.
This book is the one-volume version of *IVOVSS* (by the same editorial collective—P. N. Pospelov, et al.), of the six-volume official Soviet history of Russia's participation in World War II. Appearing five years after vol. I of the larger work, the editors were able to add details of Stalin's misperception of the German threat and faulty evaluation of the intelligence warnings.

Vollmacht des Gewissens. Frankfurt: Alfred Metzner Verlag. Vol. I [1960] and vol. II [1965].
Collections of articles on the wartime German resistance movement.

Voronov, *Chief Marshal of Artillery* **N[ikolai] N. (1899–   )**
Na Sluzhbe Voennoi [On service in the war]. Moscow: Voenizdat, 1963.
Memoirs from the Spanish Civil War until the victory at Stalingrad. Voronov was Marshal Kulik's First Deputy Chief of the Main Artillery Directorate from early 1941 until the German invasion. Includes important testimony on the degree of surprise on 22 June 1941. Not seen by me except for key excerpts in English translation in Bialer (1969), 159–161, 207–212, and other fragments in Nekrich (1968) and Salisbury (1969). A relevant portion of this memoir also appeared in *Voenno-istorichesky zhurnal,* 1961, no. 9.

Walker, David E. (1907–1968)
Lunch with a Stranger. London: Wingate, 1957.
An excellent memoir of S.O.E. and P.W.E. In all, Walker spent seven years in British secret services while working under "cover" as a foreign correspondent for the *London Daily Mirror.*

Warlimont, Walter (1895–   )
Inside Hitler's Headquarters, 1939–1945. New York: Frederick A. Praeger, 1964.
Translation of the original German edition of 1962. One of the few perceptive and carefully documented German World War II memoirs. Preceding BARBAROSSA, Warlimont was the colonel in charge of Section L of the WFSt in OKW.

Weinberg, Gerhard L. (1928–   )
Germany and the Soviet Union, 1939–1941. Leiden: E. J. Brill, 1954.
Even now, eighteen years after its publication, this is still the most comprehensively documented monograph on Russo-German relations between the 1939 pact and BARBAROSSA-*Tag.* The excellence of Dr. Weinberg's study is doubly remarkable given the fact that it was also the *first* academic study of the subject. Yet it is largely overlooked by its successors.

Weizsäcker, Ernst von (1882–1951)
Memoirs. London: Victor Gollancz, 1951.
The original German-language edition appeared in 1950. Despite his anti-Hitler claims, Baron von Weizsäcker was at best an uneasily compliant career diplomat. Served as State Secretary in the Foreign Office, 1938–1943. Con-

demned in 1949 to seven years' imprisonment by the Nürnberg Military Tribunals but amnestied in 1950.

Welles, Sumner (1892–1961)
The Time for Decision. New York: Harper, 1944.
A memoir-history of the events leading into U.S. involvement in World War II by the then Undersecretary of State, 1937–1943.

Werth, Alexander (1901–1969)
Russia at War, 1941–1945. New York: E. P. Dutton, 1964.
In this case, Werth's pro-Soviet bias leads him to a generally correct appraisal of Stalin's interpretation of the intelligence and warnings about BARBAROSSA. A Russian translation was published in Moscow in 1967 and was favorably reviewed in the Soviet press.

Weygand, *General* **Maxime (1867–1965)**
Recalled to Service. London: Heinemann, 1952.
Memoirs. In 1940–1941 he was Vichy's Delegate-General in North Africa.

Whaley, Barton (1928–   )
"Daily Monitoring of the Western Press in the Soviet Union and Other Communist States." Cambridge, Mass.: M.I.T., Center for International Studies, 19 March 1964, 30 pp. (Center paper D/64-13.)

Whaley, Barton
Soviet Clandestine Communication Nets: Notes for a History of the Structures of the Intelligence Services of the USSR. Multilithed. Cambridge, Mass.: M.I.T., Center for International Studies, 1969. 199 pp. + 127 pp. Appendix. (Center paper C/67-10.)
Cited as Whaley (1969a).
A history of the organization and channels of the various Soviet intelligence services. Includes bibliography and biographical appendix.

Whaley, Barton
Stratagem: Deception and Surprise in War. Cambridge, Mass.: M.I.T., Center for International Studies, 1969.
Cited as Whaley (1969b).
A comprehensive study. A revised edition is *Stratagem: Deception and Surprise* (New York: Frederick A. Praeger, forthcoming, 1973).

Whaley, Barton
"Operation BARBAROSSA: A Case Study of Soviet Information Processing Before the German Invasion." Ph.D dissertation, Massachusetts Institute of Technology, 1969.
Cited as Whaley (1969c).
This dissertation is the preliminary version of the present book, *Codeword* BARBAROSSA. It is entirely superseded by the present work except for two appendixes that might be of use to any persons doing further work on either BARBAROSSA itself or on intelligence problems in World War II. One sixty-one page appendix gives forty-eight charts covering the intelligence organizations

(as of June 1941) of the twelve countries most closely involved in the diffusion of information on BARBAROSSA. The second appendix presents in 134 pages the English translations of all sixty-seven German documents found by me to cover the deception planning of BARBAROSSA.

Wheatley, Ronald
Operation Sea Lion. Oxford: Clarendon Press, 1958.
A British scholar's historical reconstruction based on his research on the official British history of World War II.

Wheeler-Bennett, John W. (1902–   )
The Nemesis of Power: The German Army in Politics, 1918–1945. London: Macmillan Company, 1953.
A comprehensive, fully documented study by one of the leading British "Establishment" historians. During World War II he held various Foreign Office public information and secret intelligence posts.

Whitaker, John T. (1906–   )
We Cannot Escape History. New York: Macmillan, 1943.
An eyewitness account of the drift into World War II by a *Chicago Daily News* foreign correspondent.

Whitwell, John [pseud. of Leslie Arthur Nicholson] (1902–1971)
British Agent. London: William Kimber, 1966.
Authentic cynical memoirs of a senior British S.I.S. officer from 1929 through World War II. Personally obtained one of the early disclosures of BARBAROSSA. Introduction by Malcolm Muggeridge, who served "Whitwell" as his wartime chief of station in Mozambique.

Wiener, Jan G. (1920–   )
The Assassination of Heydrich. New York: Grossman Publishers, 1969.
Gives background on Paul Thummel, the Abwehr station chief in Prague, who also served Czech and British intelligence.

Willoughby, *Major-General* Charles A. (1892–   )
Shanghai Conspiracy: The Sorge Spy Ring, Moscow, Shanghai, Tokyo, San Francisco, New York. New York: E. P. Dutton, 1952.
Preface by Douglas MacArthur. A detailed account by General MacArthur's Chief of Intelligence, 1941–1951. A rather sad mishmash of documents, wide-of-the-mark interpretations, wild accusations, and egregious transcriptions of foreign names. As a top priority, major effort at research by one of the larger and better professional intelligence groups, it is quite disillusioning. Should be used only in conjunction with Johnson (1964) and Deakin and Storry (1966).

Winant, John Gilbert (1889–1947)
Letter from Grosvenor Square: An Account of a Stewardship. Boston: Houghton Mifflin, 1947.
The thinly sketched memoirs of the U.S. Ambassador to London, February 1941–1943.

Winter, Ella (1898–)
And Not to Yield: An Autobiography. New York: Harcourt, Brace and World, 1963.
Miss Winter (then Mrs. Donald Ogden Stewart) quotes (p. 261) U.S. Ambassador to Prague Laurence Steinhardt in late 1947 on his recollection of how on D-minus-3 he was tipped to the imminence of BARBAROSSA by the bizarre behavior of one of the German secretaries in Moscow, Gebhart von Walther: "This man, who was a homosexual with no family, had a beautiful dog he was attached to; one day I saw the dog sitting at the railroad station alone, with a ticket marked BERLIN hanging on his collar. His owner would not have parted with him except for a vital reason and at the very last moment." See warning 67.

Wiskemann, Elizabeth (1892–1971)
A Great Swiss Newspaper: The Story of the Neue Zürcher Zeitung. London: Oxford University Press, 1959.

Wiskemann, Elizabeth (1892–1971)
The Rome-Berlin Axis. 2nd ed. London: Collins, 1966.
A slightly updated version of Professor Wiskemann's pioneering 1949 study. She was Assistant Press Attaché at the British Legation in Berne, 1941–1945.

Wohlstetter, Roberta
Pearl Harbor: Warning and Decision. Stanford: Stanford University Press, 1962.
A model study by Mrs. Albert Wohlstetter, completed in the 1950s while she was with the RAND Corporation.

Wolfe, Bertram D. (1896–)
Khrushchev and Stalin's Ghost: Text, Background and Meaning of Khrushchev's Secret Report to the Twentieth Congress on the Night of February 24–25, 1956. New York: Frederick A. Praeger, 1957.
This version of Khrushchev's "secret" speech to the 20th Party Congress was obtained soon afterward in Poland by the CIA and publicized by the U.S. State Department. There are small differences among the several versions and translations in circulation. While the CPSU has never formally acknowledged (or denied) this document, the fact that it is accepted and cited by East European Communist organs is conclusive evidence of its authenticity.

Woodward, *Sir* Llewellyn (1890–1971)
British Foreign Policy in the Second World War. London: Her Majesty's Stationery Office, 1962.
One of the more cautiously censored volumes in the official British *History of the Second World War* series. Indeed, it is "an abridgement" of a classified study. Based mainly—perhaps exclusively—on Foreign Office archives. The section on BARBAROSSA (pp. 140–152) adds almost nothing to Churchill's account, although it can be taken as a more or less independent confirmation of Churchill's accurate use of his documents.

Woodward, *Sir* Llewellyn
British Foreign Policy in the Second World War. Vol. I. London: Her Majesty's Stationery Office, 1970.
A useful but much overrated official British history.

Wrench, *Sir* John (1882–1966)
Geoffrey Dawson and Our Times. London: Hutchinson, 1955.
An "Establishment" biography of its most worthy guardian, the Editor of *The Times,* in this case Geoffrey Dawson (1874–1944), whose editorship extended from 1912 until his retirement on 30 September 1941. This otherwise adulatory book by Sir Evelyn Wrench is saved from triviality by its heavy reliance on Dawson's own letters and diaries.

Yakovlev, *Lieutenant-General* A[leksandr] S[ergeevich] (1905–   )
Tsel Zhizni [Whole lives]. Moscow: Politizdat, 1966.
Autobiography of the famed Soviet aircraft designer. From 1940 until 1948 he was Deputy Commissar of Aviation Construction in charge of research and development. Extensive passages in English translation are in Bialer (1969), particularly pp. 116–122, 166–171, 204–207. See also the key excerpt in Salisbury (1969), 79n. A second edition was published in 1970.

Yeremenko, *Marshal* A. I. (1892–   )
V Nachale Voiny [On the road to war]. Moscow: Science Publishing House, 1964.
Memoirs of the first year of the Great Fatherland War. At its outbreak the then General Yeremenko was Commander of the 1st Special Red Banner Army in the Far East. Critical of Stalin's preparations for and conduct of the war. Not seen by me except for relevant excerpts in English translation in Bialer (1969), 146–151, 232–236.

Zhukov, *Marshal* [G. K.] (1896–   )
The Memoirs. New York: Delacorte Press, 1971.
Originally published in Russian as *Vospominaniya i razmuyshleniya* (Moscow: Novosti Press Agency, 1969).

Glossary of Abbreviations, Acronyms, Codewords, and Definitions

Note: Except as noted, all terms are as of early 1941.

Abwehr (ABW)	Popular designation of the Amt Ausland Abwehr, the foreign and counterintelligence service of the OKW (German)
ALTONA	The cancellation codeword for Operation BARBAROSSA. See also DORTMUND
APA	Aussenpolitisches Amt, the foreign policy office of the Nazi party. Headed by Alfred Rosenberg.
A.P.E.S.	Advanced Planning Enemy Section (formerly F.O.E.S. and later the Joint Intelligence Staff) of the British Joint Intelligence Committee (J.I.C.)
AUFBAU OST	German codeword for the Wehrmacht's initial deployment toward the Soviet frontier
BARBAROSSA	German codeword (adopted on 17 December 1940) for the invasion of Russia, *Fall* (i.e., "case") BARBAROSSA. Unless otherwise specified, my use of this term refers in this book to the *planning* of the invasion rather than the operation itself.
B-*Tag* (B-day)	B[ARBAROSSA]-day, the German military shorthand and cover term for the first day of the invasion of Russia. Finally rescheduled to 22 June 1941.
B.S.C.	British Security Co-ordination, the S.I.S. wartime intelligence field office in the United States
C.I.G.S.	Chief of the Imperial General Staff (British)
D.M.I.	Director of Military Intelligence (British)
DORTMUND	The go-ahead codeword for Operation BARBAROSSA. See also ALTONA.
F.O.E.S.	Future Operations (Enemy) Section. See A.P.E.S.

FRITZ	The initial codeword for the invasion of Russia. Changed on 17 December 1940 to BARBAROSSA.
GRU	Glavnoye Razvedyvatelnoye Upravleniye, Soviet military intelligence
I.G.S.	Imperial General Staff (British)
INU	Inostrannoye Upravleniye, the Foreign [Intelligence] Administration of the NKVD. Formerly called the INO.
J.I.C.	Joint Intelligence Committee (British). Chaired by Victor Cavendish-Bentinck.
KGB	See NKGB
KRU	Kontrrazvedyvatelnoye Upravleniye, the Counterintelligence Administration of the NKGB
M.I.5	The wartime cover name for the Security Service, the British counterintelligence
M.I.6	The wartime cover name for the Secret Intelligence Service, the British foreign intelligence service
Narkomindel	The Soviet Foreign Commissariat, now the Foreign Ministry (MID or Minindel)
N.I.D.	Naval Intelligence Division (British)
NKGB	Narodny Komisariat Gosudarstvennoy Bezopasnosti, the People's Commissariat of State Security, the Soviet state security and intelligence service. Split off from the NKVD from February to July 1941 as a separate commissariat. It was the old Cheka and the present KGB.
NKVD	Narodny Komisariat Vnutrennikh Del, the People's Commissariat of Internal Affairs

OKH	Oberkommando des Heeres, the High Command of the Army (German)
OKL	Oberkommando der Luftwaffe, the High Command of the Air Force (German)
OKM	Oberkommando der Kriegsmarine, the High Command of the Navy (German)
OKW	Oberkommando der Wehrmacht, the High Command of the Armed Forces. Hitler's personal military staff.
O.Qu.IV	The intelligence section of the General Staff of OKH (German)
ONI	Office of Naval Intelligence, the U.S. naval intelligence service
OTTO	*Otto-Programme* (East Program) was the Wehrmacht's program of improvement of the rail and road facilities leading toward the Russian frontier. OTTO began in October 1940 and was completed on 10 May 1941.
OUN	An anti-Bolshevik Ukrainian nationalist underground organization headed by Stephen Bandera. The OUN-M faction was a splinter group headed by Andrew Mel'nyk.
P.I.D.	Political Intelligence Department, the British Foreign Office intelligence. Formerly, and now again, called the Research Department.
P.W.E.	Political Warfare Executive. See S.O.1.
RSHA	Reichssicherheitshauptamt, the Reich Security Main Office, headed by Reinhard Heydrich. The RSHA was the security, intelligence, and counterespionage service of the Nazi SS.
SD	Sicherheitsdienst-Ausland. The foreign secret intelligence service of the RSHA (German).

SEA LION	German codeword for the projected invasion of Britain
SIM	Servizio Informazione Militar, the Italian army intelligence service
SIS	Servizio Informazione Segreto, the Italian naval intelligence service
SIS	Signal Intelligence Service, U.S. Army
S.I.S.	Secret Intelligence Service, the British foreign intelligence organization. Also called M.I.6.
S.O.E.	Special Operations Executive. British wartime organization dealing with unconventional warfare operations.
S.O.1	Branch of S.O.E. dealing with psychological warfare (subsequently reorganized as P.W.E.)
S.O.2	Branch of S.O.E. dealing with sabotage and guerrilla warfare (subsequently reorganized as S.O.E.)
Sovinformburo	Soviet Information Bureau
WFSt	Wehrmachtführungstab, Lieutenant-General Jodl's operations section of the OKW. WFSt/Abt.L and WFSt/L designate Major-General Warlimont's plans subsection.
Wi Rü Amt	The Economic Section of the OKW

Index

This index covers topics, codewords, organizations, and the 200 persons most intimately involved in the planning or forecasting of BARBAROSSA, including all such persons mentioned at more than one place in the text. Other persons connected with BARBAROSSA are identified in Appendix A, Appendix B, and the Bibliography.

Except for occasional special cases, the index omits all persons mentioned only once, any persons mentioned only in connection with codebreaking or intelligence but not directly linked to BARBAROSSA, and all historians of BARBAROSSA. The historians are cited in Table 7.1 and in the Bibliography.

Key to abbreviations (country of citizenship or affiliation):

B	British	R	Russian
C	Czechoslovak	Rum	Rumanian
Ch	Chinese	S	Swedish
F	Finnish	Sw	Swiss
G	German	T	Turkish
H	Hungarian	US	United States
I	Italian	V	Vatican
J	Japanese	VF	Vichy French
P	Polish	Y	Yugoslav

Illustration Credits